A TEXTBOOK OF
ANIMAL DIVERSITY - II

FOR
B.Sc. (Part - I) Zoology, Paper - III (Semester - II)

As Per New Revised Syllabus of Shivaji University, Kolhapur and Solapur University, Solapur.

Prin. Dr. KISHORE R. PAWAR
M.Sc., Ph.D.
K.A.A.N.M.S.,
Arts, Sci. & Com. College, Satana,
Nashik – 423301.

Dr. ASHOK E. DESAI
M.Sc., Ph.D.
Associate Professor in Zoology,
P.G. Deptt. of Zoology,
K.T.H.M. College,
Nashik – 422002.

Dr. DAMA L. B.
M.Sc., Ph.D.
D.B.F. Dayanand College of Arts and
Science, Solapur
Dist. Solapur

Dr. PATIL R.N.
M.Sc., Ph.D.
Head, P.G. Department of Zoology and
Chairman BOS, Shivaji University
SGM College Karad, Dist. Satara

ANIMAL DIVERSITY - II   ISBN 978-93-5164-907-6
First Edition : **February 2016**
© : **Authors**

The text of this publication, or any part thereof, should not be reproduced or transmitted in any form or stored in any computer storage system or device for distribution including photocopy, recording, taping or information retrieval system or reproduced on any disc, tape, perforated media or other information storage device etc., without the written permission of Authors with whom the rights are reserved. Breach of this condition is liable for legal action.

Every effort has been made to avoid errors or omissions in this publication. In spite of this, errors may have crept in. Any mistake, error or discrepancy so noted and shall be brought to our notice shall be taken care of in the next edition. It is notified that neither the publisher nor the authors or seller shall be responsible for any damage or loss of action to any one, of any kind, in any manner, therefrom.

Published By :   **Printed By :**
NIRALI PRAKASHAN   **Repro Knowledgecast Limited**
Abhyudaya Pragati, 1312 Shivaji Nagar,   **Thane**
Off J.M. Road, PUNE - 411005
Tel - (020) 25512336/37/39. Fax - 25511379
Email : niralipune@pragationline.com

DISTRIBUTION CENTERS

PUNE
Nirali Prakashan
119, Budhwar Peth, Jogeshwari Mandir Lane,
Pune - 411002, Maharashtra.
Tel : (020) 24452044, 66022708
Fax : (020) 2445 1538
Email : bookorder@pragationline.com

MUMBAI
Nirali Prakashan
385, S.V.P. Road, Rasdhara Co-op. Hsg.
Society, Girgaum,
Mumbai - 400004, Maharashtra
Tel : (022) 2385 6339 / 2386 9976,
Fax : (022) 2386 9976
Email : niralimumbai@pragationline.com

RETAIL SHOPS

PUNE
Pragati Book Centre
157, Budhwar Peth, Opp. Ratan Talkies,
Pune – 411002, Maharashtra
Tel : 2445 8887 / 6602 2707

Pragati Book Centre
676/B, Budhwar Peth,
Opp. Jogeshwari Mandir,
Pune – 411002, Maharashtra
Tel. : (020) 6601 7784, 2445 2254

PUNE
Pragati Book Centre
152, Budhwar Peth,
Near Jogeshwari Mandir,
Pune – 411002, Maharashtra
Tel : (020) 6609 2463 / 2445 2254

PUNE
Pragati Book Centre
Amber Chamber, 28/A, Budhwar Peth,
Appa Balwant Chowk
Pune : 411002, Maharashtra
Tel : (020) 20240335 / 66281669
Email : pbcpune@pragationline.com
Pragati Book Centre
917/22, Sai Complex,
F.C. Road, Shivaji Nagar,
Pune – 411004, Maharashtra
Tel. : (020) 2566 / 6602 2728

MUMBAI
Pragati Book Corner
Indira Niwas,
111-A Bhavani Shankar Road,
Dadar (W), **Mumbai** – 400028
Tel : (022) 2422 3525 / 6662 5254
Email : pbcmumbai@pragationline.com

DISTRIBUTION BRANCHES

NAGPUR
Pratibha Book Distributors
Above Maratha Mandir, Shop No. 3, First Floor, Rani Zanshi Square, Sitabuldi,
Nagpur 440012, Maharashtra, Tel : (0712) 254 7129
JALGAON
34, V. V. Golani Market, Navi Peth, Jalgaon 425001, Maharashtra,
Tel : (0257) 222 0395, Mob : 94234 91860
KOLHAPUR
New Mahadvar Road, Kedar Plaza, 1st Floor Opp. IDBI Bank
Kolhapur 416 012, Maharashtra. Mob : 9855046155

www.pragationline.com   info@pragationline.com

PREFACE

The authors are indeed very happy to present this book **'Animal Diversity - II'** for the students of B.Sc. Part I Zoology Paper III, Semester II of Shivaji and Solapur University.

The book has been written according to the new revised syllabus. Board of Studies of Zoology has thoroughly revised the syllabus which has been designed with the topic of 'Animal Diversity - II'.

There was a long felt need of the students as well as teachers community for a text book which covers the entire syllabus prescribed by Board of studies. The present book is an outcome of our sincere efforts. We tried our level best to present the subject matter in easy style and in a comprehensive manner. The text book is profusely illustrated with number of clear line drawings.

No doubt, there are several textbooks written by Indian and foreign authors on the subject, but they are costly and number of copies are very limited in the college libraries. The students can not get the matter on prescribed syllabus in one book and they also cannot afford the costly books. Therefore, we have presented all the topics in one book in a low price. We sincerely feel that this book will fulfill the requirements of students and teachers.

We are thankful to Shri. Dineshbhai Furia, Shri. Jignesh Furia, Shri. M.P. Munde and the entire staff of Nirali Prakashan for taking keen interest in publishing this book and bringing out in time.

Constructive suggestions for improvement of the book are most welcome.

Authors

– Authors

SYLLABUS

(SHIVAJI UNIVERSITY, KOLHAPUR)
B.Sc. Part - I, Semester - II : Paper III: Animal Diversity - II

Unit I
1. Classification - Salient Features and Classification of Chordates upto order of the following with suitable examples - Urochordata, Cephalochordata, Agnatha, Pisces and Amphibia. **(5)**

UNIT II
1. **Cephalochordata - Amphioxus** **(11)**
   - (a) Morphology
   - (b) Digestive System and Feeding Mechanism
   - (c) Circulatory System
   - (d) Excretory System
2. **Cyclostomata - General Characters**
3. Pisces - (a) Scales in Fishes (b) Fins in Fishes
   - (c) Structure of Gills in Cartilaginous and Bony Fish

UNIT III
1. Amphibia - Frog **(12)**
   - (a) Morphology
   - (b) Digestive System and Physiology of Digestion
   - (c) Respiratory System and Mechanism of Respiration
   - (d) Blood Vascular System
     - (i) Structure and Working of Heart
     - (ii) Arterial System
     - (iii) Venous System
     - (iv) Blood - Composition and Function

UNIT IV
- (e) Excretory System and Physiology of Urine Formation **(12)**
- (f) Reproductive System
- (g) Nervous System - Brain and Spinal Cord
- (h) Sense Organs - Eye and Ear **Total Periods: 40**

***

(SOLAPUR UNIVERSITY, SOLAPUR)
B.Sc. Part - I Zoology, Paper III, Semester - II: Animal Diversity - II

1. Classification of Chordates: Salient Features and Classification upto orders of the following with suitable examples: **(5)**
   - (A) Protochordata: Urochordata and Cephalochordata
   - (B) Craniata: (i) Agnatha, Cyclostomata, (iii) Gnathostomata: (a) Superclass: Pisces, (b) Superclass: Tetrapoda: Class - Amphibia
   - (This topic may be taught in practical classes)
2. Cyclostomata: General Characters, Ammocoetus Larva **(2)**
3. Fishes: (a) Types of Fins and Scales, (b) Structure of Gills in Cartilaginous and Bony Fish, (c) Mechanism of Gill Respiration **(6)**
4. Amphibia: Type Study - Frog (*Rana tigrina*) **(20)**
   (a) Morphology, (b) Histological Structure of Skin, (c) Digestive System, (d) Respiratory System and Mechanism of Respiration, (e) Blood Vascular System: Blood, Heart, Arterial and Venous System, (f) Excretory and Reproductive System, (g) Nervous System, (h) Embryology of Frog: Structure of Egg, Cleavage, Bastula and its Fate Map, Gastrulation and Formation of Three Germ Layers. Metamorphosis.
5. Neotany and parental Care in Amphibian. **(2)**

Total Periods: 40

***

CONTENTS

1. **Salient Features and Classification upto Order with One Example of the Following: Hemichordata, Urochordata and Cephalochordata**   1.1 - 1.40

2. **Cephalochordata and Cyclostomata**   2.1 - 2.58

3. **Amphibia - Frog:** *Rana tigrina*   3.1 - 3.78

4. **Urinogenital System**   4.1 - 4.74

5. **Neoteny in Amphibia**   5.1 - 5.12

***

Chapter 1...

Salient Features and Classification upto Order with One Example of the Following: Hemichordata, Urochordata and Cephalochordata

- 1.1 Hemichordata
- 1.2 Urochordata
- 1.3 Cephalochordata
- 1.4 Pisces - Cartilaginous and Bony Fishes
- 1.5 Amphibia - Apoda, Urodela and Anura
- ✏ Summary
- ✏ Review Questions

1.1 Salient Features and Broad Classification of Phylum Hemichordata

The hemichordates are vermiform enterocoelous coelomates. They may be colonial or solitary, with an epidermal nervous system. They show well developed circulatory system and glomerulli for excretion. They may be with or without gill slits.

General Characters

1. They are marine, solitary or colonial, mostly tubicolous, soft.
2. Body is soft, fragile, vermiform, unsegmented, bilaterally symmetrical and triploblastic.

3. Body is divisible into three distinct regions: proboscis, collar and trunk.
4. Body wall consists of a single layer of epidermis with mucous glands. Dermis is absent.
5. The coelom is enterocoelous, usually divided into protocoel, mesocoel and metacoel, corresponding to three body regions.
6. Buccal diverticulum, either considered as notochord, present in the proboscis.
7. The alimentary canal is complete, in the form of straight or U-shaped tube.
8. Foregut gives out a hollow buccal diverticulum into proboscis earlier considered as notochord.
9. Numerous pairs of gill slits are present on the dorso-lateral anterior part.
10. They are ciliary filter feeders.
11. The circulatory system is simple and well developed; closed type, usually with a contractile heart vesicle and longitudinal vessels, one dorsal and one ventral, interconnected by lateral vessels and sinuses.
12. Excretion by single glomerulus situated in the proboscis.
13. Nervous system is primitive comprising mainly of an intra epidermal nerve plexuses.
14. Reproduction is mostly sexual. Sexes are separate or united, gonads one or many pairs.
15. Fertilization is external. Development is mostly indirect through a free swimming tornaria larva. Direct development is also found in some forms.

Classification of Hemichordata

Phylum Hemichordata is divided into the following classes. Hemichordata includes about 80 known species which are generally grouped under two classes, *Enteropneusta* and *Pterobranchia*. Besides, two more classes *Plactosphaeroidea* and *Graptolita* (extinct) are included by some.

Class – 1: *Enteropneusta*

(Gr. *enteron*, gut + *pneustos*, breathed).
1. They are free swimming, solitary, burrowing animals, commonly called the 'acorn' or 'tongue worms'.

2. Body is elongated, vermiform, with no stalk.
3. Body is divisible into proboscis, collar and trunk.
4. Proboscis is cylindrical and tapering.
5. Collar without ciliated arms (Lophophores).
6. Alimentary canal is straight tube having two rows of hepatic caecae in the intestinal region. Filter feeding.
7. Several pairs of U-shaped gill slits.
8. Sexes are separate, gonads are numerous and sac like.
9. Development is indirect through tornaria larval stage.

Examples: *Balanoglossus, Saccoglossus.*

Class – 2: *Pterobranchia*

(Gr. *pteron*; feather + *branchion*, gill)

1. They are solitary or colonial, sessile and tubicolous animals having inside secreted chitinous tubes.
2. Body is short, compact with stalk for attachment.
3. Proboscis is shield shaped and the collar with hollow, ciliated arms bearing tentacles.
4. Alimentary canal is U-shaped. Anus dorsal lying near mouth. Ciliary feeding.
5. One pair of gill slits is present or absent, never U-shaped.
6. Sexes are separate or united. Gonads 1 or 2.
7. Development is direct or with larval stage.
8. Asexual reproduction by budding in some.

Examples: *Rhabdopleura, Cephalodiscus.*

Class 3: *Planctosphaeroidea*

1. This class is represented by pelagic and transparent larvae.
2. Body is spherical with branched ciliated bands on the surface.
3. The alimentary canal is L-shaped.
4. A triangular protocoel opening outside by a hydropore. Paired mesocoel and metacoel are also present.

Example: *Planctosphaera.*

Class 4: *Graptolita*

The fossil graptolites (e.g. *Dendrograptus*) were abundant in Ordovician and Siluvian periods and often placed as an extinct class under hemichordata. Their tubular chitinous skeleton and colonial habits show an affinity with *Rhabdopleura*.

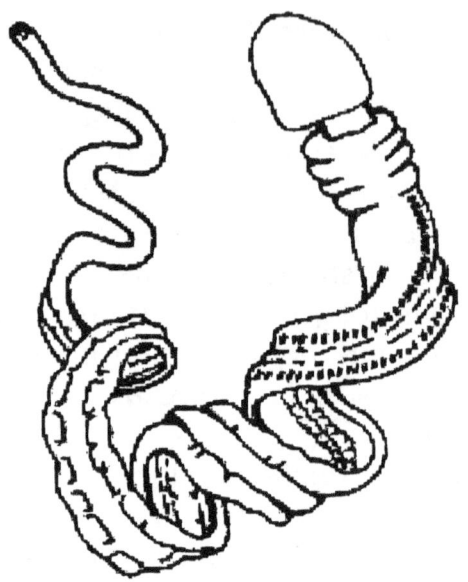

Fig. 1.1: *Balanoglossus*

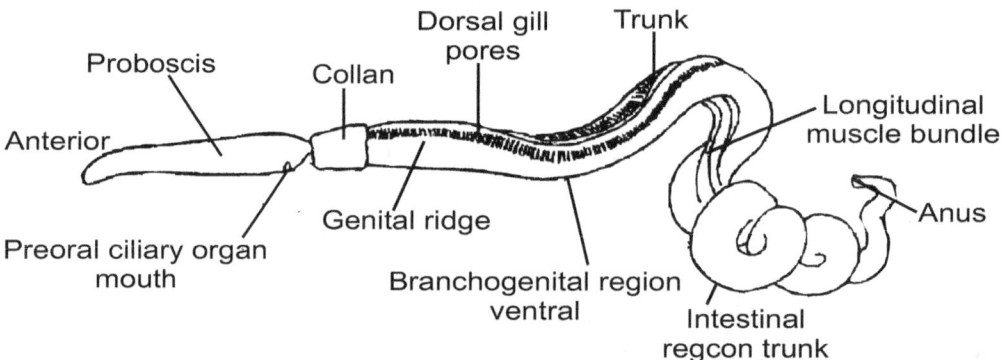

Fig. 1.2: *Saccoglossus*

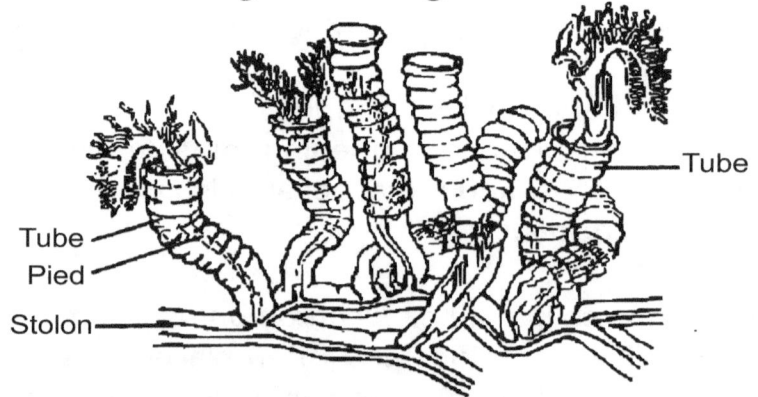

Fig. 1.3: *Rhabdopleura* and Individual Zooid

Salient Features and Broad Classification of Phylum Chordata

The animals which are characterised by the presence of a solid, unjointed, elastic, dorsal notochord; tubular, hollow nerve cord, situated dorsal to the notochord and pharyngeal gill slits are called chordate animals in the phylum Chordata. This phylum marks the climax of animal evolution. The chordates are the most familiar, most adaptable, most successful and most widely distributed animals. They exhibit great diversity of form, habitat and habits. There are some 65,000 known living chordates and most of them are free-living.

The phylum Chordata includes animals that can be grouped into two major subdivisions or sub-phyla: the *Vertebrata (Craniata)* and *Protochordata (Acraniata)*.

Three Fundamental Chordate Characters

All the chordates possess three outstanding unique characteristics at some stage in their life cycle. These three fundamental morphological features include:

1. Dorsal hollow or tubular nerve cord: The central nervous system of the chordates is located dorsally in the body. Nerve cord is tubular, hollow and longitudinal situated just above the notochord and extending lengthwise, in the body. The nerve cord or neural tube is derived from dorsal ectodermal neural plates of the embryo and encloses a cavity or canal called *neurocoel*. There are no ganglia. The nerve cord performs the functions like integration and co-ordination of the body activities. In vertebrates, the anterior part of the nerve cord is specialized into brain and protected in the cranium. The posterior of nerve cord is called spinal cord which is protected in vertebral column.

2. Longitudinal supporting rod-like notochord: It is also called chorda dorsalis. It is rod-like, flexible structure extending the length of the body. It is present beneath nerve cord and just above the digestive system. It is originated from the endodermal roof of the embryonic archenteron. It is formed by large vacuolated notochordal cells containing gelatinous matrix and surrounded by outer fibrous and an inner elastic sheath. It gives support to the body or act as internal skeleton. In vertebrates, it is replaced by vertebral column.

3. Pharyngeal gill slits: In all the chordates, at some stages of their life history, a series of paired lateral gill clefts or gill slits leading outward from the pharynx. They are also known by different names like pharyngeal clefts or pouches, branchial or visceral clefts. They are endodermal in origin. They are useful for water passage from pharynx to outside, thus, bathing the gills for respiration. The water current secondarily aids in filter feeding by capturing food particles in the pharynx. In protochordates (e.g. *Branchiostoma)* and lower aquatic vertebrates the gill slits are functional throughout the life.

Other General Characters

1. **Cephalization:** Formation of head by concentration of nervous tissue and sense organs at the anterior end. The posterior end is called tail. Thus, body shows anteroposterior axis.
2. **Bilateral symmetry:** Anterior and posterior ends and dorsal and ventral surfaces are distinguishable. Right and left sides are mirror images of each other. This is called bilateral symmetry seen in all chordates and majority of non-chordates.
3. **Triploblastic condition:** All chordates show triploblastic condition. They have three germ layers, namely ectoderm, endoderm and mesoderm.
4. **Coelom:** All chordates are coelomate animals because they have a true coelom lined entirely by mesoderm. A secondary body cavity or true coelom exist between body wall and the digestive tube.
5. **Closed circulatory system:** Blood is circulated by arteries, veins and capillaries in chordates. Thus, chordates show closed circulatory system. Besides this system, there is well developed lymphatic system. Blood contains haemoglobin. The heart is ventral in position.
6. **Complete digestive system:** Chordate digestive tract always has mouth for ingestion of food and arms or cloacal aperture for egestion of faeces.
7. **Metamerism:** Metamerism is a condition in which the body is composed of a linear series of similar body segments called metameres or somites.
8. **Organ systems:** In an organ system, several organs work together for the some functions such as digestion, circulation and respiration.

9. **Endocrine glands:** The endocrine or ductless glands pour their secretion in blood.
10. **Muscles:** Two types of muscles called stripped and smooth muscles are present in chordates. They are voluntary and involuntary in function. The heart is made of the special cardiac muscles.
11. **Skeleton:** Endoskeleton is made up of bones and cartilage, which supports the body and give particular shape.
12. **Excretory system** comprising proto or meso or metanephric kidneys.
13. **Reproductive system:** Sexes are separate with rare exceptions.

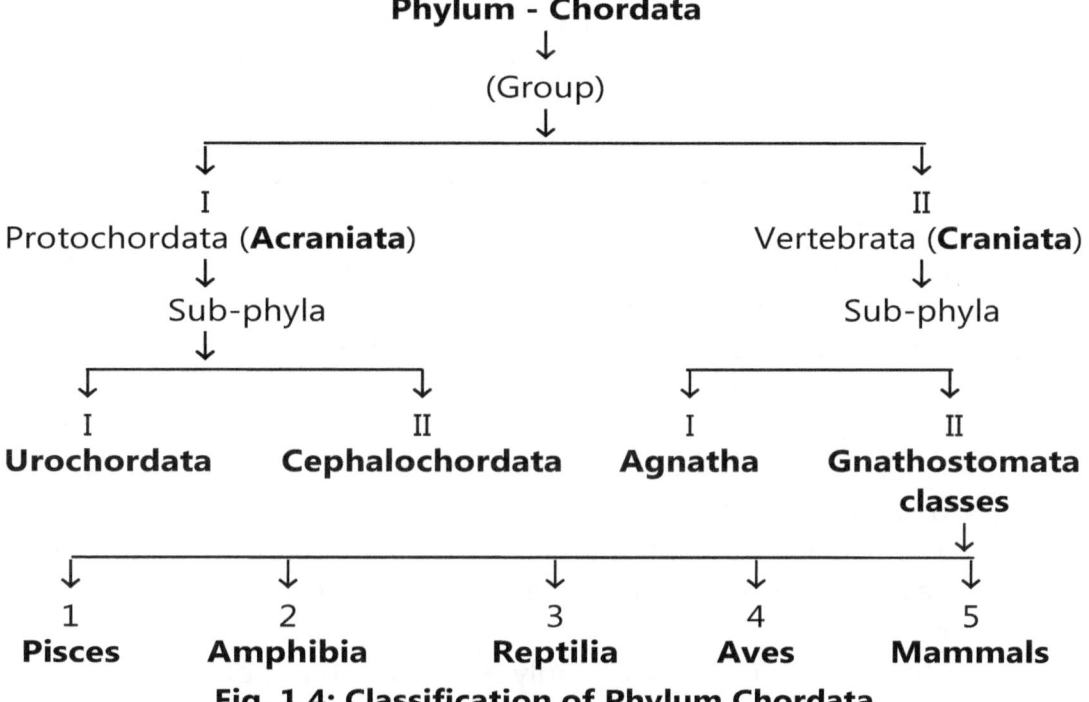

Fig. 1.4: Classification of Phylum Chordata

General Characters of Protochordata (Acraniata)
(1) They are exclusively marine and mostly of small forms.
(2) They lack head and cranium (skull).
(3) Notochord in some forms is confined to the tail in the larval stage which disappears in adult stage. But in some form like cephalochordata, the notochord extends along the entire body.

(4) Vertebral, jaws and paired appendages are absent.
(5) Dorsal tubular nervecord, notochord, gill slits and myotomes are usually present.
(6) Mode of feeding is usually ciliary.
(7) Sexes may be separate or united.

1.2 Subphylum – Urchordata

The word 'Urochordata' is adopted from Greek terminology Uros-tail, chorda-cord. They are commonly known as 'sea squirts'. Other names like tunicate and ascidia are also commonly used.

Tunicates are fixed or pelagic, solitary or colonial chordates enclosed a protective test or tunic made of tunicate.

General Characters
1. They are marine, solitary or colonial, fixed or pelagic, extending from Arctic to the Antarctic oceans. They are distributed to littoral to abyssal depths.
2. Mostly sedentary (fixed), simple, aggregated in groups.
3. The body varies in shape and size. They have different colours.
4. Adult body degenerate, sac-like, unsegmented without paired appendages and usually tail.
5. The body is covered by protective tunic or test composed largely of tunicine $(C_6H_{10}O_5)_n$ and similar to cellulose, hence name tunicata.
6. A terminal branchial aperture and a dorsal atrial aperture are usually present.
7. There is no coelom. Instead of that an ectoderm lined atrial cavity present which opens to outside through atrial aperture.
8. Notochord is present only in larval tail hence the name Urochordata.
9. Digestive system is complete. Pharynx is large with endostyle and two to several pairs of gill slits are present.
10. They are ciliary feeders.
11. Respiration through test and gill slits.
12. Circulatory system is open. Heart is simple, tubular and ventral. The blood flow is periodically reversed.
13. Excretion is by neural gland, pyloric gland and nephrocytes.

14. Mostly these animals are hermaphordite, but fertilization is cross and external.
15. Development is indirect through tadpole larva with well developed notochord.
16. Metamorphosis is retrogressive with degeneration of advanced characters of the chordates. Few tunicate larvae attain sexual maturity without metamorphosis and furnish the phenomenon of paegdogenesis.

Examples: *Hardmania, Oikopleura, Ascidia, Botryllus, Doliolum, Salpa.*

Habits and Habitat
- These animals are exclusively marine and found in shallow waters. Some forms like Ascidians are sedentary, found attached to a rocky sea bottom by broad base or embedded in the sandy flower by its extended foot.
- Group of individuals attached to one spot sometimes they are attached to the gastropod animals as commensal. Large number of animal inhabit the outer covering or test of the animal. These animals are ciliary feeders.
- Current of water passes through branchial aperture and leaves through atrial aperture. Many forms are pelagic.
- **Distribution:** These animals show world wide occurrence. Some species are found in Indian oceans. Many forms are inhabitants of coastal waters while some species live in deep waters. They are also distributed Pacific, Atlantic and Carribean oceans.

1.3 Subphylum – Cephalochordata

General Characters
1. They are marine widely distributed in swallow waters.
2. Mostly sedentary and buried with only anterior body end projecting above borvom sand.
3. They are small animals with slender and fish like body which is metameric and transparent.
4. Heal is lacking. Body is with trunk and tail.
5. Notochord and nerve cord are persistent and extend along the entire body, anteriorly right upto tip of the snout. Hence, they are called cephalochordata.

6. There is no exoskeleton, epidermis is single layered.
7. Body muscles are dorso lateral, segmented into myotomes.
8. Coelom enterocoelous, reduced in the pharyngeal region by development of atrial cavity.
9. Alimentary canal is complete. Pharynx is large perforated by numerous persistent gill slits opening into atrium. Filter feeders.
10. Respiration through general body surface. No special organs for respiration.
11. Well developed closed type of circulatory system but no heart and respiratory pigment. Hepatic portal system developed.
12. Excretion by protonephridia with solenocytes.
13. Nerve cord dorsal, tubular, without ganglia and brain. Dorsal and ventral nerve roots are separate.
14. Sexes are separate, gonads are numerous and metamerically repeated. Reproduction by sexual method.
15. Fertilization is external in sea water.
16. Development is indirect including a free swimming larva.
17. Limbs or paired fins are absent.

Examples: *Amphioxus* and *Asymmetron*.

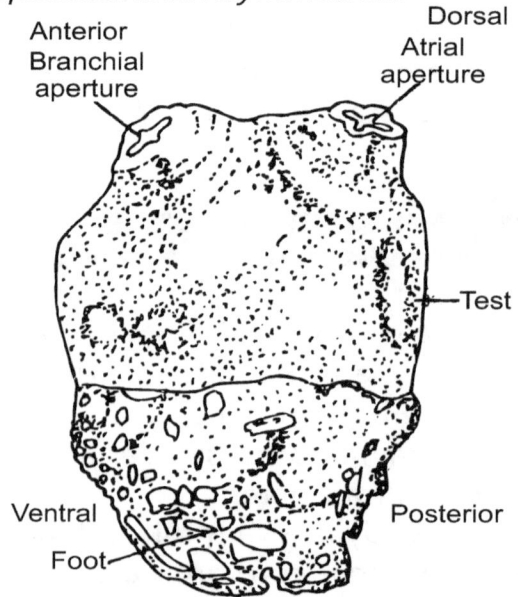

Fig. 1.4: *Hardmania*

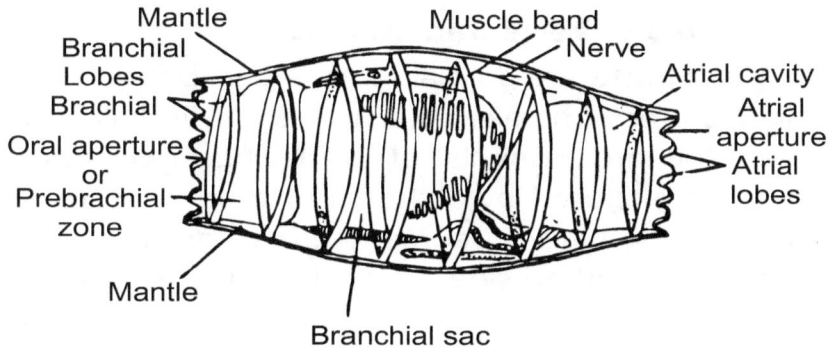

Fig. 1.5: *Doliolum*

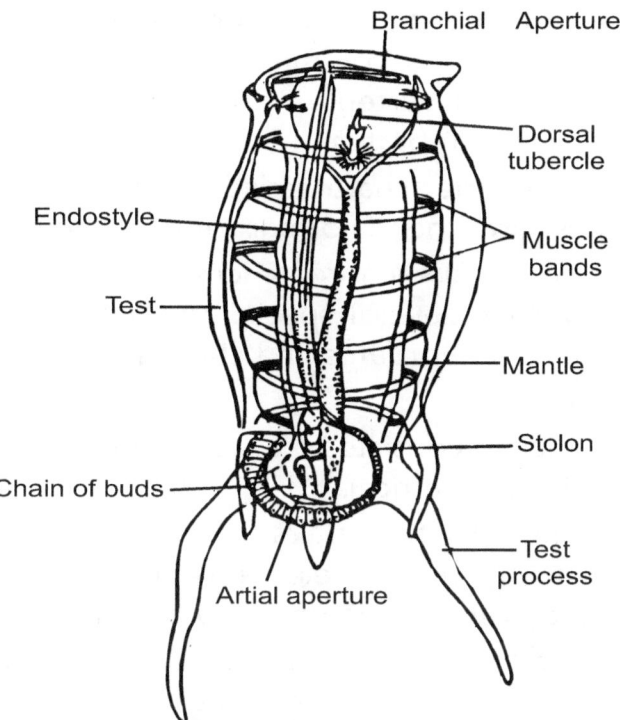

Fig. 1.6: *Salpa*

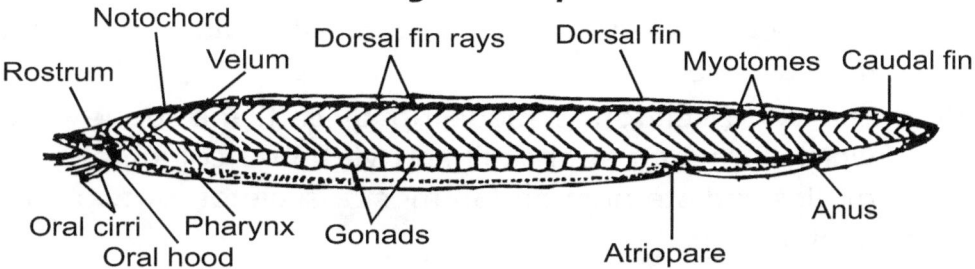

Fig. 1.7: *Amphioxus*

General Characters of Vertebrata (Craniata)

- The **Vertebrata** are animals with a backbone, but this is not exactly correct. The axial skeleton is a cylindrical rod or cord. The notochord consists of somewhat gelatinous internal substance enclosed by a sheath of tough fibrous tissue. The notochord is quite unsegmented. Its fibrous sheath extends upwards on either side to enclose the dorsal nerve cord (spinal cord).
- In the neural arch of fibrous tissue formed in this manner, minute rods or plates of cartilage are embedded.
- The little cartilages have been interpreted as vertebrae. Thus, animals without a column i.e. a longitudinal series of definitely formed vertebrae articulated to one another and are still called vertebrates.
- It is one of the characteristics of the vertebrates. The vertebrates form the major part of the phylum Chordata.
- They exhibit all the chordate characters, but in addition to these they have several special characters which distinguish them from non-chordates and chordates.

Special Characters

(1) Body typically consists of a head, neck, trunk and tail, and bilaterally symmetrical.

(2) As a rule, the two pairs of limbs or appendages are supported by skeletal elements. They may be fins, wings, arms or legs. In some form, they are modified.

(3) They have an integument basically made up of two parts, an outer epidermis and inner dermis. Epidermis may produce scales, feathers or hairs.

(4) The endoskeleton is associated with a complex musculature.

(5) The endoskeleton is made up of cartilage, bone or both which forms an axial skull and vertebral column, with ribs, girdles and sternum and in most a skeleton of two pairs of jointed limbs.

(6) Vertebrates have large coelom containing visceral organs.

(7) They have a complete digestive tract ventral to the nerve cord.
(8) Lower vertebrates have paired gills and terrestrial forms have lungs as a respiratory organs.
(9) Vertebrates have a closed circulatory system of arteries, veins and capillaries. Heart consists of 2, 3 or 4 chambers. Blood contains the respiratory pigment haemoglobin in erythrocytes.
(10) Vertebrates have a large, highly complex brain and 10 or 12 pairs of cranial nerves.
(11) Vertebrates have a pair of very complex sense organs, eyes, ears and nose.
(12) Well developed excretory organs 'kidneys' are present in vertebrates. Urinary bladder is also present in many forms.
(13) Sexes are separate. Single pair of gonads is present.
(14) In a majority of vertebrates, cloaca is present which is a common chamber for excretory, genital and rectum.
(15) There is a definite system of endocrine glands.

The sub-phylum vertebrate is divided into two infra-phyla (super classes) or sections: Agnatha and Gnathostomata.

Infra-Phylum-Agnatha *(Gnathos: Jaw, Agnatha - Jawless)*
(1) They are the earliest vertebrates.
(2) They possess no jaws (hence Agnatha).
(3) They have a distinct head and skull but cephalization is of a low order.
(4) Skull is unique and difficult to homologize.
(5) Brain is primitive.
(6) Paired appendages are absent.
(7) Vertebral column is poorly developed because there are no centra.
(8) Notochord persists permanently.
(9) They have a single median nostril into which the hypophysis opens.
(10) Some are parasitic (blood-sucking cyclostomes) while some feed on minute particles by producing food currents.
(11) Almost all extinct cyclostomes.

The Agnatha is divided into two classes: **Ostracodermi** (extinct forms) and **Cyclostomata** (living agnathans).

Class 1. Ostracodermi
   (1) Body with heavy armour of large plates on the head and small bony scales.
   (2) They are extinct agnathans with little resemblance superficially with cyclostomes.
   (3) Lack of paired appendages, head is flat and expanded.

Example: *Cephalospis (Extinct).*

Class 2. Cyclostomata
   (1) They are living agnathans, primitive in many respects but specialised in others.
   (2) Body is round with a laterally compressed protocercal tail.
   (3) Mouth is suctorial, without jaws.
   (4) In the adult state, they are parasitic or scavengers on fishes.
   (5) Skin is soft and devoid of scales.
   (6) Paired appendages are absent, but median fins are present and supported by cartilagenous fin rays.
   (7) Endoskeleton is cartilagenous with no bones, vertebral column is primitive.
   (8) They have 6-14 pairs of internal gills.
   (9) There is a single median nostril.
   (10) Buccal cavity as a muscular tongue bearing epidermal teeth by which they rasp the flesh of fishes.
   (11) Spleen is absent.

Examples: *Petromyzon, Lampetra*

Infra Phylum – Ganthostomata
   (1) They have a mouth with true upper and lower jaws.
   (2) Olfactory organs and nostrils are paired.
   (3) There is well developed endoskeleton.
   (4) Three semicircular canals in each internal ear are present.

Ganthostomata is divided into six classes: an extinct class placodermi and five living classes.

Placodermi (extinct), Chondrichthyes and Osteichthyes are together known as fishes or *Pisces*. Amphibia, Reptilia, Aves and Mammalia are grouped together and are called tetrapoda.

1.4 Pisces

General Characters
1. They are aquatic, either freshwater or marine; cold blooded vertebrates.
2. The skin is covered with scales, dermal denticles or bony plates.
3. They show generally steamlined body but some are elongated snake like and few are dorsoventrally compressed.
4. They possess pairs and unpaired fins supported by soft or spiny rays.
5. The unpaired fins are dorsal, caudal and anal fins, while the pectoral and pelvics (ventrals) are paired.
6. Tail is muscular with tail fin used for propulsion.
7. They possess paired nostril but do not open into pharynx except lung fishes.
8. Some fishes (e.g. Catfishes) possess barbles which are excellent tactile organs.
9. The endoskeleton is cartilaginous or bony.
10. Respiratory organs are gills but accessory respiratory organs may also be present.
11. Gill slits are usually in five pairs, but in some cases 6 or 7 pairs.
12. A swim bladder or air bladder is usually present but secondarily lost in some species.
13. Lateral line system is well developed.
14. The heart is two chambered containing one auricle and one ventricle.
15. Cranial nerves are present in 10 pairs.
16. Only internal ear is present.
17. The kidney is mesonephros.
18. The gonads possess true gonoducts.
19. Sexes are separate and development is indirect.
20. The fishes which are with cartilaginous endoskeleton are call cartilaginous and those with bony endoskeleton called bony fishes.

Habits, Habitat and Distribution
- Majority of the cartilaginous fishes are marine, very few sharks are found in brackish or freshwater. They are all predator fishes.

- Sharks, saw fishes are predators. They occur in warm waters of tropics. They are capacious scavengers and active swimmers. They feed on other fishes, crabs, lobsters, sea urchins and squids.
- There are few species of sharks like whale shark (*Rhincodon*) and the basking shark, though 10 metres or more long, have minute teeth. They are sluggish filter feeders living exclusively on zooplankton. Some white sharks are man eaters.
- Ganga sharks are fond of living human flesh. It is a great menace to bathers in the Hooghly at Kolkatta.
- Some sharks are viviparous. Sketes and rays are also important fishes. They are bottom dwellers.
- Sting rays inflict wound by their sharp spines on the tail and this sting may be fatal. Electric rays are able to give strong shocks to predator or food animal.
- *Chimaera* are ghost fishes or rat fishes. The lung fishes are large and inhabiting semipermanent freshwater and swamps in Africa, South America and Australia. They are all sluggish bottom dwellers and predaceous fishes.
- There are large number of bony fishes found in freshwaters as well as marine waters. Some forms can fly some distance in the sea called flying fishes (*Exocoetus*).
- Many are bottom dwellers. Sole fishes live at the bottom. Sea devils are predaceous fishes.
- Mud skippers live on the roots of mangrove plants as well as on the mud which can crawl on it.
- But they keep their tail in water for respiration. Fishes are distributed in all freshwater and marine waters. On the globe many fishes like salmon, eel show migration which is essential for breeding.

1.4.1 Class-Chondrichthyes or Cartilaginous Fishes

The chondrichthyes are commonly called as Cartilaginous fishes.

General Characters

1. Body is spindle shaped, laterally compressed or dorsoventrally flattened and disc like.

2. The skin is tough covered with minute placoid scales with mucous glands.
3. Both median and paired fins are present and supported by horny fin rays. Caudal fin is heterocercal.
4. Coelom divided into anterior small pericardial cavity containing heart and a large peritoneal cavity containing viscera.
5. Endoskeleton is entirely cartilaginous, but no bone formation, vertebrae are complete and separate notochord is persistent but reduced.
6. Five to seven pairs of gills are present for respiration, gill slits are uncovered, no operculum.
7. Air bladder is absent.
8. Heart is two chambered, hepatic and renal portal systems are present.
9. Stomach is J-shaped, intestine is short with spiral valve.
10. Brain is large, olfactory lobes and cerebellum is large, 10 pairs of cranial nerves. Well developed sense organs.
11. Kidneys are mesonephric, large amount of urea is retained in the body.
12. Sexes are separate, paired gonads, internal fertilization, some are oviparous or ovoviviparous while some are viviparous having placenta for nourishment of the embryo.
13. Most of the chondrichthyes are marine, some fresh-water and all are predaceous.

Examples: *Scoliodon, Pristis, Raja.*

1.4.2 Class-Osteochthyces or Bony Fishes

The Osteochthyces are popularly called the bony fishes and are most successful of all aquatic forms.

General Characters
1. Body is spindle shaped and laterally compressed.
2. Both median and paired fins are present and supported by cartilaginous or bony fin-rays. Caudal fin usually homocercal, single dorsal fin.
3. Body covered by either gonoid, cycloid or ctenoid scales. Skin has many mucous glands in epidermis and scales embbeded in dermis.

4. Endoskeleton is partly or wholly bony-vertebrae and many notochord often persists in a greatly reduced form. Pelvic girdle is often absent.
5. Mouth is usually terminal with numerous teeth. Jaws are well developed and articulated to the skull. Jaw suspension is autostylic. Cloaca absent but anus is present.
6. Four pairs of gills are present covered by operculum. Spiracles are generally absent.
7. An air bladder is generally present which is respiratory in lower forms but becomes hydrostatic in higher forms.
8. Heart is two-chambered.
9. Brain has small olfactory lobes and small cerebellum. 10 pairs of cranial nerves.
10. Sexes are separate, paired gonads, fertilization is external. Most forms are oviparous. Some ovoviviparous or even viviparous.

Examples: *Acipencer, Amia, Anguilla, Hippocampus, Exocoetus..*

Examples of Fishes

- *Pisces* or *Fishes* are the aquatic gnathostomes with true upper and lower jaws. There are about 30,000 to 40,000 species of fishes showing great diversity in shape, size, habits and habitat.
- They live in all the seas and brackish waters, as well as in freshwater bodies like rivers, ponds, lakes, dams, streams.
- They are generally found in almost every place where there is water.
- As far as the body form of the fishes is concerned, they have usually streamlined body, but some exhibit snake like body and most of the fishes are laterally compressed and few are ventrolaterally flattened.
- The gills are the main respiratory organs in the fishes.
- All the fishes are generally divided into two types namely cartilaginous fishes grouped in the class chondrichthyes and bony fishes included in the osterichthyes.
- The cartilaginous fishes exhibit great diversity in shape, size, habits and habitat. These fishes are mostly marine and body is covered with placoid scales.

- Their endoskeleton is made-up of cartilaginous material and often calcified. These fishes possess 5-7 gill slits on each side. There are no gill covers or opercula.

- *Scoliodon* (Dog fish), *Stegostoma Heptanchus*, *Sphyrna* (hammer headed shark), *Pristis, Raja. Tarpedo* are the some of the typical representatives of cartilaginous fishes. These fishes are called sharks.

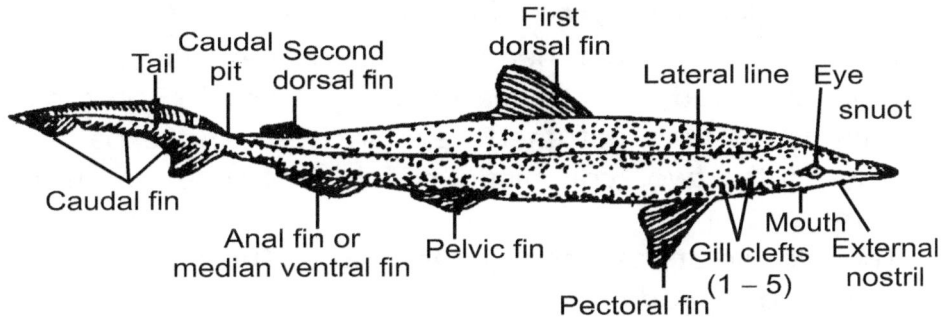

Fig. 1.8: *Scoliodon*

- The *Scoliodon* or dog fish is very well studied marine shark found in all parts of the open sea. All the sharks are carnivorous feeding on crabs, lobster and fishes.

- They are very fast swimmers and full grown animals measure from 30 to 60 cm in length. The body is perfectly streamlined with strongly compressed head dorsoventrally with wedge shaped snout.

- Mouth is on ventral side bounded by jaws which are armed with backwardly directed teeth. They show placoid scales. They show five gill slits for respiration.

- *Heptanchus* is most primitive shark which show long body and slow movements. This fish possesses 7 pairs of gill clefts. Hexanchus is another primitive shark which show 6 pairs of gill clefts.

- These fishes are viviparous but there is no placenta. They are inhabitants of warm parts of the Atlantic and Mediterranean seas.

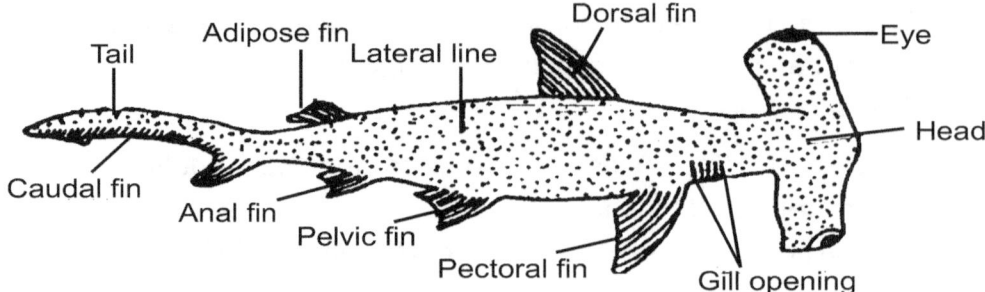

Fig. 1.9: *Sphyrna* (Hammer headed shark)

- *Sphyrna* or hammer headed shark is very large shark with elongated body which measures about 13 to 15 feet in length. This fish is with flattened head in front and expanded side ways into two conspicuous lobes, hence resembling a hammer.
- The eyes lie at the tips of lateral lobes. The other features are similar to *Scoliodon*.
- This fish is ferocious and attacks on its prey with its hammer like head. These sharks are living in deep waters and are distributed in tropical and subtropical seas.
- *Pristis* or Saw fish is a large shark which measures 10-20 feet or longer. It shows a peculiar prolonged head and skull into a long flattened rostrum and its lateral margins are equipped with series of pointed tooth like denticles giving appearance of a saw.

They are predaceous fishes and their food contains small fishes and flesh of whales and other marine animals. These fishes are found in Atlantic and Mediterranean oceans. The *Raja* or Skate is another fish which shows dorsoverntrally depressed body. The fish bears large pectoral fins which extends along the lateral margins of trunk and head forming large rhombic disc. The mouth is located on ventral side and provided with numerous sharp teeth useful for tearing the prey. These animals show caudal electric organs which are nothing but the modified caudal muscles located on each side of the terminal portion of the tail. The skates show larger or smaller spines on the body. They show marked sexual dimorphism. Male has pair of claspers present near the pelvic fin. These fishes are oviparous and egg cases are four horned with no tendrils. They catch the prey in a very peculiar manner by dropping down over prey and covering it with broad body and fins. Skates are sluggish bottom dwellers feed on crustaceaus and fishes. They are found in temperate seas but more abundant in northern hemisphere.

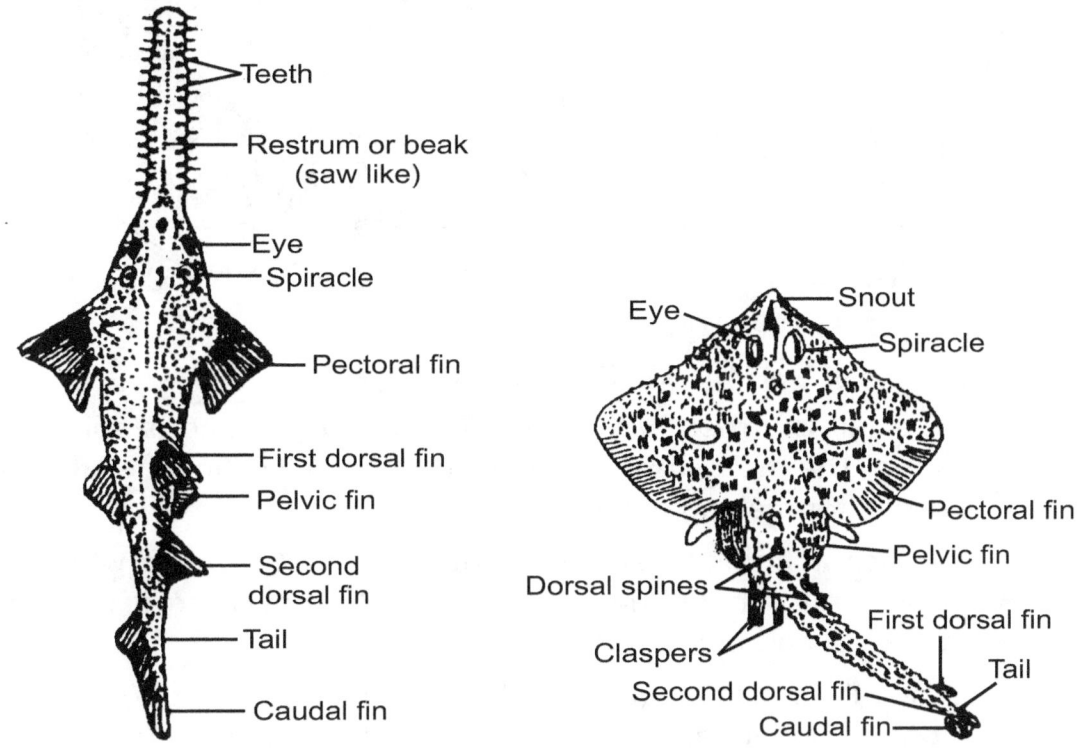

Fig. 1.10: *Pristis* **Fig. 1.11: *Raja* (Skate)**

- *Torpedo* is commonly called as electric ray with dorsoventrally flattened body and the anterior part is expanded laterally.

- Pectoral fins are large and extend in front, continuous with head which is rounded. It swims by flapping its pectoral fins up and down. The scales are absent and tail is thick with dorsal and caudal fins.

- *Torpedo* has pair of electric organs which give powerful shock of about 100 volts. They are found in Red sea, Atlantic and Pacific ocean.

- *Trygon* (Sting ray) is another flat bodied, rhomboidal shaped fish with long slender whip-like tail terminating in a small caudal fin.

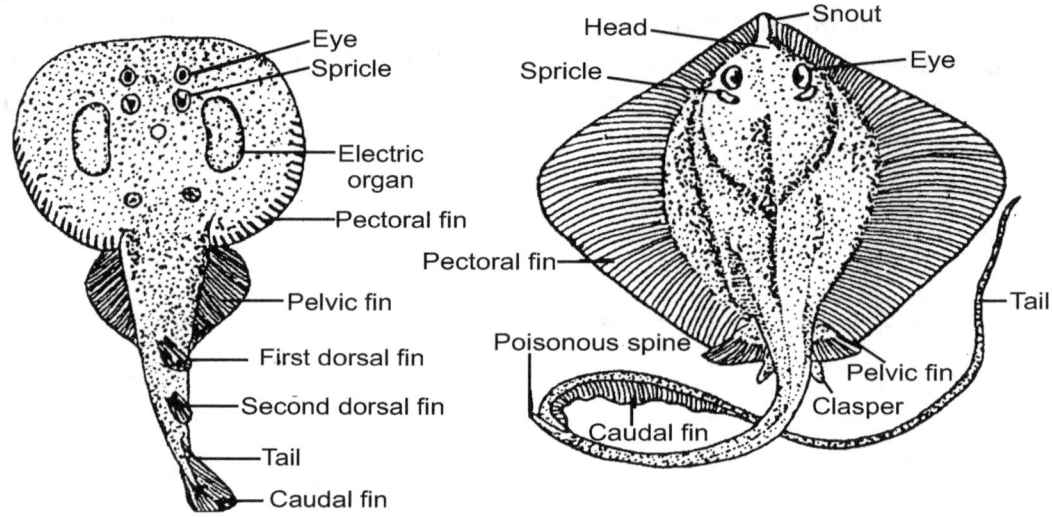

Fig. 1.12: *Trygon* and *Torpedo*

- The tail is armed with a sharp serrated poisonous spine or sting. The male shows clasper near the pelvic fin. The sting is useful for making wounds on its victims.

- The class holocephali represents the fish *Chimaera* which is called rat fish or King of herrings. It shows large fan like pectoral and pelvic fins.

- Caudal fin forms equal sized dorsal and ventral lobes. Tail is long tapering and male bears frontal clasper and pair of clasper behind the pelvic fins.

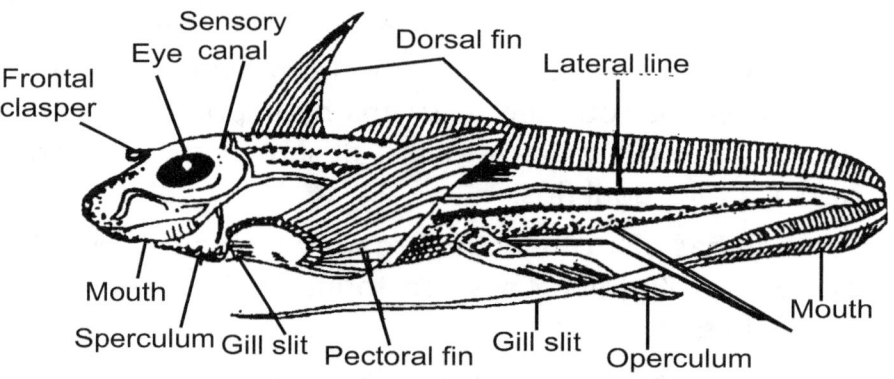

Fig. 1.13: *Chimaera*

- The class Dipnoi are specialised fishes with gills, lungs, external and internal nares and reduced scales. They are all inhabitants of freshwater and breathe air. Body long and slender covered by overlapping cycloid bony scales.
- These fishes possess paired fins which are lobe like in *Neoceratodus* whereas they are filament in *Protopeterus* and *Lepidosiren*. The dorsal and ventral fins are confluent with the caudal fin.
- These fishes show presence of air bladder which is lung like. One air bladder is present in *Neoceratodus* but there are two air bladders in other fishes. Air bladder is efficient respiratory organ.

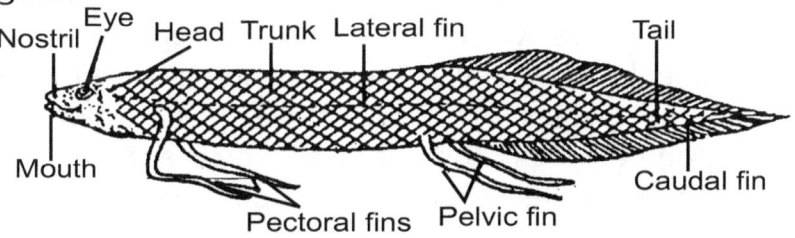

A - *Protopteus*

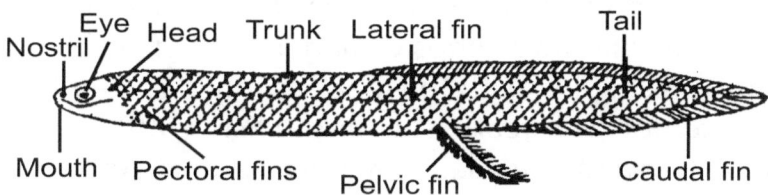

B - *Lepidosiren*

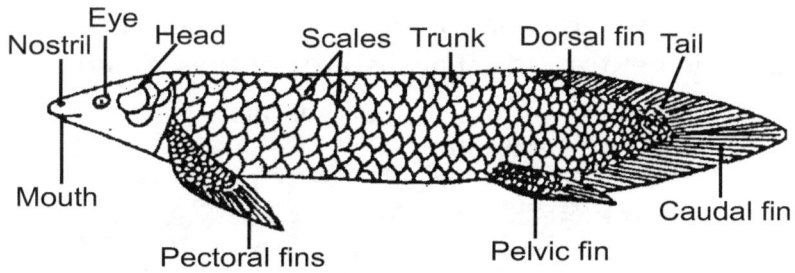

C – *Neoceratodus*

Fig. 1.14: Lung fishes

- There are three living genera. Of these *Neoceratodus* lives in pool, which becomes low and stagnant, in Queens land. *Lepidosiren* occurs in tropical and South America and *Protopteus* in tropical Africa.
- When the streams dry up in hot season they burrow deep in the mud and spend the time in a state of lowered metabolism called aestivation. They can live for 6 months in this state.
- The moist walls of the burrows protect them from drying out and a small opening brings air in for respiration. The larvae of these fishes may have sucker and external gills.
- Dipnoi resembeles the amphibians in many features but are not their ancestors.
- The class *Osteoichthyes* or *Teleostomi* includes the vast majority of fishes which show bony skeleton. Hence, they are also called bony skeleton fishes. This class represents more than 25,000 species and about 95% fishes are bony fishes.
- The *Actinopterygili* is the subclass which are popularly known as ray finned fishes. There is generally single dorsal fin which is generally divided into many parts or finlets.
- For example, *Polyptems* which is freshwater fish found in Congo and upper Nile rivers of Africa. The length of the body is about 1 metre covered with hard ganoid scales.
- The dorsal split into series of flag like finlets each consisting of a semi-erect spine with few backwardly directed fin rays.
- *Acipenser* or *Sturgeon* is a large fish with 3 metres length found in rivers and seas of Europe and Asia. It shows five longitudinal rows of large keeled bony plates called scubs and dermal denticles.
- Head shows flat, triangular rostrum bearing four slender *barbels* on ventral side. This fish resembles elasmobranchs.

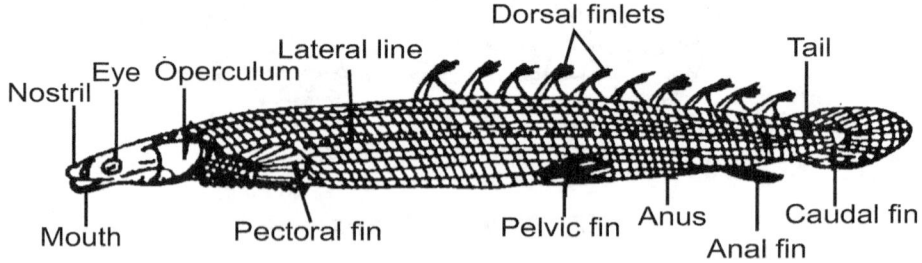

Fig. 1.15: *Poloyptems*

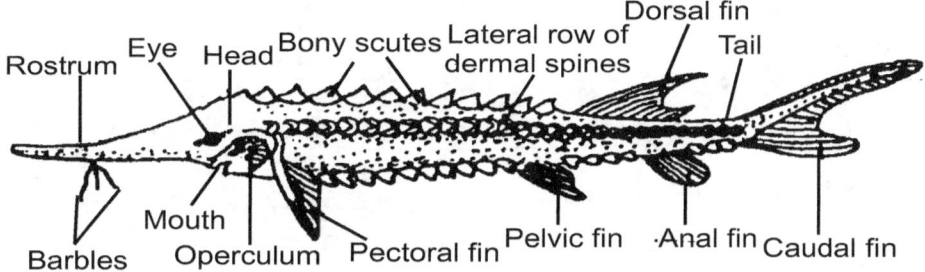

Fig. 1.16: *Acipenser* (Sturgeon)

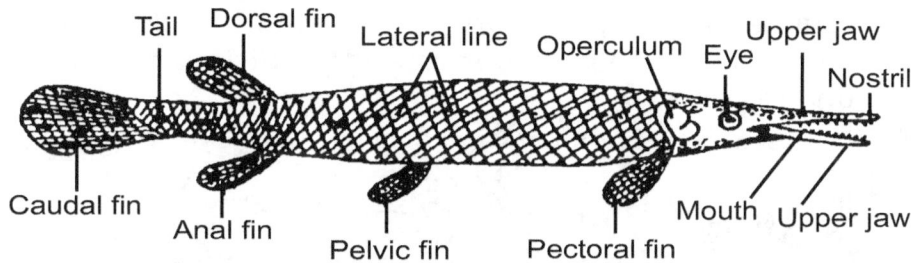

Fig. 1.17: *Lepidosteus*

- *Holostei* includes intermediate ray finned fishes. They are with air bladder connected with pharynx and it is useful as a hydrostatic organ. They are freshwater fishes.

- *Lepidosteus* or the Gar Pike is the representative which inhabits the fresh waters of North and central America. The fish shows long elongated beak like jaws and the air bladder functions as lung when water level falls or water becomes foul.

- *Amia* is another fish which retains primitive features with very long dorsal fin.

- The Teleostei is divided into 30 orders and the representative shows diverse body forms, habits and habitat.

- *Eel* or *Anguila* are snake like fish and inhabits rivers, estuaries. The fish often wriggle about on gamp grass outside water breathing through skin.

- They are well-known for their breeding migration. Breeding occurs only once in the eels life, both males and females dying after spawning.

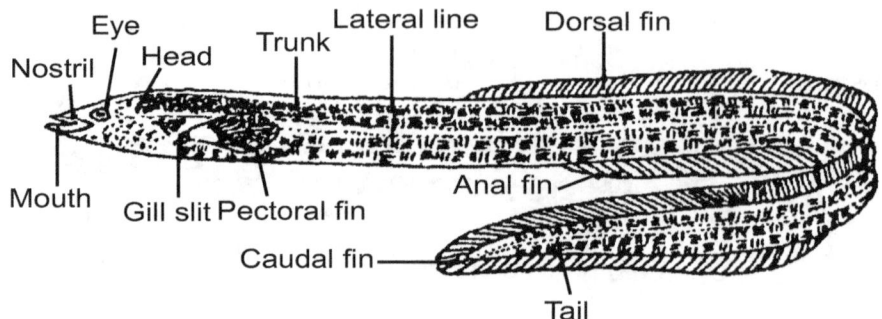

Fig. 1.18: *Eel* or *Anguilla*

- The Cat fishes, for example, *Rita*, *Wallago*, *Mystus* show presence of long sensory barbels and scales are usually lacking. These are carnivorous and predicious fishes. They are found in rivers.

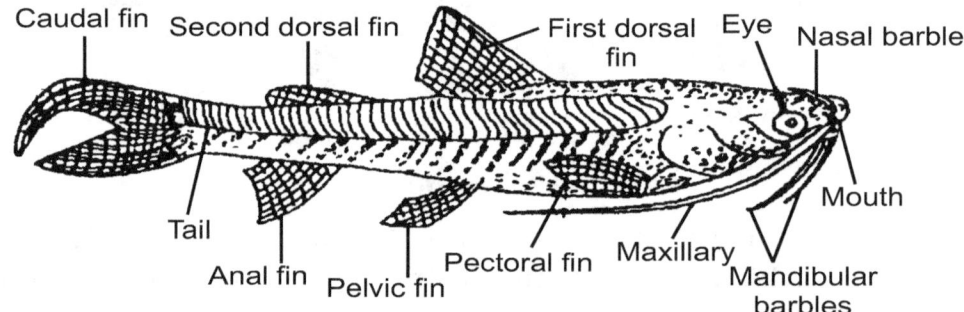

Fig. 1.19: *Cat fish*

- *Labeo*, *Catla catla*, *Cyprinus* are the carp fishes found in the rivers and streams and used as excellent food fishes. Body has cycloid scales and fins are without spines.

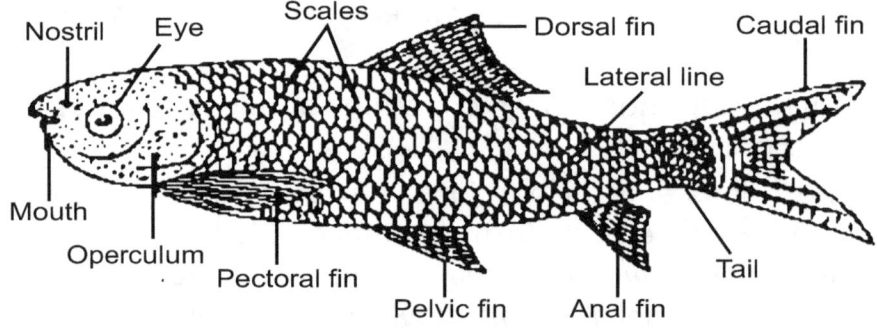

Fig. 1.20: *Labeo*

There are variety of fishes which show diverse body structure. For example: *Hippocampus* (Sea Horse), *Syngnathus* (Pipe fish) and *Fistularia* (Flute fish) are strange in appearance and body is covered by bony armour and the mouth is small and lies at the end of a tubular snout. Sea horse shows horse like appearance. Tail is prehensile. The male has a brood pouch on the belly for keeping eggs. Female lays eggs in the brood pouch of male. It is found in coastal waters of Indian and Atlantic Oceans.

Exocoetus or *Flying fish* is found in the tropical and subtropical seas. The body is covered by the cycloid scales and pectoral fins are inserted high up and are very large. Eyes are very large. The pectoral fins serve as parachute to sustain the fish in its gliding leaps. It can glide for a distance of 400 metres.

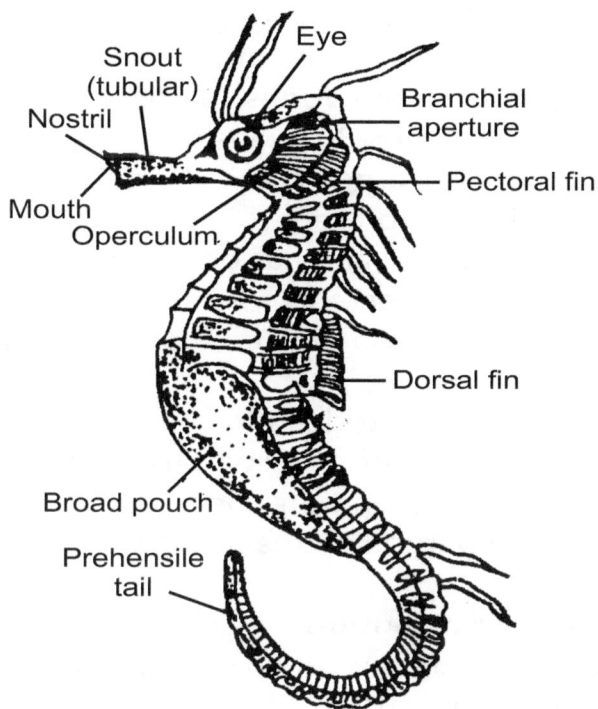

Fig. 1.21 (a): *Sea horse*

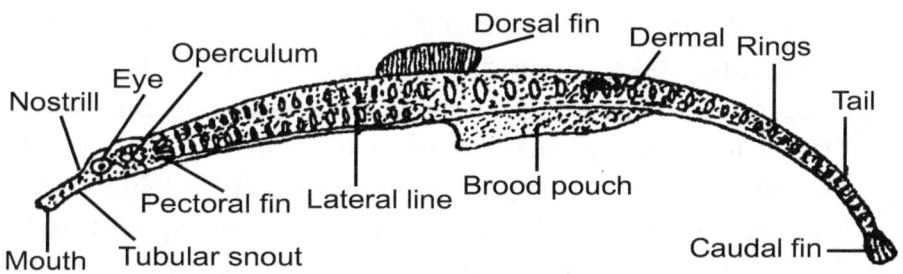

Fig. 1.21 (b): *Pipe fish*

1.5 Amphibia

Amphibians were the first vertebrates to come from water on land but not fully adapted to terrestrial life. They lead double life so they are called amphibians. (Greek *amphi* = two, double; *bios* = life).

General Characters

1. They are aquatic, only freshwater as well as terrestrial.
2. Body is divisible into head, neck and trunk.
3. Skin is smooth, moist and rich in mucous glands. Scales are absent on the skin.
4. Respiration on land by lungs but in water by skin and gills.
5. Most forms have two pairs of pentadactyl limbs with 4-5 or fewer digits. In some forms, limbs are absent. Digits are without claws or nails. But webs may be present.
6. Endoskeleton is large bony. Verterbral column, pelvic, pectoral girdles are present.
7. The skull is autostylic and has occipital condyles.
8. Heart is three-chambered.
9. Brain is well developed. Ten pairs of cranial nerves are present.
10. Cloaca has urinary bladder, Mesonephric kidneys.
11. Sexes are separate, oviparous, metamorphosis and development occurs in water only.
12. Most forms undergo hibernation in winter. Some aestivate in dry summer.

Habits, Habitat and Distribution

- Amphibians are the first animals which live on land as well as in water for reproduction. Among the amphibian frogs and toad are the anurans animals, which live on land.
- Frogs are generally found in or near water and in very damp places on land. Indian bull frog, *Rana tigrina* lives in or near freshwater lakes, ponds or streams. This is necessary for keeping skin moist to carry on cutaneous respiration.
- The animal can jump in the pond with its long hind legs to escape from its enemy. It shows leaping and swimming.
- For swimming hind legs fingers are equipped with webs. Frogs are carnivorous animals and food mainly consists of living insects, worms, molluscs and tadpoles.

- These animals are having sticky tongue attached at the tip of lower jaw, useful for catching the food material. Frogs show hibernation in winter and aestivation in summer. They live in water for reproduction. Development takes place in water.
- There are also areboreal frogs which live on trees. They shows green body colour which helps in protection. For climbing of the branches adhesive glands are present at the tips of their gingers. Some frogs can glide in air with the help of the webs present in the fingers.
- They are also called as flying frogs. Their body is very thin and slender breeding season.
- Toads are land animals, they are not living in water, but only go for reproduction in their body is not moist and mucous glands are lacking. Instead of these glands, poison glands are present in the skin which secrete poisonous secretion when attacked by enemy.
- Thus, they get protection from enemy. There are no webs present in the fingers of hind legs. Therefore, animals are unable to swim in the water. Frogs and toads are distributed on the earth.
- There are also limbless amphibians called Ichthyophis or caecilians. They mostly inhabit the tropical and subtropical regions of America, Africa and Asia. They strictly burrowing animals except few aquatic forms.
- They feed on worms and small invertebrates.
- Though they are called blind worms, but they can feel their way about by means of protrusible sensory tentacle lying in the groove between the eyes and nose. Ichthyophis is common form in South-East Asia including India.
- They show parental care some forms are found in South America.
- Salamanders and newts are tailed amphibians. They show lizard like body. Limbs are usually weak.
- Some forms retain gills and are aquatic throughout life. *Necturus*, *siven*, *proteus* are the examples of two type. Some forms lose their gills after achieving adult stage e.g. *Amphiuma*. *Amblystoma* like forms exhibit neoteny and paedogenesis.

- Its skin is poisonous and baund in U.S.A. and Mexico.
- Lack of iodine in water results in failure of metamorphosis of larva and it retains three pairs of external gills for respiration. This larva is able to reproduce because it becomes sexually mature.
- *Triturus* is European crysted newt which is terrestrial in habitat. Siren is found in North America which is permanent neotenic form Amphibians show high degree of parental care.

Adaptations for Amphibious Life

- Amphibia means double life. These animal live in water for reproduction and on land for food and shelter. Amphibia are first animals which show transition from aquatic to terrestrial mode of life.
- They are not fully terrestrially adapted animals. However, they show adaptation between aquatic and land environments. Fishes are completely aquatic animals on one hand and reptiles are fully terrestrial animals on the other hand.
- Therefore, they show transitional between these two ends. They show both aquatic as well as terrestrial mode of life, hence they are called amphibia i.e. double mode of life.

Adaptations for Aquatic Life

1. All the amphibians are generally found in or near water and in very damp places on land.
2. They live near or in the water to keep skin moist to carry on Cutaneous or skin respiration as well as to immediately jump or slip into water to escape from enemies.
3. Some amphibians swim in the water therefore their hindlimbs are long, muscular and powerful with webbed fingers. The frog swims in water by powerful backwards thrusts of its hindlimbs which act like propellers.
4. Skin is useful for respiration.
5. Some forms show external gills for respiration during larval stages. Frog and toad larva shows external gills. Siren or mud eel has three pairs of external gills and three pairs of gill slits. Mud puppy has three pairs of external gills.

Amblystoma or tiger salamander larva which is called axolot larva retain three pairs of external gills for aquatic respiration. Blind cave salamander also possess three pairs of external gills for aquatic respiration.
6. The skin of the frog is thin moist, slimy. It is kept moist by mucous glands. It is useful for cutaneous or skin respiration.
7. Eggs are protected in the gelatinous material called jelly.

Adaptations for Terrestrial Life
1. Skin is soft, moist, glandular and pigmented. Frogs are not easily noticeable by their enemies as they can change the colour or their skin to match with that of the surroundings. This type of protective colouration is known as camouflage.
2. Some amphibians are snake like adapted for burrowing mode of life. For example, *Amphiuma* or congo eel, Blind cave salamander, Mud eel. Their limbs are rudimentary. They burrow in soft mud.
3. Some amphibians are blind because eyes are of no use in burrows e.g. Blind cave salamander.
4. Terrestrial amphibians particularly frog and toads have sticky tongues for catching food.
5. Toads show rough and dry skin with poison glands when disturbed produce noxious unpalatable secretions from the skin glands, hence they are rarely eaten by enemies. There are no webs between fingers.
6. Toads concealed during day become active at night.
7. Fire bellied toad shows dorsal surface which cryptically coloured to conceal it from predator. If captured the predator will spit it out because of its bad taste.

Arboreal Adaptations
1. Some tree frogs like *Hyla* show green colour and gets protection from enemies.
2. They show terminal bones of digits are claw shaped and swollen basally into glandular adhesive discs which enable them to climb trees.
3. Large vocal sacs help in making a very loud voice which can be heard from a long distance.
4. Flying frog *Rhacophorus* has characteristic feature of large webs developed in between the much elongated digits

which also terminate in conspicuous rounded adhesive pads or discs as in *Hyla*. Webs and flattened body serve as a parachute in gliding form a higher elevation to a lower one, so that they are designated as flying frogs.

5. Their body is flat and slender with slender arms.

Amphibians as Biological Control Agents

- Amphibians are carnivorous animals living in water as well as on the land. Frogs and toads are the good friends of farmers as they feed on insects harmful to crops.
- Therefore, they are called as biological control agents. Many parts of world they are released in the crop fields to control a particular type of insect pests. Frogs are equipped with folded and sticky tongue. Its anterior end is attached to the inner border of lower jaw.
- Its posterior end is free and bifid which can be flicked out and retracted suddenly after capturing the prey with its slimy surface. There are certain tree frogs which can capture rats and swallow them.
- Thus, the harmful insects and rodents like rats who destroy stored grains as well as field crops can be controlled by these animals.
- Moreover, the frogs and toads live in water at the time of breeding. They feed on large number of mosquito eggs, larvae and pupae.
- Thus, eggs can not complete life cycle. This is helpful for controlling mosquitoes and ultimately dreadful disease malaria. Frogs and toads feed on variety of insects like grasshoppers, beetles, caterpillers, bugs etc. which are harmful to crop plants.

Examples of Amphibia

- The class *Amphibia* includes the animals that live partly in fresh water and partly on land. These are the first vertebrates to come from water on land, but not fully adapted to terrestrial life.
- They lead double life, hence they are called amphibians. They are not found in salt water. The amphibians show great diversity in their body form, habits and habitat.

- Their interesting features include ability to change the colour, power of regeneration, curious breeding habits and mode of passsing winter. There are about 25,000 species of living *Amphibia*.

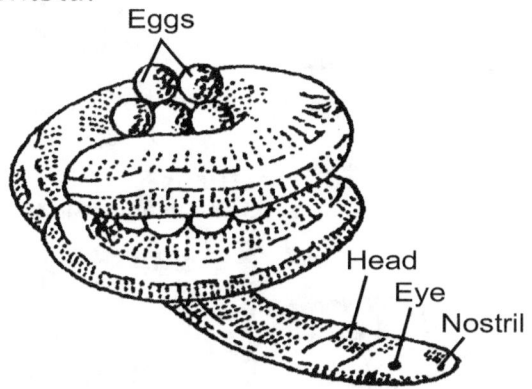

Fig. 1.22: *Ichthyophis*

- The subclass *Apoda* of *Amphibia* includes primitive burrowing forms which have no limbs and tail. They are widely distributed in the tropics.
- For example: *Ichthyophis*, *Siphonops* are vermiform amphibians with numerous small scales embedded in the skin arranged in transverse rows.
- They make burrows in the surface of soil in damp places near streams. They are completely terrestrial in the adult stage.
- They feed on worms and small invertebrates. Some forms lay large yolky eggs in moist earth; while others are viviparous.
- In case of *Ichthyophis*, mother carefully guards the eggs by coiling her body around them till they hatch. Thus it shows parental care. They are commonly called *Caecilians*.
- Subclass *Urodela* or *Caudata* includes the amphibians with well developed tail. They are mostly aquatic animals with long, narrow body divisible into head, trunk and tail.
- They use tail for locomotion on land and in water. Tail has tail fin without fin rays. Newts and Salamanders are representatives of urodela.
- *Necturus*, *Proteus* and *Siren* are the amphibian in which gills and gill slits persist in adults. *Necturus* or Mudpuppy inhabits the rivers and lakes of North America. It is a bottom dweller. The body has short and weak limbs which bear four fingers and four toes.

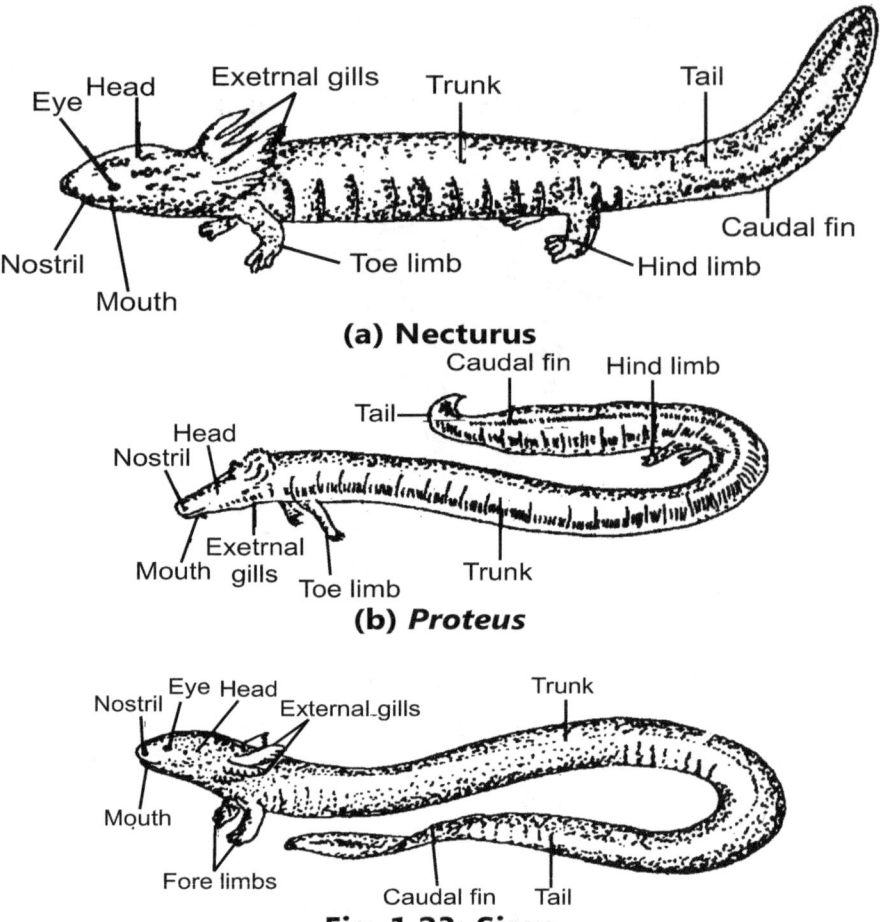

Fig. 1.23: *Siren*

- Since the aquatic form, it shows three pairs of fringed external gills and two pairs of gill slits on the sides of neck. The eyes are small and functional with no eyelids.
- *Proteus* or Blind Salamander found in the subterranean waters of deep, dark caves of Australia and Germany.
- The eyes are not functional. There are three pairs of small external gills. The limbs are small, weak and widely separated.
- The animal periodically comes to the surface for giving out foul air and gulping in fresh air.
- *Siren* or Mud eel is also inhabitants of rivers, swamps and ponds in North America. It has only forelimbs and hindlimbs are absent. It usually lives burried in mud hence called *mud eel*.

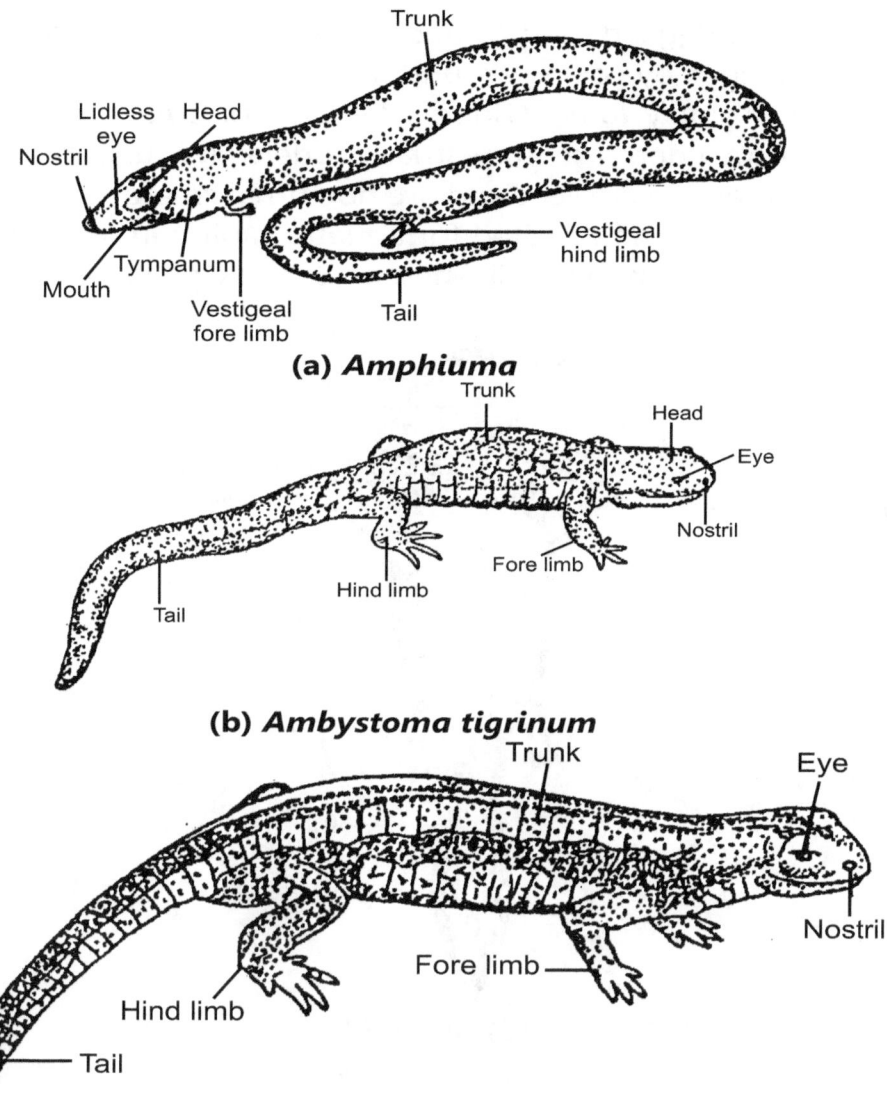

(a) Amphiuma

(b) Ambystoma tigrinum

(c) Salamandra maculosa

- In Urodela, there are representatives in which gills and gill slits disappear in adults. Tail is nearly cylindrical and usually lacks a fin.
- *Amphiuma* or Congo eel has eel like body with very short and weak limbs and it is found in swamps and rice fields in North America.

- It lays eggs in mud or under decaying leaves. Mother guards the eggs by coiling around them.
- The *Amblystoma* (Tiger salamander), *Salamandra* (Spotted Salamander) are terrestrial urodela live under stones and logs and in crevices and are nocturnal creatures.
- They are also adapted for aquatic habitat in which they swim actively with their tail. They walk slowly on land.

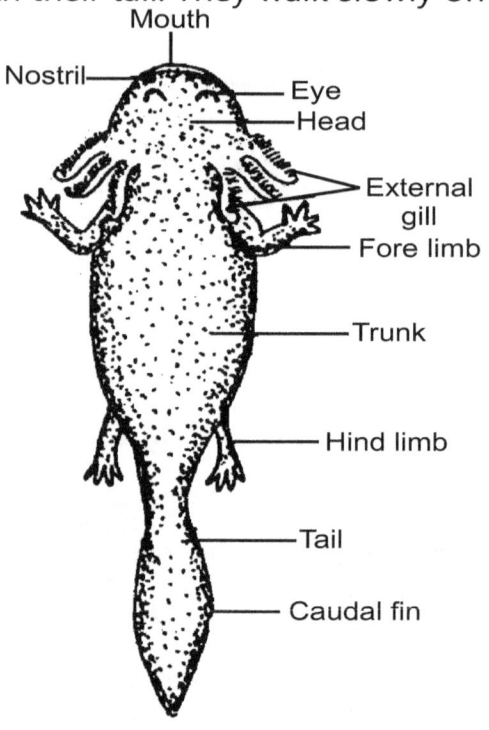

(d) *Axolotl* larva
Fig. 1.24

- In the life cycle of these animals adult like larva is present called *axolotl*. If water and food are plenty, the axolotls do not metamorphose into adults, but grow, develop gonads and start breeding like an adult. This phenomenon is called neoteny.
- If water is drying up, the larva lose gills and tail fin and develops lungs and become adult salamander.
- Another unique feature shown by salamander is that; they have great power of regeneration and can regrow lost limbs any number of times.

- *Triton* or Crested newt is found Europe and great Britain. It is very similar to salamander but its tail is strongly compressed and bears a caudal fin. It carries serrated crest on the head and back which becomes larger in the breeding season.

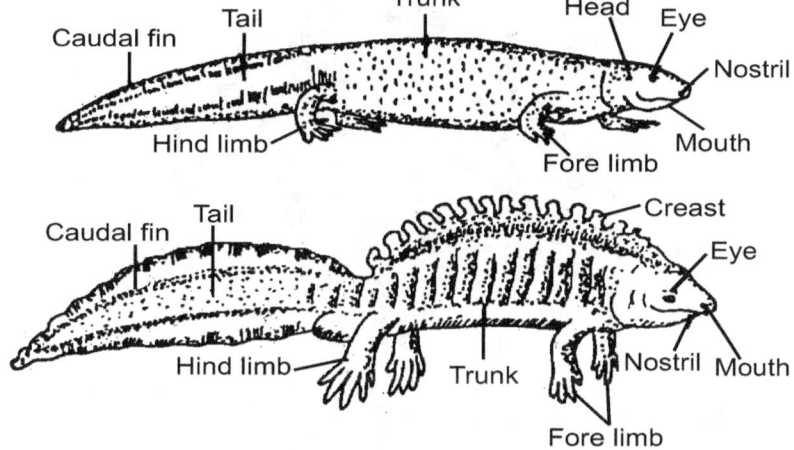

Fig. 1.25: *Triton*

- *Anuran* amphibians include the frogs and toads. Anura have a short, broad body comprising head and trunk and tail is lacking in adults. Their skin is scaleless hindlimbs are longer than forelimbs.
- Feet are webbed. They are the first vocal vertebrates. They inhabit tropical and temperate regions of the world occurring in and near ponds, rivers, marshes and streams.
- Frogs and toads show some basic difference. Toads generally live in dark shady corners of gardens hidden in grass or under stones and leaves. They visit water only for breeding. Frogs generally live in or near water.
- Toads are active at night hence nocturnal, whereas frogs are active during daytime.
- The skin of the toad is thick, dry, rough and warty, has no respiratory function and it contains numerous poison glands and very few mucous glands. The web is reduced or absent in fingers of toad.
- *Pipa* or *Surinam* toad is the found in damp forest of tropical America. It shows depressed body with triangular head. The tongue and teeth are lacking. Tympanum and eyelids are also lacking.

- The animal shows very slender fingers each ending in a four rayed star and toes are fully webbed. The female forms pockets on its back and eggs develop in these pockets.

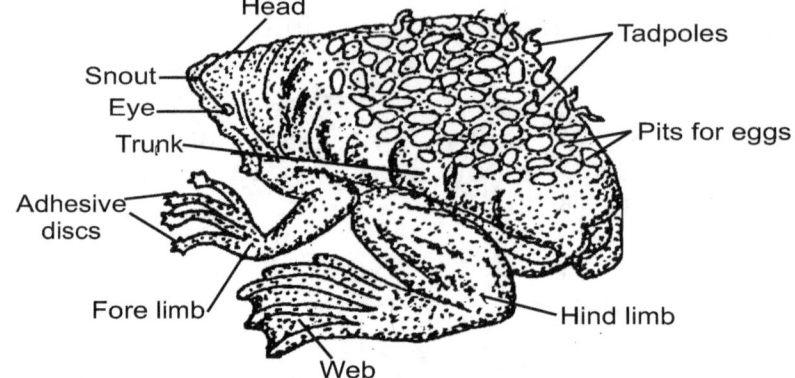

Fig. 1.26: *Pipa*

- There are other anurans which possess tongue and tymphanous include *Rana*, *Bufo*, *Hyla* and *Rhacophorus*.
- *Rana tigrina* is common Indian frog found all over the world, except South America. There are many species of *Rana*, *Bufo* etc. is a common toad found hidden in grass or under leaves, stones, logs etc. Skin is covered with ugly warts.
- *Hyla* or tree frog is found in North India. It leads an arboreal life and can change colour very rapidly to adapt with the back ground. Its limbs are very long and slender. Finger are free but toes are webbed.

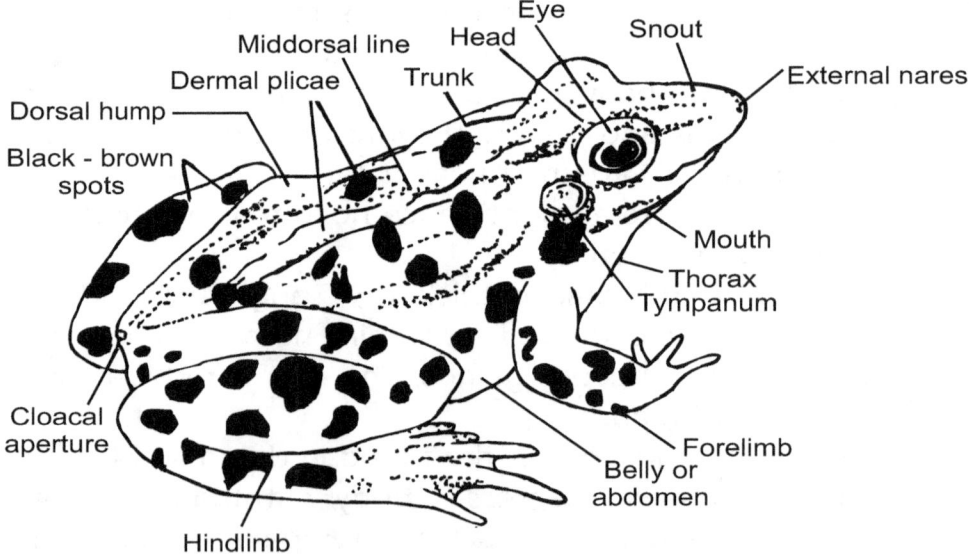

Fig. 1.27: (a) *Rana tigrina*

- All the digits have flat, circular adhesive discs at the tip. *Rhacophorus* or flying frog is found in South and East Asia.
- It is an arboreal amphibian and it can glide through the air for a considerable distance as its webs when fully expanded. It can climb trees with the help of adhesive discs.

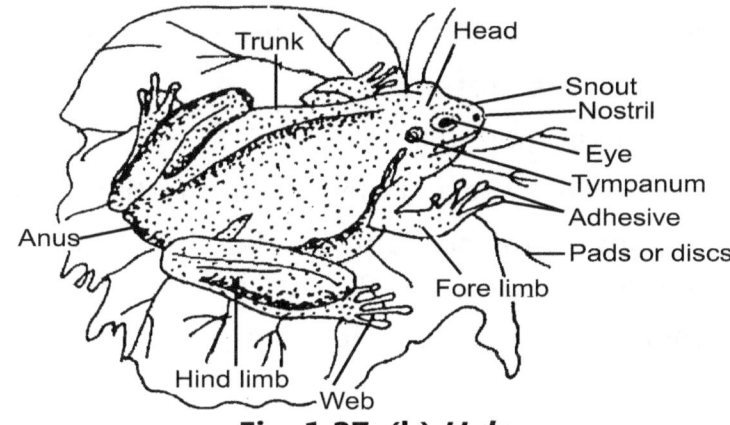

Fig. 1.27: (b) *Hyla*

- The frog genrally exhibits gliding for coming down on the ground or jumping from higher tree to a lower one. The animal is active at twilight. It make the nest of gleatinous foam in shallow water pools and rice field.
- The todpoles, when ready are dropped into water. All the amphibians show parental care.

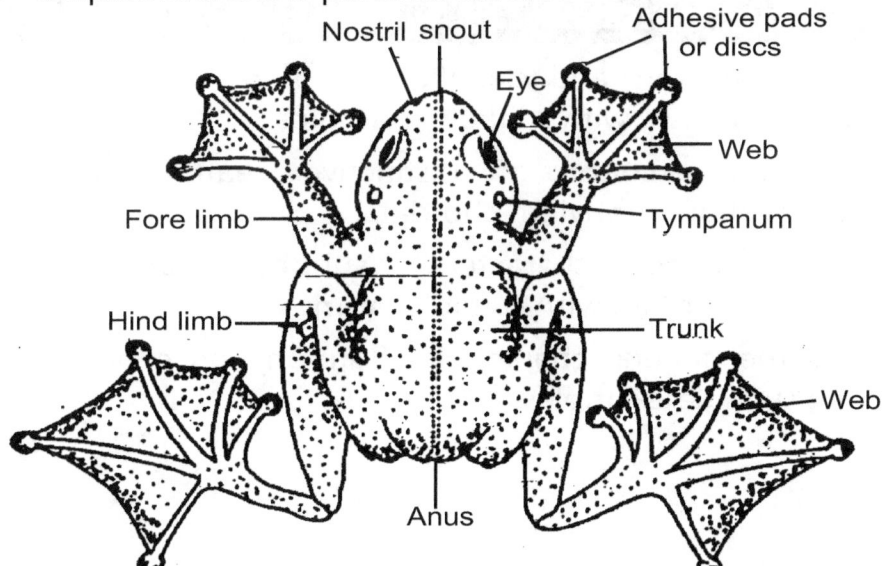

Fig. 1.27: (c) *Rhacophrus*

Summary

- Hemichordates are wormlike animals which may be colonial or solitary.
- Body is divisible into proboscis, collar and trunk.
- Coelom is divided into protocoel, mesocoel and metacoel.
- Many gill slits are present.
- Excretion by glomerulus.
- Reproduction is by sexual method and fertilization is external.
- The phylum hemichordata is classified into two classes namely *Enteropneusta* and *Pterobranchia*.
- *Balanoglossus, Rhabdopleura,* are the examples of this phylum.
- Urochordata and Cephalochordata are two subphyla of protochordata.
- *Herdmania* or sea squirts are the example of urochordata.
- Urochordata are fixed or pelagic, solitary or colonial.

Review Questions

1. Give characters and classification of phylum hemichordata upto class level with suitable examples.
2. Give an account of distinctive features and broad classification of phylum chordata.
3. Give the general characters of subphylum urochordata and cephalochordata with suitable examples.
4. Give the general characters of subphylum cephalochordate with suitable examples.

Chapter 2...

Cephalochordata and Cyclostomata

2.1 Cephalochordata - *Amphioxus (Branchiostoma)*
2.2 General Characters of Cyclostomata
2.3 Pisces
✍ Summary
✍ Review Questions

2.1 Cephalochordata - Amphioxus (Branchiostoma)

Amphioxus or *Lancelet* is the small fish like marine animal with both the ends sharply pointed. It was first discovered by P. S. Pallas in 1778 and wrongly classified as slug *Limax lanceolatum*. Later in 1834 **O. G. Costa** recognized its true position in the animal kingdom and named it *Branchiostoma lanceolatum*. It is also commonly called as *Amphioxus*.

Systematic Position

Phylum	-	Chordata
Sub-phylum	-	Protochordata
Class	-	Cephalochordata
Genus	-	*Branchiostoma*
Species	-	*lanceolatum*

The animal belongs to the *phylum Chordata* because it possesses three important chordate characters.

These are:
1. Presence of notochord
2. Presence of pharyngeal gill slits, and
3. Presence of dorsal tubular nerve cord.

The animal included in the *subphylum Protochordata* show:
1. The notochord throughout the life which is not replaced by the vertebral column.

2. No skull hence called as *acrania* (i.e. without cranium). There is no skull therefore brain is absent.
3. No true heart and excretory organs, kidneys.
4. Different embryonic development from that of vertebrates.

The animal included in the class *Cephalochordata* are:
1. Small fish like animals showing the main chordate characters.
2. The notochord extends the entire length of the body projecting beyond the nervous system to the tip of the snout (hence *Cephalochordata*).
3. They have a dorsal tubular neural tube without a defined brain.
4. Pharynx is large with numerous gill slits opening not to the exterior, but into an ectoderm lined atrium.
5. There is no definite coelom.
6. Metamerism is well marked.
7. Excretion takes place through definite protonephridia.

The class cephalochordata includes two principal genera:
1. **Branchiostoma** (*Amphioxus*) having paired sexual organs.
2. **Asymmetron** with unilateral gonads.

Habitat

Branchiostoma is marine animal found in shore water and on the sandy-beaches of the temperate, subtropical and tropical regions of the world. It is inhabitant of shallow waters. It has a wide distribution from the Mediterranean to the North sea, in the Atlantic coast of America and in the Indian Ocean. On the Chinese coast it is found in such abundance that it is sold there as a food.

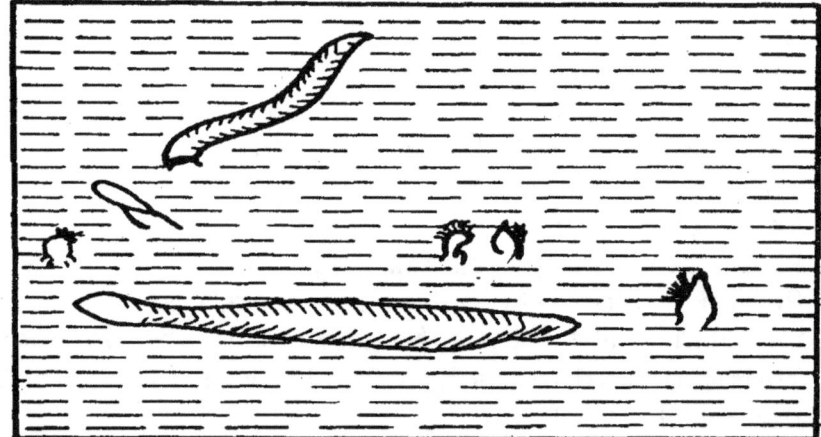

Fig. 2.1: *Branchiostoma* is in its habitat in swimming and feeding

Habit

Branchiostoma is essentially a burrowing animal but also swims actively in the water. It burrows in sand near the shore with greater part of the body burried and only anterior part of the head projecting into water. It burrows rapidly, head first, in the sand by means of vibratory action of the entire body but comes to rest with anterior end exposed to the water. It is also able to swim freely in the water by means of lateral strokes of the posterior part of the body. Often the animal lies on one side on the sand. These animals are most active at night and leave the burrows particularly at night and during breeding season. The animal shows ciliary feeding mechanism by creating water current.

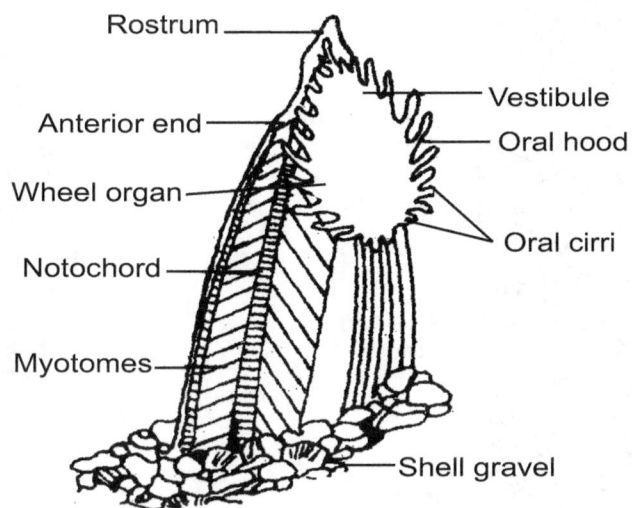

Fig. 2.2: *Branchiostoma* in its burrow

External Characters (Morphology)

Branchiostoma has fish like body ranging from one to three inches in length. The body of animal is semi-transparent in appearance, narrow, laterally compressed and pointed at both ends. The anterior end is bluntly pointed whereas posterior end is sharply pointed.

On the dorsal side, dorsal fin is running mid-dorsally along the whole length, which joined to the somewhat broader *caudal fin* around the tail. Midventrally is a *ventral fin* running from the caudal fin to an antripore. The dorsal fin is supported by a series of fin rays and the ventral fin by a series of paired fin rays. The fin rays are made up of a gelatinous substance and connective tissue. It is important to note that the structure of fins and fin rays of *Branchiostoma* are totally different from fins and fin rays of fishes. The fin rays may be absent in the anterior and posterior (caudal fin) end.

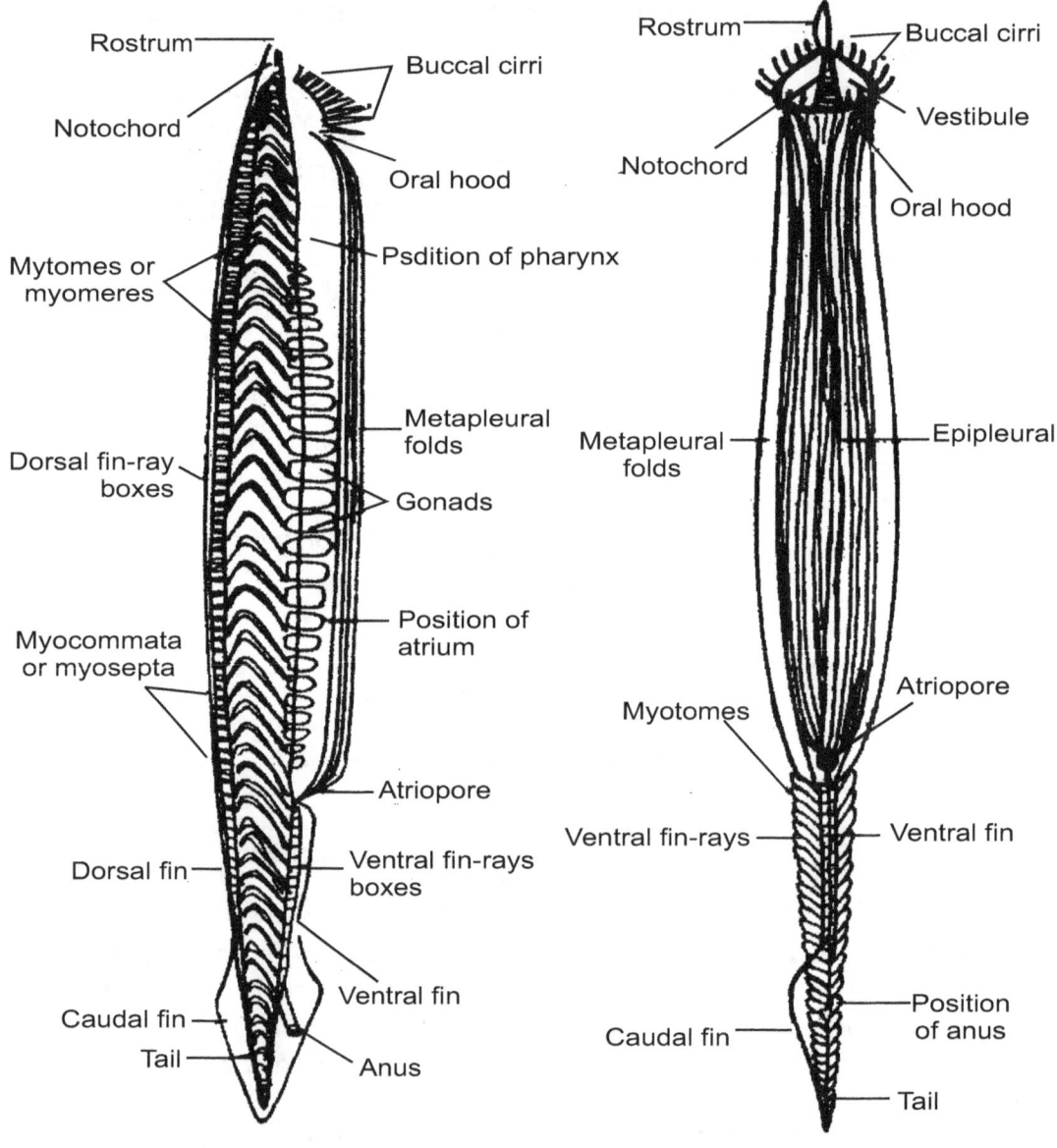

(a) Lateral view   **(b) Ventral view**
Fig. 2.3: *Branchiostoma*

For the sake of convenience, the body of the animal can be divided into four regions, the cephalic, atrial, abdominal and caudal.

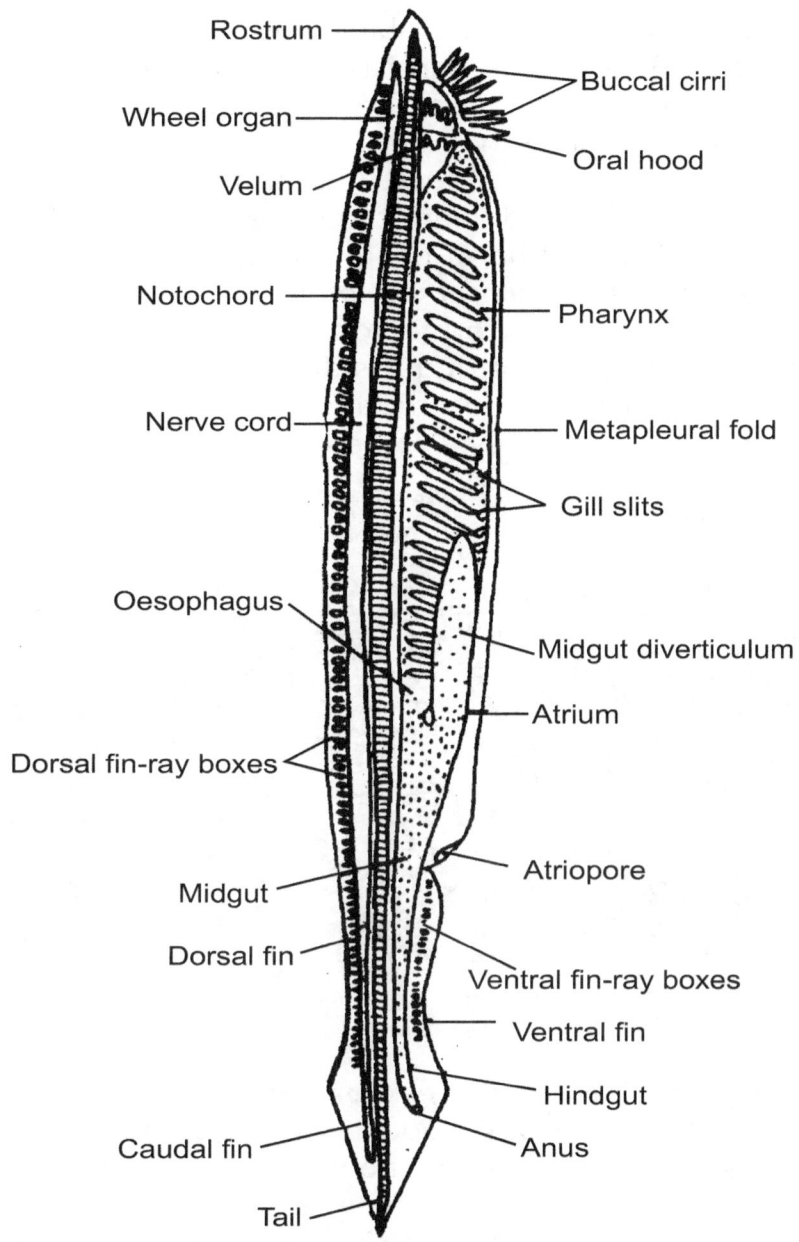

Fig. 2.4: *Branchiostoma*
Enlarge L.S. of anterior end in right lateral view

1. **Cephalic region:** This region includes the anterior bluntly pointed *snout* or *rostrum* and *mouth*. The notochord extends beyond the mouth up to the tip of the rostrum. Nerve cord is also slightly extended in the rostrum situated above the notochord. Below the rostrum mouth is present. It consists of two portions, an outer vestibule and an inner *oral aperture*, which is surrounded by a spincter with tentacles called the *velum*. The vestibule of the mouth is the space bounded by the *oral hood*. It is formed by the dorsal and lateral projections of the body and it encloses a cup shaped buccal cavity or *vestibule*. The oral hood bears twenty or more tentacle like sensory processes called *buccal* or *oral cirri*. The oral hood is supported internally by a ring formed off stiff, gelatinous pieces lying end to end, from this skeletal ring a stiff rod passes into each oral cirrus. The oral cirri may cross each other and may completely close the entrance to the mouth. They are chemoreceptors in function.

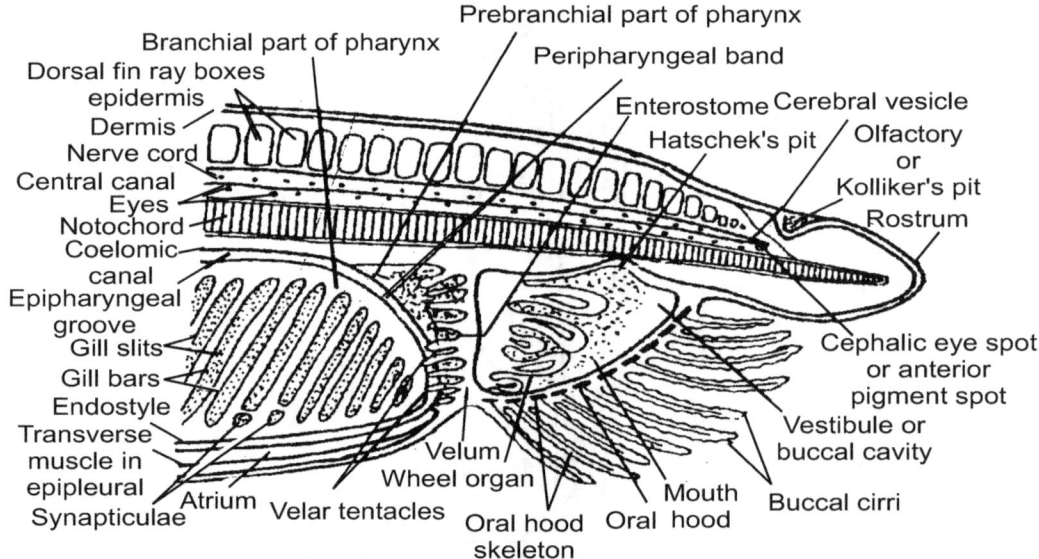

Fig. 2.5: The anterior part of *Branchiostoma*

The underside of the oral hood bears a complicated series of ciliated grooves; ridges collectively known as wheel organ, because it sets up whirling currents of water. Between the ciliated lobe of the wheel organ towards the right hand side of the notochord there is a grandular groove which secretes mucous. This is called *Hatschek's groove* or *pit*. It may be sensory because it is lined by columnar cells having stiff sensory hairs. At the posterior end of the vestibule is a vertical partition called *velum*. It is also provided with circlet of twelve velar tentacles (in some species 16) which are projecting backwards into pharynx.

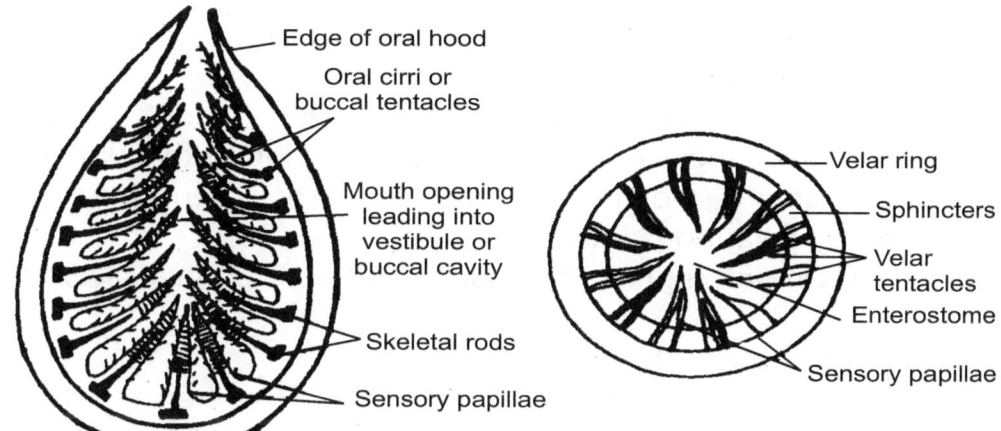

Fig. 2.6: *Branchiostoma*. Oral hood

Fig. 2.7: *Branchiostoma*. Wheel organ

The velar tentacles are sensory forming a strainer. The velum has a circular aperture called *true mouth* or the *enterostome*. On the dorsal side at the anterior end rostrum bears a pit called as *Kolliker's pit* or *olfactory pit*.

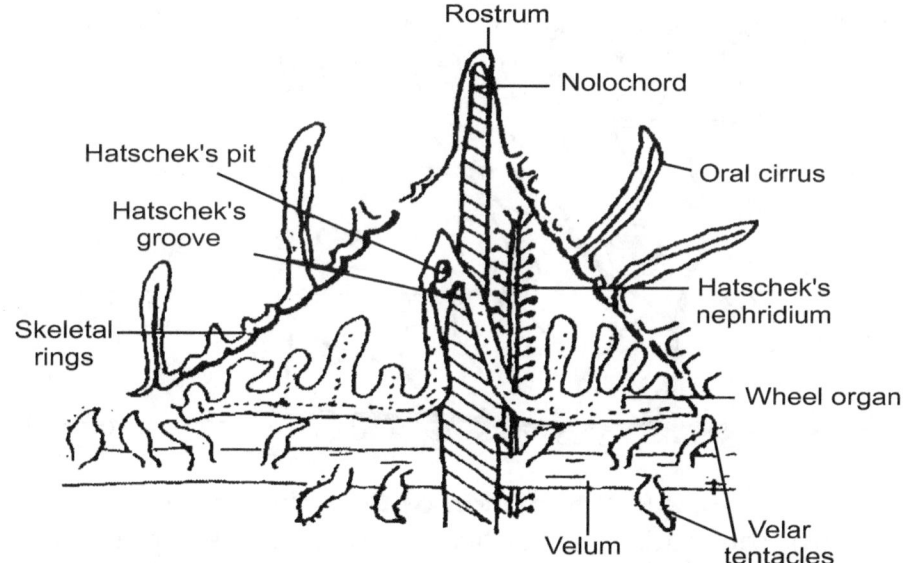

Fig. 2.8: Ventral view of anterior end of *Branchiostoma*

2. The atrial region: It extends from the mouth over about two third of the length of the body, terminating at a large median aperture, the *atriopore*. This pore is an outlet for respiratory current of water and also serves for the release of reproductive products. Hence, atrial region is also called as branchio genital region. The oral hood is continuous posteriorly with two lateral hollow membranous folds called metapleural folds running ventrally upto the *atriopore*. Within each *metapleural* fold lies continuous longitudinal lymph spate, the *metapleural canal*.

3. The abdominal region: It comprises a short stretch of body between antriopore and anus, the termination of the alimentary canal. It is characterised by the presence of a special *ventral fin* which is supported by gelatinous fin-rays.

4. The caudal region: It includes the post annual division of the trunk.

Body Wall and Musculature

The body is covered over by a thin layer of epidermis which is made up of a single layer of columnar epithelium. On the surface of epidermis a *cuticle* is perforated by pores. In between the epidermal cells, some cells are specialised as sensory cells but there are no gland cells, and chromatophores. A thin layer of tough fibrous connective tissue form a *cutis* below the epidermis.

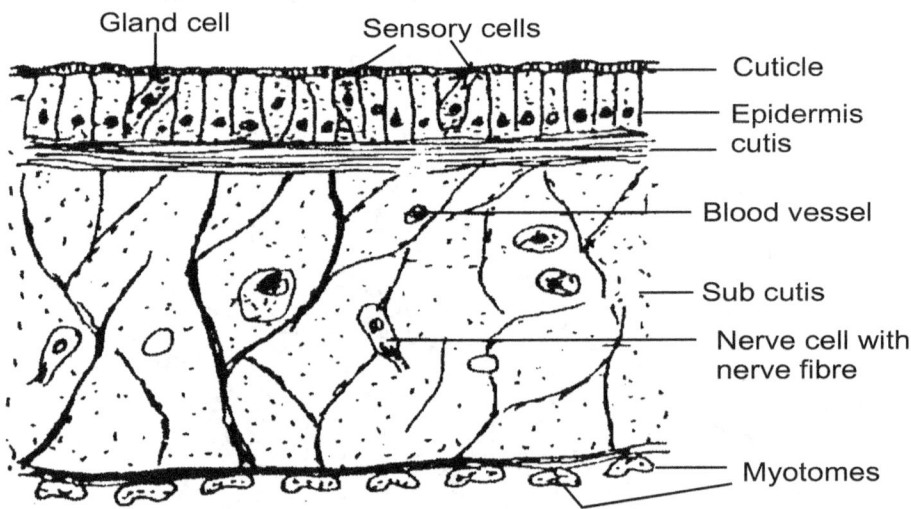

Fig. 2.9: V.S. of skin of *Branchiostoma*

Beneath the cutis is a *subcutis* layer made up of gelatinous material containing nerve fibres and blood vessels. The integument of the Amphioxus is like that of invertebrates as it is made up of only epidermis. In case of higher chordates epidermis is of multi-layered and dermis is also present. A dermis is lacking in *Amphioxus*. Due to lack of pigment cells or chromatophores the skin is more or less transparent, and underlying musculature can be seen through it.

Musculature: The body wall shows metameric segmentation being made of blocks of muscles called *myotomes* or *myomeres*.

There are about sixty myotomes on each side, but number varies in different species. Each myotome is separated from one another by partitions or coverings of dense connective tissue called *myocomma*. The myotomes are V-shaped structures with their apices directed forwards. The series of such myotomes are arranged from anterior tip of the animal to the end of the tail. Each myotome is composed of numerous flat, striated muscle fibres arranged longitudinally, so that each is attached to the successive myocommas. By means of this arrangement the body can be bent from side to side with great rapidity. The myomeres of the right and left sides of the body are not opposite to one another, but have an alternate arrangement. On the dorsal side the myotomes are very thick enclosing the nerve cord and notochord. Ventrally between the metapleural fold are *transverse muscles* in the anterior two-thirds of the body, no such muscles are seen in vertebrates.

Skeleton

The animal do not possess any exoskeleton, however there are few endoskeletal elements present within the body. The endoskeleton is not in the form of bone or cartilage but the supporting material.

Following are the components of the endoskeleton:

1. Notochord: It is the main important and prominent endoskeletal structure which is cylindrical rod extending from the every tip of the rostrum to the end of the tail. It is located just below the nerve cord (or neural tube) and above the alimentary canal. It is the main supporting structure of the body of the *Amphioxus*. The notochord is formed of alternate fibrous and gelatinous material, which makes notochord hard and turgid. The notochord is covered by means of a thick fibrous connective tissue sheath, called *notochordal sheath*. The turgid cells and sheath of notochord prevents shortening of the body when myotomes contract. But due to elastic nature of the notochord, it allows side to side bending when muscles contract.

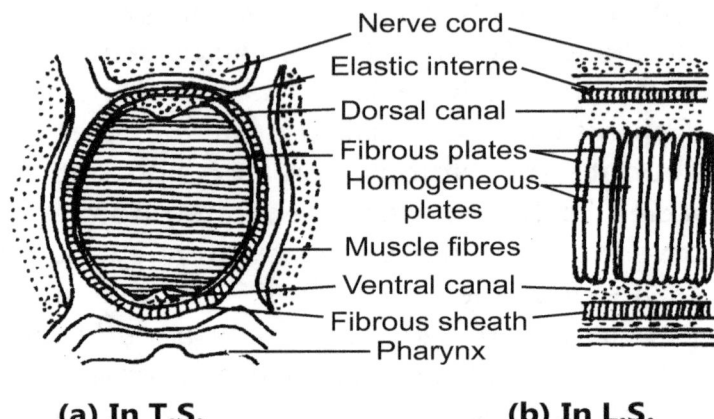

(a) In T.S. (b) In L.S.
Fig. 2.10: *Branchiostoma* Notochord

2. Connective tissue: Besides the notochord an endoskeletal function is performed by dense fibrous connective tissue. It forms distinct layer just below the epidermiss. Also it forms a sheath around the myotomes called myocommata. They form a system of strong septa throughout the length of the body and they serve for attachment of muscles. Dense fibrous connective tissue also ensheathes the central nervous system.

3. Gelatinous substance or soft cartilage: In the body of the animal is certain parts fibrous connective tissue is replaced by gelatinous substance resembling soft cartilage which provides endoskeletal support. The oral hood is supported by such a ring made up of pieces lying end to end. Each piece gives out a rod forming the axis of an oral cirrus.

Gill bars of the pharynx and endostyle also supported by skeletal rods made of elastic gelatinous substance.

The dorsal fins are also supported by single row of fin rays and while ventral fins are supported by double row of fin rays one on the left and other on the right.

The fin rays are formed by connective tissue containing gelatinous substance inside

Locomotion

Branchiostoma swims freely in the water at night. The myotomes enable it to swim rapidly with characteristic serpentine undulations of the body. The movements are brought about by the alternate contraction and relaxation of the myotomes on the both sides. As a result of contraction body bends, but the telescoping of the muscle segments is prevented by the notochord. The myotomes of the two sides (left and right) alternate with each other and are not opposite to each other. This anatomical pecularity is apparently correlated with the peculiar mode of locomotion. When the somites appear for the first time they soon undergo distortion, with the result that the somites of left side are carried forward through the length of one-half segment. For instance the 27th myotome of the left side is placed opposite to the 26th myotommata of the right side.

This arrangement is responsible for the bending of the body at varying angles as the muscles contract resulting in a forward propagation. The body, however, is not adapted for fast movement.

Digestive System

Digestive system of *Branchiostoma* is simple and consist of alimentary canal and a *digestive* and *liver* or *midgut diverticulum*. Various other structures are associated with the digestive system.

Alimentary Canal

The alimentary canal is perfectly straight tube lined throughout by ciliated epithelium. It consists of:
1. Mouth
2. Buccal cavity
3. Pharynx
4. Oesophagus
5. Mid-gut and mid-gut diverticulum (liver)
6. Hind gut
7. Anus.

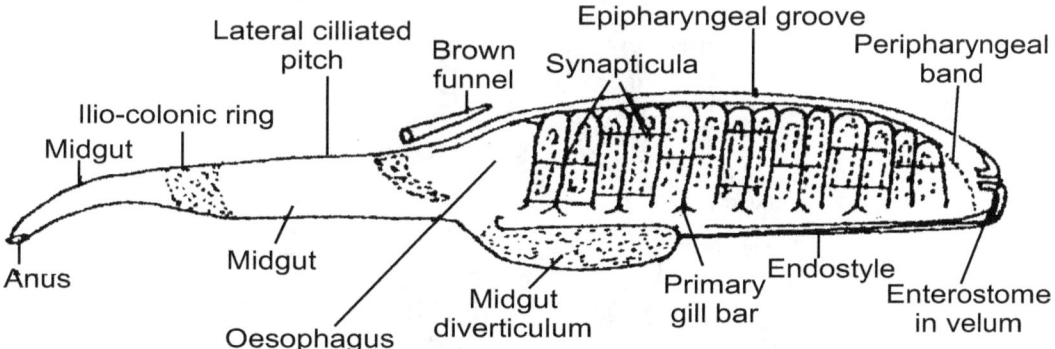

Fig. 2.11: Alimentary canal of *Branchiostoma*

1. **Mouth:** The wide opening of the oral hood is the mouth of the *Branchiostoma*. It is a large circular opening lined by ectodermal epithelium.

2. **Buccal cavity:** The mouth leads into funnel shaped buccal cavity which is also called as vestibule. It is the space enclosed by the oral hood and lined by ectoderm. At the posterior end buccal cavity is bounded by a ring of muscles called the *velum*. It bears numerous sensory tentacles called *velar tentacles*, which normally project backwards into the pharynx. The velum has a central pore or opening known as *enterostome* which leads into the pharynx. The enterostome is also called a mouth. But it opens into endoderm lined pharynx and not, into an ectoderm lined vestiule or stomodaeum. It cannot correspond to the mouth of chordates. Hence anterior opening into buccal cavity (ectoderm lined) or vestibule is a true mouth.

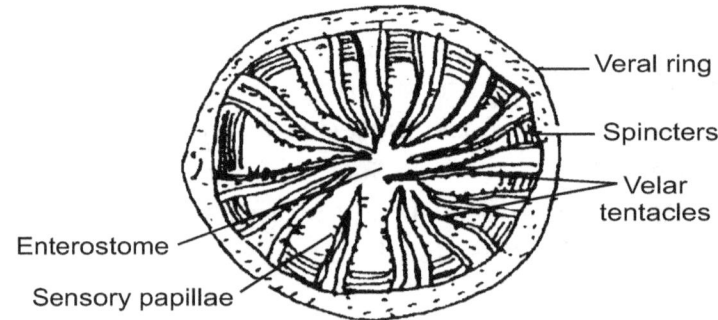

Fig. 2.12: Structure of *velum*

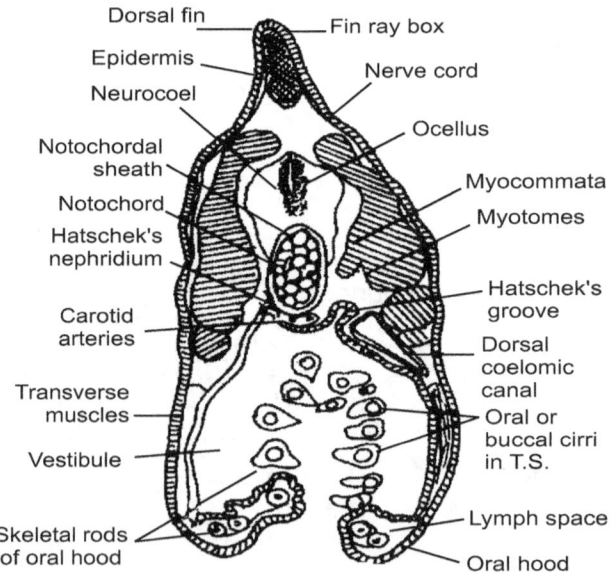

Fig. 2.13: T. S. of *Branchiostoma* through oral hood

3. Pharynx: It is a large, laterally compressed chamber where the main operation of food collection is performed. Its side walls are perforated by more than 150 pairs of oblique vertical slits or gill clefts which bear no *gills*. The number of gill clefts increases with age, the new ones being added constantly at the posterior end of the pharynx. It is through these slits that the pharynx opens to the exterior. The partitions between the adjacent gill clefts are supported by skeletal rods called *gill bars*. The gill-bars are of two types, the *primary gill bars* with forked ends and the *secondary gill bars* with unforked ends. They alternate regularly along the length of the pharynx, and differ not only in their structure but also in the mode of development. A primary gill bar is formed of the tissue between two successive gill clefts after they have perforated to the exterior. It is composed of the wall of the pharynx and the body wall of the larva, i.e. has origin of ectoderm, endoderm, and mesoderm. The secondary gill bars arise as down growth of the dorsal wall of the larval gill clefts, the wall grows downwards dividing the original gill cleft into two halves vertically. Both primary and secondary gill bars are covered on their external or outer surface by sparsely ciliated ectodermal or atrial epithelium, but on their inner, anterior and posterior surfaces by endodermal pharyngeal epithelium which is heavily ciliated. These cilia on the anterior and posterior endodermal sumacs of gill bars are long *lateral cilia* which propel water. The cilia on the inner endodermal surface of each gill bar forma long but narrow tract of *frontal cilia* which propel mucous. In the middle each gill bar has a mesodermic core of connective tissue, blood vessels and gill rods.

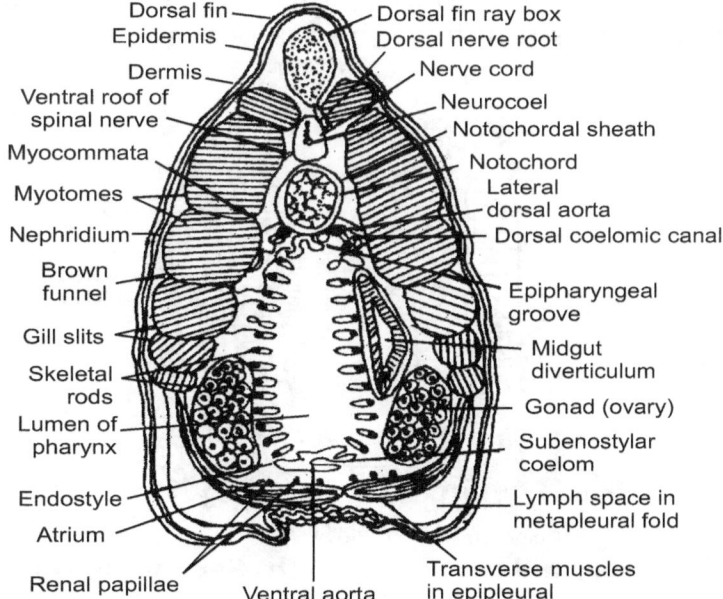

Fig. 2.14: T. S. of *Branchiostoma* through pharynx

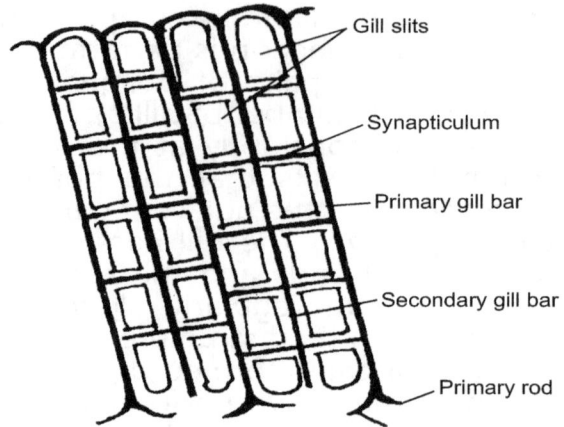

Fig. 2.15: Pharyngeal skeleton of *Branchiostoma*

The gill bars are supported internally by gelatinous skeletal gill rods. All the gill rods are united dorsally but ventrally their free ends are forked in primary gill bars and unforked in secondary gill bars. The gill bars are connected by transverse or cross bars called *synapticula* which also contains gelatinous rods and blood vessels. The synapticula develop only after the gill clefts have been completed. They make the pharynx look like a basket, which somewhat resembles the branchial sac of urochordates. The primary gill bars contain a narrow coelomic canal running throughout the length of each and communicating dorsally and ventrally with other coelomic spaces. They have also three blood vessels on each running lengthwise, however, in secondary gill bars no coelomic canal but only two blood vessels run through each of them.

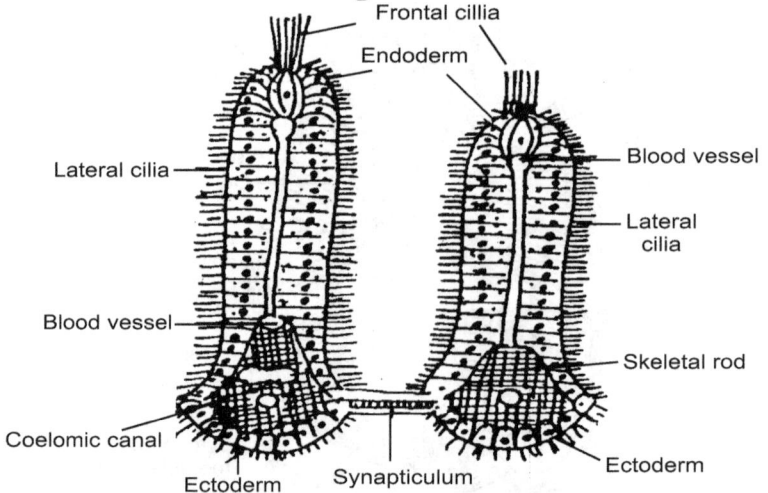

(a) Primary gill bar   (b) Secondary gill bar

Fig. 2.16: T. S of gill bars

Besides the cilia on the gill bars there are other ciliated tracts in the pharynx. On the dorsal surface of the pharynx running mid-dorsally is a ciliated groove called *epipharyngeal groove* which leads into the opening of oesophagus at the posterior end of the pharynx. It consists in food catching. In the mid-ventral wall of the pharynx is a shallow groove called *endostyle*. It is lined by four longitudinal tracts of *gland cells* which secrete mucous. These tracts are separated by ciliated cells of which the median row of the cells bear very long cilia called *median cilia*. Just below the endostyle there are two gelatinuous plates. Beneath these plates lies *subendostylar coelom* and *centrally ventral aorta*. The endostyle is V shaped structure and produce sticky mucous threads in which food panicles become entangled. The endostyle at its anterior end is joined with endostyle by two ciliated *peripharyngeal bands* each running on one side in the wall of the pharynx just behind the velum. These bands divert the food particles captured by sticky threads of the endostyle to the epipharyngeal groove in which they are conducted backwards to the oesophagus.

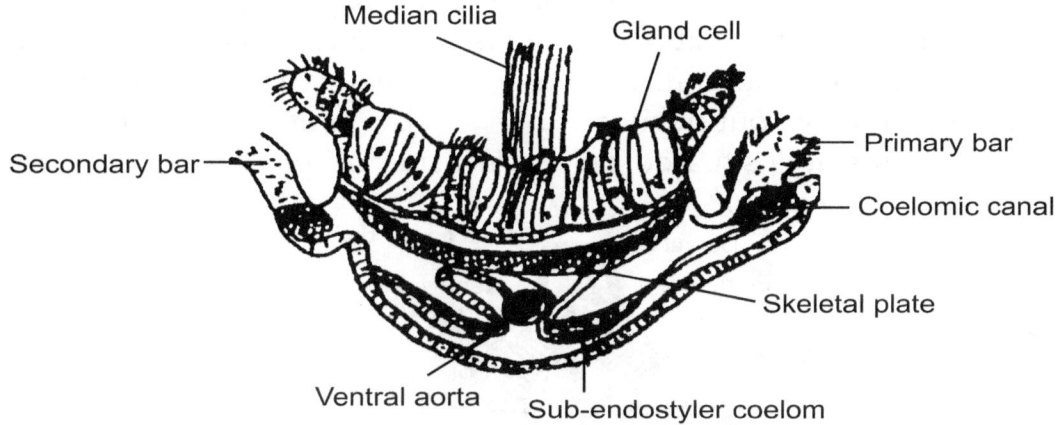

Fig. 2.17: T. S. of endostyle

4. **Oesophagus:** The oesophagus is a short region which follows the pharynx. It is also lined by ciliated cells and opens into the midgut.

5. **Mid-gut:** It is a straight tubular and broader part of alimentary canal. From the junction of oesophagus and mid-gut arising ventrally a blind pouch called *midgut diverticulum* or liver like digestive gland lies on the right of the pharynx. It does not resemble a liver in structure or function, however its blood vessels are somewhat similar to that of liver of vertebrates. It is comparable to a verebrate pancreas and secretes digestive enzymes. The diverticulum is lined by ciliated and glandular cells.

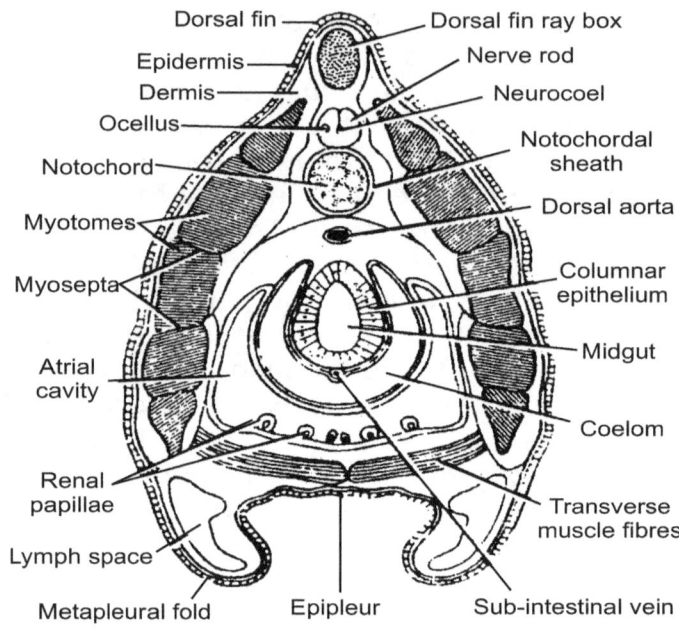

Fig. 2.18: *Branchiostoma* **T. S. through midgut**

6. **Hind gut:** Next to the mid-gut there is ilio-colonic ring followed by the hind gut. It is narrow tubular part also called as *intestine* and opens out by means of a small aperature, the anus.

7. **Anus:** It is situated on the left side of the ventral fin where the caudal fin begins.

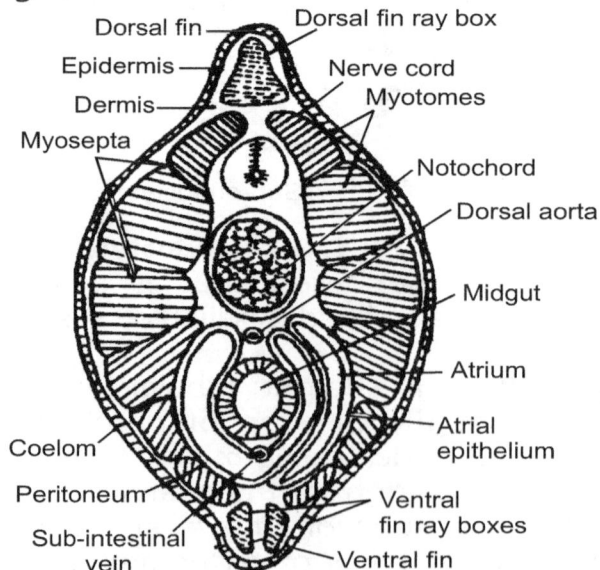

Fig. 2.19: *Branchiostoma* **T. S. of intestinal region behind atriopore**

In the alimentary canal the mid-gut and hind-gut show internally ciliated lining. In the mid-gut there is crescent shaped *lateral tract* of cilia in the mid-gut which directs food into the mid-gut diverticulum. There is dorsal tract present in the *mid-gut*. Also in between *mid-gut* and *hind-gut* iliocolonic ring is present useful for churning of food. The hind gut also possess another dorsal tract of cilia. Thus, the entire alimentary canal is ciliated useful for pushing the food towards posterior direction.

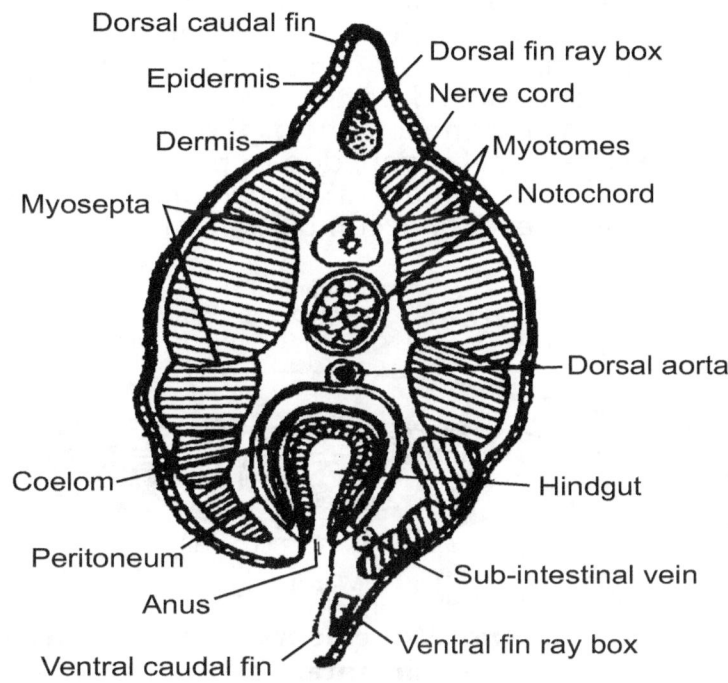

Fig. 2.20: *Branchlostonia* T. S. through pore

Food and Feeding

Branchostoma feeds upon minute organic particles chiefly microscopic animals and plants which it strains off from the surrounding sea water. The animal does not move about in search of food. The water is constantly entering the mouth and passing out in the atrium through the gills slits, it is expelled at the atriopore. This food bearing water current is produced and maintained by the action of cilia, that is why animal is described as *ciliary feeder*. The ciliary mode of feeding is believed to be primitive and it is adopted by many sedentary organisms. It is assumed that primitive chordates employed similar method for feeding.

Production of Current

The anterior and posterior faces of the each gill bar are covered with long powerful cilia the *lateral cilia*. The lashing movement of these lateral cilia drive water out of the pharynx through the gill slits into the atrium. This causes the formations of fresh water current drawn in at the mouth. The current carries particles suspended in it backwards and outwards from the mid-line towards the gill bars. This current is directed upwards from the ventral towards the dorsal mid-line by the lashing of frontal cilia on the inner (pharyngeal) surfaces of the gill bars. The buccal cirri are folded over one another to form a sieve so that larger sands particles are not allowed to enter the mouth during feeding. When there is more and more accumulation of particles on the cirri, the water current is prevented from entering in. To remove the accumulated particles a violent current of water is produced by the muscular movement of the floor of the pharynx by closing atriopore. The wheel organ, due to presence of its ciliar tracts, their peculiar movements create a vortex of water pass it to the enterostome. It also prevents accumulation of the food particles in the buccal cavity.

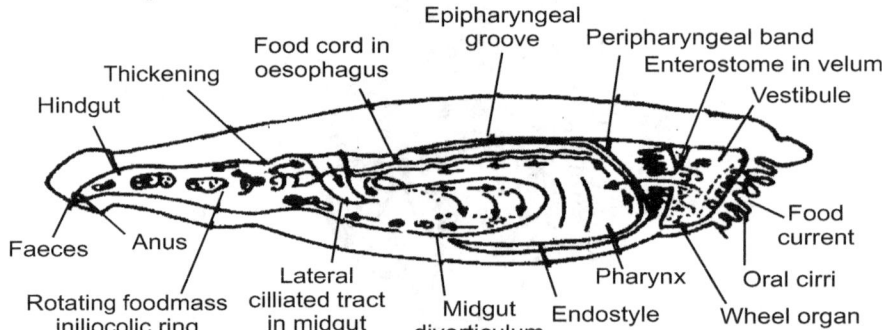

Fig. 2.21 (a): *Branchiostoma*. **Movements of ciliary currents and food in the alimentary canal**

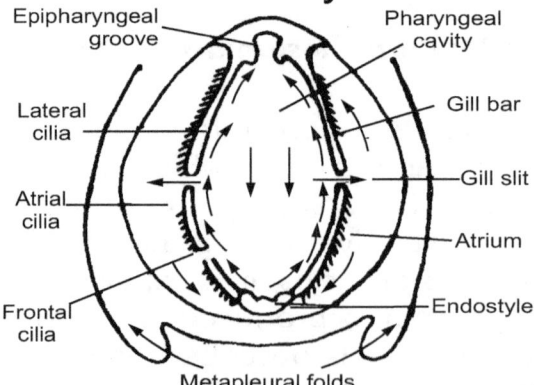

Fig. 2.21 (b): *Branchiostoma*. **Course of feeding current in diagrammatic T.S. of pharynx and atrium**

Food Concentration: When the current goes to pharynx through enterostome it contains relatively limited food particles. Therefore, food concentration mechanism is prevented in the pharynx which is assisted by endostyle. The gland cells of the endostyle secrete mucous. The median tract of the long endostylar cilia drive this mucous to the lateral endostylar cilia. This mucous is transferred to the sidewalls of the pharynx by the lateral tracts of cilia. The course of the mucous ascendng the walls of the pharynx is not definitely ventro-dorsal but somewhat oblique because the main food bringing current takes it in a backward direction. Frontal cilia along the inner surface of the gill bars beat dorsalwards carrying the mucous to the epipharyngeal groove. The cilia of epipharyngeal groove lash backwards and mucous is carried back to the opening of the oesophagus.

While passing the water current into pharynx, the suspended food particles entrapped by the mucous and carried to the oesophagus.

The food-laden mucous is carried down the gut by ciliar action, that is why the entire gut including the midgut diverticulum, is ciliated. The food is rotated as it passes slowly backwards in the gut. The rotation is brought about mainly by ciliated cells in the illio colonic ring and behind this region.

Physiology of Digestion

The large number of gland cells are present in the epithelial lining of the gut. These cells and the cells of the midgut diverticulum secrete the digestive enzymes. Digestion starts in the midgut and continued in the mid-gut and continued in the hind gut. Besides this extracellular digestion, intracellular digestion also occurs in which food particles are taken into the epithelial cells of the hind gut and digested there. Absorption of digested food takes place mostly in the hind gut and to a lesser extent in the mid-gut.

Atrium

The atrium or atrial activity is an extensive space lined by ectoderm. The gill slits do not directly open outside but open into the atrium. The atrium is the large cavity which surrounds the pharynx and anterior part of the intestine both laterally and ventrally. It opens posteriorly by a small opening, the atriopore situated ventrally just in front of the ventral fin. The atrium is formed by metapleural folds growing down and united ventrally by a transverse self, called epipleur so that a portion of the outside world becomes enclosed wthin the body (as it lined by ectoderm). At the level of posterior end of the pharynx the atrium gives rise to two forwardly directed pockets one on each side projecting into the dorsal coelomic canal. These pockets are called *brown funnels* and are of unknown function. The atrium is a protective structure. It projects the delicate pharynx while the animal is in its sandy borrow and helps to maintain an uninterrupted current of the water.

Coelom

The body cavity of *Amphioxus* is a true *coelom* lined by mesoderm. The coelomic cavity is fairly spacious in the posterior part of the body lodging the mid and hind gut regions of the alimentary canal, which are suspended by a mesentery, as in other vertebrates. In the pharyngeal region in adult condition is restricted to only a pair of dorsal *longitudinal canals*, a *mid-ventral canal* (subendostylar coelom) and the ventrally running coelomic spaces in the primary gill bars. These spaces naturally connect the dorsal and the subendostylar coelomic spaces. During the early development i.e. in the larval forms the coelom in the pharynegal region is uniform and surrounds the pharynx. As the development proceeds it becomes restricted because the gill slits arise as outgrowth of the pharynx which meet and fuse with corresponding inpushings of the body wall of that region. At the point of fusion a perforation appears on each such formation, placing the pharynx in communication with the outside. As a result of these changes the coelom is obliterated except in the dorsal and ventral regions and in the septa (primary gill bars) between the gill openings. The coelom is further reduced in higher chordates in which it is completely absent from the pharyngeal region.

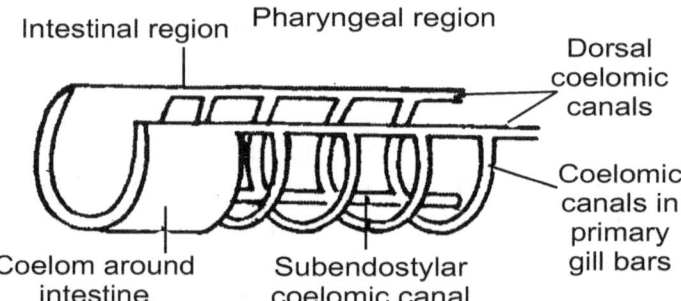

Fig. 2.22: *Banchiostoma.* **Diagrammatic representation of coelom**

Respiration

The pharynx of *Branchiostoma* is mainly an organ of feeding. In 'vertebrates the pharynx is not concerned with food collection but in some it is specialised for respiration by gills. In Amphioxus, some exchange of oxygen and carbon dioxide occurs between the water currrent and blood through the gill clefts. But this appears doubtful because blood contains no respiratory pigment. Further it has been suggested that the exchange of gases takes place through the whole body surface and particularly in the walls of the atrium.

Circulatory System

The blood vascular system of *Amphioxus* shows two very striking pecularities such as absence of heart and absence of respiratory pigment in the blood. The circulatory system in general outline is strikingly similar to that in higher chordates.

Blood

The blood in *Amphioxus* is colourless due to lack of respiratory pigment. There are also no blood corpuscles. Blood is found not only in the blood vessels but also in cavities or *lymph spaces*. The most important of these are the cavities in the dorsal and ventral fins containing fin-rays and paired canals in the metapleures. Very little amount of oxygen dissolves in the blood of the animal but it is sufficient to meet its energy needs because most of the time animals spends in the burrow and hence energy needs are meagre.

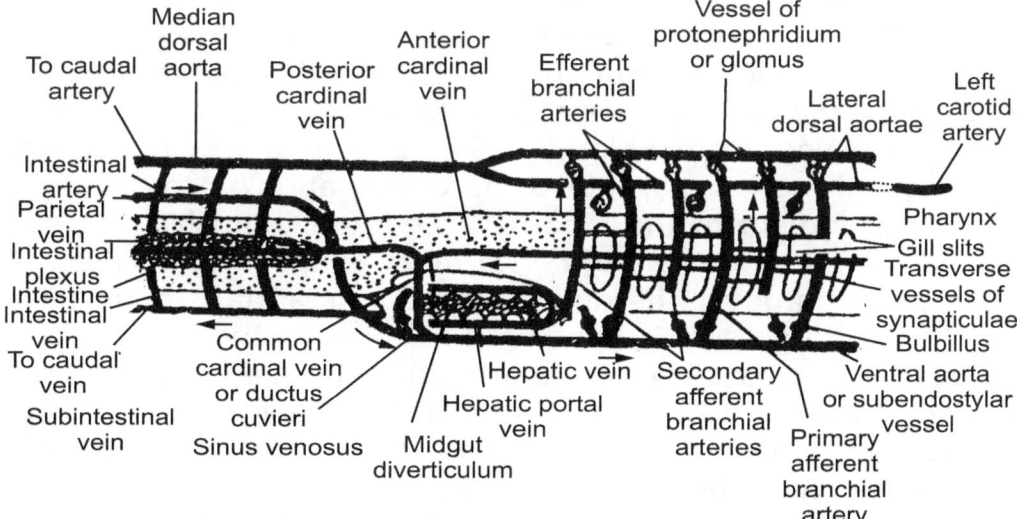

Fig. 2.23: *Branchiostoma*. Blood vascular system in right lateral view

Most of the blood vessels are similar, but due to their homologous with blood vessels of vertebrates they are called *arteries* or *veins*. The principal arteries have muscular walls and a dorsal aorta has an endothelial lining.

Arterial System

Lying in the ventral wall of the pharynx, below the endostyle, is a median longitudinal vessels called *ventral aorta*. This is contractile vessel which pumps the blood forwards by peristaltic contractions. From the ventral aorta paired *afferent branchial arteries* arise and pass upwards in the pharyngeal wall on both sides. At the bases of the afferent branchial arteries small contractile dilations are present called *bulbilli* which are also useful for pumping the blood. They pass through the primary, gill bars and through the synapticula give branches to each secondary gill bar. In this way, a network of blood vessels is formed in the entire wall of the pharynx. These vascular plexuses also supply blood to the nephridia.

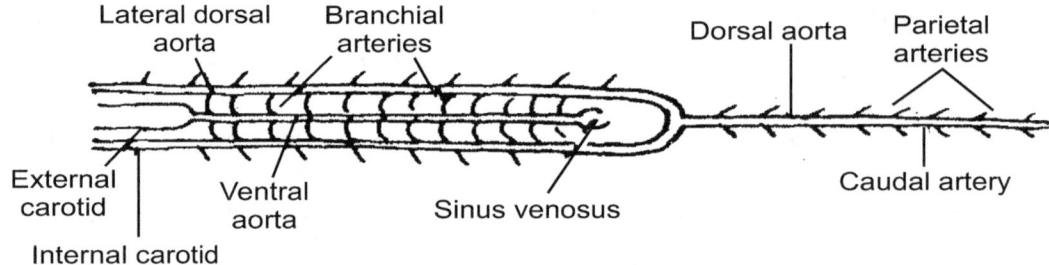

Fig. 2.24: Arteries of *Branchiostoma* (Dorsal veiw)

Blood is collected from the gill bars and nephridia by *aortic arches* or paired *efferent branchial arteries* dorsally. In the afferent and efferent vessels the blood is exposed to a respiratory water current but there is not proof of its oxygenation since there is no respiratory pigment in the blood. The efferent branchial vessels of each side open into a *lateral dorsal aorta* lying on one side of the epipharyngeal groove. The right lateral dorsal aorta is more dilated than the left one, each is continued in front to the rostrum as an *internal carotid artery*. The two lateral dorsal aortae unite behind the pharynx to form a median dorsal aorta lying below the notochord and above the intestine. The dorsal aorta gives out many small paired branches supplying blood to the intestine and the body wall. They form plexuses in lymph spaces. Then the dorsal aorta is continued backwards as a caudal artery into tail, the ventral aorta at the anterior end.

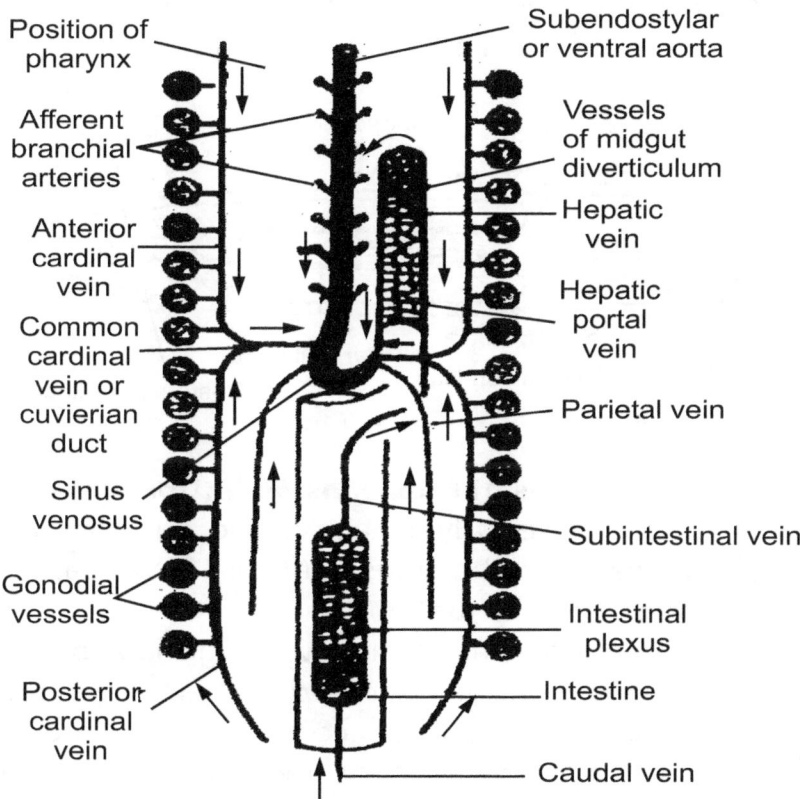

Fig. 2.25: *Branchiostoma*: Blood vascular system in dorsal view

Venous System

From the lymph space of the intestine blood is collected into a sub-intestinal vein lying beneath the intestine. For greater part of its length the sub-intestinal is not a single vein but a plexus of small vessels and in this trunk the blood flows forwards. The blood from the tail is collected by a *caudal vein* which joins the plexus of the sub-intestinal vein. The caudal vein is also jointed to both posterior *cardinal veins*.

Small vessels in the anterior part of the mid gut unite to form a short but wide hepatic portal vein which runs along the ventral border of mid-gut diverticulum and ramifies in its wall. Thus forming *hepatic portal system* similar to that of vertebrates. Small blood vessels from the mid gut diverticulum unite to form a short *hepatic vein* running along the dorsal border of the mid-gut diverticulum. The hepatic vein opens into a sac like *sinus venosus* from which arises the *ventral aorta*. The flow of blood is sub-intestinal and hepatic vein is forward and both of them are contractile vessels.

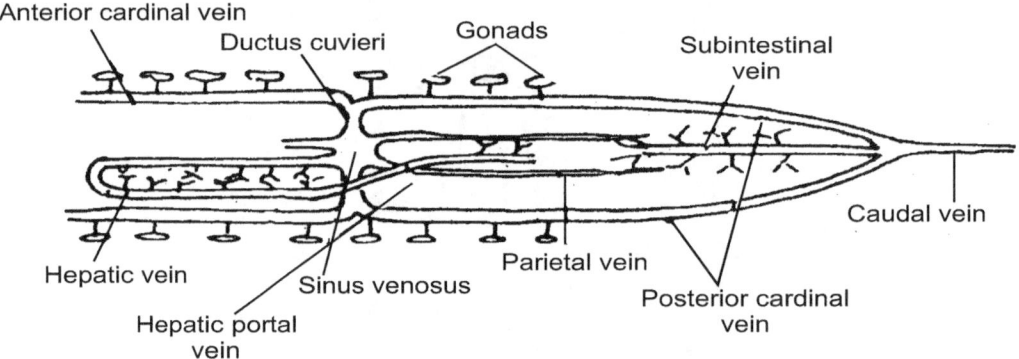

Fig. 2.26: Veins of *Branchiostoma* (Dorsal view)

A pair of *parietal veins* lying above the gut return blood from the dorsal body wall into the sinus venosus. Small paired *transverse veins* return blood to the ventral aorta.

Running in the body wall at the level of gonads on each side are an *anterior cardinal* and a posterior cardinal vein which receive blood through small segmental veins coming from the body wall, myotomes and gonads. The anterior and posterior cardinal veins of each side enter a *ductus cuvieri* or common cardinal vein just behind the pharynx. The two ductus Cuvieri pass inwards through the atrium to join the sinus venosus.

Flow of blood in the ventral vessel is from behind to forward while in dorsal aorta it flows into backward direction.

Thus, the paired dorsal aortae on the pharynx, paired afferent bronchial vessels, carotid arteries in the snout and unpaired dorsal aorta behind the pharynx are main distributing vessels. Whereas, sub-intestinal vein, hepatic vein, paired efferent branchials and anterior and posterior cardinals are the main collecting vessels.

Excretory System

The excretory system of *Amphioxus* does not agree with the class chordate plan. It consists of *protonephridia* which are found in many invertebrates such as the platyhelminthes, polychaeta annelids, branchiopods etc. Their origin is also ectodermal, however, in chordates excretory organs are always mesodermal in origin. Thus, *Amphioxus* shows invertebrate character in this regard.

There are about 90 pairs of segmentally arranged nephridia in the region of pharynx, one pair for each pair of gill slits. The nephridia lie above the gill slits.

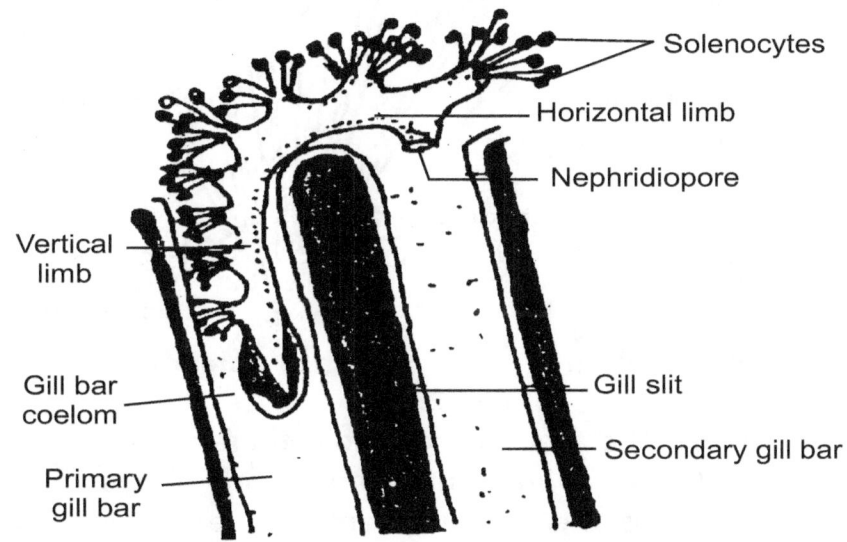

Fig. 2.27: Position of Nephridium

Each nephridium is a small bent tube consisting of two limbs. The upper horizontal limb is short while the lower limb is vertical and long. The horizontal limb is situated in coelom opens by *nephridopore* into the atrium at the upper end of gill slit, lying against a secondary gill bar. The vertical limb runs ventrally and ends blindly. From the outerside of the nephridial tube arise numerous short tubules ending into knob like structures called *solenocytes* or *flame cells*. Each solenocyte has a round, nucleated head leading into a thin tubule which contains a vibratile flagellum. Tufts of solenocytes project into the dorsal longitudinal coclomic canals and are bathed in coclomic fluid. By the flagellar vibrations the nitrogenous waste is collected by the solenocytes from coelomic fluid and pour into the nephridial tube and from it into the atrium by nephridiopore. The nephridia are also supplied with small blood vessels and hence waste products from blood are also extracted by them.

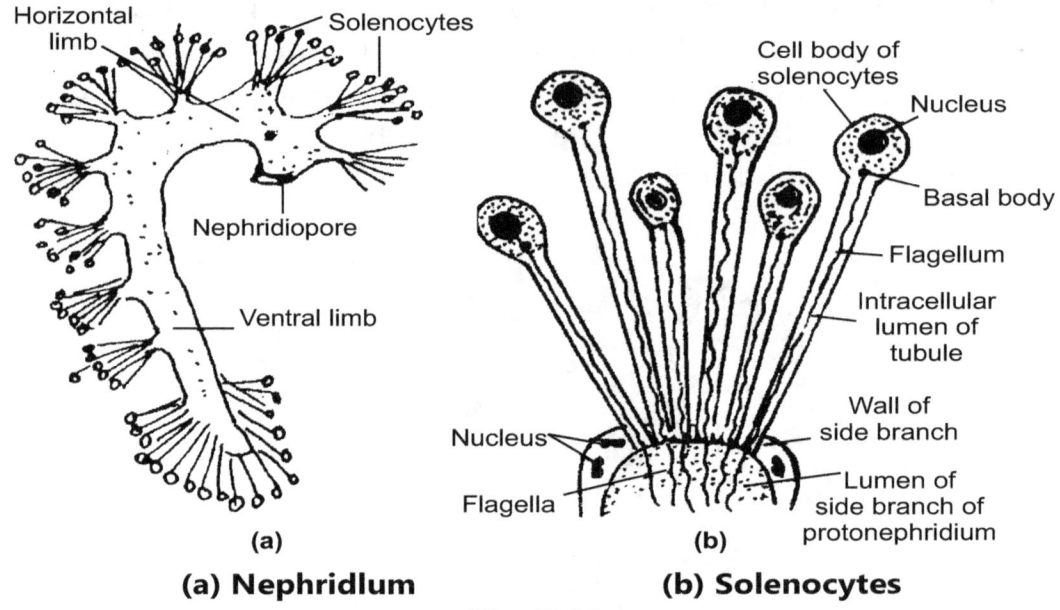

(a) Nephridium   **(b) Solenocytes**

Fig. 2.28

In addition to the paired nephrida there is a single large nephridium *Hatschek's nephridium*. It is situated above the roof of the pharynx slightly to the left and ventral side of the notochord. Structurally, it is similar with the paired nephridia. Its blind anterior end is just in front of Hatschek's pit, while the posterior end opens into the pharynx just behind the velum. The Hatschek's nephridium is associated with a network of fine blood vessels and. each solenocyte is surrounded by a small coelomic sac. It absorbs nitrogenous waste.

In the floor of the atrium are numerous small renal papillae, they are probably excretory.

Nervous System

The nervous system of *Amphioxus* is divisible into three parts:
1. The central nervous system.
2. The autonomic (sympathetic) nervous system, and
3. The peripheral nervous system.

1. The Central Nervous System: The central nervous system consists of the dorsal, hollow, tubular *nerve cord* or *neural tube*. It is situated dorsal to the notochord as in case of higher chordates. However, there is no brain formation at the anterior end. It tapers anteriorly and is broad. The dorsal and ventral roots are not united

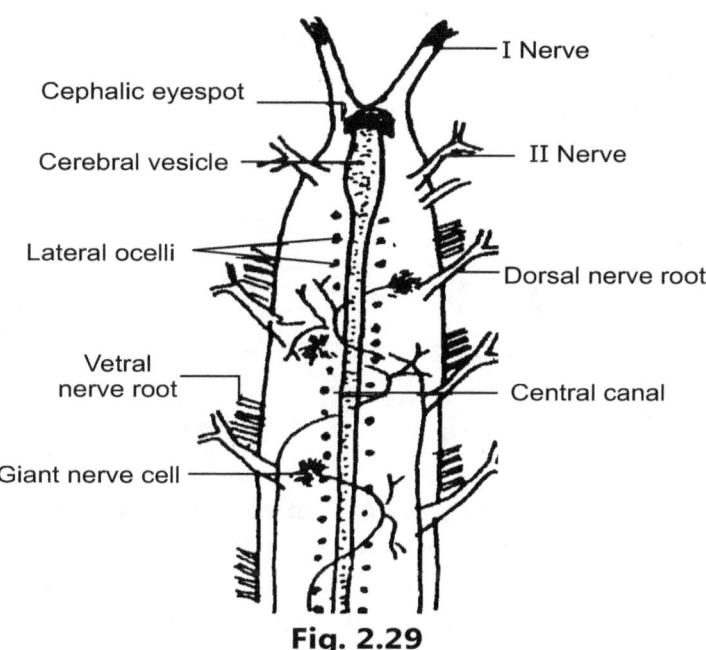

Fig. 2.29

hence there are no mixed nerves and dorsal ganglia are absent on dorsal roots. The dorsal root of a spinal nerve is slightly posterior to its ventral root and they also give fibres to the wall of the gut. The spinal nerves of the two sides do not correspond, the dorsal roots of one side are opposite the ventral roots of the other side. These nerves are non-myelinated.

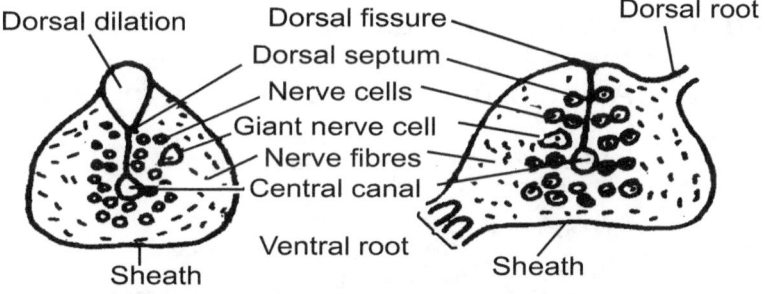

(a) Through cerebral vesicle   (b) Through nerve roots

Fig. 2.30: *Branchiostoma*. T.S. of nerve cord.

The Autonomic Nervous System

This system consists of two nerve plexuses in the smooth muscles of the wall of the intestine. These are connected to the neural tube by visceral nerves through the dorsal roots. The atrial epithelium of Amphioxus contains motor and sensory nerve fibres forming an extensive network and this is connected to the neural tube. It is also considered as autonomic nervous system, which controls various reflexes such as coughing reflex, spawning reflex etc. It also controls the unstriped muscles of the gut posterior. Hence, it differs from vertebrates.

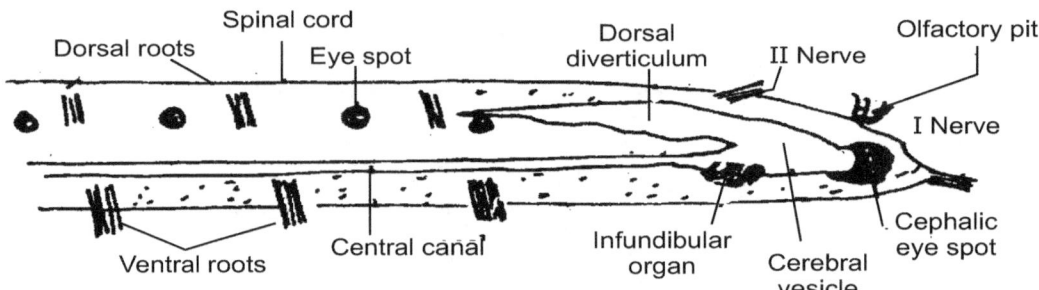

Fig. 2.31: V.S. of anterior part of neural tube of *Branchiostoma*

The neural tube is perforated throughout by a narrow *central canal* or *neurocoel*. Nerve cells are grouped around the central canal and fibres arising from nerve cells are placed superficially while in non-chordates the nerve cells are superficial and nerve fibres are placed centrally. The giant cells and the giant fibres found in running lengthwise in on the dorsal side of neural tube.

An the anterior end of the neural tube, the central canal dilates into a cerebral vesicle or ventricle, which gives out dorsally a *diverticulum*. The cerebral vesicle is supposed to represent the brain ventricle in vertebrates. Although the neural tube is narrow at the anterior end than the rest in adult, but in the larva it is much larger and broader than the remaining nerve cord. These facts indicate that the brain of the Amphioxus must have been regressed due to it sedentary life.

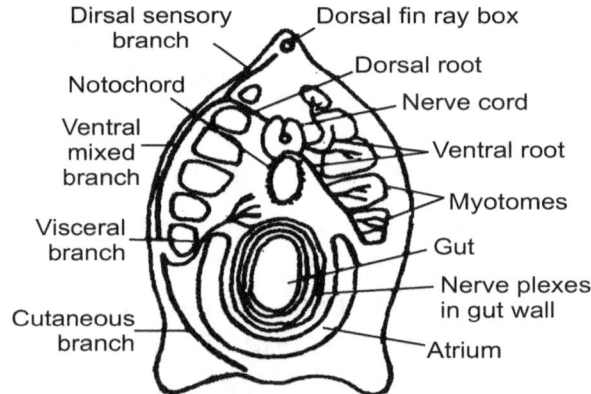

**Fig. 2.32: *Branchiostoma*
Distribution of dorsal and ventral nerve roots**

The Peripheral Nervous System

The nerves arising from the nerve cord from the peripheral nervous system. It consists of paired segmentally arranged nerves which innervate the different Parts of body and join the central nervous system.

From the anterior part of the neural tube arise a pair of sensory nerves (I pair) going to the oral hood, cirri and the sense organs. The second pair of nerves joins the neural tubes just dorsal to the cerebral vesicle. The first two pairs of nerves are sometimes described as cranial-nerves. The body behind the cerebral vesicle receives the nerves arising from the neural tube in segmental pairs called spinal nerves. Each spinal nerve has a dorsal root with afferent or sensory fibres entering and a ventral root made of several separate efferent or motor fibres leaving the neural tube. The dorsal roots originate from the receptor organs bringing impule to the central nervous system while ventral roots go to myotomes.

Sense Organs

Being a free living animal *Amphioxus* possesses different types of simple receptors or sense organs.

1. Eyes or Ocelli: Eyes or eye-spots are present along the entire length of the neural tube. These are black pigmented spots arranged in definite tracts and photoreceptors (sensitive to light). Each eye is composed of a lower sense like photosensitive, cell with a striated apical border or vitreous body and upper blackish brown cup-shaped pigmented cell. The vitreous body secretes a pigment cup.

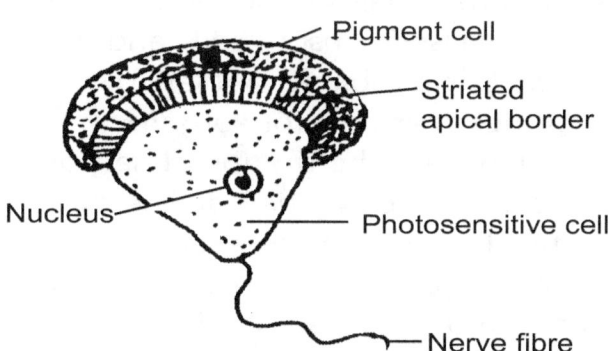

Fig. 2.33: Single eye-spot of *Branchiostoma*

Basally, the photosensitive cell receives one nerve fibre. The eyes are the photoreceptors. At the anterior end of the cerebral vesicle there is large pigment spot, however it does not show any eye like structure and is not sensitive to light. It is observed that the animal does not respond to ray of light received from in front. This indicated rays from any other directions strike, the immediately responsible for orientation of the animal as it burrows in sand.

2. Infundibular organ: It is a small depression in the floor of cerebral vesicle, which is lined by long ciliated cells. The infundibular organ detects the changes in the pressure of the fluid in the neural tube.

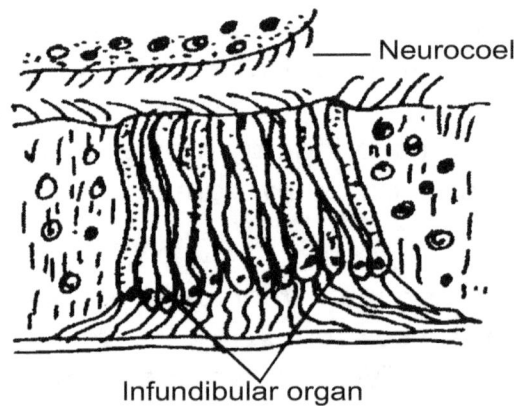

Fig. 2.34: V.S. of infundibular organ of *Branchiostoma*

3. Kollikar's pit: It is also called as *olfactory pit*. It forms a pocket of ciliated ectoderm cells above the cerebral vesicle slightly to the left side of the median pigment spot. This pit marks the position of neuropore by which the neural tube opens anteriorly in the larval stage, but the neuropore remains closed in the adult Amphioxus. The Kollikar's pit lacks specialised sensory cells and innervation from the neural tube. Hence, it is probably not an olfactory organ of the animal. But it is considered as olfactory organ.

4. Papillae: These are the groups of sensory cells located on the oral cirri and velar tentacles. The papillae occuring on the velar tentacles contain tactile and chemo-receptor cells. The tactile cells are sensitive to touch while chemoreceptors are gustatory (taste) and olfactory functions. The oral cirri are equipped with only tactile cells. These cells are having sensory hairs on their free ends and innvervated by nerve fibres at basal ends.

5. Sensory Cells: The sensory cells are found scattered all over the epidermis. These cells occur abundantly on the dorsal side of the body and on oral cirri. Each sensory has a nerve fibre at its. lower end and at the free end it has hair like sensory process projecting out from the cuticle. These cells are tactile and respond to contact. They also detect the nature of the sand in which animal will burrow. The animal generally avoid the deposit of fine sand for burrowing but prefers coarse sand. Therefore, sensory cells are important tactile receptors.

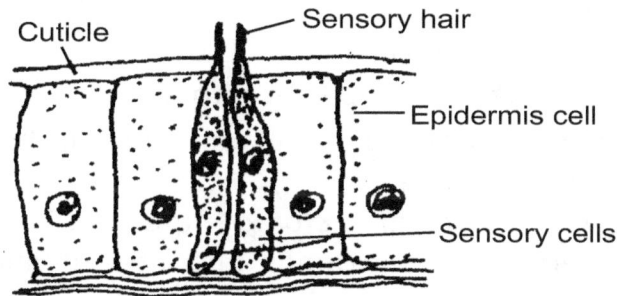

Fig. 3.35: Sensory cells of *Branchiostoma*

Reproductive System

The sexes are separated in *Amphioxus* however males and females are alike except for the gonads. The male gonads or testes occur in male and the female gonads or ovaries in female. The gonads of *Amphioxus* are hollow sacs lying in the anterior two-third of the body on the ventro-lateral sides of the body wall in the pharyngeal region. There are 26 pairs of testes or ovaries which are arranged strictly metamerically, one pair in each of the segments 25 to 51. They appear as a series of bulges protruding into the atrium on each side.

2.2 General Characters of Cyclostomata

The *Cyclostomata* or the *Marsipobranchii* are the living representatives of super class - *Agnatha*. These are characterized by the presence of suctorial mouth (without jaws). They are the most primitive of all the living vertebrates.

General Characters

1. The body is elongated, cylindrical and eel-like or worm like with compressed tail.

2. The skin is soft, smooth, slimy, containing unicellular mucous glands and without scales.
3. Median fins with cartilagenous fin-rays, paired fins are absent. Tail diphycercal.
4. Trunk and tail muscles are arranged into Z-shaped myotomes separated by myocommata.
5. Endoskeleton is cartilaginous. Notochord is persistant. Imperfect neural arches (atcualia) over notochord represent rudimentary vertebrae. A branchial basket is present in pharynx.
6. True coelom is present.
7. Jaws are absent (Group - Agnatha).
8. Mouth is ventral, suctorial and circular hence the class-name cyclostomata.
   (Gr; *Cyklos* – circular + *stoma* – mouth). Tongue is rasping. Oesophagus directly opens into the intestine. Stomach is absent.
9. Respiratory gills are 5 to 16 pairs in lateral sac-like pouches of pharynx; hence another name of class, Marsipobranchii. Gill-slits are 1-16 pairs.
10. Heart is two chambered with an auricle and a ventricle. Conus arteriosus is absent but sinus venosus is present. Many aortic arches in gill region. Blood with leucocytes and nucleated circular erythrocytes. Body temperature variable (*Poikilothermous*).
11. Brain is differentiated with a very small cerebellum. 8-10 pairs cranial or cerebral nerves.
12. Single median olfactory sac with a single median nostril. Ear may have one or two semicircular canals.
13. A pairs of mesonephric kidneys with ducts to urino-genital papilla.
14. Sexes are separated or united, Gonad single, large; without gonoduct. Fertilization is external.
15. Direct or indirect development with a larval stage.
16. Class-cyclostoma is divided into two sub-classes:
    (a) Petromyzontia and (b) Myxinodea.

Affinities of Cyclostomata

Cyclostomes are the most primitive members among living vertebrates. Ammocoete larva shows the primitive characters like cephalochordata while the adults have certain specialized as well as degenerate features due to parasitic mode of life. Thus, the affinities of cyclostomes can be discussed under the primitive and specialized characters.

I. Primitive Characters
(a) Resemblances with Cephalochordata:
1. Head is indistinct.
2. Skin is naked without any exoskeleton. Paired fins are absent.
3. Numerous gill-slits are present.
4. Persistent and continuous notochord.
5. Segmental muscles or myotomes with little modification.
6. Alimentary canal is straight without stomach.
7. Separate dorsal and ventral roots of spinal-nerves. Nerves are unmyelinated.
8. Gonoducts are absent. Fertilization is external.
9. Development indirect with a larval stage. The ammocoete larva resembles *Amphioxus* in; continuous median fin; presence of endostyle; filter feeding; ciliated gut; and vestibule anterior to mouth.
10. Jaws are absent.

(b) Differences from Fishes (Vertebrates):
Both cyclostomes and fishes are aquatic vertebrates, but cyclostomes shows many primitive characters in which they differ from fishes, such as:
1. Absence of biting jaws, scales, true teeth, paired appendages, true fin-rays, girdles, ribs, stomach, spleen, gall-bladder and gonoduct.
2. Caudal fin is diphycercal.
3. Continuous median dorsal fin.
4. Incomplete or poorly developed cranium, and vertebral column.
5. A single median nostril.

6. Poorly developed pancreas, brain, spiral valve, sympathetic nervous system and lateral line system.
7. Heart ' S ' shaped tube without conus-arteriosus.
8. 9th and 10th cranial nerves not enclosed by cranium.
9. 1 or 2 semi-circular canals in membranous labyrinth instead of third of advanced vertebrates.
10. Non-medullated nerves.

(c) Affinities with Ostracoderms:

Ostracoderms are the oldest fossils of vertebrates. Palaentologists belive that they are the fore runners of higher fish. The fossil ostracoderms and living cyclostomes are grouped together under Agnatha because of the following structural similarities.

1. Absence of biting jaws.
2. Single nasal opening.
3. Pineal eye.
4. No paired limbs.
5. Pouch-like branchial sacs.
6. Membranous labyrinth with two semi-circular canals.
7. Poorly developed lateral line system.

II. Advance or Vertebrate Characters

Cyclostomes are undoubtedly vertebrates because they have many advance but simple features similar to fishes and higher vertebrates. These are:

1. Head with paired sense-organs like Eyes and Ears.
2. Differentiated brain like embryonic vertebrates with 10 pairs of cranial nerves.
3. Cranium for the protection of brain.
4. Beginning of segmental vertebrae.
5. Dorsal root ganglia on spinal nerves.
6. Stratified and multilayered epidermis.
7. Gills for respiration and not for food collection as in *Branchiostoma*.
8. Presence of large bilobed liver, gall-bladder, bile duct, pineal and parietal eyes, pancreatic cells in midgut wall.
9. Blood contains RBCs and WBCs.
10. Well developed circulatory system with a heart and lymphatic system also present.
11. Mesonephric kidneys.
12. Lateral line sense organs.
13. 'E' shaped myotomes as in fishes.

III. Specialized Characters

Adult cyclostomes are too specialized in many respect. These are adaptations for parasitic mode of life. These are:

1. Suctorial mouth is present at the bottom of funnel which helps in leading a parasitic life to the animal.
2. Powerful, muscular tongue bearing horny teeth serves as a rasping organ while feeding.
3. Production of anticoagulant in saliva to feed on blood and body fluids of prey.
4. Peculiar sac-like gill-chambers located far behind the head.
5. Complete separation of ventral sac-like respiratory pharynx from the dorsal oesophagus.
6. A special supporting skeletal structure called the branchial basket is present around the gills in the pharyngeal region.
7. A definite liver is present.
8. A single median naris is present.
9. Large number of mucous glands are present in *Myxine*.

IV. Degenerative Characters

1. Simple, cylindrical eel-like body form compared to broad fish-like shape of ostracoderms.
2. The exoskeletal structures such as scales are absent.
3. Paired fins and girdles which support them are absent.
4. Reduced liver and disappearance of gall-bladder and bile-duct in adult lamprey.
5. The eyes are poorly developed (i.e. vestigial) and without eye-lids but covered by thick skin and muscles in hagfishes.

1. *Petromyzon*: The Lamprey

Petromyzon is one of the most primitive living vertebrate and its study is thus important, besides being interesting, in the understanding of vertebrate evolution.

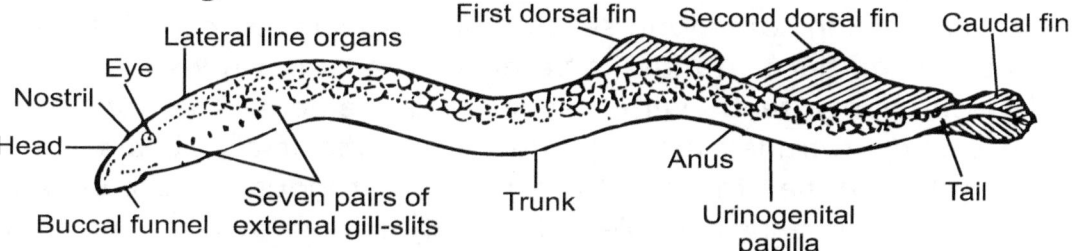

Fig. 2.36: Sea lamprey *Petromyzon marinus*

Petromyzon marinus is the common species distributed all over the world and found in salt water. There are other species like *Lampetra fluvatilis* and *Lampetra planer* are the common fresh water lampreys. They are distributed in temperate zones of Northern Hemisphere, coasts of North America, Canada. As well Europe, West Africa and Japan. *Petromyzon* usually lives at the bottom.

Habits: *Petromyzon* is a sanguivorous (blood sucking) ectoparasite of healthy fish. It attaches to the undersurface of a large fish by suction of its buccal funnel and use of buccal teeth. Its tongue is toothed which is helpful in grasping the body of the host. Blood clotting is prevented by the secretion of anticoagulant from the special buccal glands and sucks the blood. The host may be killed due to excessive loss of blood. The life cycle of the *Petromyzon* includes two quite different phases. The larval phase called ammocoete is a fresh water, sedentary, filter feeding and microphagus creature. The adult swims about near the bottom of salt or fresh water by undulations of its body. In autumn, the adult. *Petromyzon* usually migrate in the rivers to spawn in the spring after which they die.

External Characters

The *Petromyzon* has a long, slender eel-like body with a soft, slimy, scaleless skin. It is mottled green-brown in colour and about one metre in length. The body is distinguishable without any clear demarcation into three regions; head, trunk and tail. Head and trunk are cylindrical, while the tail is laterally compressed.

Head: The head bears a mouth, a single naris, a pair of eyes and seven pairs of gill slits. Mouth is present at the anterior body end or head which ventrally directed large cup like depression called the sucker or buccal funnel. The buccal funnel is bordered by a fleshy marginal membrane which bears numerous small processes called *oral fimbriae* and some long sensory processes called *cirri*. The inner surface of the buccal funnel is beset with radiating rows of conical, yellowish, horny teeth with definite arrangement. The tongue is mobile and protrudes through the mouth and it also bears horny teeth but large than those in the funnel. The tongue is muscular and powerful, which rasps a whole in the body of host by back and forth movements for sucking the blood. On the dorsal surface of the head there is naris or nasohypophyseal aperture. It leads into an olfactory sac, which serves only as an organ of smell. Just behind the naris (nostril) a transparent area of skin indicates the position of the pineal organ.

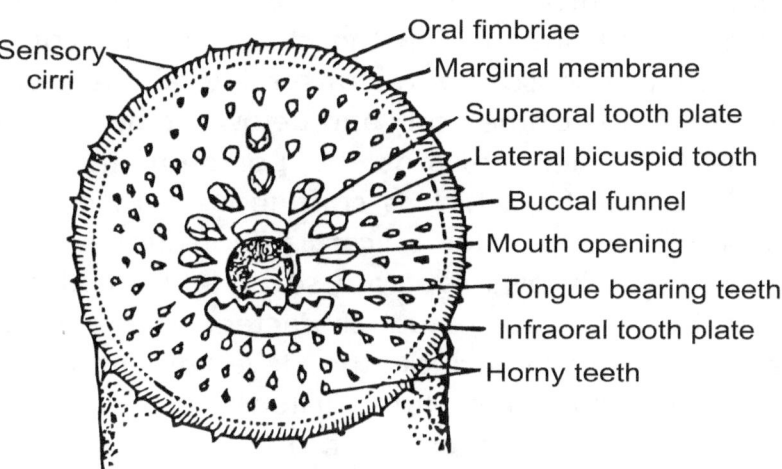

Fig. 2.37: *Petromyzon.* **Buccal funnel in ventral view**

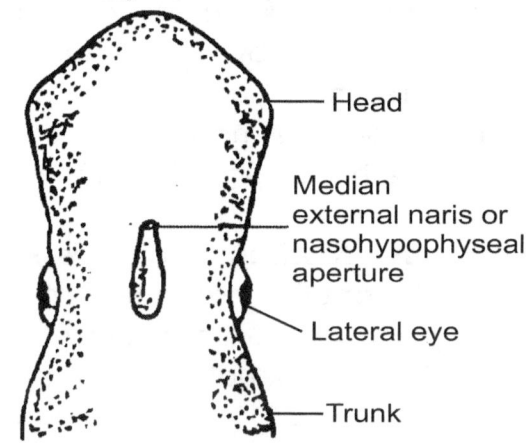

Fig. 2.38: *Petromyzon.* **Head in dorsal view**

On the each lateral side of head one prominent eye is present. The eyes are without eyelids but are covered by transparent skin. There are seven small rounded apertures of external gill slits form a longitudinal row on each lateral side of the head just behind each eye. Water enters and leaves them alternately for respiration.

Trunk: There are no paired appendages on the trunk. It bears two unequal median dorsal fins first and second, are located near the posterior end. Around the tail there is a caudal fin, the upper lobe of which is continuous with the second dorsal fin. The fins are supported by thin cartilaginous rods, the fin rays. On the ventral side, at the junction of trunk and tail is a slit-like depression called cloaca. A urinogenital papilla bearing on its tip a minute urinogenital aperture protrudes through the cloaca. Just infront of urinogenital papilla lies the small anus within the cloacal depression. There are also numerous small sensory pores of the lateral line system extend along each lateral side of the body and below the head.

Tail: The tail tapers towards the posterior end and bears a vertical caudal or tail fin; which is continuous with posterior dorsal fin. The tail fin is also supported by cartilaginous fin rays.

The *Petromyzon* shows separate sexes and are distinguishable when mature by secondary sexual characters. The secondary sexual characters of the female include the development of an anal fin behind the urinogenital aperature, distension and reddening anal margin. In case of male, there is formation of penial tube and thickening of the base of the dorsal fin.

Musculature: The muscles of the body are arranged in zig-zag or Σ-shaped myotomes separated by myocommas.

Skeleton: There are no true bones in *Petromyzon* but endoskeleton is of cartilage. The notochord is rod-like gelatinous enclosed by a tough sheath composed of inner fibrous and outer elastic layer.

Digestive system and feeding: Mouth is suctorial and opens into large buccal cavity. It contains prominent muscular and toothed tongue. Tongue is rasping organ. *Petromyzon* is ectoparasite and sanguivorous animal. Buccal glands are present which secrete anticoagulant substance prevents clotting of blood.

Respiration: There are seven gills in spherical gill pouches on either side between respiratory pharynx and body wall. Each gill pouch contains a series of gill filaments or lamellae. In gill pouches, exchanges of gases occurs.

Circulation: Heart is enclosed in a thick walled pericardial sac. Auricle and ventricle are present. Blood contains erythrocytes and leucocytes. Blood vessels circulate the blood in the body.

Excretion: Kidneys are mesonephric type, which filter the nitrogenous wastes through uriniferous tubules and urine is discharged through urinogenital papilla.

Nervous system: The brain of *Petromyzon* is very primitive but shows typical plan of the vertebrate brain. Spinal cord is dorsoventrally flattened. Sense organs are olfactory sacs, pituitary pouch, eyes, pineal eye and lateral line sense organs.

Reproduction: Sexes are separate. In summer, they migrate in fresh water stream for breeding. The sperms and eggs are released in the water. Fertilization is external. The adults die after spawning. A tiny larva called *ammocoete* hatches from the egg.

Ammocoete larva: The larva is different from parents but resembles *Amphioxus* in structure as well as mode of life. The small larva (7 mm in length) lives in nest but as it grows (15 mm). It quits the nest and burrows in mud and sand in quiet water. It starts living as a filter feeder in a U-shaped burrow made in sand. The larval period lasts from 3 to 7 years and gains the length about 17 mm. The larva differs in several respect from adult.

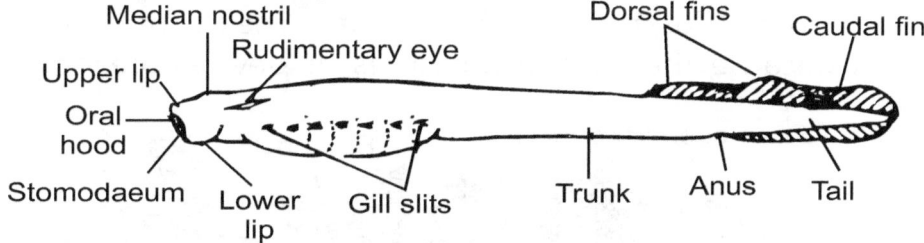

Fig. 2.39: Ammocoete larva. External features in lateral view

It has continuous single median dorsal fin. It is blind and toothless and non-parasitic filer feeder. Mouth is not suctorial for feeding it comes out of the burrow at night. It feeds on organic ooze, containing unicellular algae and bacteria which are caught on the floor of pharynx in mucous strings secreted by a tubular endostyle. Paired eyes remain hidden under thick skin and muscles.

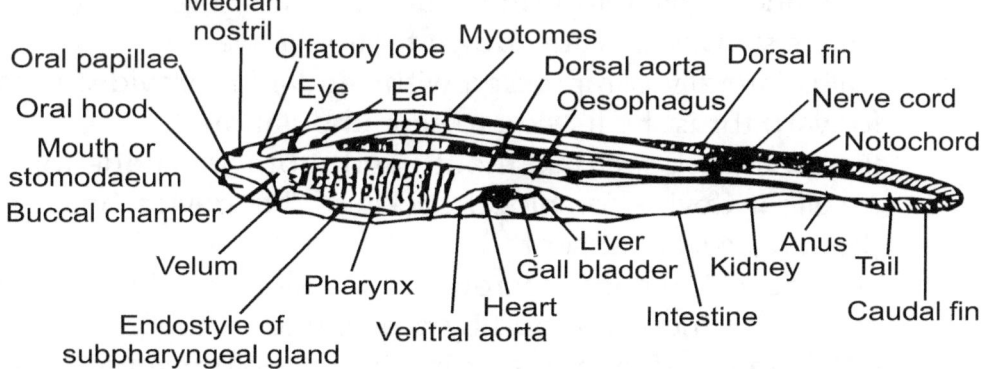

Fig. 2.40: Ammocoete larva showing general internal structure

During metamorphosis the larva undergoes several radical structural changes to become semiparasitic adult form. The suctorial buccal funnel is formed with strong and sharp teeth. Gill develop into gill pouches. The continuous fin breaks into two dorsal and a caudal fin. It stands seaward journey. Reaching the sea, it becomes adult and takes to free swimming and blood sucking life. The lampreys thus, has two phases in its life-history: a filter feeding larval stage and a blood sucking adult stage.

Economic Importance: Lampreys have posed a great economic problem to the fisheries in some regions. Since they are ectoparasites and feed on the blood and body fluids of fish. Such fishes become victim of other predators and diseases. The scars on the body of fish render them unfit for the market. *Petromyzon* flesh is also used as a food in Europe and America to some extent. The larvae of Lampreys are used tor bait. Thus, lampreys are harmful. Their control is not fully successful because the control measures or devices are not wholly effective.

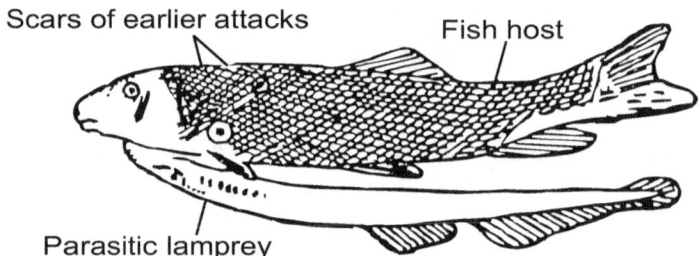

Fig. 2.41: *Petromyzon* **attached to a bony fish for feeding**

Adaptations in *Petromyzon*

1. Body is long, slender and limbless which offers minimum resistance to water during progression.
2. Skin is slimy which cuts down friction in water.
3. Tail is laterally compressed with caudal fin provides greater forward thrust by its side to side undulations.
4. Buccal funnel, suctorial mouth and toothed tongue form an excellent device for blood sucking. This device holds prey though jaws are absent.
5. The buccal glands secrete anticoagulant which ensures continuous flow of blood by preventing clotting.
6. Influx and outflux of water in gill slits help respiration even during feeding.

7. It lives in coastal water which provides easy concealment under sea weeds and stones. This gives protection to the animal.
8. Active swimming helps in escaping from predators and searching for suitable prey.
9. The eyes are covered by transparent skin which helps the animal to see in water and also gets protection from salt water.
10. Fat is stored beneath the skin which acts as a reserve food when alimentary canal atrophies prior to breeding.
11. Female lays very large number of eggs about 236,000 compensates her inability to breed more than once in her life-lime and counteracts mortality of larvae during migration.
12. Larva leads burrowing life which gives protection from its enemies.
13. Larva is filter feeder which suits its nearly sedentary life in burrows.

Systematic Position

Petromyzon belong to the:

Phylum	– Chordata	because it has notochord.
Sub-phylum	– Vertebrata	because it has vertebral column, though incomplete.
Section	– Agnatha	because it lacks jaws.
Class	– Cyclostomata	because it has circular mouth.
Order	– Petromyzontia	because it has suctorial buccal funnel, dorsal closed nasal sac and larval stage.
Family	– Petromyzontidae	Do
Genus	– *Petromyzon*	
Species	– *marinus*	because it lives in the sea and grows to a metre in length.

2. Myxine Glutinosa

Myxine belongs to the order Myxiniformes and the members of this order are commonly called hagfishes. *Myxine* is exclusively marine and found off the coasts of America, Africa, Europe and Japan. It is the bottom dweller and lives in colonies. Its food consists of polychaete worms. Myxine has an eel-like body which is elongated, pinkish and scaleless which measures about 50-60 cm. Body is differentiated into head, trunk and tail. The mouth lies in a depression on the ventral side near the anterior end. There is a single, large, median, palatine tooth above the mouth opening tongue. It shows suctorial mouth with soft wrinkled lips like those of an old ugly woman or hag hence the common name hag fish. The eyes are vestigial, being sunk beneath the skin. The naris is almost terminal and communicates by a canal with the pharynx to send the water current to the gills. There are four pairs of sensory tentacles around the anterior end of the body. They are supported by the cartilage. The tongue is protrusible and it is bordered by two multitoothed horny plates. The tongue serves as a powerful rasping organ. Close to the mouth lies a single median nostril. Six pairs of gill pouches are located far behind the head region and their efferent ducts join into a single pair of external gill slits, probably an adaptation to burrowing. A longitudinal row of small pores on each side marks the position of slime or mucous glands inside. The glands secrete large amount of slime hence it is also called by the common name, the slime eel. There are poorly developed midventral and caudal fins.

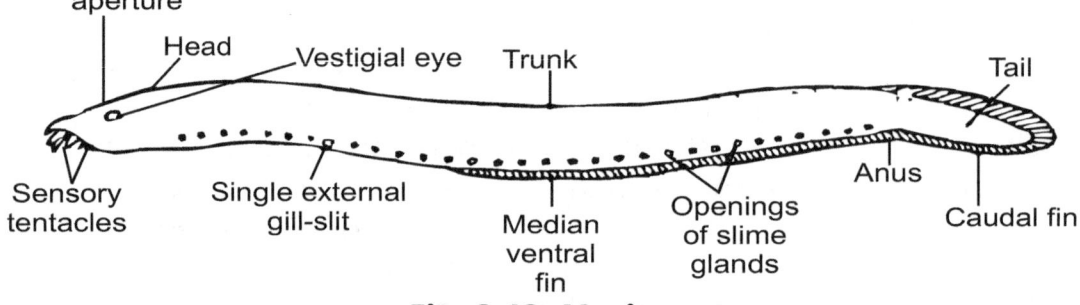

Fig. 2.42: *Myxine*

Myxine generally attacks the injured or dead fishes and the fishes caught in nets and on lines. It burrows in the body of victim through mouth or opercular outlet and consumes all soft parts of the body. Therefore, it is also called as borer. The tongue helps in boring and *Myxine* leaves only a shell or skin and bones. It is actually an internal parasite. The fishes usually attacked are cods and flounders. When not feeding, the *Myxine* lives in the mud at the bottom of sea at depths ranging to nearly 625 metres. It also shows rapid swimming by eel-like undulations. The sexes are perhaps separate in *Myxine* but differentiation of sex cells occurs quite late in the life as in the lampreys. The spawning occurs on the floor of ocean. The female lays large-shelled eggs with hooked processes at each pole. By these process, the eggs cling to one another and also to sea weeds.

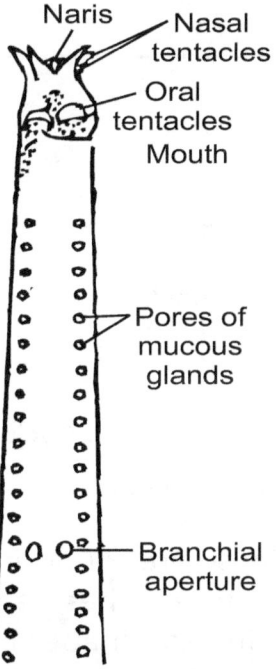

Fig. 2.43: *Myxine*

Development is direct i.e. eggs hatch into miniature adults without passing through a larval stage.

Since *Myxine* is a parasitic animal, it may pose a serious threat to fisheries in some regions.

2.3 Pisces

(a) Scales in Fishes

In many vertebrates, the exo-skeletal covering of body is made of two types of scales i.e. epidermal and dermal. The *epidermal scales* are cornified and are developed from the malpighian layer of epidermis. They are present in reptiles, birds and mammals. The *Dermal* scales are mesenchymal in origin and well developed in the fishes. The skin of fish consists of two layers. The outer layer is the epidermis and the inner the *dermis* or *corium*. The dermis plays a main role in the formation of scales hence, fish scale are termed as dermal scales; these are small, thin, cornified, calcareous or bony plates which fit closely together. The scales vary in size and shape in different species. The present classification of scales of fishes is based on *Lagler et. al.* 1977 and *Weichert,* 1970.

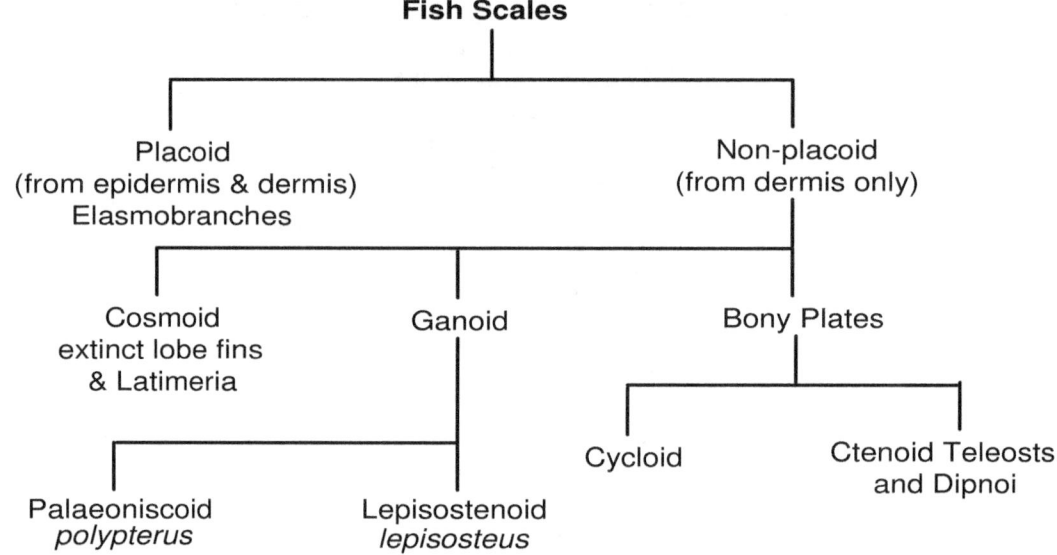

(1) Placoid scales: These are found in Elasmobranch fishes only and also called dermal denticles. These are closely set together but not overlap each other giving sandpaper like appearance to the skin. Each *placoid scale* consists of two parts a rhomboidal *basal plate* embedded in the dermis and a flat *trident spine*, projecting outward and backward through the epidermis.

The *basal plate* consists of a calcified tissue. According to *Weichert* (1970), it is a bony plate, which indicates the remain of ancestral bony armour. It is anchored into the dermis by connective tissue fibres called the Sharpley's fibres. The trident spines are curved and directed towards the tail end. This is to minimise friction with water. Each spine consists of *dentine*. This is covered with a hard layer of *vitrodentine*. The dentine encloses a pulp cavity. This opens below through the basal plate. Through this opening, blood vessels and nerves enter the pulp cavity. The pulp cavity contains many odontoblasts which are dentine forming cells. Fine canaliculi arise from the pulp cavity and reach the dentine.

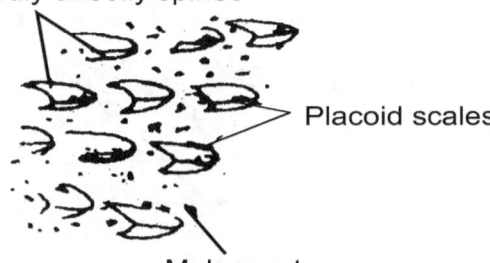

Fig. 2.44: Placoid scale

(2) Cosmoid scales (Gr. Kosmos, ornament and oide, like): These type of scales were characteristic of certain ostracoderms, placoderms and extinct sarcopterygians (lobe finned fishes and lung fishes but do not occur in living fishes). Each cosmoid scale consists of three layers as follows:

(i) **Isopedine:** This is the inner (deepest) layer consisting of layere bone. It is pierced by channels for blood vessels.

(ii) **Vascular layer:** This is the middle layer consisting of spongy bone. It contains numerous vascular spaces.

(iii) **Cosmine:** This is the outer layer consisting of dentine contain in pulp cavities.

(3) Ganoid scales (Gr. Ganio, brightness and oide, like): Ganoid or rhomboid scales are thick, usually diamond shaped plates closely fitted side by side, like tiles, providing a bony armour to the fish. In some fishes, they may be overlap. Ganoid scales are two types.

(i) **Palaconiscoid ganoid scales:** In this type, the layered bone isopedine is present. The spongy bone is absent and the cosmine layer reduced. The cosmine layer is a hard multilayered ganoine. This gives, lustrous metallic shining. Ganoid scales are characteristics of chon drosteans (Examples: *Polypterus, Acipencer*).

(ii) **Lepidosteoid ganoid scales:** In this type, both spongy bone anti-cosmine layers are absent so that ganoine contains many tubules. Such scales are arranged closely together, like tiles on a floor in diagonal rows. This type of scales are characteristics of holosteans
(Example: *Lepidosteus*).

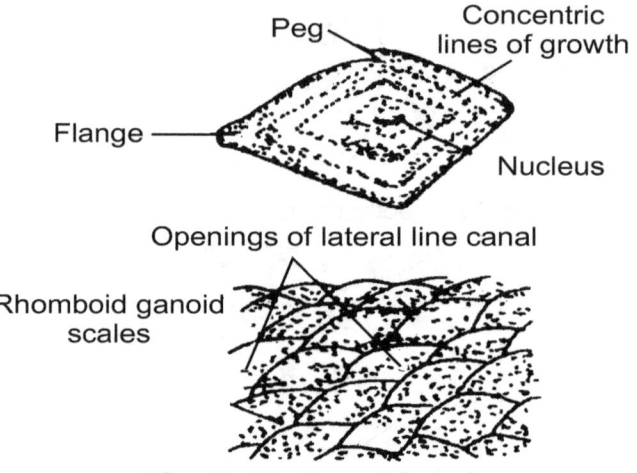

Fig. 2.45: Ganoid scale

(4) Bony - ridge scales: These are of two types namely; cycloid and ctenoid scales. The ctenoid scales differs from the cycloid in the presence of comb-like teeth or cteni in its posterior margin.

(i) Cycloid scales: These are thin, flexible, translucent plates, rather circular in outline, thicker in the centre and marked with several concentric lines of growth which can be used for determining the age of fish. They are composed of a thin upper layer of bone and a lower layer of fibrous connective tissue. They overlap each other and each scale is embedded in a small pocket of dermis. Cycloid scales are found lung fishes (Dipnoi) and some *holosteans* (*Amia*) and in the lower *teleosteans* (Carps, cods etc.)

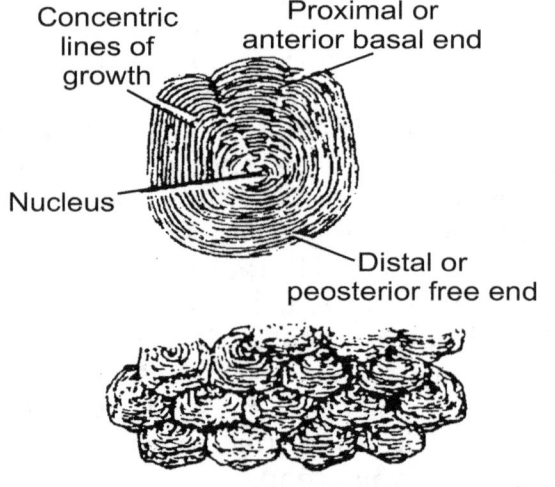

Fig. 2.46: Cycloid scale

(ii) Ctenoid scales: Structure and arrangement of these scales is similar to the cycloid scales. They are more firmly attached and their exposed free hind part is not overlapped, but bear numerous small comb-like teeth or spines (Gr. *Ctenos*, comb). Certain fishes, such as *Flounders* may bear both types of scales, ctenoid scales dorsally and cycloid scales ventrally.

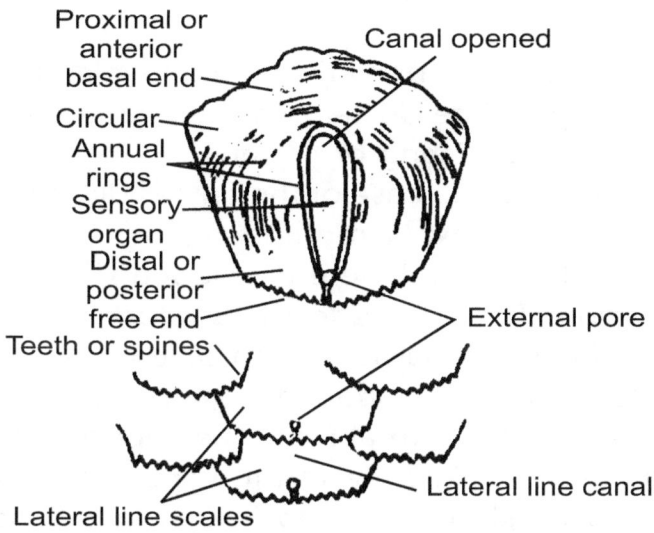

Fig. 2.47: Ctenoid scale

Uses of Scales

1. Scales are useful for the classification and identification of fishes e.g. scale counts along the lateral line are used for cyprinids (**Jones**, 1967).
2. Scales are useful for the determination of age of fish. Growth of fish is not constant. There are seasonal fluctuations in growth. In summer, when food supplies are abundant, the fish grows rapidly and so do its scales. In winter, growth slows down due to temperature - dependent metabolic processes. The wide lines of growth represents period of rapid growth and closelines, the slow growth (**Jones**, 1967). A series of wide line and a series of close lines in an area on a scale correspond to a year in the life of the fish.
3. Scales form a protective covering of exoskeleton on the body.

(b) Types of Fins in Fishes

Fins are the chief organs of locomotion in fishes, which are thin, broad folds of integument internally supported by fin rays, which may be bony, cartilaginous, fibrous or horny. Fins of adult fish are of two kinds, *median* or *unpaired* and *paired fins*.

(1) Unpaired or median fins: These include one or two dorsal fins along mid-dorsal line, a ventral anal fin behind anus or vent (Cloaca) and a tail or caudal fin around the tip of tail. Dorsal fin may be in a series or reduced or absent. Anal fin may be absent in bottom dwellers.

Among the present day bony fishes, the median fins of sturgeons are of a primitive type. The dorsal and the anal are provided with a fleshy lobe the base consisting of fin muscles. In all the higher bony fishes, the fleshy lobe at the base of the fin has disappeared.

(2) Paired lateral fins: Paired appendages were not present in the ancestral vertebrates and were developed during the course of early fish evolution. These include the pectoral fins anteriorly and pelvic fins posteriorly. The pelvic fin also called thoracic when placed below the pectoral fins and abdominal when situated just infront of anus. In some fishes, they are absent. The supporting endoskeleton of the paired fins varies greatly in different groups of fishes. The primitive types of fin skeleton found in *Ceratodus* and is known as the '*archipterygium*' and was present in the Devonian crossopterygii. Various types of paired fin skeleton in the Teleostomi may be derived from the archipterygium. The skeleton may be disappeared completely this condition called *pleuroarchic* and found in teleosts.

Caudal Fins

The caudal fin differs from the dorsal and anal fins in the naure of its supporting skeleton. The caudal fin is well developed in most fishes because it is important in direction and forward propulsion during swimming. It has different shapes in different fishes correlated with their habits and is of three main types.

(i) The protocercal (First tail): The protocercal (Diphycercal) is probably the most primitive type. The hind end of the notochord or vertebral column is straight and divides the caudal fin into two equal lobes, the dorsal epichordal and the ventral hypochordal lobe. The 'diphycercal' is also used for secondarily symmetrical tails as in Dipnoi.

Diphycercal caudal fins occurs in modern cyclostomes, primitive sharks, Holocephali (*Chimaera*), living Dipnoi (Lung fishes), living crossopterygii (*Latimeria*), many larval teleost and deep sea fishes. *Latimeria* and extinct coelacanths have unique symmetrical three lobed tail with a marked median lobe. In *Chimaera* and some deep sea fishes, the fin is called *isocercal* which is very much elongated and symmetrical.

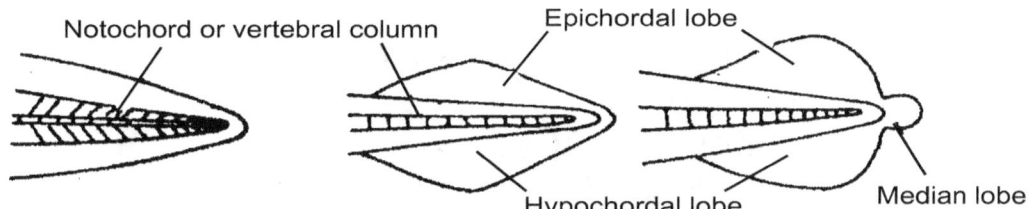

Fig. 2.48: Protocercal   **Fig. 2.49: Modified diphycercal**

(ii) Heterocercal fin: The heterocercal (unequal) tail/fin is characteristic of the chondrichthyes and some primitive bony fishes. The hind end of the notochord is bent upwards and continues almost upto the tip of the caudal fin. The ventral hypochordal lobe is much larger than the dorsal epichordal, so that the caudal fin is asymmetrical both externally and internally. It is peculiar in flying fish, some primitive fishes and ostracoderms larger ventral lobe helps the flying fish *(Cypselurus)* to attain maximum speed for gliding, as it leaves the water.

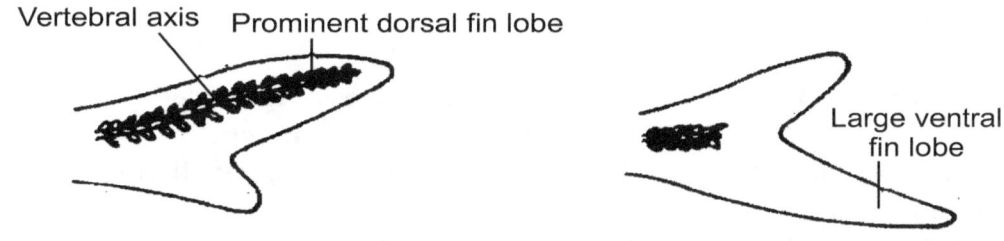

Fig. 2.50: Heterocercal   **Fig. 2.51: Hypocercal**

Heterocercal caudal fin is the characteristic of bottom feeders, with ventral mouth and without swim bladder. The strokes of larger dorsal lobe in swimming serve to direct fish towards bottom.

(iii) The homocercal fin: This is characteristic of most higher bony fishes. It is symmetrical externally consisting of equal sized epichordal and hypochordal lobes. But internally, the tail is asymmetrical and the hinder end of the vertebral column is turned upward and greatly shortened. The end of the vertebral column does not reach the posterior limit of the fin. Actually, the epichordal lobe is much smaller than in the heterocercal tail the homocercal tail is derived from the heterocercal type and intermediate types are found in many bony fishes. This transition is seen many fossil bony fishes and in the living primitive Teleostomes like *Amia*, *Lepidosteus*, and *Polypterus*.

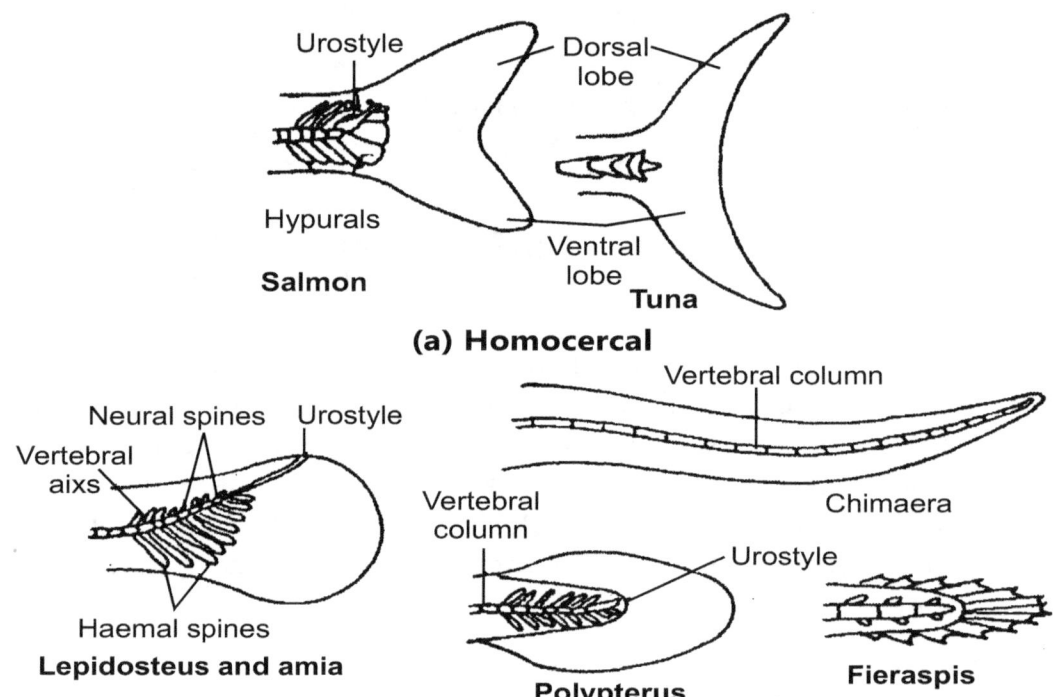

(a) Homocercal

(b) Abbreviated Homocercal   (c) Gephyrocercal

Fig. 2.52: Types of Homocercal fins

Homocercal type caudal fin is characteristic of fishes with a terminal mouth.

Homocercal type has several variations. In *Cod* and *Tuna*, the upturned. Urostyle of vertebral column is reduced or absent. In some deep sea fishes, the terminal part of vertebral column is straight and greatly elongated to form isocercal tail. In Fieraspis vertebral column and fin itself become reduced and vestigeal form a gephyrocercal tail.

Uses of Fins

Fishes swim mainly by the lateral movements of caudal fin and other fins used as steering devices and rudders. When the body is at resting position, the paired lateral fins serve to maintain equilibrium. Fins are also modified to serve other purposes i.e. lungfishes use it as legs in walking. The flying fish use their large and extended hypocercal fin for gliding. Pelvic fins in some chondrichthyes became modified as claspers and in some teleosts the anal fin forms an intromittent organ or ovipositor.

C. Respiratory System

(c) Structure of Gills in Chondricthys Fishes and Mechanism of Gill Respiration

Like most fishes *Scoliodon* is adapted to aquatic respiration and breathes by means of gills borne in a series of gill clefts on the either side of pharynx. There are five pairs of lateral *gill clefts*, each *gill cleft* communicates with the large pharynx through a large internal branchial aperture and with the outside mucous membrane lining the gill clefts is raised into a series of horizontal folds called *branchial lamellae*. The branchial lamellae are richly supplied with blood capillaries and they have a very thin covering membrane through which blood is exposed to sea-water for exchange of gases. Each gill cleft has two sets of gill lamellae, one on its anterior and the other on its posterior wall. A single set of lamellae is called a half gill or hemibranch, so that each gill cleft has two hemibranches. Successive gill clefts are separated from one another by stout fibromuscular partitions called the *interbranchial septa*. The interbranchial septa extends well beyond the branchial lamellae, then each bends posteriorly to protect the lamellae. The inner part of each interbranchial septum has a supporting visceral arch from which cartilaginous gill rays arise in a single row and project into the interbranchial septum for further support.

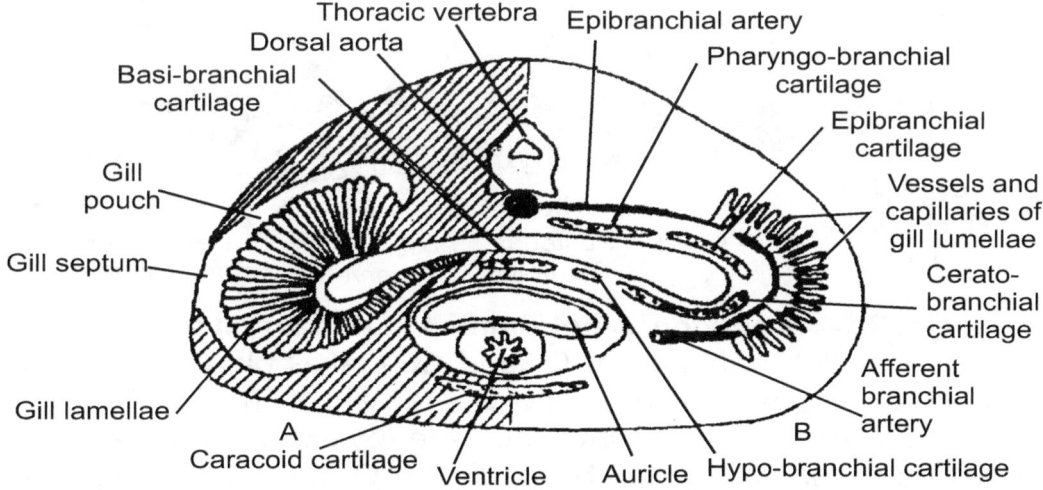

Fig. 2.53: Respiratory organs of *Scoliodon*

Visceral arches also give out rigid comb-like gill *rackers* which project inwards to protect the internal branchial aperture from food. The hyoid arch bears gill lamellae on its posterior border only, and therefore supports only a hemibranch. The first four branchial arches, bear gill lamellae on both their anterior and posterior surfaces and therefore each supports a holobranch. The fifth branchial arch is entirely gill-less. The spiracles are vestigeal gill clefts in the pharynx with no lamellae or external branchial apertures.

Mechanism of respiration: The floor of the buccopharyngeal cavity is depressed by the contraction of its hypobranchial muscles and the mouth is opened and water rushes in to fill the buccal cavity. The cavity of the pharynx is next enlarged by expansion of gill arches, while the external gill-slits are still tightly closed.

Entry of water into external branchial apertures is prevented by an anterior fold of the skin on each gill cleft. The buccopharyngeal Boor is then raised and the mouth is closed and contraction of the wall of the pharynx forces the water into internal branchial aperture, the oesophagus being closed and then into the gill clefts where it baths the branchial lamellae and goes out of the external branchial apertures. The flow of the blood in branchial lamellae is from tip to base, that is in a direction opposite to that of the water current. So blood comes in contact with high concentration of oxygen and low concentration of CO_2.

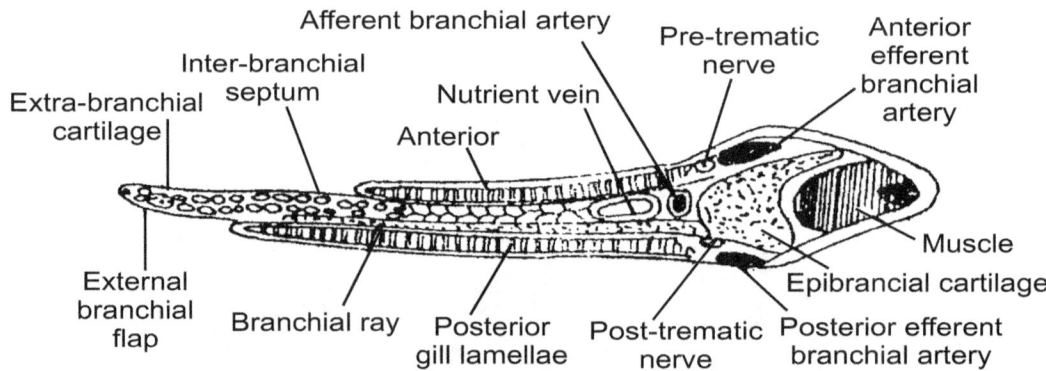

Fig. 2.54: *Scoliodon*. A holobranch in horizontal section

Thus, an efficient exchange of O_2 and CO_2 takes place between the blood and sea water. The oxygen is taken in the blood by endosmosis and CO_2 passes into the water by exosmosis. The oxygen is supplied to all parts of the body, while CO_2 brought to the gills in the venous blood is eliminated by the water of the out-going respiratory current. There is quick gaseous exchange as blood makes complete circuit in the capillaries of the gills in a very short time.

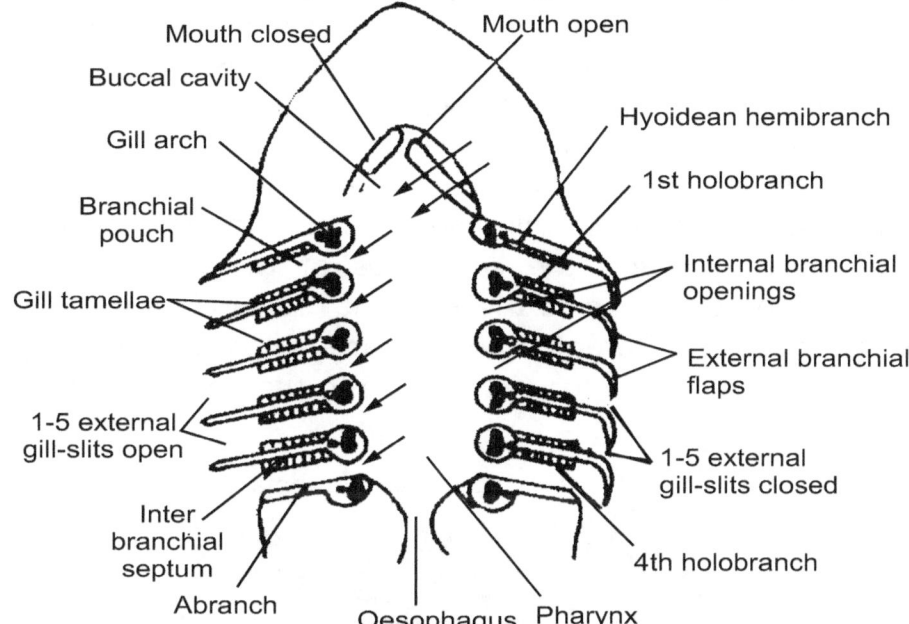

Fig. 2.55: *Scoliodon*. Breathing mechanism

Structure of gills in bony fishes and mechanism of gill respiration:

The bony fishes posses four pairs of gills. For example, *Labeo*. The hyoid and the fifth branchial arches are gillless. The gills are borne on the interbranchial septa. Each gill is made up of two rows of slender processes, the gill filaments. The row is atched to the anterior side and the other to the posterior side of the interbranchial septum. Therefore, all the gills in bony fishes are thus *holobranches*. As the interbranchial septa are reduced, the gill filaments lang out freely into the branchial chambers.

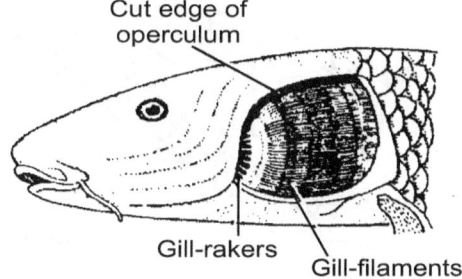

Fig. 4.56: Gills in the gill chamber after removal of the operculum

The gill filaments are covered with very thin and delicate respiratory epithelium overlying a network of capillaries. In *Labeo*, the gills with freely hanging gill filaments are described as *filiform* or *pectinate* gills whereas the gills in chondrichthyes (e.g. *Scoliodon*) are called *amelliform gills,* because they are attached to the interbranchial septa by their entire length.

The afferent branchial artery supply the blood to each gill through its branch to each gill filament. The blood gets oxygenated when it passes through the capillaries of the filament and then collects in a vessel that joins the efferent branchial artery. The latter leaves the gill. The efferent branchial arteries carry the oxygenated blood to the dorsal aorta for distribution to the body.

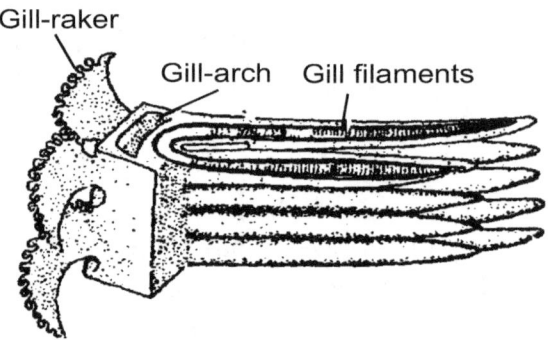

Fig. 2.57: A part of gill magnified

Mechanism of gill respiration: The fish exhibits deifnite rhythmic breathing movements to pass a current of water over the gills through the respiratory tract. The branchiostegal membranes are pressed against the body closing the branchial apertures. The opercula are then raised, enlarging the branchial chambers.

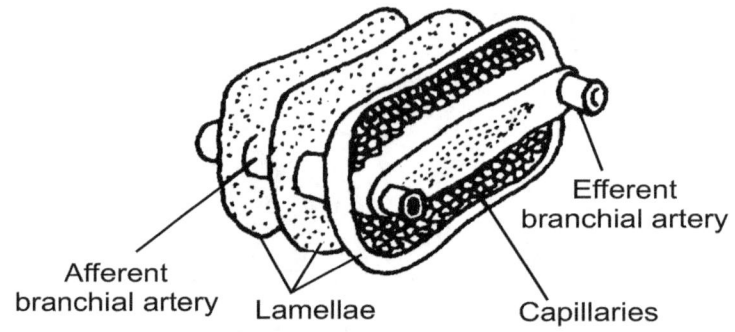

Fig. 2.58: A part of gill filament

The branchial chambers act as suction pumps so that the oral valves open and water current from outside flows through the mouth into the buccal cavity; pharynx and branchial chambers. Now, the opercula are lowered. This increases the pressure on the intenral water. This results into closing of the valves and opening of the branchial aperaturs. Hence, the water is forced out through the gill slits over the gill filaments into the branchial chambers, when it leaves via branchial apertures. During this the blood flowing in the capillaries of gill filaments gives up its carbondioxide to water and absorbs oxygen from the water flowing over them by diffusion through their thin respiratory epithelium. During this process, the oesophagus kept closed by the oesophageal valve and entry of the water is prevented into it.

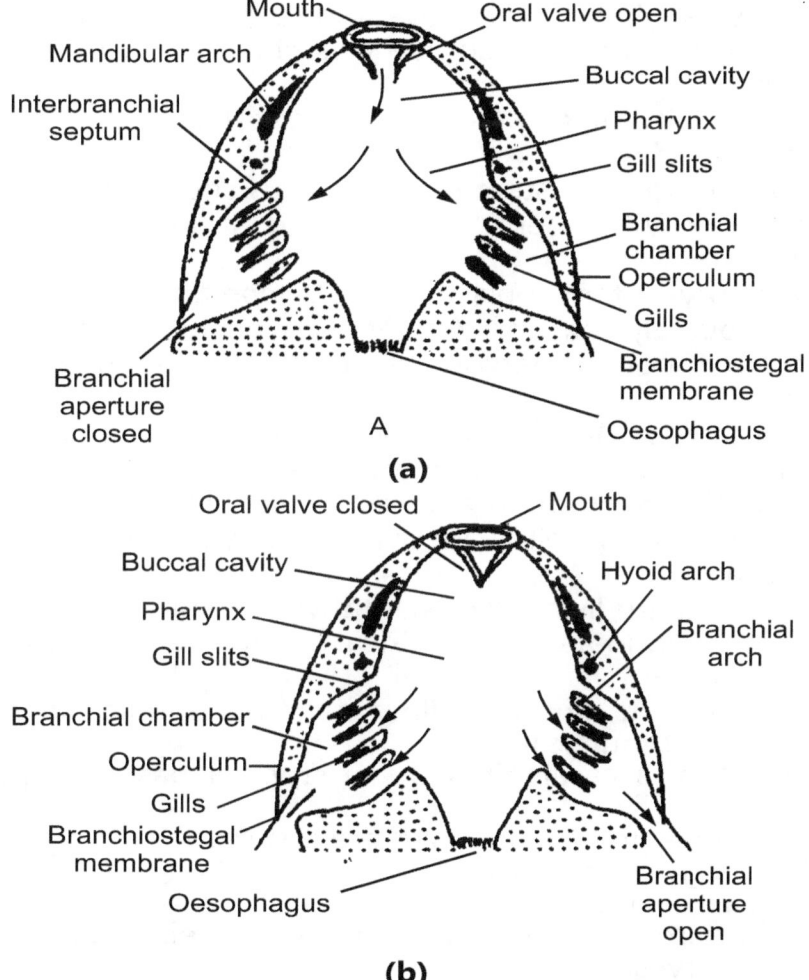

Fig. 2.59: Respiratory mechanism in bony fish

Therefore, the fish requires a constant supply of oxygen rich water. If it is removed from water or if it is left in water depleted of oxygen, the fish dies of asphyxiation (suffocation).

Summary

- *Cephalochordata* belongs to phylum chordata because it possesses three important characters viz.: presence of notochord, pharyngeal gill slits and tubular nerve chords.
- *Branchiostoma* is fish-like burrowing animal but swims actively in the marine water.
- The body of animal can be divided into four regions, cephalic, atrial, abdominal and caudal.
- The digestive system of Branchiostoma is simple and consists of alimentary canal and a digestive and *liver* or *midgut diverticulum*. It feeds on minute organic particles chiefly microscopic animals and plants.
- The body cavity of *Amphioxus* (*Branchiostoma*) is a true coelom lined by mesoderm.
- The blood vascular system of *Amphioxus* shows absence of heart and respiratory pigment in the blood. It includes arterial and venous system.
- The excretory system consists of *protonepridia*.
- The nervous system of *Amphioxus* includes central nervous system, autonomic nervous system and peripheral nervous system.
- Sense organs of *Amphioxus* comprises eyes, infundibular organ, Kollikar's pit, papillae and sensory cells.
- **Reproductive System:** The sexes are separate male gonads and testes and female gonads are ovaries. They are 26 pairs.

Cyclostomata:

- Cyclostomata are living representatives of super class - *Agnatha*. They are elongated, cylindrical and eel-like worm with compressed tail.
- The skin is soft, smooth, slimy containing unicellular mucous glands and without scales.
- Endoskeleton is cartilaginous. A branchial basket is present in pharynx.
- True coelom is present and jaws are absent.
- Respiratory gills are 5 to 16 pairs.
- Heart is two chamber.
- Brain is differentiated into very small cerebellum and 8-10 pairs of cranial nerves.
- A pair of mesonephric kidney.
- Sexes are separate, single gonad, fertilization is external.

Pisces
- The exo-skeleton covering of body of fishes is made of two types of scales i.e. *epidermal* and *dermal*.
- Epidermal scales are cornified and developed from malpighian layer of epidermis while dermal scales are mesenchymal in origin.
- Dermal scales are small, thin, cornified, calcareous or bony plates.
- *Lagler et. al.* (1977) and *Weichert* (1970) classified scales of fishes into placoid and non-placoid. The non-placoid scales are further subclassified into cosmoid, ganoid, cycloid and ctenoid scales.
- Scales are useful for the determination of age of fish.
- Fins are the chief organs of locomotion in fishes, which are thin, broad fold of integument internally supported by fin rays - which may be bony, cartilaginous, fibrous or horny.
- Fins of adult fishes are of two kinds - median or unpaired and paired fins.
- Unpaired (median) fins include 1 or 2 dorsal fin, ventral anal fin and tail or caudal fin.
- Paired fins includes pectoral fins and pelvic fins.
- The caudal fins are of three types viz. protocercal fin, heterocercal fin and homocercal fin.
- The respiration of chondricthys and osteichthyes fishes takes place by gils.

Review Questions
1. Describe the habit, habitat and external characters of *Amphioxus*.
2. Describe the digestive system of *Amphioxus*. Add a note on food and feeding.
3. With suitable diagram, explain the structure of alimentary canal of *Amphioxus*.
4. Give an account of circulatory system of *Amphioxus*.
5. Describe the excretory system of *Amphioxus*.
6. Give an account of nervous system of *Amphioxus*.
7. Explain the various sense organs of *Amphioxus*.
8. Explain the general characters of cyclostomata.
9. Describe the affinities of cyclostomata with other verebrates.
10. Describe the various types of scales found in fishes.
11. Explain types of fins in fishes.
12. Describe the structure of gills in cartilaginous and bony fish.
13. Write short notes on the following:
    (a) Systematic position of *Amphioxus*
    (b) Habit and habitat of *Amphioxus*

(c) Structure of body wall of *Amphioxus*
(d) Food, feeding and physiology of digestion of *Amphioxus*
(e) Arterial system of *Amphioxus*
(f) Venous system of *Amphioxus*
(g) Structure of nephridium of *Amphioxus*
(h) Central nervous system of *Amphioxus*
(i) Autonomic nervous system of *Amphioxus*
(j) Sense organs of *Amphioxus*
(k) Affinities of cyclostomata
(l) Specialised characters of cyclostomata
(m) Placoid scale of fishes
(n) Cosmoid scale of fishes
(o) Ganoid scales of fishes
(p) Cycloid scales of fishes
(q) Uses of fish scales
(r) Types of fins in fishes
(s) Caudal fins in fishes
(t) Structure of gill of cartilaginous fish
(u) Structure of gill of bony fishes

14. Sketch and label
    (a) Anterior part of *Branchiostoma*
    (b) V.S. of skin of *Branchiostoma*
    (c) Alimentary canal of *Branchiostoma*
    (d) T.S. of *Branchiostoma* through oral hood
    (e) T.S. of *Branchiostoma* through pharynx
    (f) T.S. of gill bars of *Branchiostoma*
    (g) T.S. of *Branchiostoma* through midgut
    (h) T.S. of *Branchiostoma* through intestine
    (i) Structure of Solenocytes of *Amphioxus*
    (j) CNS of *Amphioxus*
    (k) Single eye-spot of *Branchiostoma*
    (l) Placoid scale of fishes
    (m) Ganoid scale of fishes
    (n) Cycloid scale of fishes
    (o) Ctenoid scale of fishes
    (p) Protocercal fin fishes
    (q) Heterocercal fin fishes
    (r) Homocercal fin fishes
    (s) Respiratory organs of *Scoliodon*
    (t) Holobranch H.S. of *Scoliodon*

✱✱✱

Chapter 3...

Amphibia - Frog: *Rana tigrina*

3.1 Systematic Position, Habit and Habitat
3.2 External Characters and Sexual Dimorphism
3.3 Digestive System, Food, Feeding and Physiology of Digestion
3.4 Circulatory System
3.5 Central Nervous System
3.6 Sense Organs
3.7 Reproductive System
✍ Summary
✍ Review Questions
✍ University Questions

Introduction

Rana tigrina is the most common and largest frog, found in India. Because of its loud voice and considerably large size, it is often called as the Indian bullfrog. This frog is usually seen in the rainy season around ponds, ditches, muddy soil and human localities. Although, there is a ban on frog catching, this animal was the most ideal material for dissection purposes in laboratories. Since, a long time, the frog has been used as a dissecting vertebrate animal all over the world. Therefore, it has been extensively studied. There are several reasons for including this animal as a study animal. Firstly, it is very common, secondly, it is easily available in all parts of India and thirdly, it can be easily maintained in laboratory conditions for several days, and can be reared in a laboratory provided with pond facilities.

Besides, its body structure is simple, dissection is also simple. Moreover, the frog shows many structural similarities with man. The study of frog provides us fundamental knowledge of different organs and parts of different animals. Hence, the frog is the best dissecting as well as study animal. The genus *Rana* is found all over the world except in Australia, New Zealand and Southern South America. There are several species of *Rana* in the world.

Of these *Rana tigrina* is the most common and extensively studied animal. The other species are namely *Rana cyanophlyctis, Rana hexadactylus* and *Rana pipen, Rana catesbiana, Rana clamitans, Rana sylvatica* and *Rana temporaria*.

3.1 Systematic Position

Phylum	-	Chordata
Sub-phylum	-	Gnathostomata
Group	-	Craniata
Section	-	Gnathostomata
Super-class	-	Tetrapoda
Class	-	Amphibia
Order	-	Anura
Sub-order	-	Diplasiocoela
Family	-	Ranidae
Genus	-	*Rana*
Species	-	*tigrina*

The *Rana tigrina* belongs to the phylum Chordata because it has a notochord during the embryonic stage. It is included in Vertebrata or Craniata because it has a vertebral column and skull. It belongs to the section Gnathostomata because it has a jaw bordering the mouth.

The frog *Rana* has four limbs, hence it is included in super-class 'Tetrapoda'. This frog belongs to class Amphibia because it can live in water as well as on land i.e. amphibious mode of life.

There is no exoskeleton. It belongs to the order Anura because it lacks a tail and the body is short and broad. The legs are much longer than the arms. The sub-order Diplasiocoela shows characters such as sacral vertebra with a convex centrum anteriorly and a double convex posteriorly.

The Eighth vertebra is biconcave. There are no ribs. The Rana tigrina belongs to family *Ranidae* because it lacks cartilagenous discs between the centre of the vertebrae and has teeth only in the upper jaw. The frog belongs to genus *Rana* because its sternum is largely bony.

The species of the frog is *tigrina* because its upper surface is olive-green, mottled with dark spots, under surface is white, and a cutaneous fold borders the tympanum dorsally and fifth toe externally.

3.1.1 Habitat and Habits

The habitat of frog *Rana tigrina* is fresh water and moist land. It is generally common in and near ponds, ditches, lakes, pools, marshes and streams.

Rana tigrina prefers to live near or in water because in such an environment it can keep its skin moist which is essential for cutaneous or skin respiration.

Moist skin is useful for absorption of water as well as to escape from enemies by jumping into water. Moreover, it lays eggs in water and development takes place in it.

The larval stages are aquatic. The frog is amphibious (*amphi* = dual; *bios* = life) in nature i.e. adapted for aquatic as well as land life. The frog gets shelter in water and protection from a land enemy at the time of danger.

These frogs are cosmopolitan in distribution except in Australia, New Zealand and Southern South America.

Rana tigrina is a solitary animal, except during the breeding season. During the breeding season many frogs, both males and females generally gather together near or in a pond or lake.

The frog shows the following important habits:

1. Croaking Sound: During the rainy season or breeding season a loud croaking sound is heard near ponds which is only produced by males. At other times, they are silent. Croaking in frogs is a call for pairing i.e. a inviting signal to mates. The males croak at night or when the weather is wet. The male frog croak in air as well as in water. While croaking under water the air from the lungs is forced pass the vocal cords into the mouth-cavity and back again. The croaking sound is produced by a special apparatus called *vocal sacs*. These organs are present in male frogs on the throat. The vocal sacs are bag like structures which are distensible and swell up like balloons. They serve to increase the pitch of the sound.

2. Squatting Posture: While resting on land frogs exhibit a characteristic posture called the *squatting posture*. In this posture, the fore limbs hold the front part of the body on the ground and the long and slender hind limbs are closely folded beside the hinder part of the body.

3. Floating Posture: When a frog is in water, it relaxes in water by a passive floating posture near the surface of water. In this posture, the frog keeps the tip of the snout projecting out of water, the body hangs in a slanting manner, long hind limbs are partly extended and the fore limbs are held out on the sides.

4. Locomotion: *Rana tigrina* shows three modes of locomotion. They are walking and leaping on land and swimming in water.

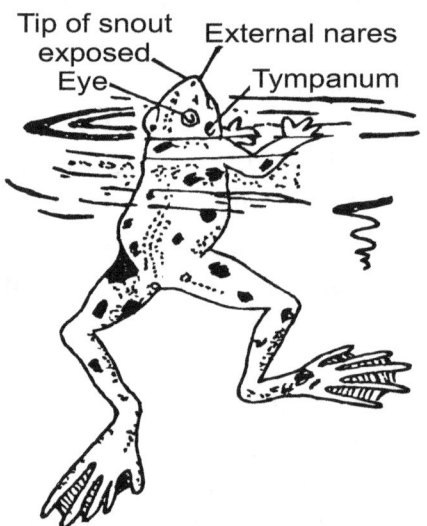

Fig. 3.1: A Frog Floating in Water

(i) Walking: When a frog is on land while walking the propulsive force is due to the reaction of each foot against the ground. During walking each limb is lifted, swung forward and placed on the ground again. The frog also exhibits the walking pattern of all other four-footed animals. The limbs move forward in a diagonal pattern i.e. the left fore foot is followed by the right hind foot and the right fore foot is followed by the left hind foot. When one limb is being lifted and carried ahead, the remaining three limbs rest on the ground.

(ii) Leaping: It is a very important mode of locomotion in *Rana tigrina* and the long, slender and powerful hindlimbs play a vital role in it. In leaping, the hindlimbs are employed to lift the body off the ground and the forelimbs suddenly become straight from a fully folded condition. This produces an upward and forward thrust which is responsible for throwing the body of the frog into the air. This also carries the body in a forward direction. As compared to the forelimbs the hindlimbs are very long and powerful so that the feet may remain on the ground to transmit the thrust generated by the legs to the body.

Fig. 3.2: Frog. Stages of Leaping on Land

While the frog is still in the air the hindlimbs are again folded. The forelimbs meet the ground first on completion of the leap. These obsorbed limbs are bowed out at the elbows to the shock of landing. In a single leap a frog can cover a distance of more than a metre. This type of locomotion is generally used by the frog when it is in danger or when escaping from an enemy.

(iii) Swimming: Swimming is employed by the frog when it is in water. The long powerful hind limbs with large webbed feet play the main role in swimming. During swimming the hind limbs are folded and extended alternately. When a frog gives backward stroke i.e. extension, the toes of feet are spread apart and the webs between them are expanded. This backward stroke produce forward thrust, which pushes the animal ahead. The short fore limbs usually take no part in swimming and are kept clasped below the trunk. But when a frog is padding around leisurely, the right and left fore limbs may be moved alternately. The sequence of limb movement in that case is the left fore limb, right hind limb, right fore limb and left hindlimb.

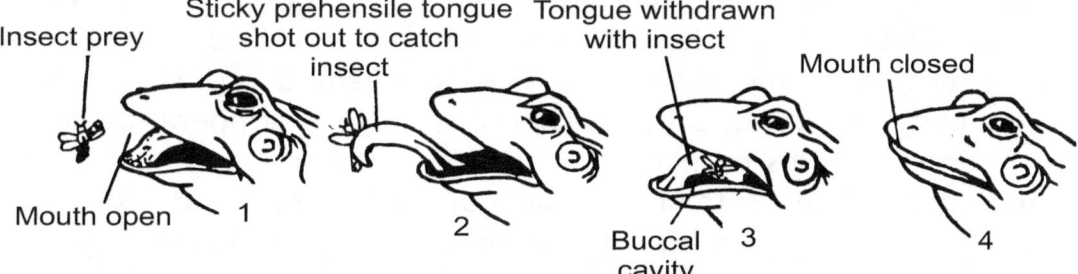

Fig. 3.3: Frog. Mechanism of Capturing Prey with its Sticky Prehensile Tongue

5. Feeding: *Rana tigrina* is a carnivorous animal which feeds on small animals such as insects, worms, spiders, crustaceans, *molluscs*, snails, tadpoles and even small frogs and fish. Frogs feed only on living or moving organisms while motionless food is ignored. Sometimes, it uses tadpoles as food hence it is a cannibal also. The food is caught by its tongue which is sticky, bifid and attached infront and free behind. This type of tongue is most suitable for a predatory mode of life. Once the prey is detected and when it is within reach the frog suddenly ejects its tongue with a great force, the prey sticks to the tongue. (Fig. 3.3.), the tongue is then quickly withdrawn in the mouth along with the prey. The food is not chewed but swallowed whole.

6. Hibernation and Aestivation:

The frog is a cold-blooded animal or poikilotherm i.e. the temperature of its body changes with the change in temperature of the environment. During adverse environmental conditions in severe cold winter or dry hot summer days the frog undergoes a dormant condition. It becomes inactive and sluggish. In winters when the temperature of the environment decreases the body temperature of the frog also decreases. This results in the slowing down of all vital activities of the body making the frog sluggish. In such adverse conditions for protection from its enemies, it goes deep down in the moist mud burrowing upto 30-60 cm. It passes winter hidden in this burrow. The frog remains inactive as if sleeping.

During this period it does not move, lung respiration is suspended, but skin respiration continues. Its mouth and external nares become closed thus is unable to take food and respire by lungs. The heart beats become slow. During this period the stored food i.e. glycogen in the liver and fat in the fat bodies is consumed. Skin respiration is sufficient to provide oxygen for body. This period of inactivity or state of dormancy is called *hibernation* or *winter sleep*. At the end of winter or on the onset of spring the temperature of the environment begins to increase which becomes suitable for the frog. It then comes out of its hiding place of winter sleep and restarts an active life. The mouth and external nares are opened and they start their function. But this favourable environment only lasts for a few months. In summer, the temperature of the environment becomes hot which leads to drying up of the water bodies. This is also an adverse condition for the frog because it lacks a device for cooling the body. In hot environmental conditions other organisms like insects, worms also disappear and hence the life of the frog becomes hard. To overcome this problem the frog undergoes dormancy. It either lies quietly in deep cool water or buries itself in the mud, near a pond. This period of inactivity is called *aestivation* or *summer sleep*. In the rainy season favourable conditions like suitable temperature, water, moisture and food appear and the frog comes out and becomes active and remains so till hibernation. According to Fischer-Sigwarts frogs do not show true aestivation.

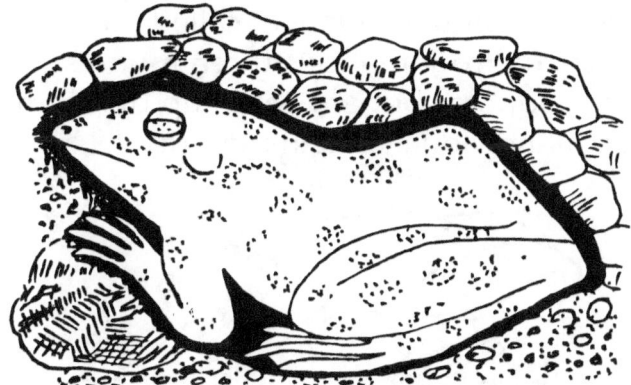

Fig. 3.4: Frog in Hibernation or Aestivation

7. Camouflage or Colour Change: *Rana tigrina* is not easily noticeable by its enemies as it can slowly change the colour of skin to match with the colour of the surroundings. This phenomenon is called protective colouration or camouflage. Changes in colour are possible due to dispersion or concentration of chromatophores or pigment cells present in the skin. The camouflage is useful for protection of frogs as well as to approach its prey unnoticed.

8. Breeding: The frog *Rana tigrina* breeds in the rainy season, i.e. from July to September. Male frogs gather in appropriate shallow and quiet waters and start croaking to attract females for mating or copulation. When both the male and female come together the male mounts upon the back of the female and grasps firmly around her thoracic region by his forelimbs. During the breeding season the nuptial pads of the male located on the bases of inner fingers become active and fully developed.

These nuptial pads are useful holding devices to hold on to the slippery female. This pairing is called *aplexus*, which lasts for several days, until the female deposits several hundred ova or eggs through her cloaca into water. (Fig. 3.5) At the same time, the male frog also drops seminal fluid containing spermatozoa on the egg to fertilize them. The fertilization in *Rana tigrina* is external then the male releases its grip and leaves the female. The mass of the eggs is called *frog's spawn*. The eggs are embedded in a gelatinous material which swells when it comes in contact with water. Jelly is a protective transparent material.

There is no parental care. Within two weeks the zygote develop into free swimming aquatic larva called tadpoles. A tadpole metamorphoses into a frog in about three months time. Most of the eggs develop into tadpoles but are eaten up by enemies. Thus a very small percentage of individuals attain maturity.

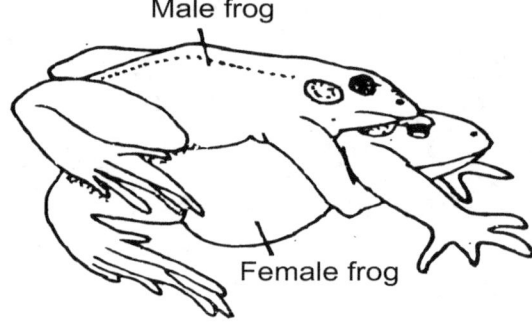

Fig. 3.5: Frogs in Apexus

9. **Enemies:** There are many natural enemies of frogs such as snakes, mongoose, crows, cranes, herons, kites, fishes and man. Large frogs also eat up the smaller ones and tadpoles. Man is also a great enemy of the frog, as he kills frogs in large numbers for scientific study and for frog legs. Many enemies destroy eggs and tadpoles and adult frogs thus reducing their numbers. Tadpoles fall a prey to aquatic insects, fish and water fowls. Frogs also serve as hosts for different kinds of parasites, such as protozoans *(Opalina, Nyctotherus, Balantidium, Trichomonas, Entamoeba)* and nematodes *(Rhabdias)*.

10. **Moulting:** During the active season, once in a month a frog casts off the outermost layer of its skin as small shreds or thin sheets. This casting off skin is called moulting or ecdysis. The skin castings may be eaten up by the frog.

11. Waste Matter Discharge: The faeces of frog is black and semisolid in nature. Urine is clear and colourless. Both are discharged through the same aperture called *cloacal opening*.

12. Economic Importance: *Rana tigrina* is a beneficial animal to man. It feeds on insects which are harmful to crops. It acts as a biological control agent, hence it is of great use to farmers. It also serves as human food. The muscular hindlimbs of the frog are used as a delicious food item in many three star and five star hotels in Western countries. Frogs are rared in frog farms in some countries to meet the demand for frogs. Frogs are used for laboratory study all over the world. This animal is widely used for research in physiology and pharmacology, human pregnancy tests and as a fish bait. Dried frogs are also used for medicinal purposes in various parts of the world particularly in the Orient. A frog in its adult and young stages has long been recognised as an ideal laboratory animals. Frogs have made great contribution in our most fundamental discoveries in experimental embryology, endocrinology and general physiology.

3.2 External Morphology and Sexual Dimorphism
3.2.1 External Characters
Shape, Size and Symmetry

The body of the frog *Rana tigrina* is somewhat ovoid or spindle shaped; pointed towards the anterior end and rounded at the posterior end. The body is also slightly flattened dorsoventrally. It is streamlined for swimming in water. It has bilateral symmetry. The size of the adult Rana tigrina varies from 12 to 18 cm in length and 5 to 8 cm in width.

Skin and Colour

The skin of the frog is thin, naked, smooth, moist and slimy. It fits loosely on the body with a thin film of mucous secreted by the glands present in it. There are no scales or any hard exoskeletal material on the skin. The skin is attached to underlying muscles at certain places only. It has dorsolateral folds or thickenings called *dorsal plicae*. These wrinkles are formed. Due to loose skin, on either side of the body. The skin is loosey fit over the body of the frog because of the space present between the skin and the muscles. This space is filled by a colourless, viscoid fluid called *lymph*. This fluid is similar to that of blood but lacks haemoglobin. Colour of the skin is dark green or olive-brown with black or brown patches or spots on the dorsal side.

The dorsal side of the animal is more pigmented but a lighter pale yellow on ventral side. On dorsal side there is also a light median streak, called the vertebral line, which runs from the tip of the snout to the cloacal opening on the back. The skin of the ventral surface is almost white or slightly yellowish, except for a few red patches at vascular areas.

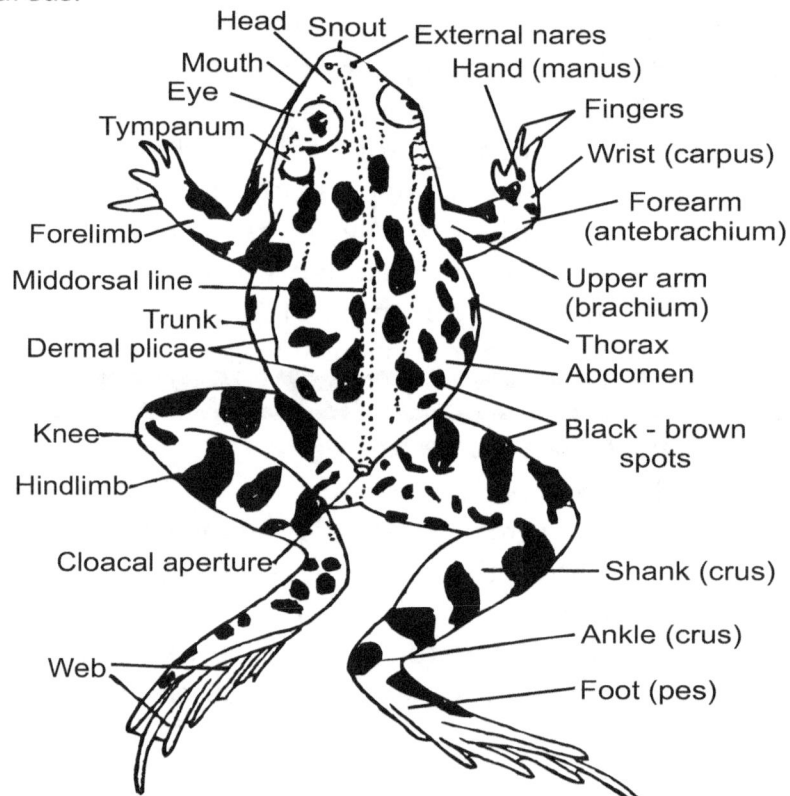

Fig. 3.6: *Rana tigrina*. External Features in Dorsal View

Body Divisions: The body of the frog is divisible into two regions only: the *head* and the *trunk*. The neck is absent because there is no demarcation between the two regions. There is also no tail.

1. HEAD

The head of the frog is flat and somewhat triangular. It is narrow infront and broad behind and thus is triangular in shape. The narrow and blunt anterior end of the head is called *snout*. The head bears various organs, such as nostrils, eyes, brow spot and tympana on the upper side and throat on the lower side.

(i) Mouth: The mouth is a wide, semioval slit. It extends along the entire border of the head. The mouth gap is large which extends from 2-4 cm behind the tip of the snout. Because of a very large mouth gap the frog is able to swallow large sized prey. The mouth is bounded by upper and lower jaws. The jaws are bounded by the skin called upper lip and lower lip. The lips are non-muscular and immovable. The upper jaw is fixed and immovable; and is armed with a row of small conical teeth. There are no teeth on the lower jaw. The frog keeps its mouth closed except during feeding.

(ii) Nostrils: There is pair of small openings just a little above the mouth called the *external nostrils* or *external nares*. Each nostril lies on either side of the median line. These are used in respiration. They open into the buccal cavity through narrow nasal passages and the internal openings are called *internal nares*.

(iii) Eyes: Two very large, spherical and protruding eyes are situated dorsolaterally on the top of the head. They are placed on the highest point of the head to compensate for the deficiency of neck. The frog is able to see on all sides without moving its body all around. They also enable it to come to the surface of water and see without exposing the rest of the body. Each eye has a thick pigmented and almost movable *upper eyelid* and movable *lower eyelid*. The upper part of the lower eyelid is transparent and is called *nictitating membrane* or *third eyelid*. It is freely movable and is nothing but the prolongation of the lower eyelid. When the eyes are open the nictitating membrane remains folded in the lower part of the eye. The frog can retract the eyes into the eye sockets in the head by special muscles. The nictitating membrane can be then moved upwards to cover them. This nictitating membrane keeps the eyes moist in the air and protects them from mud particles in water. Because of the transparent nature of the nictitating membrane, the frog can see them when its eyes are covered with it.

(iv) Brow Spot: Just near the anterior borders of the eye, a small light coloured patch is present in the median line called *brow spot*. It is a remnant of the third eye present in the ancestors of frogs. It is believed that the third eye was functional in ancestors of frogs living about 300 million years ago. But gradually this eye became functionless and reduced to only a black spot. It has been recently suggested that the brow spot is sensitive to the light of longer wavelengths, producing colour changes in the skin. Thus, it is photo sensitive.

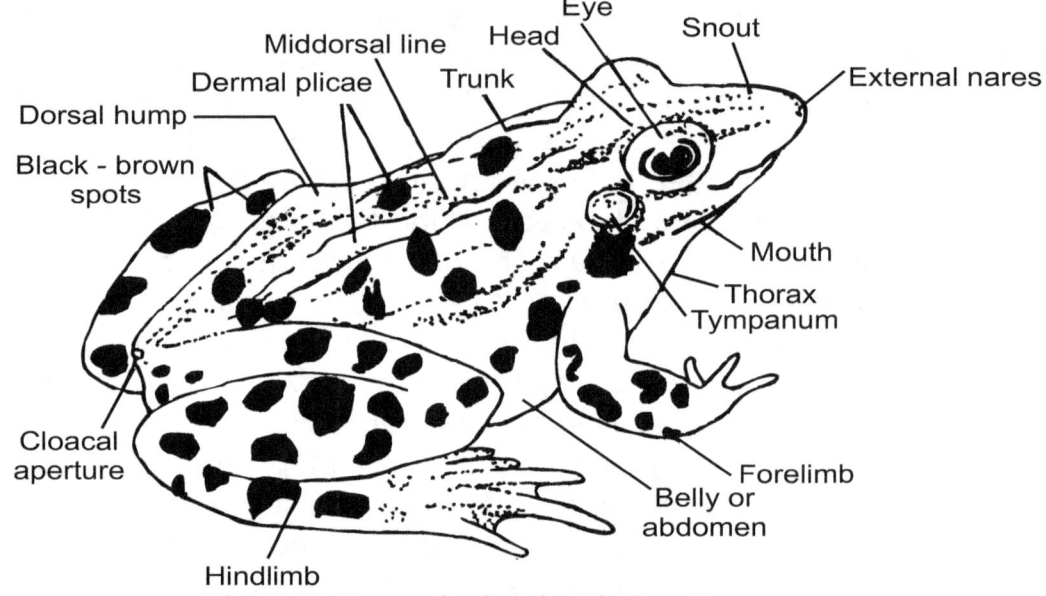

Fig. 3.7: *Rana tigrina* **in Sitting Posture**

(v) Tympana: A little behind and below each eye is a prominent, flat and deeply pigmented circular patch of the skin. This is called the *tympanic membrane or tympanum* (plural - tympana). There is no external ear in frog, but the tympanum or eardrum is fitted over a round cartilagenous ring, which is slightly raised. It is the part of the ear and serves to receive sound waves.

(vi) Vocal Sacs: In frogs, on the underside of the head is a soft throat. It rises and fails alternately in a living frog to help in breathing. In male frog, there are two patches of bluish wrinkled skin on the posterior part of the throat called *vocal sacs*. These are sac like structures and can be expanded with air. By inflating these vocal sacs the male produces a croaking sound. These structures act as resonators to intensify the croaking during breeding season. The croaking sound is nothing but the call for a female mating partner.

2. TRUNK

The trunk lies behind the head. It is also flattened like the head. The dorsal side of the trunk has a characteristic bulge in the middle of the back, the *hump* or *sacral prominence*. The hump appears prominent when the frog is squatting. The trunk widens laterally upto the hump region and then becomes narrow behind it. On the ventral side, the trunk is distinguishable into two regions: the anterior stout walled *thorax* and the posterior large, soft walled *abdomen*.

The skin on the dorsal surface of the trunk shows longitudinal wrinkles, called *dermal plicae*. At the posterior end of the trunk is a small circular cloacal aperture or vent. It is a common outlet for discharge of faeces, urine and gametes (ova and sperms). On each lateral side, the trunk bears two pairs of appendages; *forelimbs* at the anterior end and *hindlimbs* at the posterior end.

(i) Forelimbs

The forelimbs are shorter in size than the hindlimbs. Each forelimb is composed of three segments by movable joints. The proximal segment is the *upper arm or brachium*. The middle part is *fore arm* or *antebrachium*. The distal part is *hand* or *manus*. The hand is further divided into three regions: the *wrist* or *carpus*, the *palm* or *metacarpus* and four *fingers* or *digits*. There are no webs between the fingers. The wrist is very short. The first digit, corresponding to the *thumb* or *pollex* of human hand is rudimentary and invisible externally. In male frogs, the base of the first inner finger is rough, thickened with a rough swelling called the *nuptial pad* or *amplexusory pad*. These pads become specially enlarged during the breeding season.

They are useful for clasping the female during aplexus. There are small thickenings on the under surface of all the digits at the joints called *articular pads*. They are probably developed due to friction with ground. The forelimbs perform many functions such as, to hold up the front part of the body when the frog is at rest, break the fall after a leap and in males they are used for grasping the female during mating.

(ii) Hindlimbs

The hindlimbs are much elongated and more powerful than the forelimbs. They arise close together posteriorly from trunk. Each hindlimb is divisible into three parts: The proximal stout *thigh*, the long middle *shank* or *crus* and the distal *foot* or *pes*. The foot is further divided into three regions: the *ankle* or *tarsus*, the *instep* or *metatarsus* and five *toes* or *digits*.

The ankle is very long. The toes are joined together by a thin fold of the skin called the *webs*. All the toes, like the fingers possess small articular pads at the joints on the underside. A rudimentary additional digit or *sixth toe* or *prehallux* is present close at the base of first toe or *hallux*. The hindlimbs are the most important locomotory organs useful for leaping, walking and swimming. All the digits, fingers as well as the toes are without claws.

3.2.2 Sexual Dimorphism

There are some differences in external characters by which male and female frogs can be distinguished. These characters are called sexual dimorphic characters. Usually, sexual dimorphism is not very evident but during the breeding season the sexual dimorphic characters become conspicuous.

Following are the important characters distinguishing male and females:

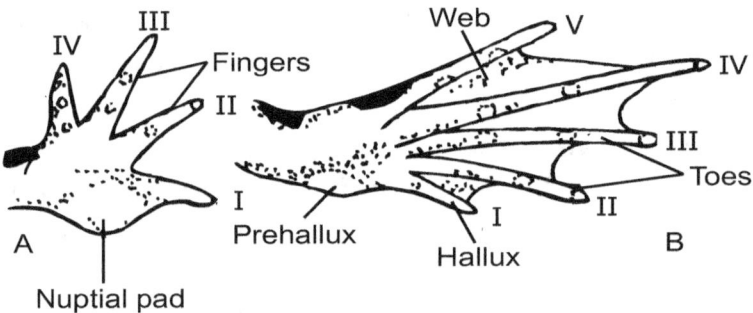

Fig. 3.8: Frog. A - Underside of Right Hand of male in Breeding Season showing Nuptial Pad., B - Foot showing Web.

Male	Female
1. The male is generally smaller in size.	1. The female is larger in size.
2. Skin colour is darker.	2. Skin colour is less dark.
3. The male is slim.	3. The female is strong and stout.
4. Vocal sacs are present.	4. Vocal sacs are absent.
5. The male croaks loudly.	5. No croaking in the female.
6. Nuptial pads are present which develop in breeding season for grasping the female.	6. Nuptial pads are absent.

Coelom and Viscera

Inside the trunk of the frog the body wall encloses a spacious body cavity called *coelom* or *splanchnocoel*. The coelom is lined by *peritoneum*. The visceral organs are situated in this large and spacious cavity. This cavity extends from behind the head to the cloacal aperture. Except the brain all other organs like alimentary canal, lungs, kidneys, urinogenital organs are situated in this cavity. These organs are called visceral organs or viscera. The heart is situated in a separate cavity called pericardial cavity or coelom.

It is also the part of the coelom which is separated from the abdominal cavity with the help of a transverse septum called *septum transverse*. Thus, coelom is divided into two unequal parts - the anterior small pericardial cavity which encloses the heart and the posterior large perivisceral cavity or pleuroperitoneal cavity which contains all the remaining internal organs except the kidneys.

The dorsal peritoneum encloses above it a large space, the subvertebral lymph sinus. The space full of lymph contains the kidneys. The kidneys therefore, have peritoneum on the ventral side only, hence called retroperitoneal.

The pericardial and abdominal cavities are lined with a thin membrane called *peritoneum* or *parietal peritoneum*. The peritoneum covers the visceral organs and is therefore called *visceral peritoneum*. In the middorsal line of the body cavity the peritoneum becomes double and forms the *mesentery*.

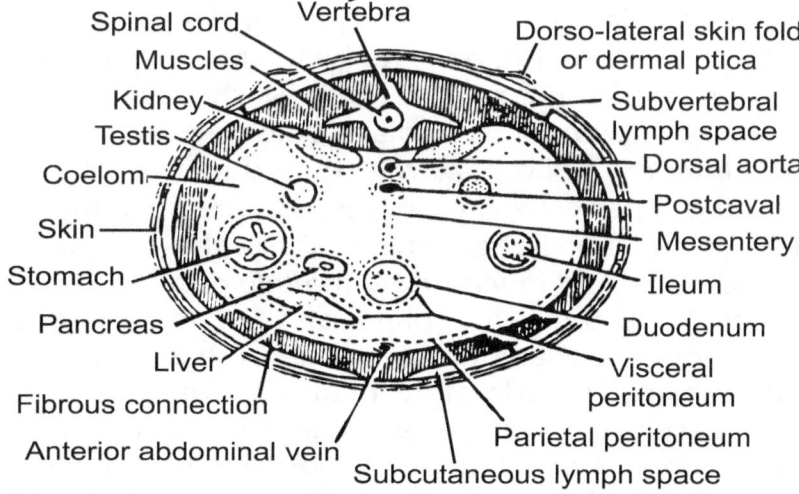

Fig. 3.9: Frog. Diagrammatic T.S. of Trunk showing Coelom, Peritoneum (Broken Lines) and Viscera

The mesenteries are useful in keeping the alimentary canal in a suspended position and slight movement. The abdominal and the pericardial cavities are filled with a transparent jelly like fluid called the coelomic fluid. Its composition is similar to that of lymph. There is no communication between the two coelomic compartments. The watery coelomic fluid present in these cavities is secreted by peritoneum. The coelomic fluid keeps the internal organs moist and prevents friction between the organs.

Thus, injury is avoided. The fluid is viscous which allows the smooth movement of the organs and offers least resistance. In addition to the number of mesenteries, there is another elastic membrane which also attaches different organs called *omentum*. This membrane is recognized by different names. For example, the membrane which connects the alimentary canal with the liver is called gastrohepatic omentum. The gastrosplenic omentum is the membrane which connects the part of alimentary canal and the spleen.

Viscera of Frog

The trunk or large body cavity or coelom consists most of the internal organs. These are collectively called *visceral organs* or *viscera*. When a frog is dissected can be seen two cavities: the pericardial cavity and the abdominal cavity. In the pericardial cavity there is only one organ, the *heart*. The heart is conical in shape and deep red in colour. It is enclosed in a thin membrane called pericardial membrane. In between the heart and pericardial membrane the fluid is present which protects the delicate heart from external shocks. The *abdominal* or *perivisceral cavity* lies behind the pericardial cavity. In this cavity lies a brown or chocolate coloured bilobed organ, the *liver*. The left lobe of the liver is larger than the right lobe. It is further divided into two lobes. The dark green coloured, round *gall bladder* present in between two lobes which stores the bile juice. The bile juice is poured into the *duodenum* by the *bile duct*.

Above the liver, there are pairs of thin, membranous, hollow reddish ash coloured organs present called *lungs*. A large elongated sac like organ lies by the side of liver called *stomach*. The *oesophagus* which is the part of the alimentary canal lies above the stomach. There is no neck in frogs hence, the oesophagus is very short, is partly covered by the left lobe of the liver. The position of the liver is dorsal while the stomach is on the ventral side. The next part of the alimentary canal extends posteriorly called the *duodenum*. It shows a

U-shaped position. At the junction of the stomach and duodenum there is a constriction called pyloric constriction or pylorus. The duodenum continues as a narrow tube called small *intestine or ileum*. The small intestine is a coiled structure which extends to the posterior region of the body cavity. Its diameter becomes more and this part is called *large intestine or rectum*. It becomes narrow towards the posterior end and passes through the pelvic girdle and opens outside into the cloacal aperature.

The entire alimentary canal remains suspended in the body cavity by the thin elastic membranes called *mesenteries*. The *pancreas* or digestive gland is situated in the U shaped loop of the duodenum. The secretion of this gland is carried by the *pancreatic duct* into the duodenum. The red, rounded *spleen* is associated with the digestive system, but is not a part of it. Close to the rectum, a thin walled colourless bag like structure is present called the *urinary bladder* which is part of the excretory system.

In the middle of the abdominal cavity, on either side of the vertebral column lies a pair of dark brown coloured elongated kidneys. From each kidney originates a narrow thin tube called *ureter* which opens into the cloaca by a separate opening. Each kidney bears on its ventral surface a yellow coloured elongated gland called *adrenal gland*. Very close to the anterior part of each kidney there may be testes (in male) or ovaries (in female). The testis may be elongated or oval attached to the kidney by a membrane called *mesorchium*. In case of female the ovaries are suspended in the abdomen with the help of a special membrane called mesovarium.

From each testis *vasa efferentia* originate which opens into the ureter or *urinogenital* duct which is the common duct for both the excretory and genital system. In female, pair of long, white, coiled tubes are present called *oviducts* which open separately into the cloaca. During the breeding season the ovaries enlarge and occupy most of the abdominal cavity.

A large number of eggs are present in the lobes of the ovaries. Because of the large number of eggs, the ovaries appear black in colour. There are also finger like yellow or cream coloured *fat bodies* attached to the anterior end of the testes. Fat bodies store the food and also make the body light for floating in water. On the dorsal side in the middle line of the body the *vertebral column* is present. It is made up of many ring like structures called *vertebrae*. The spinal cord passes through the vertebral column from the brain to the last vertebra.

On either side of the vertebrae white glands are seen called the glands of *swammerdam*. The spiral nerves originate through these glands from the spinal cord.

Body Wall

The body of the frog is covered by skin. The skin is thin, coloured, moist and quite tough. Beneath the skin there is a layer of muscles. The muscular layer is thickened more on the dorsal side than on other parts of the body. The skin is not continuously attached to the muscle layer but attached at certain places only. Therefore, there are spaces formed between the two points. These spaces are filled by a watery fluid called *lymph*.

These spaces are therefore known as subcutaneous lymph sinuses. The thin peritoneum covers the muscular layer internally. The peritoneum is not in contact with the muscular layer on the dorsal side. The skin, muscles and peritoneum together form the body wall. It protects the internal organs. The skin performs a number of functions. The muscles are important for body movements and the peritoneum secretes coelomic fluid.

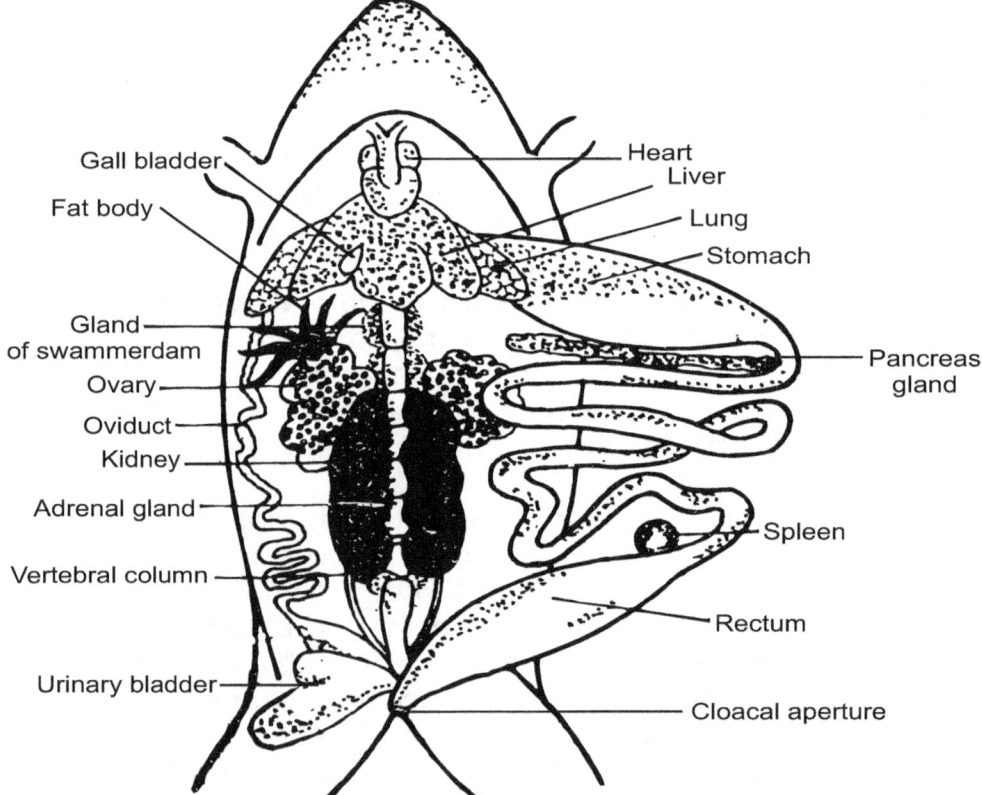

Fig. 3.10: Frog - Coelom and Viscera of a Female

Skin or Integument

The outermost covering of the body of the animal is called *skin* or *integument*. The integument of a frog helps the internal organs of the body and is also responsible for maintaining the shape of the body. The skin of the frog is smooth, moist and loosely fitted. There are no exoskeletal structures such as scales, feathers and hair on the skin.

Frog skin is thick on the dorsal side and thin on the ventral side. Frog skin has dark green patches on the dorsal side whereas it is light yellow on the ventral surface. The integument is formed by stratified epithelium and connective tissues. Histologically, frog skin consists of two layers: an outer *epidermis* and an inner *dermis*.

1. Epidermis

Epidermis is the outer thin, non-vascular stratified layer of cells. It has an ectodermal origin; as it develops from the ectoderm of the embryo. It is stratified epithelium.

Epidermis is composed of several layers of thin flattened epithelial cells which are periodically changed by moulting. The moulting occurs about once a month during the active season. The ecdysis or moulting is controlled by the pituitary and thyroid glands.

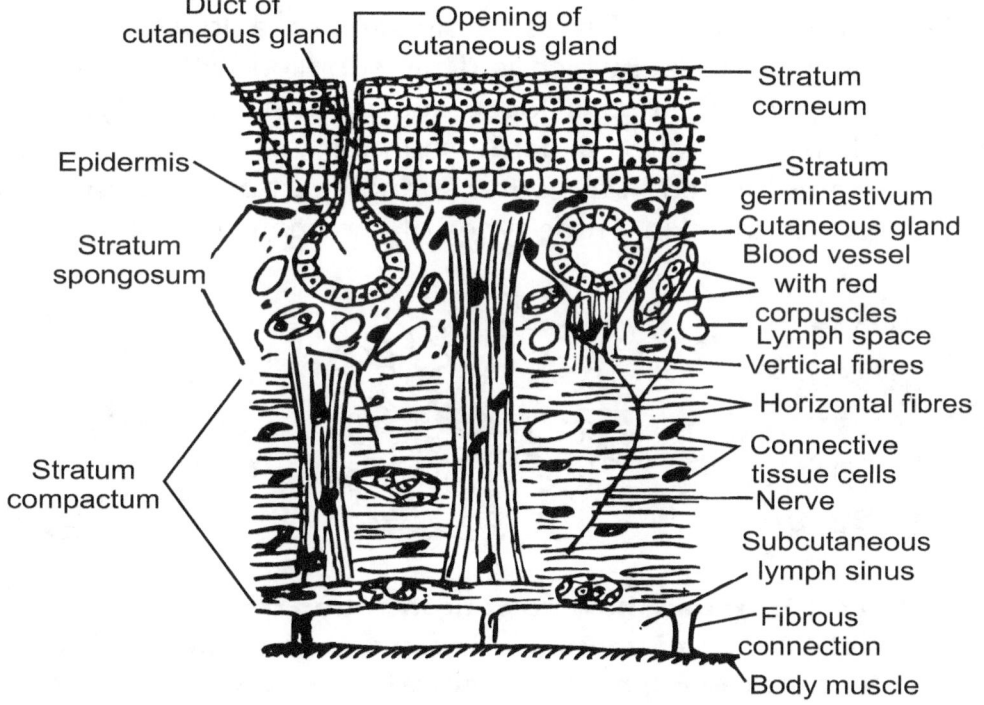

Fig. 3.11 (a): V.S. of Skin

The outermost layer of the epidermis is called *stratum corneum*. It is a dead layer. This layer of cells is formed by the innermost layer called *Malpighian* layer or *stratum germinativum*. This layer consists of columnar epithelial cells which are active protoplasmic cells.

The cells of this layer are divided by repeated mitotic divisions and give rise to columnar epithelial cells. These new cells gradually migrate towards the outer surface. During this outward migration, the cells become gradually flat and their cytoplasm is slowly replaced by a hard substance, the *keratin* or *horn*. By the time they reach the surface of the epidermis, they become extremely thin and nearly dead. Therefore, these cells are called *keratinized* cells or *horny cells* and the cells layer is called *stratum corneas*. This dead cell layer forms an efficient protective covering of the body.

2. Dermis

Beneath the epidermis, the dermis is present. It is the inner, thick and vascular region of the skin. Dermis is mesodermal in origin. i.e. it develops from the mesoderm of the embryo. Dermis is further composed of two layers: the outer loose *stratum spongiosum* and inner denser *stratum compactum*.

The stratum spongiosum is composed of a loose network of fibrous connective tissue, which is richly supplied with *lymph spaces* and *blood capillaries*. In this loose space most of the glands are present. There are also a large number of *pigment cells* or *chromatophores* located in the outer spongy part of the dermis which impart colour to the skin. Three types of chromatophores are seen in the layer.

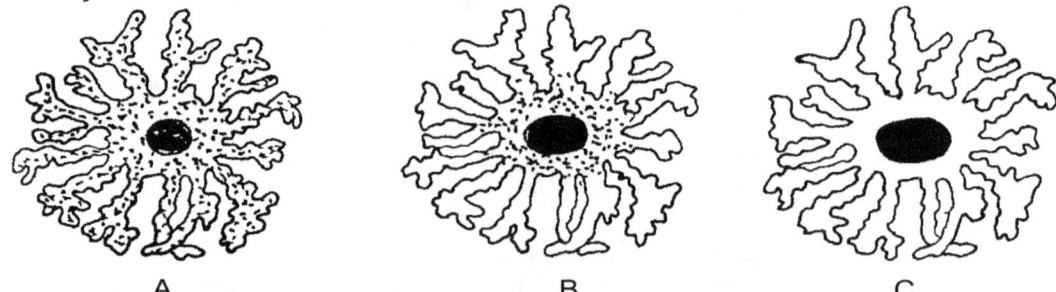

A   B   C

Fig. 3.11 (b): Stages showing concentration of pigment in the pigment cells. When pigment is dispersed as in A, the skin is darker in colour. As the pigment concentrates from B to C, the skin becomes progressively light.

They are *melanophores* with black and brown pigment, *lipophores* with red and yellow pigment and *guanophores* with crystals of guanine. Skin colour is exhibited due to the combination of the pigment and reflection of light from guanine crystals. For example, a frog shows green skin colour; it is produced by the combination of yellow pigment and reflection of blue light by guanophores. Changes in the colour are brought about by movement of pigment in the chromatophores. The movement of the pigment is partly under hormonal control and partly under the control of the nervous system.

When the pigment is dispersed the skin imparts a dark colour. As the pigment in the chromatophore gets contracted or concentrated the skin becomes progressively light or pale. External and internal conditions are responsible for colour changes in the animal. The external environmental factors like low temperature, dampness and darkness darken the skin whereas higher temperature, drying and intense light make the animal pale. There is hormonal and nervous control on pigmentation. The endocrine gland pituitary secretes the hormone *intermedin* which darkens the skin and adrenal gland hormone *adrenalin* makes the skin lighter. In the stratum spongiosum a number of mucous glands are present. The glands are flask-shaped cavities lined with glandular cells and open outside through a narrow tube called the *neck*. The mucous or cutaneous gland has a narrow duct, which passes outwards through the epidermis, opens out by a small pore on the surface of the skin. These glands, though present in the dermis, are epidermal in origin. They are formed by sinking in of the malpighian layer.

The mucous glands are abundantly present all over the skin. They are made up of a thick wall and secrete slimy mucous. The mucous spreads over the skin as a thin film, and thus makes the skin moist and slippery. The mucous makes the skin soft and moist which helps in *cutaneous respiration*. Poison glands are absent in *Rana tigrina*, but they are mostly found in toads and the secretion protects the animal from enemies. The lower layer called stratum compactum is composed of a dense layer of connective tissues which are made up of *horizontal* and *vertical fibres*. The bands of white collagen fibres predominate. The bands are mostly horizontal. There are also nerves and blood vessels. Beneath these layers, there is a layer of subcutaneous connective tissue. The connective tissue remains separated by large lymph spaces or *lymph sinuses*.

Functions of Skin

The skin or integument performs a number of functions in the frog *Rana tigrina*. The important functions are summarised below:

1. **Protection:** The skin forms a firm protective covering to the body of the animal. The internal organs are protected by the skin from mechanical injuries. It serves to protect body organs from external shocks, friction and pressure. The skin also protects the animal from external factors like extreme cold or heat. It also prevents entry of disease causing microorganisms and other foreign bodies. It also prevents evaporation of water.
2. **Secretion:** The large number of cutaneous glands present in the skin secrete mucus which makes the body slippery to facilitate its escape from the enemy's grip. The moist and slippery skin also reduces the resistance when frogs swim in water. It also prevents excessive water absorption.
3. **Colour change:** The chromatophores of the skin enable the frog to change its colour resembling those of its surroundings. This helps in escaping from enemies.
4. **Respiration:** The skin acts as an additional respiratory organ. This respiration is called cutaneous respiration. The moist skin is richly supplied with blood capillaries and gaseous exchange takes place through the skin. Thus, respiration occurs through it.
5. **Sensitivity:** The skin is tactile in function. It is supplied with nerve endings making it sensitive to touch and responsive to various external stimuli such as temperature, pressure, humidity etc.
6. **Absorption:** The body of the frog needs water but it is unable to drink it. However, the skin absorbs water and fulfils the water need of the body.
7. **Temperature Regulation:** Frog is a poikilotherm animal i.e. the body temperature changes as per the temperature of the environment. The large number of mucous glands secrete the mucous on the skin which evaporates and cools the body when the frog is on land. This results in a slightly lower body temperature than that of the surrounding

temperature. Thus, skin performs cooling of body temperature.

8. **Locomotion:** There are webs or skin folds present in the toes or the hindlimbs which helps the frog in swimming.
9. **Hatching:** The skin of larval frogs produces hatching enzymes which are useful for dissolving the egg membranes, so that hatching may take place.
10. **Formation of Bones and Teeth:** Certain bones are developed in the dermis of the skin and which then fuse with the skeleton. These bones are called *membrane bones*. These bones are partly developed from the epidermis and partly from the dermis.
11. **Prevention of Evaporation:** The skin also prevents the evaporation of body fluids.
12. **Excretion:** The skin performs the function of excretion through ecdysis or moulting.
13. **Sexual Selection:** The skin also plays the role of sexual selection due to its colour.

3.3 Digestive System

The digestive system includes the organs of ingestion, digestion and assimilation of food. All these organs combine to form the *alimentary canal*. Thus, the digestive system is formed by the alimentary canal and the associated digestive glands. The digestive system of the frog *Rana tigrina* consists of:

1. Alimentary canal and 2. Associated digestive glands.

3.3.1 Alimentary Canal

The alimentary canal of the frog is a coiled tube which includes the following parts:

(i) Mouth,
(ii) Buccopharyngeal cavity,
(iii) Oesophagus,
(iv) Stomach,
(v) Small intestine (Duodenum),
(vi) Large intestine (Rectum) and
(vii) Cloaca.

1. Mouth: The alimentary canal begins with the mouth opening. The mouth is a wide semioval slit. It extends along the entire margin of the head. Its wide gap enables the frog to capture large prey. Mouth is bounded by upper immovable and lower movable jaws covered by immovable lips. The lower jaw can move freely up and down to close or open the mouth. The mouth leads into the buccopharyngeal cavity.

2. Buccopharngeal Cavity: It is the space formed in the head bounded above by the skull and below by the throat. The buccopharyngeal cavity is wide from side to side but low dorsoventrally. This cavity is lined with ciliated epithelium. There are a large number of mucous glands present in the epithelium, which secrete mucous for lubricating food. The mucous glands are abundant on the tongue and on the roof. There are no salivary glands in the frog. The buccopharyngeal cavity is differentiated into two parts anterior *buccal cavity* and the posterior *phyrynx*. There is, however, no demarcation between these two regions.

(a) Buccal Cavity: The buccal cavity is a spacious cavity which contains several organs, such as teeth, subrostral fossae, internal nares, tongue and prelingual elevations.

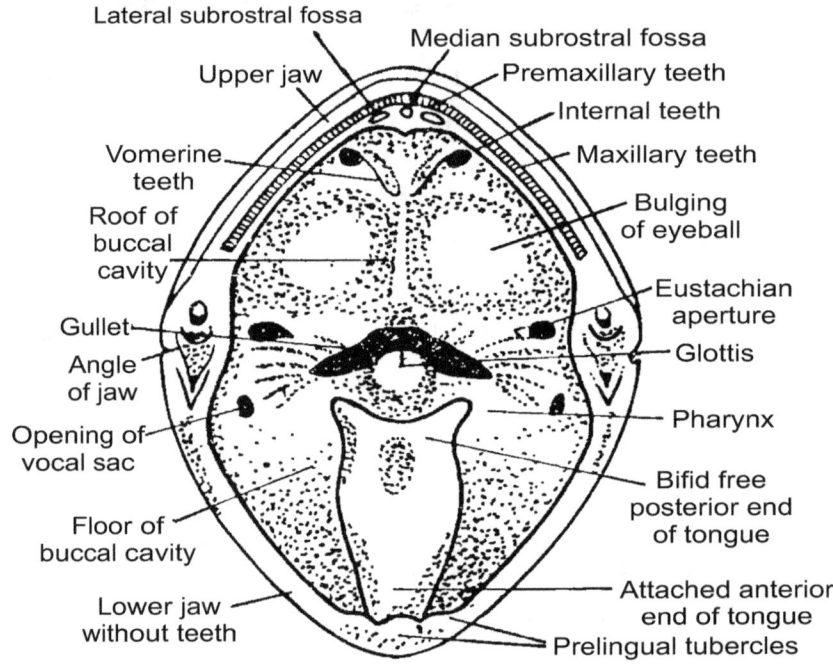

Fig. 3.12: Frog. Buccopharyngeal Cavity of Male

(i) Teeth

The teeth are present only in the upper jaw. The lower jaw lacks teeth. In the upper jaw the teeth occur in a single oval row along the margin. They are called maxillary teeth because they occur on the premaxillae and maxillae bones of the upper jaw. Besides, these, there are two small bones in the roof of the mouth called vomers. The frog also bears two groups of *vomerine teeth*. They are located near the anterior end, each on either side of the median line. The teeth of frog are not used for chewing or mastication of food. They are only useful to hold the prey and to prevent it from escaping.

All the teeth of frog are similar in structure, they are therefore called homodont teeth. They are small, conical and backwardly pointed. These teeth are not fixed in the sockets of the jaw bones by cement hence are called *acrodont*. These teeth if broken, are replaced by new ones any number of times. Thus, they are called *polyphyodont teeth*. The frog tooth consists of two parts: a base and a crown. The base is made up of bone like material. The free part or crown of the tooth is made of a hard ivory-like substance known as *dentine*. The tip of the crown is covered by a very hard, resistant and glistening substance, called the *enamel*. The tooth is hollow and the cavity is called *pulp cavity*. The pulp cavity is filled with *blood* capillaries nerve endings, odontoblast, and the soft tissue pulp consists of connective tissue. The pulp nourishes the tooth during growth.

The odontoblast cells produce new material for the growth of the tooth.

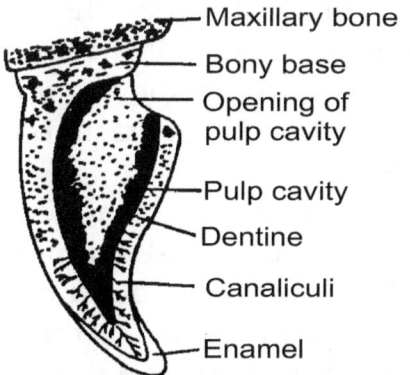

Fig. 3.13: Frog. A Maxillary Tooth in V.S.

(ii) Subrostral Fossae

Near the tip of the upper jaw within the maxillary teeth, three shallow pits are situated. There are two lateral and one median pits or fossae. The middle is larger called *median subrostral fossae* and the two lateral are smaller, known as the lateral *subrostral fossae*. These fossae are useful in keeping the mouth firmly closed during respiration.

(iii) Internal Nares

The internal nares are a pair of small openings lying close to the lateral sides of vomerine teeth. They help in respiration.

(iv) Bulgings of Eyeballs

On the roof of the buccal cavity there are two large, pale, oval areas behind the vomerine teeth, called bulgings of eyeballs. They play an important role in swallowing.

(v) Tongue

On the floor of the mouth cavity lies a large, soft and muscular tongue. It is covered with sticky mucous. Its anterior end is attached to the inner border of the lower jaw and its posterior end is free and bifid which can be thrown out and taken back into the buccal cavity suddenly after capturing the prey with its sticky surface. The *genioglossus muscles* are responsible for the extension of the tongue. These muscles arise from the lower jaw and are inserted in the tongue.

The protrusion of the tongue is again aided by sudden and simultaneous filling up of the large lymph sac present in the floor of the buccal cavity. This mechanism is useful for catching prey. The immediate withdrawal of the tongue occurs by a pair of *hyoglossus muscles*. These muscles originate from the posterior cornua of the hyoid apparatus. They meet infront of the larynx and extend forward to the root of the tongue, where they enter the tongue and pass backwards to its tip. The tongue bears taste buds on the papillae.

(vi) Prelingula Elevations

These are there small elevations or projections located at the tip of the lower jaw just infront of the attachment of the tongue called *prelingual elevations*. The lateral two elevations are smaller than the middle one. When the mouth is closed, they fit into the subrostral fossae of the upper jaw. Thus, they form the locking arrangement.

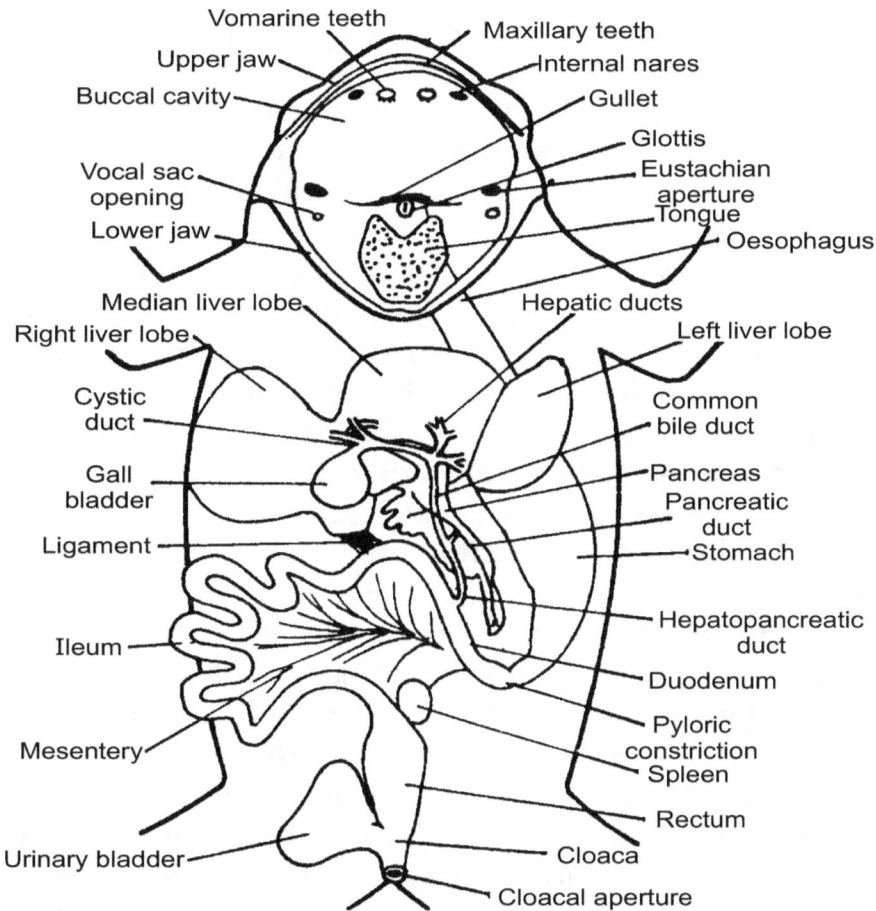

Fig. 3.14: Frog. Digestive System in Ventral View

(b) Pharynx: Posteriorly, the buccal cavity passes without demarcation into a short pharynx. There are different apertures opening into the pharynx. The median oval elevation on the floor bearing a longitudinal slit-like aperture called the glottis. It leads into the lungs. Air goes into the lungs through the glottis. On either side, behind the glottis, is present a pair of *openings of vocal sacs* which are found only in male frogs. The vocal sacs act as resonators during croaking. A pair of wide apertures is located on the roof of the pharynx, almost at the angles of the jaws called Eustachian apertures which lead into the Eustachian tubes. These apertures connect the pharynx with the middle ear and help in keeping the air pressure equal on both sides of the tympanic membrane. Posteriorly, the pharynx tapers, abruptly into the oesophagus. At the junction of the roof and floor of buccopharynx is a wide opening, the *gullet*, which leads into the oesophagus.

3. Oesophagus: The buccopharyngeal cavity opens into the oesophagus through an aperture gullet. The oesophagus is a short muscular but wide tube. It is because of the absence of a neck. The mucous membrane or internal lining of the oesophagus is longitudinally folded. The folds keep the oesophagus closed to prevent the entry of air, but allows expansion during the passage of food. Hence, it is a highly distensible tube. Posteriorly, oesophagus elongates to merge with a large sac like stomach.

4. Stomach: The stomach is a broad, thick walled sac like tube which lies on the left side of the body. It is attached to the dorsal body wall by a mesentery called *mesogaster*. The inner surface of the stomach is thrown into longitudinal folds, which allows considerable expansion of the sac of the stomach as food accumulates. These folds also increase the surface area of the stomach for secretion of gastric juice and for absorption of the digested food. The stomach is differentiated into two parts. The large broader anterior part is called *cardiac stomach;* while the short, narrower posterior part is called the *pyloric stomach*. The posterior or the pyloric end of the stomach is slightly constricted and its opening into the small intestine is guarded by a circular ring-like sphincter muscle called *pyloric valve* or *pyloric sphincter*. This valve guards the premature escape of food from the stomach into the small intestine. There is also a *cardiac sphincter* or *valve* at the cardiac end. It controls the entry of food into the stomach and prevents its regurgitation i.e. the food coming back into oesophagus.

The mucous membrane of the stomach contains a large number of multicellular *gastric glands* and the unicellular *oxyntic glands*. The gastric glands secrete the enzyme pepsinogen, hydrochloric acid and mucous. The stomach is an organ for storage and digestion of food.

5. Small Intestine: The stomach passes into a narrow tube 'the *intestine*' through a pyloric *valve*. The small intestine is distinguished into two parts. The anterior part, next to the stomach is called *duodenum* which runs forward parallel to the stomach forming a U with stomach. It receives a common *hepato-pancreatic duct* from the liver and pancreas bringing bile and pancreatic juice. The posterior part of the small intestine is called ileum which is the longest part of the alimentary canal. It is coiled and makes several loops and accommodated within the body cavity. The inner surface of the small intestine is thrown into several longitudinal folds. The great length and the longitudinal folds of the ileum increase the area of secretion and absorption of the digested food. The ileum leads abruptly into the rectum.

    6. Large Intestine or Rectum: The large intestine is a short, wide tube. It runs straight behind and opens into the cloaca by the anus which is guarded by a *anal sphincter*. Its inner lining forms numerous low longitudinal folds. The rectum absorbs water from the stored faeces.

    7. Cloaca: The cloaca is a small terminal chamber. It serves as a common passage for the digestive and urinogenital systems. The cloaca opens out by the cloacal aperture which is situated at the end of the trunk between the hind limbs.

Histology of the Alimentary Canal

The wall of the alimentary canal in every part, consists of four layers or coats which are stated below.

    1.   Mucosa or Mucous Membrane,
    2.   Submucosa,
    3.   Muscular coat and
    4.   Visceral Peritoneum or Serosa

The arrangement of these layers is in sequence from the inner side to the outer side.

    1. Mucosa: The mucosa is the innermost layer of the intestine. It is further divisible into three layers: The innermost *columnar epithelium*, the middle *lamina propria* and the outer *muscularis mucosae*. The mucosa is very much folded and thus increasing the secretory and absorptive area. The columnar epithelium rests on the thin basement membrane and it contains mucous secreting *goblet cells*. Each goblet cell contain a big vacuole which is filled with mucous. These cells secrete mucous which is discharged on the inner surface of the intestine as a thin film. The columnar cells are absorptive in function. The *lamina propria* consists of a thin sheet of reticular connective tissue.

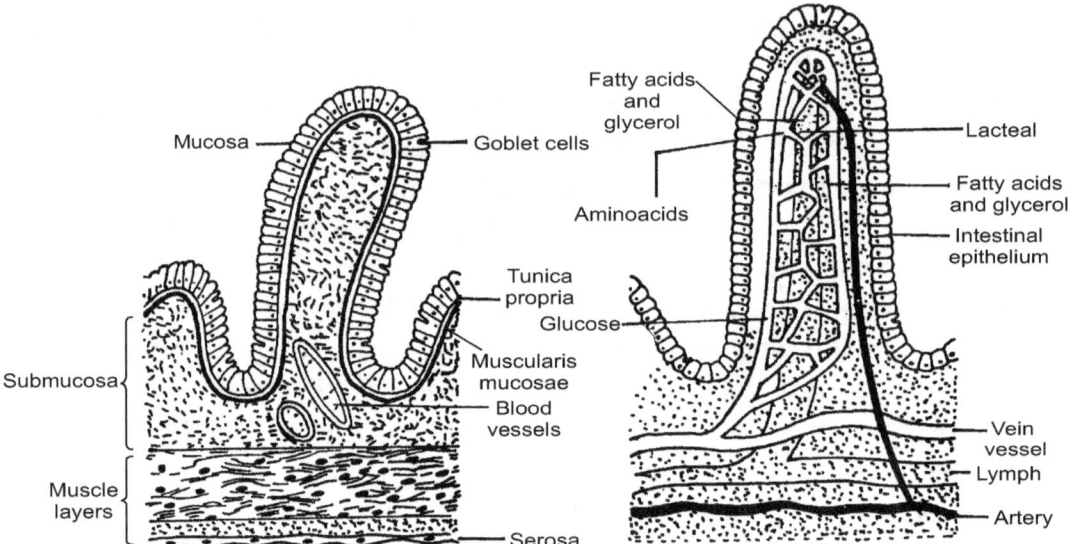

Fig. 3.15: Frog - T. S. of Intestine **Fig. 3.16: Frog - Diagrammatic Section of a Villus of the Intestine showing the Absorption of Digested Food**

It contains fine capillaries, lymph vessels and nerves. The muscularis mucosae is a thin layer of smooth muscles; made up of circular muscles. Mucosa performs the function of secretion and absorption.

2. Submucosa: This layer lies next to the mucosa. It is made up of dense connective tissue with both white and yellow fibres. It also contains larger blood vessels and lymph vessels or lacteals. These vessels send their branches to the mucosa on the inner side and muscular coat on the outside. The plexus of nerve cells and fibres called *submucous plexus* of *Meissner* are also found in the submucosa. The submucosa carries blood and lymph vessels for absorption of food. It also provides elasticity for expansion of the intestinal lumen.

3. Muscular Layer: It surrounds the submucosa and formed by unstriated muscle fibres. This muscular layer consists of two parts; the inner thick layer of *circular muscles* fibres and the outer thin layer of *longitudinal muscle fibres*. Between these two muscle layers lies a network of nerve cells and fibres; called *plexus of Auerbach*. These muscle layers undergo contraction and relaxation which helps in mixing of the food digestive juices and push that material towards the rectum.

4. Peritoneum or Serosa: The peritoneum or serosa is made up of tesselated epithelium which covers the muscular coat by a thin sheet of connective tissue. The peritoneum forms a protective covering of the digestive tract. This layer is continuous with the mesentery and suspends the intestine from the dorsal body wall.

Histological Structure of Stomach

The stomach wall is made up of the four coats. They are mucosa, submucosa, muscular coat and peritoneum.

(i) Mucosa: The mucosa layer again consists of three layers: epithelial layer, lamina propria and muscularis mucosae. The epithelial layer is made up of columnar epithelium forming invaginations into the underlying connective tissue layer. They form either simple or branched tubes of glandular cells called *gastric glands*. These glands are formed by two types of cells which secrete different types of secretions. The cuboidal cells are called *peptic cells* or *chief cells* which secrete an enzyme called *pepsin*. The other type of cells are ovoid in shape called *oxyntic cells* which secrete *hydrochloric acid*. Gastric juice is nothing but mixture of hydrochloric acid and pepsin. The muscularis mucosae is well developed and consists of an inner layer of circular and outer layer of longitudinal muscle fibres.

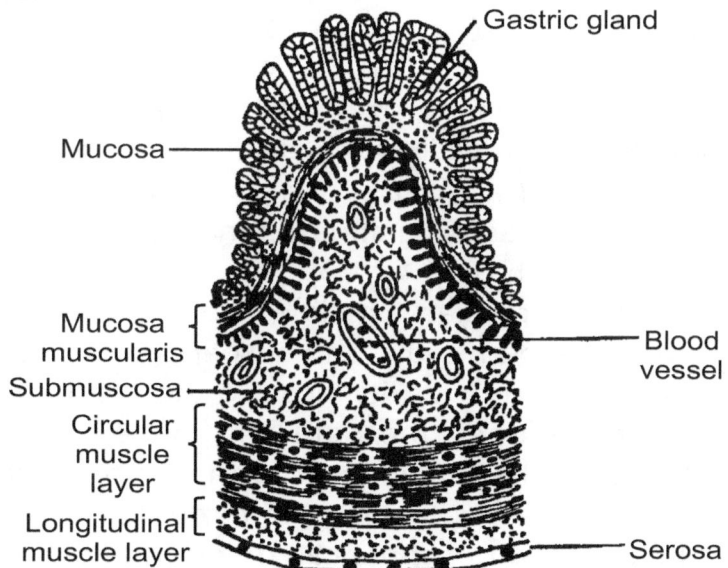

Fig. 3.17: Frog - T. S. of stomach

(ii) Submucosa: Next to the mucosa is the submucosa. It is a connective tissue; containing blood vessels and lymph vessels. This layer is similar to that of intestinal submucosa.

(iii) Muscular Coat: This layer is also very well developed in the stomach. Three types of muscle fibres are present in this coat. They are, *oblique* muscle fibres inside, *circular* muscle fibres in the middle and *longitudinal* fibres outside. These muscles are more developed because the stomach has to hold a large quantity of food and has to churn it effectively.

(iv) Peritoneum: Muscular coat is covered by the peritoneum or the serosa.

Histology of Oesophagus

The histological structure of the oesophagus is more or less similar to that of the stomach and intestine. However, slight changes or modifications are seen. There is no peritoneum. The mucous membrane consists of stratified *squamous epithelium* instead of columnar epithelium. The muscle fibres are striated in the beginning but gradually become unstriated towards the posterior end.

Digestive Glands

The digestive system of the frog consists of the following digestive glands:

1. Gastric glands,   2. Liver,
3. Pancreas and   4. Intestinal glands.

Gastric Glands: The gastric glands are very small and microscopic located in the wall of the stomach. These glands secrete a secretion called *gastric juice*. It is a mixture of pepsin and hydrochloric acid. The gastric glands discharge their secretion into the lumen of the stomach.

Liver: The liver is the largest digestive gland of the digestive system. It is a bilobed, dark red gland suspended by a mesentery in the anterior part of the body cavity close to the heart and lungs. The gland forms two main lobes, the right and the left. The left lobe is larger than the right. The left lobe is further sub-divided into two lobes. Thus, the liver of a frog consists of three lobes. In between the two lobes is situated a large, spherical, greenish and thin walled sac called the *gall bladder*. The bile juice produced by the liver is stored in the gall bladder.

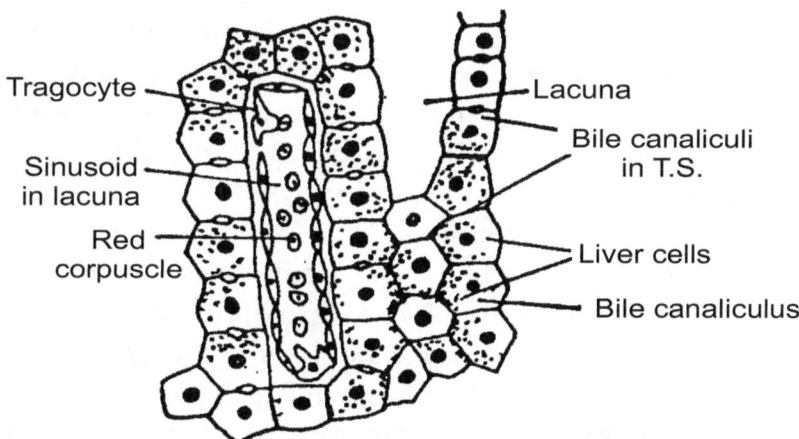

Fig. 3.18: A Part of Section through Liver

The bile is greenish liquid and it is brought to the gall bladder by small hepatic ducts. The *bile duct* or *cystic duct* carries bile from the gall bladder to the duodenum. Some hepatic ducts directly open into the bile duct. The hepatic and bile ducts form *common bile duct*. It runs backwards through the pancreas and receives *pancreatic duct* to form *hepatopancreatic duct* which ultimately opens into duodenum. It is also called *common bile pancreatic duct*.

The liver is composed of a large number of *polygonal hepatic cells*. Each hepatic cell has a prominent central nucleus and a granular cytoplasm with glycogen granules and fat droplets. The hepatic cells are arranged in a single layer round a network of spaces called *lacunae*. These lacunae are filled with blood capillaries and their walls are made up of discontinuous squamous epithelium. The blood spaces are also called as *sinusoids* in which blood from the hepatic vein and artery passes. There is direct contact of blood and hepatic cells hence they regulate the amount of food material in the blood. The hepatic cells secrete bile which is collected by the fine *bile ductules* and many ductules unite to form the main bile ducts.

Functions of Liver

1. The liver secretes bile juice which do not contain digestive enzymes. However, it only emulsifies fats and helps in the digestion of fats.
2. The liver takes up excess of sugar and converts it into glycogen. Glycogen is again converted into glucose; when there is need of blood sugar. Thus, liver maintains a constant blood sugar level.

3. The liver also converts protein into glycogen and glycogen into glucose when there is lack of blood sugar.
4. It separates ammonia from proteins and amino acids. Ammonia is converted into an excretory product urea which is excreted through kidneys.
5. It acts as excretory kidneys.
6. The liver converts toxic substances into non-toxic substances hence is called a detoxifying organ.
7. In the embryonic stage, the liver acts as a haemopoietic organ i.e. production of blood corpuscles.
8. It also produces blood proteins such as prothrombin and fibrinogen which play an important role in blood clotting.
9. The liver also produces *heparin* which does not allow blood to clot in the blood capillaries.
10. The old RBCs are destroyed in the liver.

Pancreas: Pancreas of the *Rana tigrina* is a much branched, irregular, flattened and yellow-coloured gland lying in the mesentery between the stomach and duodenum. It is a duplex gland because it consists of both the exocrine as well as the endocrine gland. The exocrine part of the gland secretes *pancreatic juice*. This juice is discharged by several small, branched *pancreatic ducts* into the bile duct. Both form the common *hepatopancreatic duct*. The endocrine part is formed by scattered *Islets of Langerhans* which secrete the hormone *insulin* directly in the blood.

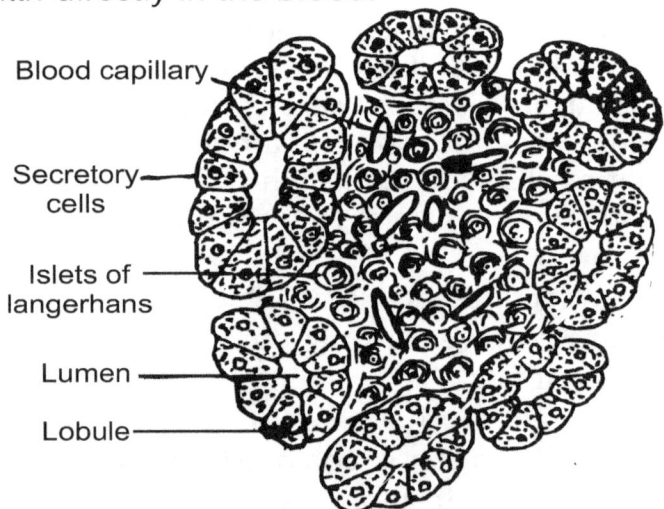

Fig. 3.19: T. S. of Pancreas

The histological structure of the pancreas shows a large number of minute rounded masses called *lobules* or *acini*. These acini are arranged like grapes in a bunch. The acini or lobules are held together by the connective tissue. The connective tissue contains blood capillaries, lymph vessels and nerve fibres. Each lobule or acinus consists of a central narrow cavity which is enclosed by a single layer of columnar epithelial cells. The columnar cells have a distinct nucleus and granular cytoplasm. The cells are secretory in function and secrete pancreatic juice. The cavities of the adjacent lobules join together and open into fine ductules which are also lined by epithelial cells. The ductules unite together and form pancreatic ducts which then open into the bile duct. In between the acini groups of small closely packed cells, called islets of Langerhans occur, scattered in the connective tissue. These cells secrete the hormone insulin which regulates, blood sugar. In case of deficiency of insulin *diabetes* is caused.

Intestinal Glands: These glands are microscopic and lie in the wall of the intestine. The glands secrete a secretion called intestinal juice in the lumen of the intestine. In addition to these digestive glands, a large number of unicellular mucous secreting cells are located in the mucous membrane of the entire alimentary canal.

Food and Feeding

The frog is a carnivorous animal. Its food consists of small insects, caterpillars, earthworms, crustaceans, worms and spiders. It can also feed on molluscs, small fishes and tadpoles. The small prey is captured by the tongue. The food of the frog consists of proteins, fats, carbohydrates, salts, minerals and vitamins, a complete diet.

Ingestion of food: The food catching mechanism of frogs is quite peculiar and interesting. The food catching act is very quick and rapid. On finding a prey within reach, the frog opens its mouth which is very wide. The tongue plays an important role in food catching. It is a large, bifid, sticky, muscular organ attached in front and free from behind. Both the mouth and tongue help in ingestion. Whenever, the prey lies near the mouth of frog, the mouth is opened, the tongue is flicked out and stricken at the prey. Since, the tongue is sticky, the prey adheres to the tongue, which is suddenly withdrawn and the mouth closed. The flicking and withdrawal movements of the tongue are so quick that they require hardly 1/10 of a second. The attachment of the tongue in the mouth is in such a way that it can be extended to some distance from the mouth. The larger prey is gripped with the jaws. Its escape is prevented by the backwardly directed maxillary and vomerine teeth. Thus, these teeth help in holding the prey firmly in the mouth. There is no mastication of food in the mouth because teeth for mastication are absent. Hence, food or prey is directly swallowed which is brought about by upward pressure of the throat and downward pressure of the eye balls, followed by peristalsis in the oesophagus. There are no salivary glands present in the buccal cavity but mucous for lubricating food is secreted from the lining of the bucco-pharyngeal cavity and oesophagus. This mucous lubricates the food and helps in swallowing. The bucco pharyngeal cavity is also lined by ciliated epithelium and any small food particle left in it gets entangled with mucous and is pushed back into the oesophagus and stomach.

Physiology of Digestion

Digestion is a process in which the insoluble, and indiffusible complex organic substances are converted into simpler, soluble and diffusible forms. Thus, it is a complex physiology process.

Digestion of food takes place in different parts of the alimentary canal. It begins in stomach, continues in the duodenum and is completed in the ileum.

Gastric Digestion: Since, there is no mastication of food in frogs digestion does not start in the buccopharynx. In oesophagus, there are certain glands which secrete mucous and a *proteolytic enzyme*, *pepsin*. But it does not act on food in the oesophagus. The food stays in the stomach for a considerable time (2 to 3 hours). In the stomach the gastric glands secrete *gastric juice*. The gastric juice contains 90% water, an inactive enzyme *pepsinogen* and free *hydrochloric acid*. In the presence of hydrochloric acid the inactive enzyme pepsinogen changes into an active enzyme *pepsin*. The hydrochloric acid is useful for killing bacteria and fungi and also dissolves inorganic salts. Pepsin acts on proteins in the acidic medium and breaks them into *polypeptides, peptones and proteases*. Muscular contractions of the stomach wall also assist in digestion and mixing of digestive enzymes with food. Food is also reduced to fine particles, and becomes soft. In the presence of food, the stomach also produces a hormone *gastrin*, which activates cells secreting hydrochloric acid. Now the semidigested acid food is called *chyme*. From the stomach the food is pushed into the duodenum through the *pyloric valve* or *sphincter* in small quantities for digestion in the intestine.

Intestinal Digestion: The acidic chyme in the duodenum causes production of several intestinal hormones, which in turn induce secretion of *pancreatic juice* from the pancreas and *bile juice* from the gall bladder respectively. These hormones are 1. Enterogastrone which reaches the stomach through blood to stop production of more gastric juice with HCl. 2. Cholecystokinin causes the gall bladder to contract and release bile into the duodenum through the hepatopancreatic duct. 3. Secretin and 4. *Pancreozymin* working together stimulates the pancreas to secrete pancreatic juices into the duodenum. 5. *Enterocrinin* activates the secretion of an intestinal juice *succus entericus*.

Thus, all the three substances mix up with food in the intestine. It is necessary for completion of digestion in the intestine. These three juices are secreted from three different sources: They are bile, pancreatic juice and intestinal juice.

(i) **Bile:** It is a greenish alkaline fluid secreted by the liver. It is alkaline and does not contain any digestive enzymes. Bile juice contains bile salts such as *sodium bicarbonate, sodium glycocholate* and *sodium torocholate etc.* Since, bile is alkaline in nature, it neutralizes acidity of the chyme. It also emulsifies fats, stimulates peristaltic movement of the intestine and activates pancreatic lipase.

(ii) **Pancreatic juice:** The pancreatic juice is a watery and alkaline fluid which contains three enzymes namely *trypsinogen, amylopsin* and *lipase*. All these enzymes act best in an alkaline medium and hydrolyse proteins, carbohydrates and fats.

(a) *Trypsinogen* is inactive and it becomes active *trypsin* by intestinal *enterokinase* which is found in the succus entericus. Trypsin is a proteolytic enzyme and acts on the remaining proteins, peptones, polypeptides and proteases and converts them into simple amino acids.

(b) *Amylopsin or amylase* converts starch or polysaccharides into maltose a disaccharide sugar.

(c) *Lipase or steapsin* converts fats into *glycerol* and *fatty acids*.

(iii) Succus entericus: It contains water, an activator of enterokinase and several enzymes which act on all classes of food stuffs. *Erepsin, maltase* and *lipase* are the important enzymes.

    (a) *Erepsin or Peptidases:* Converts polypeptides into amino acids.

    (b) *Maltase:* It converts maltose to glucose; *sucrase* or *invertase* converts lactose to glucose and galactose.

    (c) *Lipase:* Splits fats into fatty acids and glycerol.

Absorption

Though digested and semidigested food is present in the alimentary canal it should be absorbed by it or utilised by the body. Thus, absorption of digested food from the intestine is called absorption. It occurs only in the intestine by its wall. The intestine wall bears a large number of villi which increase the internal absorptive surface area. The villi are richly supplied with blood capillaries lymph vessels, the *lacteal*. The actual mechanism of the absorption is not fully understood. However, osmotic forces and other factors seem to play an important role in absorption. Water, mineral salts and other nutrients in solution are directly absorbed by the epithelial lining of the mucosa layer. Carbohydrates are absorbed in the form of glucose and fructose and proteins as amino acids. They are absorbed through the epithelium of mucosa by diffusion into the blood capillaries, then into the hepatic portal system and finally into the liver. In the liver excess of sugar is stored in the form of *glycogen*. The excess of amino acids are converted into urea by the process of *deamination*. The urea is excreted out by the kidneys as urine. The fatty acids and glycerol are absorbed by the lymphatic capillaries or lacteals and are ultimately passed into the blood.

Assimilation

After absorption of food in the blood it should be utilized by the body tissues. This is called assimilation. The absorbed end products like amino acids, fatty acids, glycerol, glucose and fructose are transported to the various tissues of the body by blood capillaries. The absorbed food stuff is used for two basic purposes of nutrition, (i) liberation of energy during respiration or (ii) assimilation as a part of the intimate structure of animal. The excess of glucose sugar is stored in the liver and muscles as *glycogen* or converted to fat or incorporated in the living protoplasm. The surplus fatty acids and glycerol are converted into fats which are deposited into adipose tissues. The amino acids form body proteins for growth and repair or undergo deamination, resulting in the formation of urea which is excreted by kidneys with urine.

Egestion

After the absorption of digested food in the intestine, the undigested part of the food is slowly pushed towards the large intestine or rectum for storage and preparation of faeces. The water is absorbed by the wall of the large intestine. At intervals the faecal matter passes into the cloaca and egested out through the cloacal aperture in the form of semisolid *faeces*.

In *Rana tigrina*, during summer, excess of food is stored in the liver and the fat bodies which is used during hibernation in winters. Due to storage of the food in the liver, it becomes enlarged and lighter in colour. By spring, the stored food is practically consumed and hence the liver becomes small and dark. The fat bodies are also largest before hibernation and far reduced after breeding. In case of females the reserved food in the fat bodies is used in the formation of gametes.

3.4 Respiratory System

All living organisms require constant energy for performing a number of body functions. Energy is produced by oxidation of food stuff in the body which needs constant supply of oxygen. During this process carbon dioxide and water are the end products formed which are expelled out from the body. Thus, a process in which oxygen is taken for energy production from the surrounding atmosphere and carbon dioxide is removed out with the help of blood is known as respiration.

The organs which help in the intake and supply of oxygen to the body tissues and remove the carbondioxide from the system is called the *respiratory system*. The organs which play an important role in respiration are called *respiratory organs*. Energy is released in the cells of living tissues, but a set of organs concerned with exchange of gases from the respiratory system of the animal. Frog *Rana tigrina* is an amphibious animal i.e. it lives on land as well as in water. The larval stages of the frog are fully aquatic. Hence, the frog shows both aquatic and aerial respiration. During the larval stages tadpoles respire by means of external gills. This respiration is called as *branchial respiration*. The thin respiratory epithelial cells on the gill are responsible for gaseous exchange. The dissolved oxygen is taken by the gills from water. Branchial respiration is limited only in the larval stage.

The adult frog has three modes of respiration; depending on the organs involved in respiration. They are:
1. Cutaneous Respiration,
2. Buccopharyngeal Respiration and
3. Pulmonary or Lung Respiration.

1. Cutaneous Respiration: Cutaneous respiration takes place with the help of skin or integument. Thus, respiration which occurs through skin is called cutaneous respiration. This type of respiration goes on all the time whether a frog is in or out of the water. It is practically the only mode of respiration when a frog is under water hibernating. The skin fulfils all the requirements of the respiratory surface. It is thin, moist and richly supplied with blood capillaries. The skin is kept moist either by the mucous secreted by the mucous glands or by water. It is so thin, that it is permeable to gases like oxygen and carbon dioxide. There are no impervious layers on it like keratin, scales etc. The outermost layer of the skin is with a very thin layer of keratin which forms the outermost layer of the epidermis.

Mechanism: Skin is the ideal organ for gaseous exchange. The oxygen in the air first dissolves in the moist surface of the skin and diffuses into the blood capillaries of the skin. In water, oxygen is present in a dissolved condition and diffuses directly into the blood capillaries of the skin and *haemoglobin* of the blood is converted into *oxyhaeomoglobin* which provides oxygen to the tissues. After utilization of oxygen by the tissues carbon dioxide is given out which is again carried back to the skin and finally diffused out through it, either in air or in water.

Importance: Cutaneous respiration goes on without any effort on the part of the frog. It is the most important type of respiration found in frogs. This respiration has special significance because it occurs in water as well as on land. This is the only form of respiration that can occur when a frog is submerged in water. Moreover, during winter sleep or hibernation, frogs depends exclusively on this mode of respiration to conserve stored food in the liver and fat bodies.

2. Buccopharyngeal respiration: Buccopharyngeal respiration takes place in the *buccopharyngeal cavity*. This cavity opens into the exterior by two short passages called *respiratory tracts*. Air enters and leaves the cavity (through these respiratory tracts). This tract is composed of *external nares, nasal chambers and internal nares*. The external nares are situated on the snout and open into the nasal olfactory capsules of the skull. Through the internal nares, nasal chambers open into the buccopharyngeal cavity. The internal nares are situated on the anterior part of the roof of the buccopharyngeal cavity.

The respiratory organ, the buccopharyngeal cavity of the frog is lined by a thin mucous membrane which is always kept moist with the mucous secreted by mucous glands. The mucous membrane is permeable to gases and is highly vascularised.

Mechanism: Buccal respiration takes place when the frog is in a resting position; but it has to make some efforts for this respiration. In this respiration, a frog has to lower and raise the throat or floor of the buccal cavity rhythmically. Lowering of the throat is brought about by the *sternohyal muscles*. When the throat is lowered the buccopharyngeal cavity becomes enlarged. This results into reduction of air pressure in the buccopharyngeal cavity. The pressure outside the cavity is greater than inside. Thus, fresh air rushes from the outside higher pressure area to the lower pressure area of the buccopharyngeal cavity through the external nares, nasal chambers and internal nares. The fresh air which contains oxygen, first dissolves in the thin film of mucous layer covering the surface of the buccopharyngeal cavity. Then the dissolved oxygen diffuses through the mucous membrane lining and passes into the fine blood capillaries, lying below it. The blood capillaries carry carbon dioxide which diffuses into the air of the buccal cavity. Thus, the air in the buccopharyngeal cavity becomes foul.

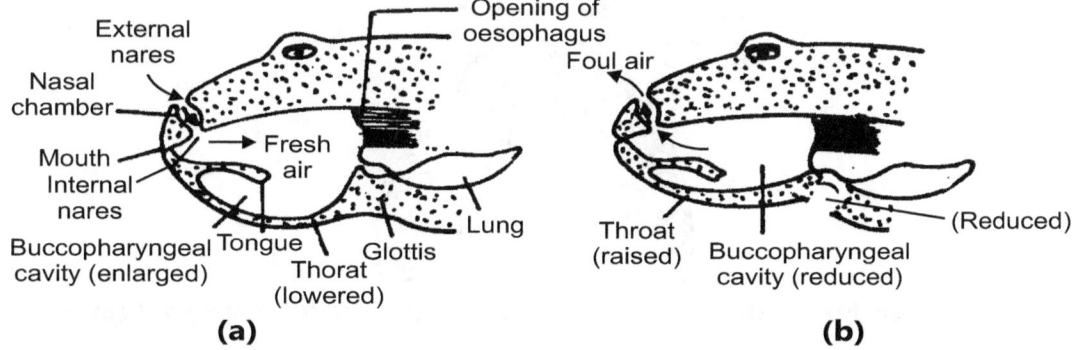

Fig. 3.20: Mechanism of Buccopharyngeal Respiration

The raising of the throat is brought about by the contraction of the *petrohyal muscle bands*. This reduces the buccopharyngeal cavity and increases the pressure of the air in it. The pressure of this air is greater than that of atmospheric air. Therefore, the foul air is expelled outside through internal nares, nasal chambers and external nares. This process is repeated regularly and thus lowering and raising of the throat occurs rhythmically.

During buccopharyngeal respiration the external nares remain open, the mouth and glottis are closed and thus the air is not able to enter the lungs.

Significance: Buccopharyngeal respiration supplements cutaneous respiration in summer, when frogs become active. This respiration takes place when frogs are on land or when they floats leisurely in water with the snout exposed to air.

Cutaneous and buccopharyngeal respiration provide normal supply of oxygen but whenever oxygen requirement is more the lungs are also used for respiration. This is called pulmonary respiration.

3. Pulmonary Respiration: Pulmonary respiration takes place by the two lungs. Breathing on land in atmospheric air with the help of lungs is called *pulmonary respiration*. The passage through which air enters and leaves the lungs is called the *respiratory tract.*

(i) Respiratory tract: It begins from the external nares, which are a pair of small apertures situated on the snout, just above the mouth. The external nares open into small sacs, called *nasal chambers*. They are situated in the skull. These nasal chambers open into a large cavity the *buccopharyngeal cavity* through small openings called internal nares. The buccopharyngeal cavity communicates behind through a slit called *glottis*. The median slit-like glottis on the floor of the pharynx opens into a small thin-walled chamber called *larynx* or *laryngo-tracheal chamber*. Its walls are supported by cartilages. (2 arytenoid + 1 cricoid).

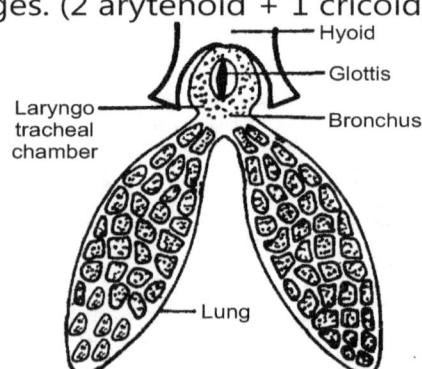

Fig. 3.21 (a): Frog Lungs alongwith Bronchus and Laryngo-Tracheal Chamber

Its internal lining forms a pair of elastic horizontal bands, the vocal cords, for sound production, hence it is also called *voice box*. This chamber opens into the lungs by a pair of very short tubes, the *bronchii*.

(ii) Lungs: In frog the lungs are a pair of oval, pinkish, thin walled and highly elastic sacs. They are suspended freely inside the peritoneal body cavity, one on either side of the heart. They are covered externally by the peritoneum. The inner surface of each lung is divided by a network of the folds or *septa* into many small air sacs or *alveoli*. The septa and alveoli increase the inner surface of the lungs, thereby adding to their efficiency. The histological structure of wall of the lung shows three layers. The outer layer *peritoneum*, the middle layer of *connective tissue* and the inner *epithelium*. The outer peritoneum is protective in function. It consists of very thin cells. The connective tissue contains unstriated muscle fibres and blood capillaries. This layer supports the blood vessels and provides elasticity to the lungs. The innermost layer is of the epithelium which is composed of thin cells. Thick cells are present on the septa. Numerous mucous secreting gland cells are scattered in the epithelial cells. The mucous keeps the inner surface of the lungs moist for the absorption of oxygen.

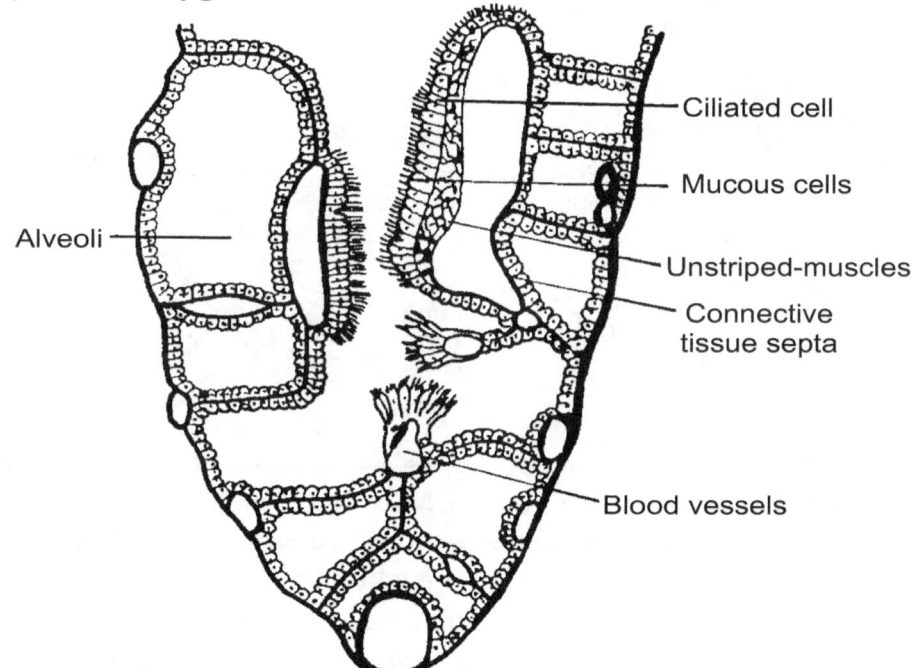

Fig. 3.21 (b): Frog - T. S. of Lung

Mechanism of Pulmonary Respiration

For pulmonary respiration, a frog has to take efforts. The up and down movement of throat is responsible for sending air into and out of the lungs. The whole mechanism involves three steps:
1. Aspiration,
2. Inspiration and
3. Expiration.

1. Aspiration: The passage of air from outside into the buccopharyngeal cavity is called aspiration. The up and down movement of the floor of the buccal cavity or throat is brought about by the contraction and relaxation of the sternohyal and petrohyal muscles. On contraction of the sternohyal muscle the throat is lowered down which results into enlargement of the buccopharyngeal cavity. This reduces the pressure of air present in it. The pressure of the outside air is greater than the inside air hence fresh air from outside with greater pressure rushes in the buccopharyngeal cavity through the external nares, nasal chambers and internal nares. This passage of air into the buccopharyngeal cavity is called aspiration.

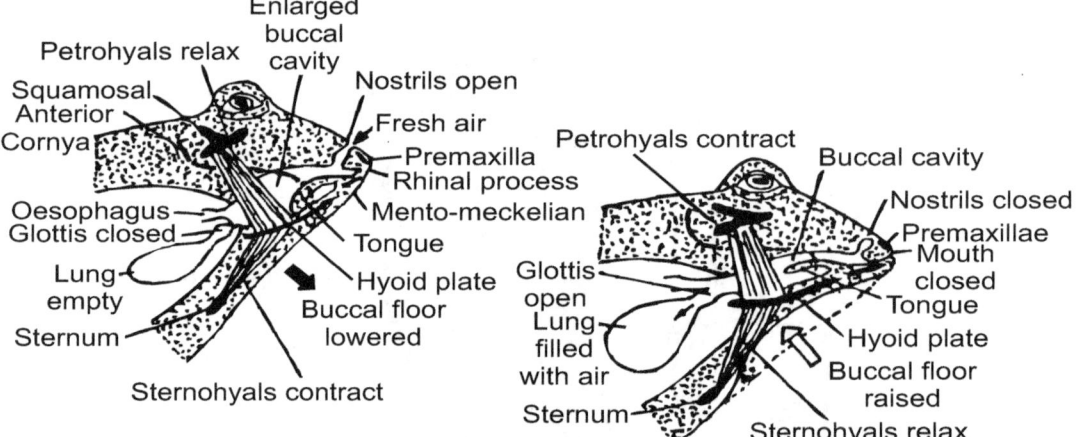

Fig. 3.22: Frog. Diagrammatic Representation of the Respiratory Mechanism Involving Two Sets of Muscles. The Two Stages bring Inspiration. Reverse Sequence will result in Expiration

2. Inspiration: The air which rushes into the buccopharyngeal cavity enters into the lungs. The passage of air from buccopharyngeal cavity into the lungs is called *inspiration*. Now the glottis opens and the mentomeckelian bones of the lower jaw push upwards the premaxillae bones of the upper jaw so that the external nostrils or nares are closed. The petrohyal muscles contract raising the hyoid apparatus and the floor of the buccal cavity. The space of the cavity becomes smaller and the pressure on the air in it increases considerably. When the external nares, mouth and oesophagus are being closed, the compressed air in the buccal cavity forces open the glottis and passes into the lungs through laryngo-tracheal chamber and the bronchi. The lungs expand with this air. Thus, buccopharyngeal cavity acts as a *force pump* to push air into the lungs. The process by which lungs are filled with air is called inspiration.

   3.   Expiration: Inspiration is followed by expiration. After the gaseous exchange which occurs in the lungs, the buccopharyngeal cavity is lowered by contraction of the sternohyal muscles. Because of this, a partial vacuum is created in the buccopharyngeal cavity. The glottis is opened by the air in the lungs and it comes into the buccopharyngeal cavity. This is facilitated by contraction of the wall of the lungs and body wall muscles. Thus, the lungs become empty. The floor of the buccal cavity is usually raised and lowered several times so that the same volume of air is passed into and out of the lungs more than once. This act though reduces the efficiency of gaseous exchange but minimizes the loss of water from the respiratory surface. In the next step, the tips of the jaws move down and the external nares open. The floor of the buccal cavity is pushed upwards thus foul air is expelled out through the external nares. The passage of air from the lungs to the exterior is known as *expiration*.

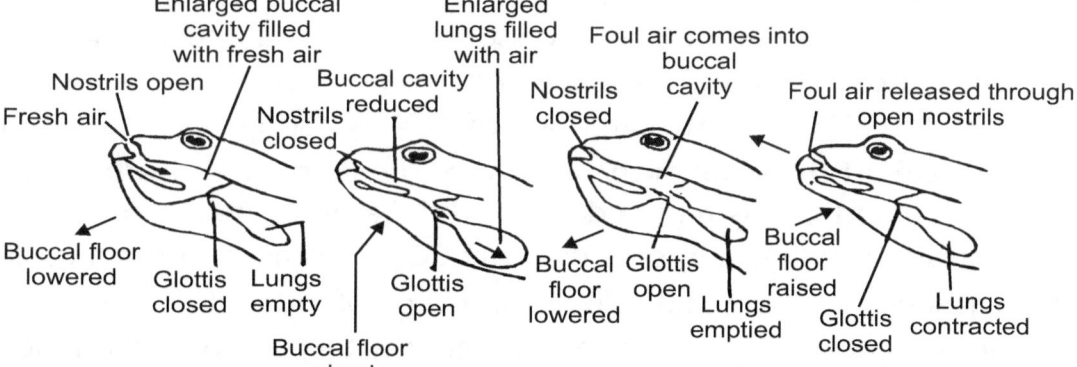

Fig. 3.23: Frog. Breathing Movements during Ventilation of the Lungs. Black Arrows indicate Pathway of Air in and out of Lungs. While Arrows show up and down movements of the Buccal Floor.

According to recent findings, the external nares of the frog always remain open during pulmonary respiration. Only the mixed air of the buccopharyngeal cavity, not rich enough in oxygen moves into and out of the lungs the several times. This indicates that lungs of frogs are not efficient for respiration.

Gaseous Exchange

The walls of the lungs are thin and richly supplied with blood capillaries. The exchange of gases takes place through them by diffusion. The alveoli are covered by a capillary network. The fresh air contains more concentration of oxygen and lower concentration of carbon dioxide as compared to the concentration of gases in the blood capillaries around the alveoli. The oxygen from the air dissolves in the film of mucous covering the inner surface of the alveoli. It then diffuses into the blood flowing through the capillaries. This diffusion takes place due to high concentration of oxygen in the air and low concentration of oxygen in the blood capillaries. The blood contains haemoglobin in the erythrocytes which has a strong affinity with oxygen. Hence, oxygen combines with haemoglobin and forms oxyhaemoglobin.

$$Hb + 4O_2 \rightarrow Hb(O_2)_4$$

Haemoglobin + Oxygen $\rightarrow$ Oxyhaemoglobin

Due to oxygen, blood becomes oxygenated and red.

At the same time the carbondioxide and water brought by the blood from tissues are at a high concentration in the blood capillaries than in the alveoli. A part of CO_2 dissolves in plasma and a little part of CO_2 is brought along the plasma as sodium bicarbonate. In the erythrocytes (RBCs) a little amount of CO_2 is carried as potassium bicarbonate. At the respiratory surface of the lungs the bicarbonates are split up and CO_2 is released which diffuses into the alveoli where concentration of CO_2 is less. In this way CO_2 is released in the alveoli.

Thus, gaseous exchange takes place between blood and the air in the alveoli. As a result of the gaseous exchange, the blood in the lungs becomes oxygenated and the air in the alveoli becomes foul due to CO_2 and water. Therefore, the air expired from the lungs, always contains more of CO_2 and very less of oxygen.

Tissue Respiration

The oxygen taken in the blood at the respiratory surface in the form of oxyhaemoglobin is distributed to all the parts of the body by arterial blood. The RBCs perform the function of transport of oxygen to tissue cells. The solubility of O_2 in the water is low, very little amount of O_2 is dissolved in the plasma, but a major amount of O_2 is loaded in the red blood cells. The O_2 concentration in the tissue cells is rather low as compared to the concentration in blood. It is because whatever O_2 is received in the tissue cells is immediately used up for the production of energy. On the other hand concentration of CO_2 in the tissues increases due to constant oxidation of food. The oxyhaemoglobin of the blood is an unstable complex which dissociates into original haemoglobin and free O_2. Thus, haemoglobin combines with O_2 in the lungs and liberates oxygen in the tisues.

In Lungs:

$$Hb + 4O_2 \xrightarrow[\text{Low } CO_2]{\text{High } O_2} Hb(O_2)_4$$

(Haemoglobin) (Oxyhaemoglobin)

In Tissues:

$$Hb(O_2)_4 \xrightarrow[\text{Low } O_2]{\text{High } CO_2} Hb + 4O_2 \uparrow$$

The concentration of O_2 in the tissues is less than that of oxygenated blood which reaches the tissues. At the same time the concentration of CO_2 in the tissues is higher than that in the blood. As a result of this the O_2 of the blood diffuses into the tissues and CO_2 of tissues diffuses in the blood. The gaseous exchange which takes place between tissues and blood hence is called *tissue respiration* or *internal respiration*. The O_2 which comes to the tissues combines with carbohydrates and fats. The food is oxidised by O_2 in the presence of certain enzymes releasing energy, CO_2 and water. The glucose is acted upon by enzymes called *dehydrogenases* so that some of its hydrogen atoms are activated and liberated. The free hydrogen is transferred to a protein called *cytochrome* which acts as a hydrogen acceptor. By this transference the cytochrome is converted into reduced cytochrome.

Glucose + Dehydrogenase → Free hydrogen (H)
Cytochrome + Free H → Reduced Cytochrome.

Another enzyme called *cytochrome oxidase*, oxidises the reduced cytochrome at the expense of oxygen which is given to the tissue. It is thus brought to its original cytochrome condition. This results in the release of energy, CO_2 and water.

$$\text{Reduced cytochrome} + CO_2 \text{ cytochrome oxidase} \rightarrow \text{Cytochrome} + \text{Energy} + CO_2 + \text{water.}$$

Transport of Carbondioxide

During tissue respiration CO_2 is released as a waste product which should be removed from the body. Being highly soluble CO_2 dissolves freely in the tissue fluid surrounding the cells. Then it is received by the blood and dissolves in the blood plasma forming Carbonic acid.

$$CO_2 + H_2O \rightarrow H_2CO_3$$

But hardly 5 to 10% of CO_2 is carried in this state. This is because a major amount of carbonic acid immediately dissociates into hydrogen ion (H^+) and bicarbonate ion (HCO_3^-)

$$H_2CO_3 \rightarrow (H^+ \; HCO_3^-)$$

The bicarbonate ion combines with sodium ions in the blood plasma to form sodium bicarbonate.

$$Na^+ + HCO_3^- \rightarrow NaHCO_3$$

In the form of sodium bicarbonate about 50% of CO_2 is carried by the blood. The rest of CO_2 is carried by the erythrocytes as potassium bicarbonate. In the erythrocytes CO_2 combines with haemoglobin to form *carbominohaemoglobin*.

$$Hb + CO_2 \rightarrow HbCO_2$$

The bicarbonate of sodium and potassium from the erythrocytes and plasma are converted into CO_2 and water by an enzyme *carbonic anhydrase*. In the lungs the oxygenation of haemoglobin into oxyhaemoglobin brings about the break down of carbamino haemoglobin into haemoglobin and CO_2. The CO_2 formed is removed by the process of diffusion into the alveoli. Finally, along with water both are eliminated out by expiration.

Sound Producing Organ

In frogs, the laryngo-tracheal chamber acts as the sound producing organ. This chamber is situated between the posterior cornua of the hyoid apparatus. Anteriorly it communicates with the bucco-pharyngeal cavity through the glottis. At the posterior end it opens into the lungs by a pair of short *bronchii*. The sound producing organ is supported and kept distended by three cartilages, a *cricoid* and two *arytenoids*. The cricoid bone is an oval ring like structure with a spine like median process at the hind end. In addition to this there are two slender lateral processes at the sides. On the ventral side of the laryngo-tracheal chamber, the lateral processes turn backwards downwards forming a loop by uniting together on a transverse bridge. The arytenoid cartilages are semilunar in shape.

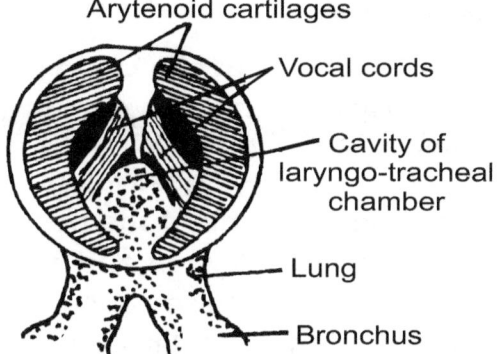

Fig. 3.24: Frog. Laryngo-Tracheal Chamber Opened to show Vocal Cords

These cartilages are situated in the cricoid ring and glottis is enclosed between them. The lining of the laryngo-tracheal chamber forms a pair of folds called *vocal cords*. The *rima glottis* is a narrow slit between the inner free edges of the vocal cords. The air passes through this slit on its way to and from the lungs. The vocal cords are elastic structures. They can be stretched by special muscles which are connected with the cartilages. When air from lungs is vigorously passed through the edges of the vocal cords; vibrations are produced which in turn produce sound. The pitch of the sound is controlled by the tension of the vocal cords. The male frogs during breeding season produce croaking sound to attract females. Therefore, the male frog has a pair of *vocal sacs* and they communicate with the bucco-pharyngeal near the angles of the mouth. The vocal sacs act as resonators i.e. they intensify and prolong the sound. Air is pumped in the vocal sacs from the lungs and again driven back passing between the vocal cords, each time producing sound.

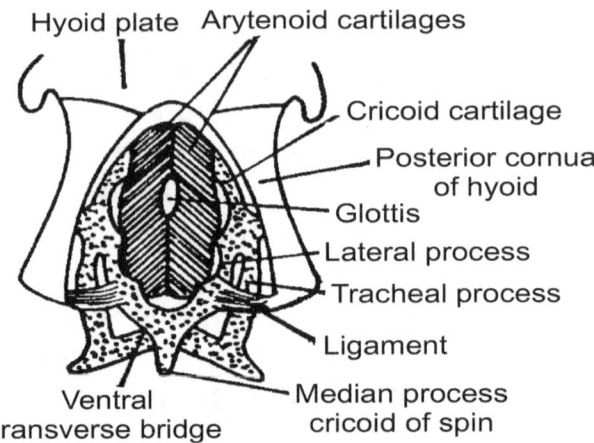

Fig. 3.25: Frog. Skeletal Cartilages of the Laryngo-Tracheal Chamber

3.5 Circulatory System

The circulatory system like the digestive and respiratory systems, is one of the most important systems of the body. Living cells need a constant supply of nutrients and oxygen and continuous removal of waste products formed in them. These functions are performed by the circulatory system. Thus, the circulatory system is the transport system in the body of higher animals. The food and oxygen acquired through the digestive and respiratory systems are distributed through the circulatory system. Another important function of the circulatory system is the maintenance of *homeostasis* through transportation of electrolytes, the control of fluid volume, pH and regulation of body temperature. The blood stream also carries different hormones which are required for the co-ordination of body functions. Moreover, blood carries gases and antibodies foreign organisms. The circulatory system also transports waste matter or excretory products to the excretory organs which eliminate them.

In frogs, the circulatory system is of *closed type*. The blood which remains within a completely closed system of vessels and circulated to the various body parts by blood vessels under pressure is called *closed circulatory system*. In frogs and higher vertebrates, there are two types of circulating fluids namely, blood and lymph. They are constantly circulated flowing through a network of vessels. Thus, the circulatory system is divisible into two types:

1. *Blood vascular system* which consists of blood, heart and blood vessels, the arteries and veins.
2. *Lymphatic system* which consists of lymph, lymph vessels and lymph heart.

The circulatory fluids blood and lymph are responsible for transport of nutritive substances absorbed in the alimentary canal to the various tissues.

Blood Vascular System

The circulatory fluid blood which is circulated to various body parts through blood vessels is called the *blood vascular system*. This system conveys various materials from one part of the body where they are formed or taken in, to another part where they are required to get rid off. Thus, blood plays an important role in the transport of oxygen and food material to the various parts of the body.

It also carries waste and unwanted metabolic products to the excretory organs from where they can be eliminated. For effective transport of food, oxygen, water and waste products there must be constant circulation of blood. This circulation is maintained by the rhythmic contraction of the *heart* with its connected blood vessels. The blood vessels which carry blood from the heart to the different organs are called *arteries*. The arteries divide into thinner vessels called *arterioles* which branch into extremely thin and small *capillaries*.

The arteries have thick muscular and elastic walls, while the capillaries are thin walled made up of a single layer of endothelial cells. Blood does not come in contact directly with tissue cells, but exchange of substances (O_2, food, etc.) between the blood and cells of the body take place through the capillary walls. This exchange is done through lymph contained in tissue spaces between cells. The capillaries reunite in the organs forming small vessels which in turn join with one another to form venules. Many *venules* unite to form a *vein* which carries the blood from organs to the heart. The walls of the veins are thinner than those of arteries and less muscular.

Thus, the blood vascular system consists of:
1. Blood,
2. Heart,
3. Arterial system and
4. Venous system.

I. Blood

Blood is a red coloured *fluid connective tissue* which flows through blood vessels and capillaries to reach different organs of the body. It is heavier than water because of higher specific gravity than the water. It is alkaline in nature and salty to taste. The blood consists of two components, the straw-coloured fluid part called *plasma* and a large number of blood cells called *corpuscles* which are suspended in plasma.

(A) Plasma: It is a straw-coloured and structureless liquid. It is a slightly alkaline fluid, containing about 90% water, 10% other substances. The plasma contains a number of organic and inorganic constituents in the dissolved condition. Thus, it is a liquid of complex chemical composition.

The organic constituents are:
1. **Plasma proteins:** The plasma proteins constitute about 7% of the plasma. They are albumin, globulin, and fibrinogen. All these proteins are present in plasma in a colloidal form making the blood viscous. Globulin plays an important role in the defence mechanism, while fibrinogen is responsible for blood clotting. Albumin regulates osmotic pressure of the blood. The nutrients like amino acids are also present.
2. **Carbohydrates:** Glucose, fructose and glycogen are the energy producing sugars present in plasma.
3. **Fats:** Cholesterol, fatty acids and neutral fats.
4. **Nitrogenous waste products:** Urea, uric acid, ammonia, creatine and creatinine.
5. Vitamins, enzymes and hormones.

The inorganic constituents of plasma are:
1. **Salts:** In plasma, chlorides, carbonates and phosphates of the sodium, potassium, calcium and magnesium are present which make blood alkaline.
2. **Gases:** Dissolved gases like oxygen, carbon dioxide and nitrogen are present in plasma. When the protein fibrinogen is removed from plasma (in the form of fibrin) the residual plasma is called *serum*. Thus, serum = Blood – All corpuscles and fibrin.

The chemical composition of plasma is not constant because of continuous exchange of chemical substances between the tissue and the blood. Plasma is the chief transporting medium supplying water, oxygen and metabolites to all cells and collecting nitrogenous waste products and CO_2 from them.

(B) Blood Corpuscles: The blood corpuscles are suspended in the plasma and are of three types. They are:
1. Erythrocytes or Red Blood Corpuscles,
2. Leucocytes or White Blood Corpuscles and
3. Thrombocytes.

1. Erythrocytes: These are red blood corpuscles which are numerous, about 300 to 500 thousand per cubic millimetre of blood. They are elliptical, biconvex, nucleated and immobile. Each cell has an oval nucleus in the centre. The central portion therefore appears slightly bulging. Each red blood corpuscle consists of a central spongy mass of cytoplasm called *stroma* surrounding the nucleus and a red coloured pigment called *haemoglobin,* an iron compound. Each corpuscle is bounded by a thin elastic lipoid layer. Haemoglobin or the respiratory pigment is complex substance containing the protein globulin a combined with haematin, an organic substance containing iron. Haemoglobin has strong affinity with oxygen forming an unstable bright red coloured complex called oxyhaemoglobin.

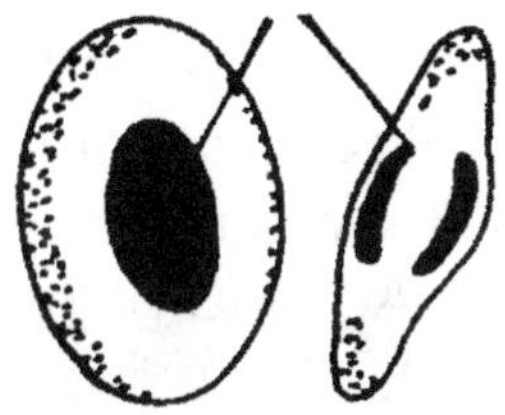

Fig. 3.26: Frog: Erythrocytes

$$Hb + 4 O_2 \rightleftharpoons Hb (O_2)_4$$

Haemoglobin + Oxygen $\rightleftharpoons$ Oxyhaemoglobin

The oxyhaemoglobin readily dissociates into haemoglobin and oxygen when there is deficiency of oxygen in the tissues. It can also combine with CO_2 to form carbomino/ haemoglobin, which is also an unstable complex. Therefore, the haemoglobin in the erythrocytes plays an important role of transport of gases, O_2 and CO_2. Actually erythrocytes with their haemoglobin pigment carry the O_2 from lungs to the tissues and CO_2 from tissue to the lungs. The life of the erythrocytes is of 100 days, after that they are destroyed in the spleen by phagocytes. These cells are produced in haemopoietic tissues of kidneys and liver. The break-down of haemoglobin occurs in liver, iron is separated and reused for the formation of new erythrocytes. The remaining haemoglobin is used for the formation of bile pigments *bilirubin* and *biliverdin*. The functions of RBCs are: (i) to carry oxygen in the form of oxyhaemoglobin from the respiratory organs to all the cells of the body and also (ii) to carry CO_2 in the form of potassium bicarbonate from the tissue cells to the respiratory organs.

2. Leucocytes: These are white blood corpuscles (WBCs) which are less numerous; about 3 to 8 thousand per cubic millimetre of blood. They are colourless, nucleated, amoeboid and motile. These are nucleated cells but without haemoglobin. The leucocytes are not confined to the blood vessels only, but can pass through the walls of the capillaries and migrate anywhere in the body. Since, they destroy disease causing organisms and bacteria, they are called phagocytes.

These cells are capable of amoeboid movement. The leucocytes show considerable differences with respect to shape, size of their nuclei and nature of cytoplasm and functions. They are classified according to the form of nucleus, the nature of strong reactions of the cytoplasm and the presence or absence of granules in the cytoplasm. The leucocytes also produce antibodies and antitoxins which are highly specific in reaction. These cells are produced by the spleen, liver and bone marrow in frog. When they are worn out they are disintegrated in the blood stream and engulfed by other phagocytes. The leucocytes are mainly of two types:
(A) Granulocytes and (B) Agranulocytes or lymphocytes.

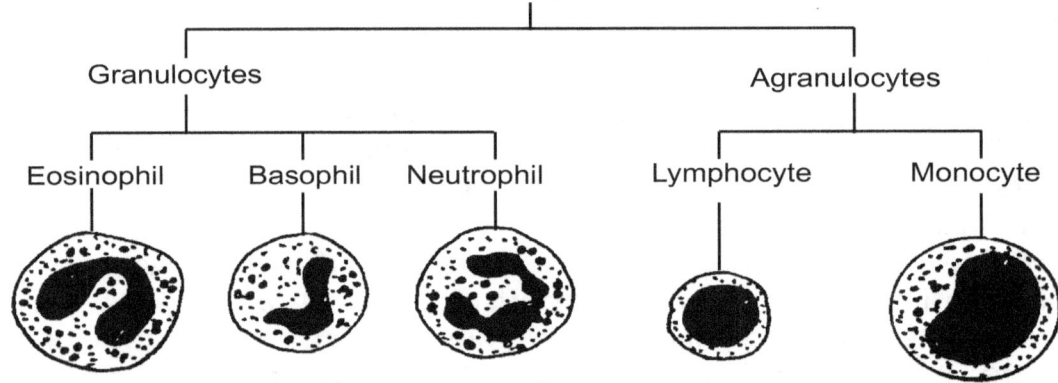

Fig. 3.27: Frog. Types of Leucocytes

(A) Granulocytes: They are distinctly amoeboid containing numerous granules in the cytoplasm and a lobed nucleus in each cell. The cells possess granules in the cytoplasm hence they are called granulocytes. The granules may be fine or coarse. The granulocytes have an affinity for neutral, acidic or basic dyes. According to their staining properties they are classified into neutrophils, eosinophils and basophils. They are further characterised by the presence of a many lobed (polymorphous) nucleus, hence they are called *polymorphonuclear leucocytes*. The nuclear lobes are connected by delicate chromatic strands.

Following are the different types of leucocytes:

(i) Eosinophils: These cells are large in size with abundant large granules in the cytoplasm. The granules stain intensely with eosin or other acid dyes. The nucleus is polymorphous but generally bilobed. Their number is about 5% of the total leucocytes, however, their percentage increases during infection or allergic conditions. Eosinophils have immunizing effect.

(ii) Basophils: The cytoplasm contains a variable number of coarse granules which are stained with basic dyes, (methylene blue) hence cells are called basophils. The nucleus is relatively large and bilobed. These cells are present in an almost negligible quantity forming 0.5% to 1% of the total number of leucocytes. Since, they contain heparin they prevent clotting of blood while flowing. Their exact function is not clearly known however, they show limited phagocytic action.

(iii) Neutrophils: The granules of these cells are stained with neutral dyes. These cells contain 3 to 5 lobed nuclei connected by fine chromatic strands. They form 70% of the total leucocytes. These cells are more active and show amoeboid movement. Neutrophils are phagocytic in function and form the first line of defence against germs and bacteria. They are also concerned with removal of worn out tissues and cells debris. In metamorphosis, they are concerned with reabsorption of the tissue of the tail.

(B) Agranulocytes: These cells contain clear cytoplasm i.e. cytoplasm is without granules, thus called agranulocytes. These cells are with a single nuclei and the nuclei are not lobed. Due to the large size of the nucleus in the agranulocytes the cytoplasm is less in proportion. The agranulocytes are formed in the lymph nodes by special cells. Agranulocytes are of two types: Lymphocytes and Monocytes.

(i) Lymphocytes: These are small cells with a comparatively large spherical nucleus in each. They form about 25% of the total leucocytes. The cytoplasm of the cell is basophilic. These cells live in blood for longer periods. The lymphocytes are not phagocytic in function but they produce antibodies and antitoxins which play an important role in immunological reactions.

(ii) Monocytes: These are larger cells with an ovoid, kidney or horse-shoe shaped nucleus. The nucleus is usually eccentrically placed. They are phagocytic in function. They are about 1 to 3% of the total leucocytes.

3. Thrombocytes: These are small, spindle-shaped and nucleated cells. They are also called thromboplastids or blood platelets. They are unstable. In fresh blood, their shape is round or ovoid, in fixed preparations they are often appear stellate.

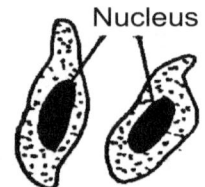

Fig. 3.28: Frog: Thrombocytes

These cells have a centrally placed nuclei and granular area and a peripheral hyaline zone. On coming in contact with a foreign body they disintegrate and release the enzyme *thromboplastin* which plays an important role in clotting of blood. Thromboplastin transforms *prothrombin* into *thrombin* and later in turn transforms fibrinogen into fibrin. They are about 20 to 25 thousand per cubic millimetre of blood.

Coagulation or Clotting of Blood

When the animal is wounded or blood vessels is cut open, the resulting bleeding stops after a certain period by the formation of a semi-solid jelly like natural plug. This phenomenon is called coagulation or clotting of the blood and the semisolid jelly like substance is called *clot* or *thrombus*. The blood clot plugs the wound, stops further loss of blood and prevents the entry of harmful germs into the wound. Sometimes after formation of the clot, a clear straw coloured fluid called *serum* oozes out of it.

It is very important that blood should not coagulate within the vessels. Blood usually never coagulates in the blood vessels because of insufficient concentration of thromboplastin and the inactive enzyme *prothrombin*. Formation of prothrombin takes place in liver cells in the presence of vitamin K. In the absence of vitamin K prothrombin is not synthesized and the animal may have a tendency to bleed. For the process of blood clotting various substances like prothrombin, fibrinogen, calcium ions and vitamin K and thromboplastin are essential. The prothrombin, fibrinogen and calcium are present in the plasma of blood while the thromboplastin is provided by the thrombocytes or platelets. The main steps in clotting are as follows:

1. When a blood vessel ruptures, the thrombocytes come in contact with cut edges of the blood vessel and disintegrate. They release the enzyme thromboplastin (or thrombokinase).

2. The thromboplastin makes *heparin* ineffective and acts on the inactive prothrombin present in the blood. The inactive prothrombin is converted into active *thrombin* by thromboplastin in the presence of calcium ions and vitamin K. The blood flowing in the vessels does not coagulate, because thrombin remains in the form of inactive prothrombin. Also an anticoagulant like heparin which is produced by liver works as *antithrombin* that prevents coagulation of blood within the vessels.

3. The active thrombin acts as soluble fibrinogen, a plasma protein to form insoluble fibrin in the form of a network of fibres.

4. The fibrin fibres form a network in which the dead RBCs get entangled. These together form the blood clot sealing the ruptured blood vessel and stop further bleeding. The clot or thrombus once formed gradually contracts and squeezes out a clear straw coloured fluid known as serum. This serum is similar to plasma but without fibrinogen. The process of blood clotting can be summarized in the following stages.

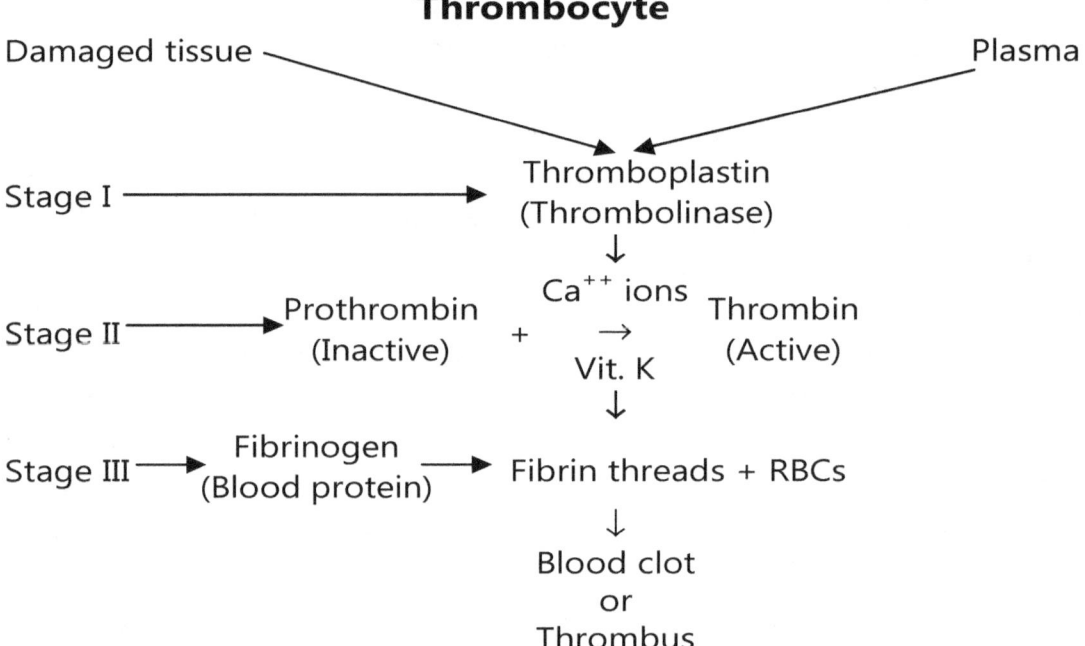

It is quite clear from the above, that, if any one of the substance is absent or action of one of them is neutralised, blood clotting will not occur. There are a number of chemicals which prevent coagulation of blood when added to blood. These chemicals are known as *anticoagulants*. Substances like oxalates and citrates precipitate calcium ions present in the blood, thereby, preventing the activation of prothrombin into thrombin and hence clotting. The saliva of leech contains hirudin which is also an anticoagulant.

Clotting is a natural phenomenon of physiological importance in the following respects:

(a) It prevents undue loss of blood from the body.
(b) It also prevents entry of bacteria or disease causing organisms into the body when a blood vessel is ruptured.
(c) It is a sort of adaptation for emergency repair of blood vessels.

Functions of Blood

Blood, the fluid connective tissue performs a number of functions

1. **Transport of respiratory gases:** Blood carries oxygen from the respiratory organs to the different parts of the body with the help of the respiratory pigment haemoglobin. It also collects and conveys carbon dioxide from different tissue cells to the respiratory organs.

2. **Transport of digested food:** The digested soluble food substances are absorbed by the blood and carried and distributed to different parts of the body.
3. **Transport of excretory products:** Nitrogenous waste substances such as urea, uric acid, ammonia etc. are formed in the liver mostly by the process of deamination. These waste products are carried by blood to the kidney for excretion.
4. **Transport of hormones:** Hormones are secreted by the endocrine glands, and are important for vital processes in the body. Each hormone is carried from its place of origin to its target organ for its proper functioning.
5. **Equalization of temperature:** Blood distributes heat energy generated by active parts of the body. Thus, it maintains uniform temperature all over the body by even distribution of heat.
6. **Prevention of desiccation:** Blood supplies adequate quantity of water to all cells and prevents the desiccation of tissues due to evaporation of water.
7. **Formation of clot:** Blood shows property of clotting which prevents the loss of blood from an injured tissue. Thrombocytes and fibrinogen, the plasma protein play an important role in clotting of blood.
8. **Prevention of infection:** The leucocytes protect body against the attack of bacteria and other microorganisms. These cells fight and engulf the pathogenic organisms entering the body. Thus, these cells play an important role in the protection of the body.
9. **Immunity and defence mechanism:** The lymphocytes of the blood produce antibodies and antitoxins in the blood. The antibodies act against antigens (bacteria) and kill them; antitoxins neutralise the toxins and poisonous substances released by pathogens in the body of the animal.

(II) Heart

The heart of the frog is a red hollow, muscular organ, roughly triangular in shape. It is situated in the anterior region of the trunk in the midventral line, between the sternum and the oesophagus.

Ventrally, it is supported by the pectoral girdle. The heart is enclosed in a thin double walled, transparent membranous covering called *pericardium*.

The inner pericardial membrane is called the *visceral pericardium* and the outer the *parietal pericardium*. The space between these two membranes is called the pericardial cavity. The pericardial cavity is filled with a fluid, the *pericardial fluid*. The fluid prevents the desiccation of the heart by keeping it moist and protects it from external shocks and injuries. Thus, pericardial fluid facilitates free movements of the heart and also functions as a shock absorber.

External Structure of Heart

The heart of a frog is a thick, muscular, almost triangular organ. Its broad base lies towards the anterior end while the pointed apex is directed backwards. The heart of a frog consists of three main chambers, two *auricles* and one *ventricle*.

It is also supplemented by two accessory chambers namely, the *sinus venosus* and *truncus arteriosus*. In the dorsal view, the heart shows two auricles (left and right auricles) infront and a conical ventricle behind with its apex directed backward.

In addition, it also shows a triangular, thin walled sac like structure called sinus venosus formed by the confluence of three large veins, two *left* and *right precavals* and one *postcaval*. The sinus venosus collects blood coming from different parts of the body. Anteriorly, in front of sinus venosus, it also shows a pair of *pulmonary veins* joining and opening into the left auricle. The auricles are thin walled chambers, whereas the ventricle is a large thick walled, muscular and conical chamber.

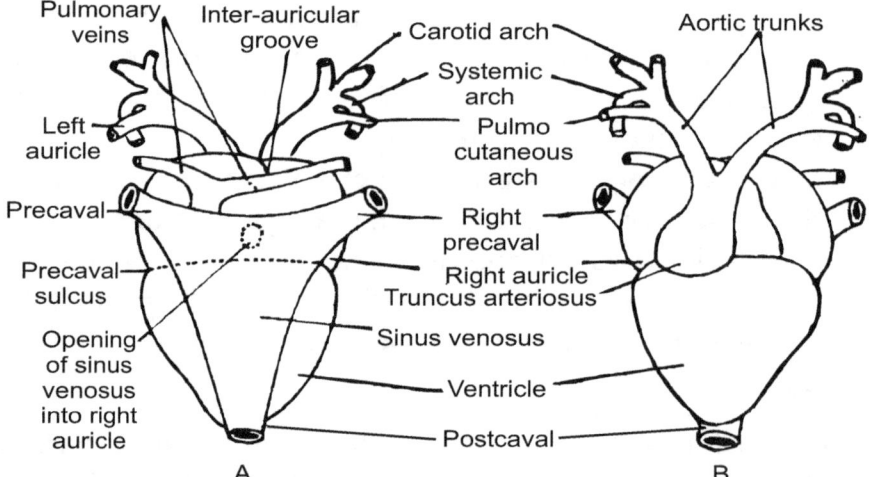

Fig. 3.29: Frog. Structure of Heart: A - Dorsal view. B - Ventral view.

In the ventral view, heart also shows two left and right auricles and one ventricle. Externally the auricles and ventricles are differentiated by a shallow transverse groove called *coronary sulcus*. It also shows a slightly muscular tubular *truncus arteriosus*. Truncus arteriosus arises from the right side of the base of the ventricle and runs forward obliquely and at the margin of the auricles bifurcates into two trunks.

It takes blood away from the heart for distribution to the different parts of the body. The two auricles are externally demarcated by a very faint longitudinal *inter auricular groove*.

Internal Structure of Heart

The internal structure of the heart is seen in its longitudinal section. The internal structure of the heart is so designed as to propel and maintain the flow of blood under pressure in one direction and back flow is prevented by the valves present in it.

(a) Sinus venosus:

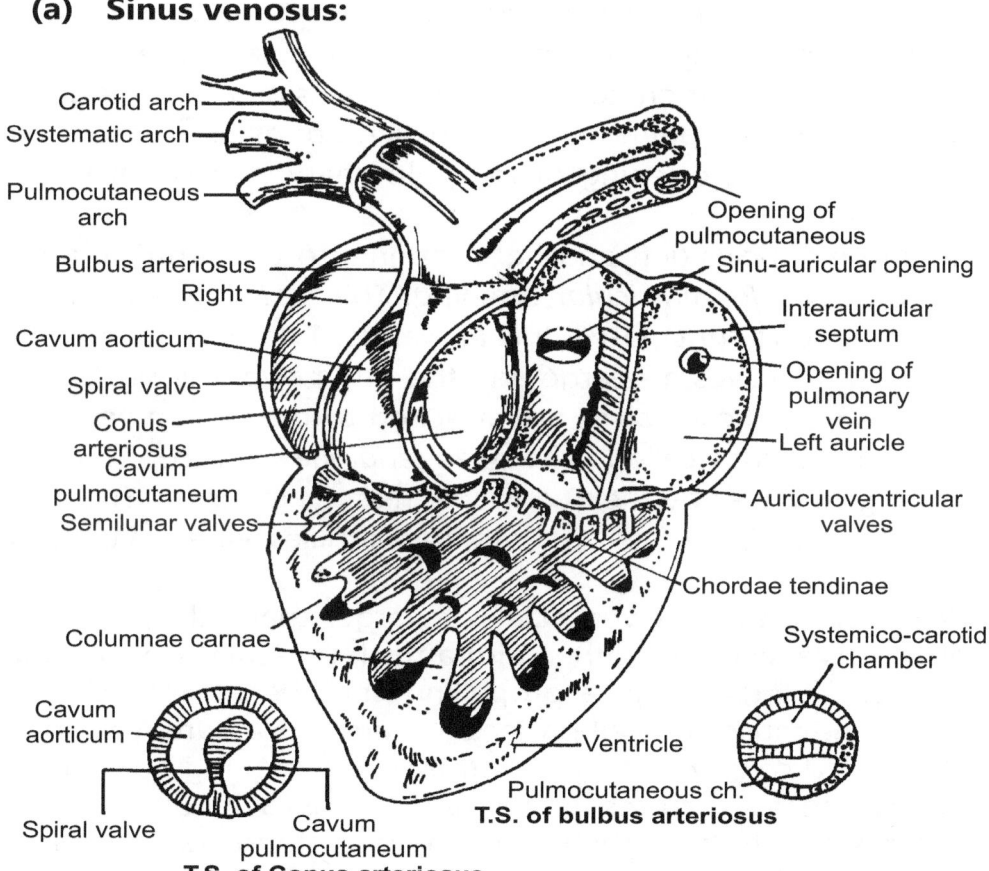

Fig. 3.30: Frog - Internal Structure of Heart

The sinus venosus is a thin walled triangular chamber present on the dorsal surface of the heart. Its base is at the anterior end and the apex is directed backward. It receives deoxygenated blood through two left and right precavals and a postcaval. The precavals bring blood from the anterior part of the body and the postcaval brings from the posterior part of the body. The sinus venosus opens into the right auricle through a *sinuauricular aperture*. This opening is guarded by a pair of lips like muscular *sinu auricular valves*. These valves open into the right auricle and prevent the back flow of blood from the right auricle to the sinus venosus.

(b) Auricles: The auricles are thin walled receiving chambers. Internally, the left and right auricles are separated by a vertical partition called inter *auricular septum*. The right auricle is larger than the left auricle. The sinus venosus opens into the right auricle through the *sinuauricular opening* near the inter-auricular septum. The opening is guarded by a pair of sinuauricular valves. The right auricle receives deoxygenated blood from the sinus venosus. Into the left auricle opens the pulmonary vein which brings oxygenated blood from the lungs. The opening of the pulmonary vein is not provided with valves.

Both the auricles (left and right) open into the ventricle through a common *auriculo-ventricular* opening. This opening is guarded by four membranous *auriculo-ventricular* valves. Two of them, the dorsal and the ventral valves are large and the other two, the right and left valves are small. These valves are attached to the wall of ventricle by fine fibrous cords called *chordae tendinae* which control the functioning of valves by their contraction and expansion. These cords prevent the pushing of valves into the auricles when the ventricle contracts.

(c) Ventricle: The ventricle is a large, triangular and spongy chamber. It is a single chamber with a thick muscular wall. Its apex is directed backwards. Being a propelling chamber, it is thick walled. Moreover, the muscular wall projects inwards by a number of muscle columns called *columnae* corner or *trabeculae* forming open pouches or fissures. These structures greatly reduce the cavity of the ventricle. The fissures help to keep the two streams of blood coming from two auricles. Anteriorly on the right side the ventricle communicates with the *truncus arteriosus*.

(d) Truncus arteriosus: (Fig. 3.31). The truncus arteriosus is a thick muscular tube which runs obliquely from the base of the ventricle. The opening of the ventricle is guarded by three cup shaped *semilunar valves* which prevent the back flow of blood from the truncus into the ventricle. The truncus arteriosus is differentiated into a long proximal portion called globular *conus arteriosus* enclosing a cavity called *pylangium* and a distal tubular part *bulbus arteriosus* containing a space called *synangium*. The second row of three *semilunar* valves is present at the anterior end of the pylangium. The pylangium contains a wavy, longitudinal fold, the *spiral valve*. The spiral valve runs obliquely, and is attached by its dorsal edge, though free ventrally. Anteriorly, the spiral valves are attached to one of the semilunar valve. Thus, the spiral valve divides the pylangium into a right *cavum aorticum* and a left *cavum pulmocutaneum*. The cavum aorticum begins on the right side and curves round to become ventral and the cavum pulmocutaneum begins on the left side and curves round to become dorsal. Because of this arrangement blood from the ventricle first enters cavum aorticum and then overflows into cavum pulmocutaneum.

The bulbus arteriosus is also divided by a horizontal septum called septum principale into a dorsal *pulmocutaneous* and a ventral *systemicocarotid chambers*. The pulmocutaneous chamber is communicated behind with the cavum pulmocutaneus and leads in front into the pulmocutaneous arches of both the sides while the systemicocarotid chamber communicates behind with the cavum aorticum and leads in front into the carotid and systemic arches of both sides. The opening of the pulmocutaneous arch lies immediately at the base of the spiral valves while the openings of the carotid and systemic arches lie after the bifurcation of ventral aorta. All these openings are guarded by valves. The distal right and left branches or trunks appear externally to be single vessels but internally, each is made up of three channels which eventually form three separate arches on either side.

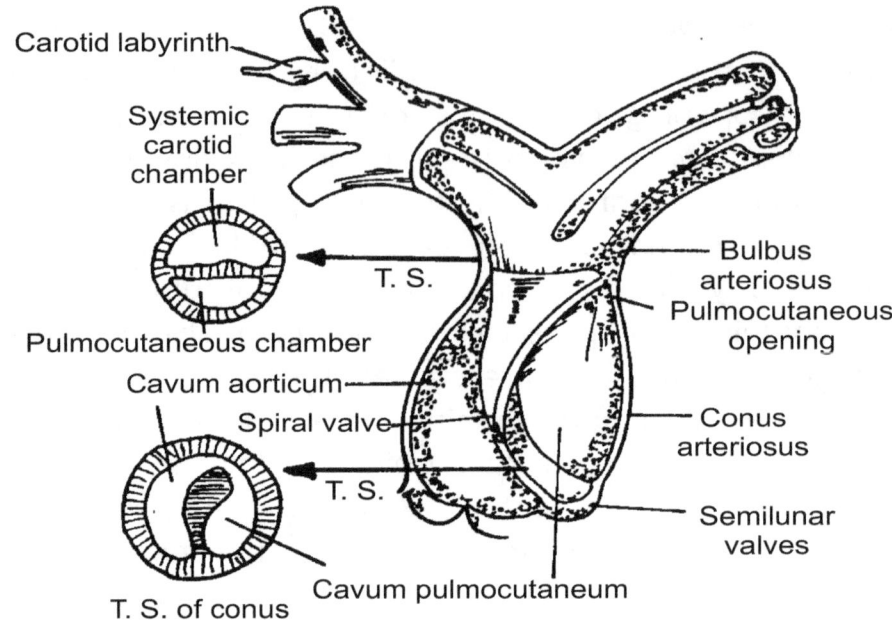

Fig. 3.31: Frog. Internal Structure of Truncus Arteriosus

Working Mechanism of the Heart

The heart is made up of a special type of epithelial cells which form its inner layers. This layer is called as *endocardium*. Its outer layer is called myocardium which is formed of special type of striated muscles called as *cardiac muscles*. Thus, the walls of the heart are composed of special type of muscles called cardiac muscles.

The cardiac muscles are found only in heart and not anywhere in the body. They show involuntary, autonomic (self regulating) and rhythmic actions. The heart muscles have an inherent property of rhythmic contraction and relaxation. The heart is a pumping organ which drives the blood to all parts of the body.

The heart receives the blood under low pressure through caval veins, but it pumps the blood under great pressure through arteries so that the blood reaches even the distant parts of the body. The contraction of the heart is called *systole* and the relaxation as *diastole*. Between the systole and diastole there is a lapse of time called *pause*. The rhythmic contraction and relaxation of the heart is called *heart beat*. The heart beat maintains circulation of blood. The heart of the frog is *myogenic* as its contraction is initiated by modified muscle plexus situated in the wall of the sinus venosus.

The heart beat is initiated in sinus venosus at a particular point called as *sinuauricular node*. It is situated in the wall of the right auricle close to the sinuauricular aperture. It is also called 'pace maker'. This sinuauricular node or plexus not only initiates heart beat but also sets up pace or rhythm hence this is called pace maker. It supplies the impulse for starting the contraction in all directions. The wave of contraction spreads over both the auricles; therefore both the auricles contract.

The wave of contraction of heart follows a regular sequence from the sinus venosus to the auricles, from auricles to the ventricles and finally to the truncus arteriosus. Each of these chambers contracts and relaxes alternately so that blood passes from one chamber to the next in succession as described below:

1. Sinus venosus receives deoxygenated blood from various parts of the body through precavals and the postcaval. The sinus venosus contracts and the deoxygenated blood enters the right auricle through the sinuauricular aperture. At the same time the left auricle receives oxygenated blood coming from the lungs.

2. The wave of contraction quickly passes over to both the auricles. The sinus venosus then relaxes. Both the auricles then contract simultaneously (auricular systole) and the blood from them is forced into the ventricle through the auriculo-ventricular aperture. Reverse flow of blood is prevented by auriculo-ventricular valves.

3. Now pressure within the ventricle increases making it contract (ventricular systole) and the blood enters the truncus arteriosus. The back flow of blood is prevented by the semilunar valves.

4. Then truncus arteriosus contracts and the blood is forced into three arches. These three arches (carotid, systemic and pulmocutaneous) carry blood to the different parts of the body.

5. As the entire blood from the auricles enters the ventricle, the two auricles relax (auricular diastole) and again receives blood through the sinus venosus and pulmonary veins. Similarly, when the entire blood from the ventricle enters the

truncus arteriosus, the ventricle relaxes (ventricular diastole) and is ready to receive blood from the auricles. In this way the heart-cycle continues.

Since, the ventricle is undivided the streams of blood coming from the two auricles enter the single chamber of the ventricle. There is difference of opinion as regards the mechanism of blood circulation in the ventricle.

According to the old theory of "selective distribution of blood" put forward by **Bruke** (1857) the blood received from the right and left auricles does not mix in the ventricle but is stored in the right and left parts of the ventricle respectively.

Thus, the right columnae cornae possess impure blood, middle columnae cornae contain mixed blood and the left columnae cornae contain pure blood.

When the ventricle contracts the blood is selectively distributed. The impure blood goes into the systemic arch and pure blood goes into the carotid arch. This sequence is maintained by the spiral valve.

However, this theory is now completely discarded.

According to the new theory called 'free mixing of blood' proposed by **Van der Vael** (1933) and **Foxon** (1951), blood mixes completely in the ventricle and is forced into the parts of the conus arteriosus.

According to them blood flows simultaneously on both the sides of the spiral valve and enters the three arches.

These three arches therefore carry mixed blood to all parts of the body. The opening of pulmocutaneous arch lies earlier than the openings of systemic and carotid arches, the blood goes first into the pulmocutaneous arch.

The rest of the blood goes into the systemic and carotid arches.

This theory is based on the following facts:

(i) Aquatic respiration is more prevalent than the aerial respiration in frog. The blood which comes in the sinus venosus from the veins is more oxygenated than the one which comes into the left auricle from the lungs.

(ii) There is complete mixing of the blood in ventricle and it passes through conus arteriosus from where it is distributed simultaneously into the three arches.

(iii) The spiral valve which is present in the truncus arteriosus is to check the collapsing of the tube and not to separate the oxygenated and deoxygenated blood.

(iv) The carotid labyrinth is sensitive to pressure changes.

According to **Simons** (1959) and **Nigam** (1975), the blood does not mix much in the ventricle. The spiral valve keeps the oxygenated and deoxygenated blood separate. The deoxygenated blood enters the pulmocutaneous arch and it carries the blood to the lungs and skin for oxygenation. The oxygenated blood goes in the carotid and right systemic. The carotid carries oxygenated blood to the brain. The two systemics join to form dorsal aorta and it carries mixed blood to the different parts of the body. This view is supported by the work of **Long** (1962) on Rana pipens by gas analysis.

Nigam (1975) in *Rana tigrina* has shown that most of the deoxygenated blood goes to the pulmocutaneous arch and a little quantity goes to the left systemic arch. Rest of the blood goes to carotid and right systemic trunk.

Actually, how this selective distribution of blood takes place is still a matter of controversy. Some workers are of the opinion that, this is done by spiral valve but others claim that spiral valve prevents only collapsing of truncus arteriosus and nothing to do with selective distribution of blood. But this is certain and proved beyond doubt that deoxygenated blood does not enter the carotid trunk and right systemic trunk because on contraction of truncus arteriosus, the spiral valve and septum medial together form a complete partition. In the frog mixing or non-mixing of blood in the ventricle is of little importance as the oxygen contents of two streams of blood coming from two auricles is practically the same.

The blood coming from sinus venosus is not completely deoxygenated because it also receives oxygenated blood coming from skin and buccal cavity. Similarly, the blood coming from lungs is not always completely oxygenated as lung respiration takes place at intervals and there is no lung respiration under water and during hibernation. Therefore, the entire blood in the right auricle is not completely deoxygenated. It is also a fact that the frog being a sluggish animal can do with mixed blood.

3.5.1 Arterial System

The blood vessels which carry oxygenated or pure blood to the various organs of the body from the heart are called *arteries*. The arteries are divided into smaller branches the *arterioles* and finally into the *capillaries*. The arteries, arterioles and capillaries form the *arterial system*.

Arteries carry blood away from the heart. They are thick walled and without valves. For convenience the arterial system is divisible into two parts:

(A) Anterior or precardiac arterial system.

(B) Posterior or postcardiac arterial system.

(a) Anterior Arterial System

The arterial system in frog begins with the truncus arteriosus. It arises from the ventricle, runs across the right auricle and infront of the heart divides into the right and left branches or trunks. They are also called as lateral *aortae*. Each branch further divides into three main arteries or *aortic* arches, namely *carotid*, *systemic* and *pulmocutaneous*. These arteries supply blood to different parts of the body and they are further sub-divided as follows:

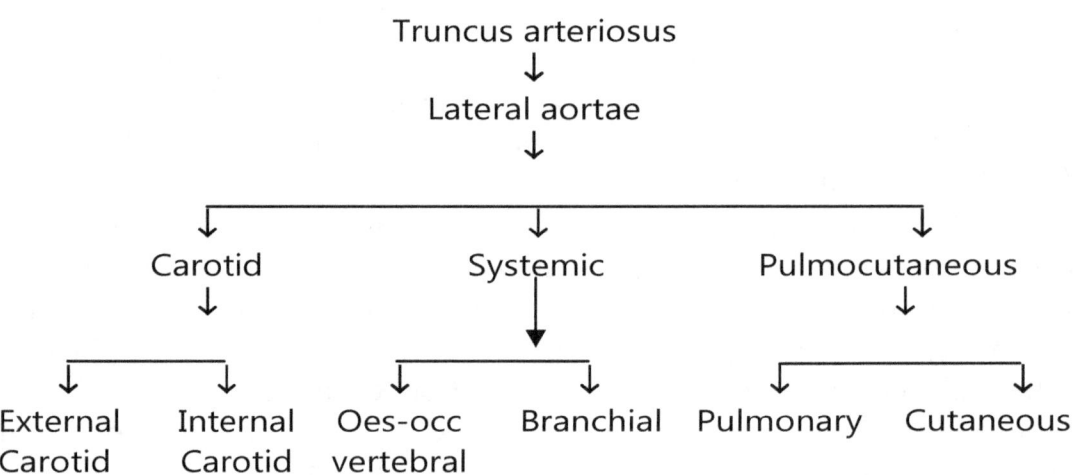

1. **Carotid arch:** It is the anterior most arch going to the head. It is a short vessel running forward and outward, but soon divides into two branches; external and internal carotids.

    (i) **External carotid:** It is also called the lingual, supplying blood to the tongue and the muscles of hyoid apparatus and the lower jaw.

    (ii) **Internal carotid:** It is the larger outer branch supplying blood to the roof of the buccal cavity, eye muscles and brain. At its base, there is a swelling called carotid labyrinth which detects and regulates the pressure of the blood going to the brain. It also responds the chemical changes, i.e. decrease of O_2 or increase of CO_2 and it stimulates the motor centres in the brain to increase the rate of respiration.

2. **Systemic arch:** It is the middle and longest of the three arches. The systemic arches of the sides curve round the heart and pass backwards to meet each other to form the *dorsal aorta* in the mid dorsal line. Before forming the dorsal aorta each systemic arch gives off three small branches - oesophageal, occipito-vertebral and subclavian.

    (i) **Oesophageal artery:** It is a small artery which provides blood to oesophagus. It may arise from occipito-vertebral artery.

    (ii) **Occipito-vertebral:** It sends one branch, occipital artery to the posterior part of head i.e. occipital region and another branch called *vertebral artery* supplying blood to the vertebral column and spinal cord.

    (iii) **Subclavian:** It is a large artery supplying blood to the shoulder region and then continues as the brachial artery in the forelimb.

3. **The pulmocutaneous:** It is a posterior short trunk dividing immediately into two branches; pulmonary and the cutaneous.

    (i) **Pulmonary:** It carries blood to the lungs.

    (ii) **Cutaneous:** It provides blood to the skin.

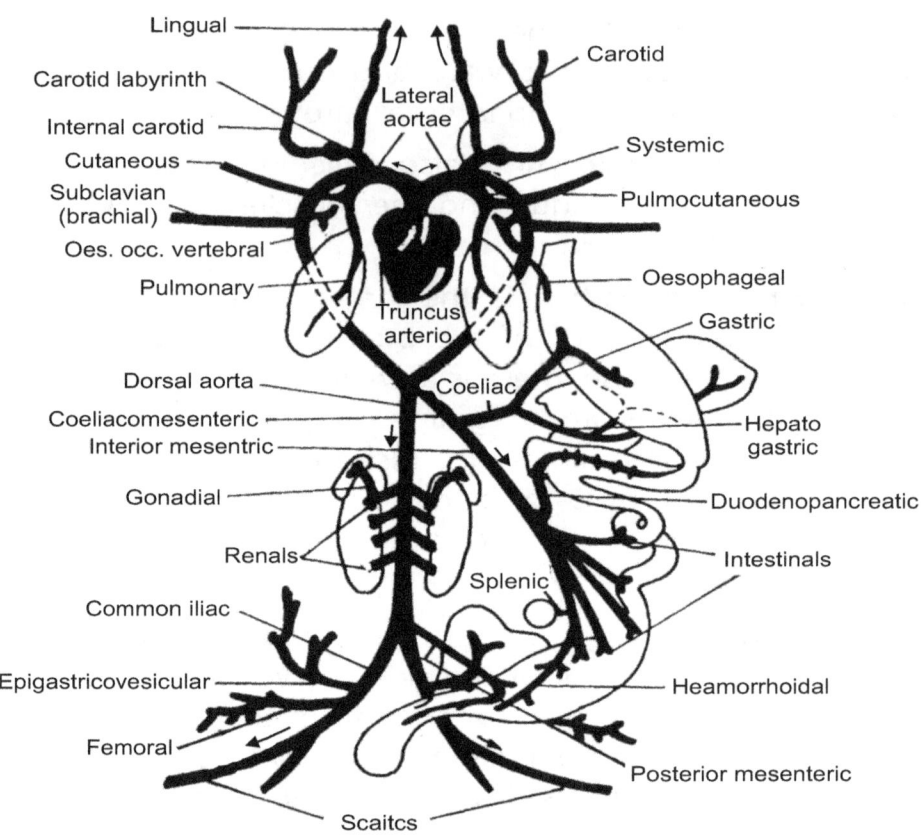

Fig. 3.32: Frog - Arterial System

(b) Posterior Arterial System or Dorsal Aorta and its Branches

The Dorsal Aorta: The dorsal aorta is formed by the union of two systemic arches. It runs posteriorly upto the base of legs, ventral to the vertebral column. It gives off the following branches:

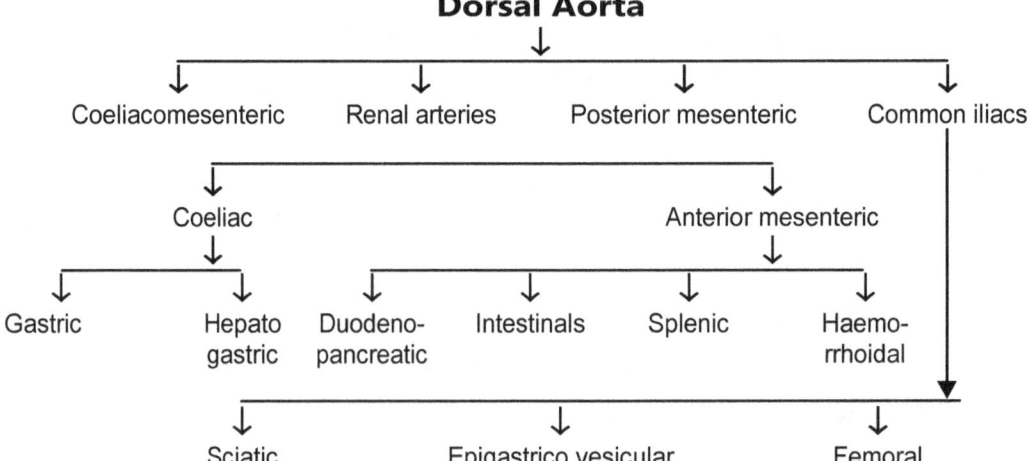

1. Coeliacomesenteric: It arises from the place where two systemics unite. It soon divides into: (i) the *coeliac* and (ii) the *anterior mesenteric*. The coeliac further divides into the *gastric* supplying the stomach and the *hepatogastric* going to the stomach and liver. The antero-mesenteric gives out *duodeno pancreatic* to the duodenum and pancreas, three or four *intestinals* to the coils of intestine, a short *splenic* to the spleen and the *haemorrhoidal* to the rectum.

   2. Renal arteries: These are four to six pairs of short arteries given out from the dorsal aorta in between the kidneys and they supply blood to kidneys. From the first renal artery is given out the *gonadal artery* namely spermatic in males or *ovarian* in female and goes to the testis or ovary respectively.

   3. Posterior mesenteric artery: It is a short, unpaired artery given out by the posterior bifurcation of the dorsal aorta and supplies blood to the rectum.

   4. Common iliac: These are pairs of arteries formed by the bifurcation of the dorsal aorta posteriorly.

Each iliac runs into the leg on its side and on its way gives out the following branches.

   (i) Epigastrico Vesicular: Supplying blood to the ventral body wall and urinary bladder.
   (ii) Femoral: Supplying blood to skin and muscles of thigh.
   (iii) Sciatic: It supplies blood to the lower leg.

All the arteries after entering the respective organs divide and redivide to form capillary network in the organ. Then these capillaries join and rejoin to form veins which leave the organs with deoxygenated blood.

3.5.2 Venous System

Venous system consists of veins which are thin walled blood vessels with valves and collect deoxygenated blood from different parts of the body and bring it to the heart. It can be divided into two parts: anterior and posterior venous system.

(a) Anterior Venous System

The anterior venous system includes (A) pulmonary veins and (B) Precaval veins and their tributories.

(A) Pulmonary Veins: These are pairs of short veins collecting and carrying blood from the lungs to the heart. The two pulmonary veins unite and open through a single aperture into the left auricle. They bring oxygenated blood from lungs.

(B) Precavals: These veins are also called *anterior* or *superior venae cavae*. There are pairs of precavals which are short and broad vein opening into the anterior corners of the triangular sinus venosus.

Each precaval veins is formed by the following branches:

1. External jugular: It is formed by *lingual* and *mandibular*. Lingual brings blood from tongue and hyoid apparatus and mandibular collecting blood from muscles of lower jaw.

Precaval
↓
┌─────────────────┼─────────────────┐
↓ ↓ ↓
External jugular   Innominate   Subclavian
↓ ↓ ↓
┌───┴───┐ ┌───┴───┐ ┌───┴───┐
↓ ↓ ↓ ↓ ↓ ↓
Lingual Mandibular Internal Subscapular Brachial Musculo-
jugular cutaneous

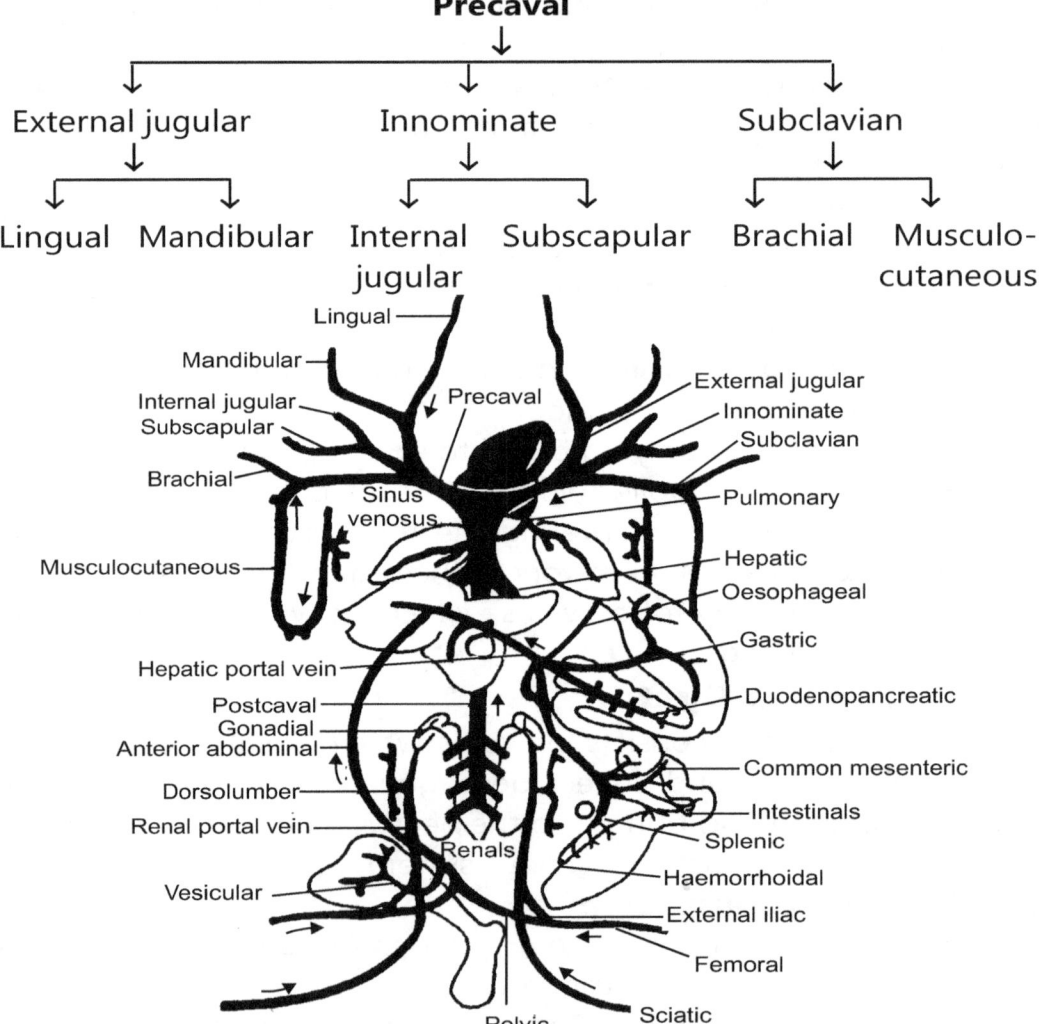

Fig. 3.33: Frog - Venous System

2. Innominate: It is formed by *internal jugular* and *subscapular*. The internal jugular brings blood from the brain and muscles of eyes. The subscapular collects blood from below the shoulder region and the back of the forelimb.

3. Subclavian: It is formed by the joining of the *brachial* and the *musculocutaneous* veins. Brachial collects from the forelimbs and musculocutaneous from the skin, buccopharynx and the muscles of the body wall. It brings oxygenated blood from the skin and buccopharynx and deoxygenated blood from muscles, it contains mixed blood.

(B) Posterior Venous System

The posterior venous system is formed by the postcaval and portal systems. The blood is collected in the heart from the posterior parts of the body.

Postcaval: It is also called *posterior* or *inferior vena cava*. Postcaval brings blood from the posterior end of the kidneys. It is formed by the joining of four to six pairs of *renal veins*. The first renal vein also receives the gonadial veins from the gonads (*spermatic* or *ovarian* from testis or ovaries). The postcaval then runs forward and enters the liver. It emerges out arteriorly without dividing into capillaries in the liver. Post caval receives a pair of *hepatic veins* bringing blood from the liver after which the postcaval opens into the sinus venosus.

Portal systems: These are the veins which carry blood from one organ to the other before going to the heart. They form a capillary network in the organs in which they enter. The veins which leave the organ also start with capillaries. Such veins are called portal veins and the system formed by them is known as a *portal system*. The organ from which blood is taken, serves as a 'port' or exchange of materials hence the name. Normally an artery divides to form arterioles which merge into capillaries. The capillaries unite to form veins. A vein arises as venules from the capillary network. A vein may join another vein or may open into the heart. But in the venous system of frog, two veins the *renal portal* and the *hepatic portal* veins show peculiarity. The renal and hepatic portal veins when traced towards either end both of them show a capillary network at both ends. One set of capillary network is situated in the organs from which the vein arises and the other in the kidney or liver in which the vein terminates. Thus, these veins form capillary network before sending their blood into the heart. The organ liver or kidney cuts as a port or a check post of exchange of material.

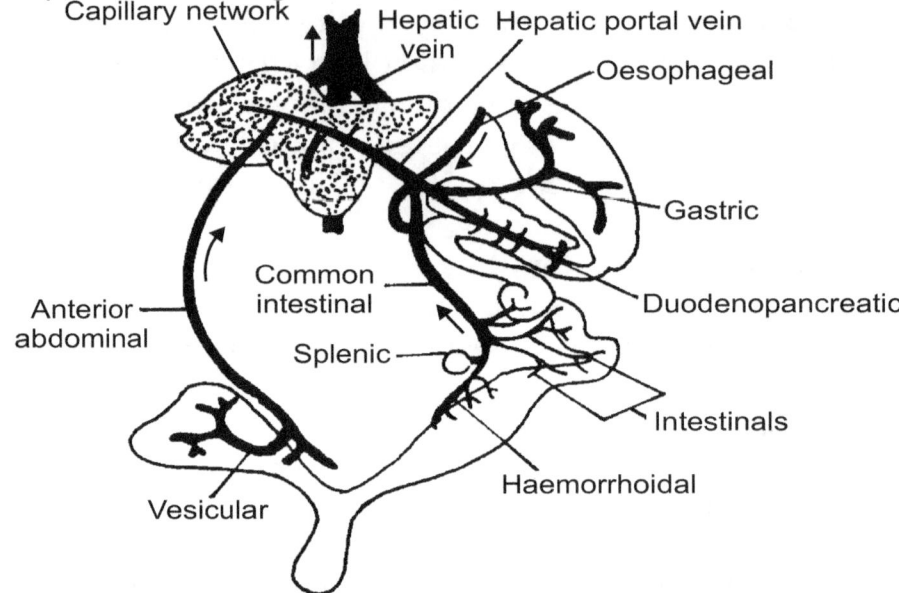

Fig. 3.34: Frog - Hepatic Portal System

In the frog there are two portal systems namely, *hepatic portal system* and the *renal portal system*.

1. Hepatic Portal System: It takes blood to the liver and consists of the *hepatic portal vein* and the *anterior abdominal vein*.

(A) The Hepatic Portal Vein: It collects blood from the alimentary canal and takes it to the liver. The hepatic vein is formed by the union of the following veins bringing blood from the different parts of the alimentary canal.

(i) **Gastric:** Collects blood from the stomach.

(ii) **Duodeno-pancreatic:** Receives blood from the duodenum and pancreas.

(iii) **Common intestinal or mesenteric:** Carries blood from the oesophagus and the intestinal coils.

(iv) **Splenic:** Collects blood from the spleen.

(v) **Haemorrhodial:** Brings blood from the rectum.

In the region of the liver the hepatic portal vein gives out branches which enter the liver. The hepatic portal vein carries with blood a large amount of sugar to the liver. In the liver sugar is converted into the glycogen and stored in the liver cells.

(B) Anterior abdominal vein: This vein is formed by the union of two pelvics (the branches of femorals) at the base of the hindlimbs. It collects blood from the hindlimbs and bring to the liver. On its way, the anterior abdominal collects blood from the urinary bladder through the *vesicular vein* and several pairs of small veins from the abdominal muscles. It then joins one of the branches of the hepatic portal vein.

After entering the liver lobes, the branches of the hepatic portal vein and the anterior abdominal vein divide and redivide to form a second network of capillaries, a characteristic feature of the portal system.

2. Renal Portal System: The renal portal system brings blood from the hindlimbs and dorsal body wall to the kidneys. It consists of (a) Renal portal veins, (b) Dorso-lumbar vein and in females oviducal veins.

(a) Renal portal veins: These are pairs of veins bringing blood from the legs to the kidneys. Each renal portal vein is formed by a *femoral* and sciatic vein. From the leg region, blood is collected by the femoral from the anterior side and the sciatic vein from the posterior side. The femoral on each side, after entering the abdominal cavity, divides into two branches, outer *external iliac* and *inner pelvic*. The two pelvics join to form the anterior abdominal (the part of hepatic portal system) but the external iliac on each side joins the sciatic to form *renal portal vein* on each side. The renal portal on each side runs forward along the outer margin of the kidney in which it enters.

(b) Dorsolumbar: The dorsolumbar veins are also pair of veins joining the renal portal veins in the region of kidneys on the outer sides. They collect blood from the muscles of the dorsal body wall and lumbar region.

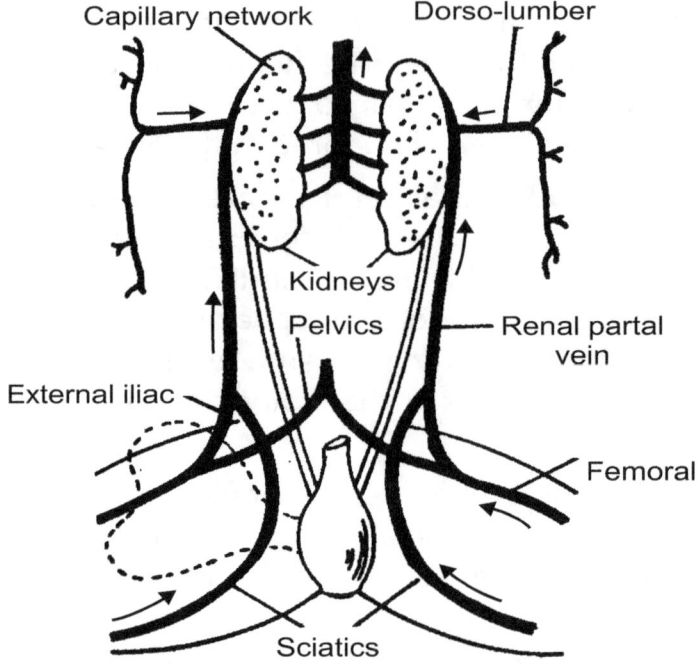

Fig. 3.35: Frog-Renal Portal System

(c) The oviducal vein: Present only in females coming from the oviducts, also unite with renal portal veins.

The renal portal veins which enter the kidney, divide and redivide forming a second capillary network. These capillaries again rejoin and form 4 or 6 pairs of renal veins which carry blood from kidneys to the heart.

The blood in the renal portal vein contains many harmful substances such as urea, uric acid etc. These substances are removed from the blood by the kidneys. Thus, the blood is purified to some extent in the kidneys by the removal of toxic substances. Blood goes to the heart.

Significance of Portal System: The portal system plays a significant physiological role in the frog as shown below:

1. Liver and kidneys are port like organs which act as 'sensor organs' or 'check posts' not allowing any waste or toxic unwanted substances to remain in the stream of blood. In the liver and kidney, toxic waste and harmful substances are removed after which blood is sent to heart.
2. The main significance of the portal system is to increase the area of diffusion and absorption by dividing into capillaries

into the organs like liver and kidneys to facilitate the effective functioning. The capillary network in these organs that blood is exposed to a larger area and individual cells. The increased area also increases the rate of diffusion of substances from blood into those organs.
3. More blood flows through liver. Glucose and amino acids are brought into the liver from the alimentary canal. Excess of glucose is converted into glycogen and stored in liver cells. Glycogen breaks down into glucose (sugar) and is released into the blood stream when required. Excess of amino acids are decomposed to ammonia and urea by deamination and it is made non-toxic by the process of detoxification. Thus, liver acts as an organ for conversion and storage of excess of sugar and deamination and detoxication.
4. The renal portal system enables the kidney to eliminate nitrogenous wastes and excess of any salts. Blood is purified and osmotic balance is maintained.
5. The portal system helps to carry, in general circulation, new erythrocytes formed by haemopoetic tissue in the liver and kidneys of frog.

Histology of Artery and Vein
Arteries

The arteries are thick walled and highly contractile. The wall is made up of three layers, namely, tunica externa, tunica media and tunica interna.

(i) **Tunica externa:** It is the outermost layer made up of connective tissue. The connective tissue makes this layer firm and elastic to withstand blood pressure. The elastic nature of arteries prevent the bursting.

(ii) **Tunica media:** It is the middle layer made up of collagen fibres and unstriated muscles. As per the need of blood, contraction and relaxation of vessels takes place. These arteries regulate the blood quantity in organs.

(iii) **Tunica interna:** It is the innermost layer composed of flat epithelial cells called *endothelium* and connective tissues. This is a strong and stout layer because maximum blood pressure is on this layer. In some arteries this layer is still more strong called inner elastic membrane.

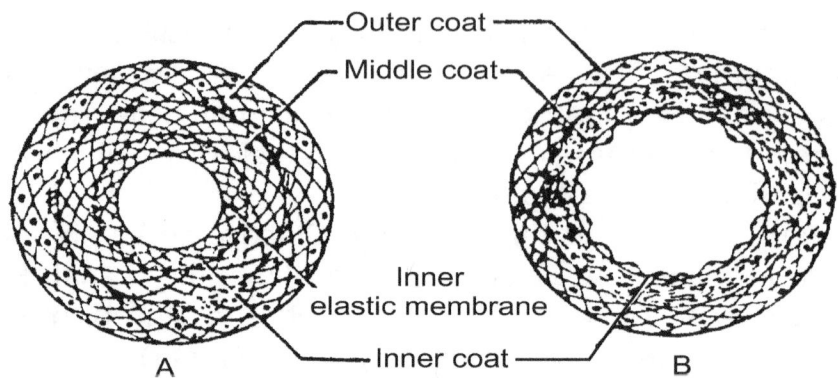

Fig. 3.36: Transverse section of A - Artery B - Vein

Veins

Histological structure of the vein is similar to that of arteries but their walls are comparatively thinner and more elastic.

Tunica externa, which is the outer layer contains lesser collagen fibres and is thin. The middle layer of muscles is also very thin. There is no inner elastic membrane. Veins have valves which allow the flow of blood in one direction only. The valves are semi-lunar in shape. In case of blood capillaries an elastic membrane is present and they are very thin walled. Therefore, exchange of substances takes place by diffusion.

Differences between Artery and Vein

	Artery		Vein
1.	They carry blood from the heart to different organs of the body.	1.	Veins collect blood from organs and carry it to the heart.
2.	Blood flows rapidly with pressure.	2.	The blood flows slowly with less pressure.
3.	Colour is pink or dark red.	3.	Colour is dark blue.
4.	Situated deep away from the skin.	4.	Situated superficially near the skin.
5.	They possess valves.	5.	Valves are absent.
6.	They do not contract even when blood is drained.	6.	They contract when blood is drained.
7.	The wall is thick, muscular, stout and non-contractile.	7.	The wall is thin, non-muscular and contractile.

Chapter 4...

Urinogenital System

4.1 Urinogenital System
4.2 Excretory System
4.3 Reproductive System
    4.3.1 Male Reproductive System
    4.3.2 Female Reproductive System
4.4 Central Nervous System
4.5 Sense Organs
✍ Summary
✍ Review Questions

4.1 Urinogenital System

The excretory and reproductive systems are functionally unrelated. In vertebrates the ducts of excretory organs and genital organs are common. In males, the excretory products (urine) as well as genital products (sperms) pass out through common urinogenital ducts. Thus the excretory and genital system are generally described together under the same heading i.e. *urinogenital system*. In frogs, sexes are separate and sexual dimorphism is conspicuous.

4.2 Excretory System

Metabolism is one of the important features of all living organs. Metabolic activities going on in the tissue cells produce a number of waste products such as nitrogenous by-products like ammonia, urea and uric acid. These waste products are toxic and harmful and should not to be accumulated in the body of the animal. To carry on the life processes smoothly, these poisonous and harmful substances must be eliminated from the body by specialised organs. The separation, collection and elimination of nitrogenous waste products such as urea, uric acid, resulting from metabolic activities going on in cells along with mineral salts and excess of water is called *excretion*.

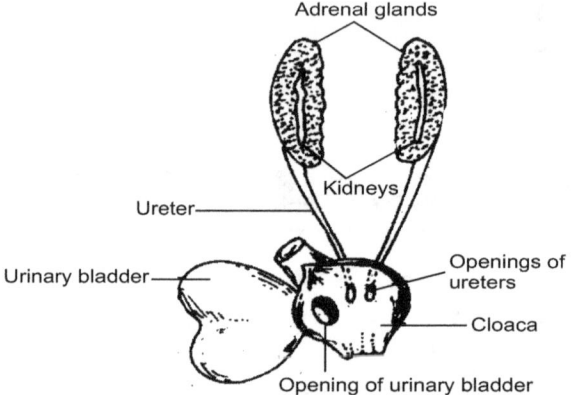

Fig. 4.1: Frog - Excretory system

The organs concerned with excretion constitute the excretory system. The excretory system of frogs consists of (1) a pair of kidneys, (2) a pair of ureters (3) a single urinary bladder and (4) cloaca.

1. Kidneys: The two kidneys are situated dorsally in the sub-vertebral lymph space, one on each side of the vertebral column and covered ventrally by the peritoneum. The kidneys are *mesonephric*. They are elongated, flat and reddish brown structures. The outer edges are smooth and convex but the inner edges are notched and straight ventro-medially. On each kidney lies a yellow irregular, longitudinal strip-like structure called *adrenal* or *supra renal gland* which is the endocrine gland. Kidneys receive blood through renal arteries as well as renal portal veins and are drained by the renal vein.

Histology of Kidney: Each kidney is made up of about 2000 coiled tubules called *nephrons* or *uriniferous tubules*. Between uriniferous tubules lies *connective tissue* and blood capillaries which form a compact organ. The longitudinal section shows longitudinal *Bidder's canal* along the inner margin and ureter along the outer margin, joined by transverse collecting tubules. There are a large number of microscopic, convoluted uriniferous tubules. On the ventral surface of each kidney there are a number of ciliated funnels called nephrostomes which open into the coelom in early stages.

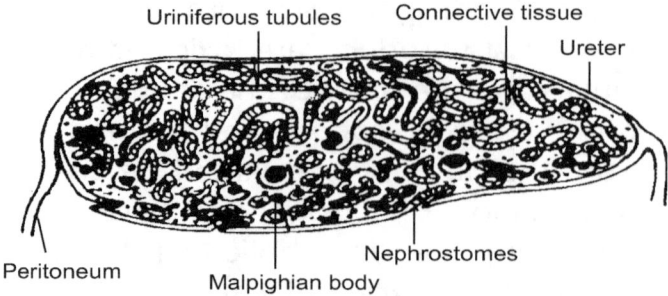

Fig. 4.2: Frog - T.S. of kidney

Structure and functions of uriniferous tubules: The nephrons or uriniferous tubules are the functional units of kidneys. It is structurally differentiated into three regions such as (i) Bowman's capsule (ii) neck and (iii) body of the tubule.

(i) Bowman's capsule: It is an anterior dilated double walled hollow, cup-like structure. It is lined by a single layer of flattened epithelial cells. The Bowman's capsule encloses a bunch of capillaries called *glomerulus*. The inner wall of the Bowman's capsule is closely applied to the capillaries of glomerulus. This intimate contact facilitates filtration. The glomerulus is formed by the *afferent arteriole* a branch of renal artery that enters the Bowman's capsule and divides into capillaries. The capillaries of afferent arteriole reunite to form *efferent arteriole* which leaves the Bowman's capsule. The diameter of the afferent arteriole is greater than that of the efferent arteriole. Bowman's capsule and glomerulus together form *Malpighian body*.

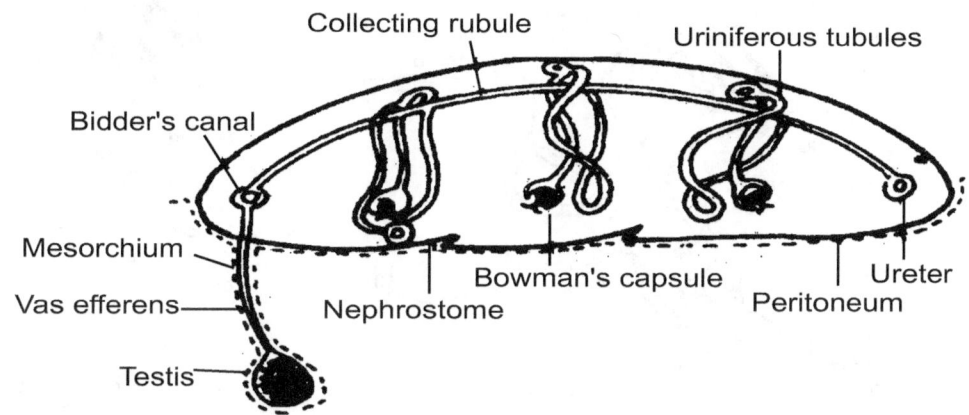

Fig. 4.3: Frog - T. S. kidney showing the course of the uriniferous tubule (diagrammatic)

(ii) Neck: Next to Bowman's capsule, is a short and narrow neck which is lined by cuboidal epithelium beset with long cilia. They are useful for pushing contents filtered by the Bowman's capsule.

(iii) Body of the tubule: It is long, convoluted, lined by tall glandular cells ciliated at intervals and rich in mitochondria. It runs up and down and becomes coiled on the ventral surface. During its course it shows a proximal convoluted part and distal convoluted part which ultimately opens *into transverse*.

Collecting tubule: The collecting tubules in turn open on the inner side into Bidder's canal and the outer side into the *ureter* or *urinogenital duct*.

Blood supply to uriniferous tubule: Each tubule receives arterial as well as venous blood. The afferent arteriole brings blood into the glomerus and the efferent arteriole drains out the blood. The body of the tubule receives venous blood through capillaries of the renal portal vein and efferent arteriole to form a dense network of capillaries around the tubule and ultimately unite and reunite to form renal venules which join to form the renal vein that leaves the kidney.

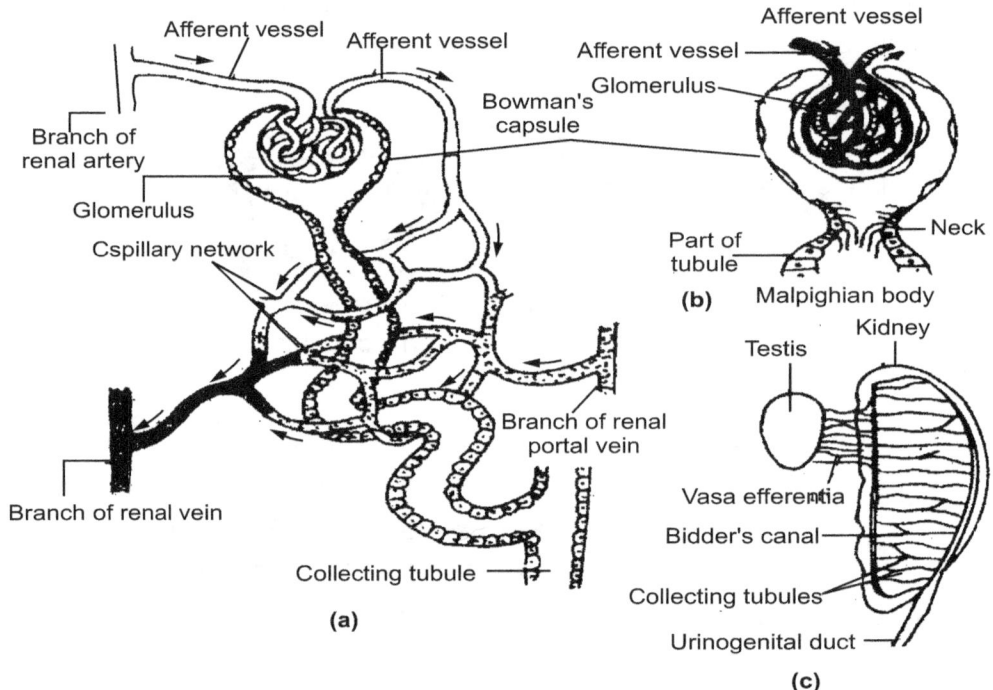

Fig. 4.4: Frog - (A) Structure of uriniferous tubule and its blood supply. (B) Structure of Malpighian capsule. (C) L. S. of kidney of male.

Physiology of excretion: The formation of urine takes place in three stages. (i) Ultrafiltration, (ii) Selective reabsorption and (iii) Renal secretion.

(i) Ultrafiltration: Ultrafiltration takes place in the Malpighian body. The blood enters the kidneys through renal arteries. The afferent arteriole carries blood into the glomerulus and it leaves the glomerulus via. the efferent arteriole. Since the diameter of the efferent arteriole is smaller than that of afferent arteriole, blood in the glomerulus is under great pressure. Filtration which takes place under pressure is called as *ultrafiltration*. As a result of filtration certain substances which are useful to the body are also filtered. The filtrate contains water, glucose, urea, uric acid, salts etc. except blood proteins and blood corpuscles. The filtrate in the Bowman's capsule is called *glomerular filtrate*. It is also called *deproteinised plasma* since it contains all the constituents of the plasma except plasma proteins.

The process of ultrafiltration takes place on the principle of pressure difference. The blood in the glomerulus is separated from the cavity of the Bowman's capsule by thin semipermeable membranes. Membranes are formed by the endothelial lining of blood vessel and the epithelial lining of the Bowman's capsule.

(ii) Selective reabsorption: It occurs in the body or tubular region. Since only useful substances are reabsorbed it is called selective reabsorption. It is a physiological process in which oxygen is utilized. When the glomerular filtrate reaches the tubule the cells of the tubule show selective reabsorption and reabsorb only useful substances like glucose, amino acids, some salts and requisite quantity of water from the filtrate and put them back into blood in the surrounding capillaries. Thus, whatever useful substances are lost from blood through the Bowman's capsule by ultrafiltration, are regained by blood in the cells of tubules. Some water, salts, urea and uric acid remain in the glomerular filtrate. This forms the *urine*.

(iii) Renal or tubular secretion: Some harmful substances like urea, uric acid may escape ultrafiltration and pass into the blood of the efferent arteriole and blood capillaries surrounding the tubular region. These capillaries also bring metabolic waste materials from the renal portal vein. From this network of blood capillaries, the cells of the tubules by active absorption also separate substances like amonia, potassium and hydrogen ions, creatinine and discharge them into the filtrate of the tubule. Thus, the tubular secretion is supplementary to glomerular excretion, increasing the efficiency of the excretory system. Most of the urea in frogs is received by tubular secretion. Frog being an amphibian, is in constant danger of osmotic flooding as water enters through its permeable skin due to endosmosis. As kidneys eliminate more water, hence the urine of frog is *hypotonic* to blood. The chief excretory material being urea, frog is also called an *urotelic* animal. Urine enters in the transverse collecting duct and then into the ureter.

Functions of Kidneys

1. Kidneys act as efficient filters, which extract nitrogenous waste materials from blood in the form of urine.
2. They regulate the acid-base balance or pH of blood and body fluids.
3. They also maintain the composition of blood with respect to salts and water contents. Thus, they perform the function of osmoregulation.
4. In frogs, kidneys also act as haemopoietic tissue producing erythrocytes (RBCs.).
5. In male frogs, they also serve as a path way for sperms.
6. Thus kidneys maintain a internal environment (constant) and balanced i.e. they maintain *homoestasis*.

2. Ureters: There are pairs of ureters or kidney ducts each running along the outer margin of the kidney. The anterior part of ureters is embedded in the kidney but they emerge out from the middle of the kidneys. They run posteriorly upto the cloaca into which they open separately on the dorsal side.

In case of female frogs, these ducts are useful only for carrying urine hence they are called ureters. While in male frogs they carry both urine as well as sperms hence called *urinogenital ducts*.

3. Urinary bladder: It is a thin walled bilobed sac like organ opening ventrally into the cloaca. It arises from the cloaca hence it is also called as cloacal bladder. The wall of the urinary bladder is made up of smooth muscle fibres. It is an elastic bag and hence much distensible. The cloacal spincter keeps the cloacal aperture closed, therefore the urine trickles down the ureters back up into the urinary bladder where it is stored. When the bladder is full by sudden contraction of body muscles and the urinary bladder itself, urine is expelled out by forcing open the cloacal aperture. Urine is often expelled when frogs leap about on land.

The function of the urinary bladder is therefore, temporary storage of urine. Besides this, it also serves as a temporary reservoir water to prevent dehydration under adverse conditions of dryness.

4. **Cloaca:** It is the terminal small chamber of the rectum. It does not only receive undigested matter but also receives urine and genital products hence receives the name cloaca meaning common chamber. It opens outside by a cloacal aperture guarded by a cloacal spincter which controls the elimination of urine along with faecal matter and genital products.

4.3 Reproductive System

Reproduction is one of the characteristic features of all living organisms. In all vertebrates, male and female reproductive organs are developed for this purpose. The frog is an unisexual animal i.e. male and female reproductive organs are present in separate individuals. It shows sexual dimorphism.

The male can be distinguished from the female by the following characters:

1. A male frog is smaller than a female frog.
2. A pair of vocal sacs is present in the male which act as resonators for amplifying croaking. These are thin walled, bluish black, distensible pouches, one on each side of the throat. Vocal sacs are absent in female.
3. The male frog has *nuptial pads* which is a muscular swelling on the innermost digit of each forelimb. The nuptial pads become more conspicuous during the breeding season are useful for clasping the female during amplexus.

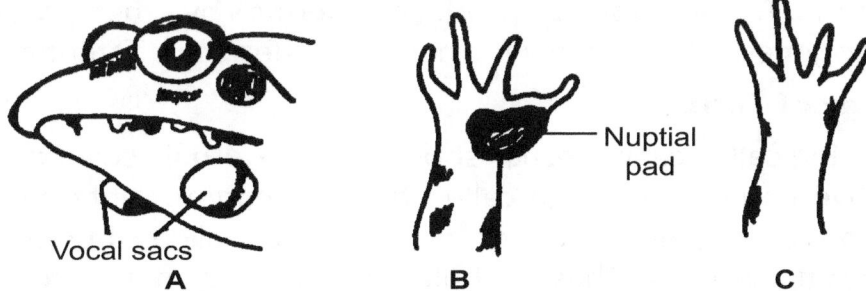

Fig. 4.5: Frog - Sexual Dimorphism; A - Head of Male Frog showing Vocal Sacs. B - Forelimb of Male Frog. C - Forelimb of Female Frog

4.3.1 Male Reproductive System

The male reproductive organs are a pair of testes, vasa efferentia, a pair of urinogenital ducts, cloaca and fat bodies.

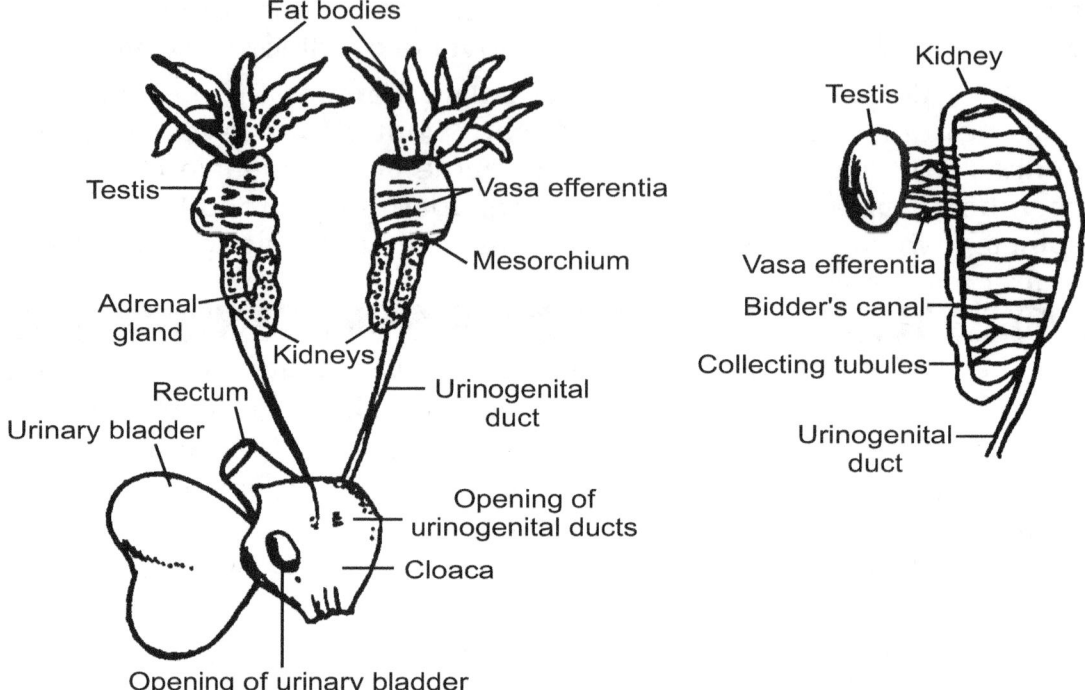

Fig. 4.6: Frog - Male Reproductive System

(i) Testes: Testes are a pair of essential male reproductive organs which are capsule like, light yellow coloured bodies. They are attached to the anterior and ventral surface of the kidneys by a double fold of peritonium called mesorchium. The size and colour of the testes varies according to the season. Internally each testis is made up of a large number of seminiferous tubules lined by germinal epithelium. These tubules produce sperms by the process of spermatogenesis. The sperms further enter the vasa efferentia.

Histology of Testis

Histologically each testis shows an external covering of a connective tissue membrane called *tunica albuginea*. Internally each testis consists of hundreds of microscopic coiled tubules called seminiferous tubules. These tubules are packed in the connective tissue in which there are groups of cells embedded called *interstitial cells* or *cells of Leydig*. These cells are endocrine glands which secrete a sex hormone called *testosterone* which controls the development of secondary sexual characters.

Each seminiferous tubule is lined by germinal epithelium. In between the germinal epithelium another type of cells called *cells of sertoli or nurse cells* are present. In the seminiferous tubule the cells of the germinal epithelium undergo the process of *spermatogenesis* which produce rounded cells *spermatogonia* primary spermatocytes, secondary spermatocytes and spermatids. The spermatids undergo metamorphosis or spermiogenesis to produce *sperms* or *spermatozoa*.

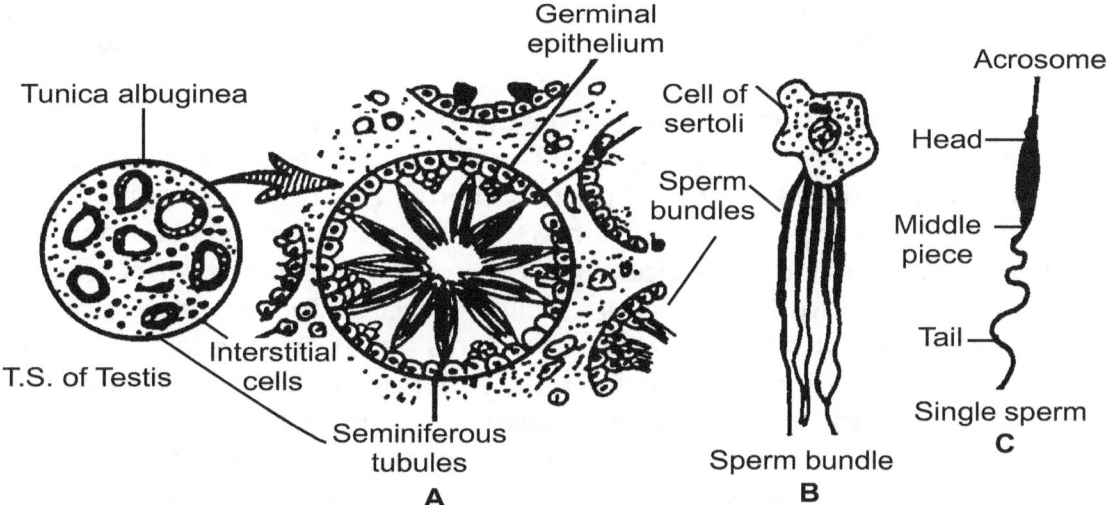

Fig. 4.7: Frog - Histology of Testis

Each sperm consists of a small, rod-like head, with a nucleus and a long whip like cytoplasmic tail. It is a motile male gamete provided with a head capped by acrosome, mid-piece and vibratile tail. The immature sperms adhere to the cells of sertoli with their heads towards the periphery and tails towards the centre. The cells of sertoli play an important role of nourishment to the developing sperms. Once the sperms become mature they are released in the seminiferous fluid in the lumen of the seminiferous tubules from where they enter the vasa efferentia.

(ii) Vasa efferentia: These are 10-12 fine delicate, thread-like tubules running from the inner border of each testis to the kidney through the mesorchium. Inside the kidney they open into the

Bidder's canal. The Bidder's canal is a longitudinal tube running along the inner margin within each kidney. The canal ultimately opens into the urinogenital duct through transversely placed collecting tubules. Thus, the function of vasa efferentia is to carry sperms from the testis to the Bidder's canal and ultimately into the urinogenital ducts through collecting tubules.

(iii) Urinogenital ducts: These are a pair of thin transparent ducts. They carry urine as well as sperms thus are called urinogenital ducts. They are also called vas deferens. Each vas deferens or urinogenital duct opens separately into the cloaca. They are slightly dilated on the posterior ends in some species called *seminal vesicles*. The sperms are stored in seminal vesicles and are expelled out during copulation. The urinogenital ducts run backwards and finally open into the cloaca through its dorsal wall by separate apertures.

(iv) Cloaca: It is a small posterior chamber in which urinogenital ducts open. The cloaca opens outside by the cloacal aperture, guarded by the spincter. Sperms from the testes enter in the urinogenital ducts and finally into the cloaca from where they are expelled out through the cloacal aperture, at the time of *amplexus*.

(v) Fat bodies: These are yellow or orange coloured, ribbon-like structures attached to the anterior side of the testes. They are made up of adipose tissue. Their function is mainly to provide nourishment to the developing testes during hibernation. The fat bodies also reduce the specific gravity of frog and help to maintain floating position in water. They also act as reserve food for the animal during hibernation and aestivation.

4.3.2 Female Reproductive System

The female reproductive system consists of (1) a pair of ovaries, (2) a pair of oviducts (3) cloaca and (4) fat bodies.

(1) Ovaries

These are a pair of irregular shaped essential female reproductive organs. They are attached to the kidneys ventrally and anteriorly by a double fold of peritoneum called *mesovarium*. The ovaries are small and yellowish in colour for most of the year but during the breeding season are greatly enlarged and blackish in colour. The eggs can be seen as black or yellowish spots depending on whether the yellow vegetal half or the black pigmented animal half is facing outward. Each ovary contains about 2000 eggs. The ovaries are hollow and lobulated organs.

When they are immature they are small, yellow and semi-transparent. But when they become mature, the wall of the ovary ruptures, the eggs or primary oocytes are released in the body *cavity*. This process is called *ovulation*.

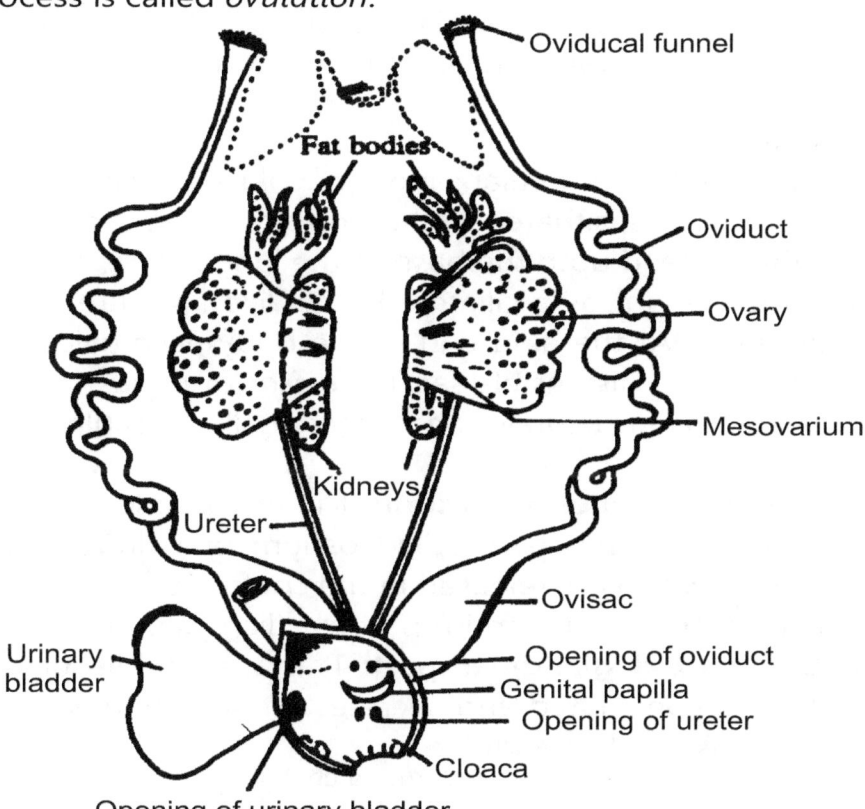

Fig. 4.8: Frog: Female Reproductive System

Histology of Ovary

Histologically, the ovary is a hollow organ filled with lymph and is divided into several compartments by septa. The wall of the ovary is made up of double epithelium with connective tissue called *stroma* in between. The outer wall is called *theca externa* whereas the inner wall is called *theca interna*. The stroma which lies in between these two membranes is connective tissue.

It contains blood capillaries, nerves and groups of germ cells called *germ patches*. The cells of the germinal epithelium give rise to globular masses of cells called ovarian follicles. They are formed by the proliferation of the germinal epithelium. Large number of ovarian follicles are seen in the ovary at different stages of development. They project from the inner wall of the ovary. During development one of the cells of the follicle distinguishes itself as primary *oocyte* or *ovum*, which is surrounded by a non-cellular vitelline membrane. The remaining cells surround the ovum to form a follicular membrane. These follicular cells play an important role for secreting female sex hormone and provide nourishment to the developing ovum. After the release of ovum, ovarian follicles contract and forms a compact body.

(2) Oviducts

These are highly muscular and convoluted yellow or cream coloured long tubules; situated in the body cavity above the ovaries. Anteriorly, they extend upto the base of the lungs. Here, each oviduct opens into the coelom by a ciliated, funnel like aperture, the *ostium* or *oviducal funnel*. At the hind end of the body each oviduct dilates to form a thin walled distensible sac, the *ovisac* or *uterus*.

Each oviduct is structurally and functionally divisible into three regions:

(i) Oviducal funnel or ostium: It is the anterior, straight and broad funnel like ciliated part called ostium or oviducal funnel. It receives the ova, which are released in the coelomic cavity and carries them further towards the posterior part by ciliary action.

(ii) Convoluted glandular part: It is the middle part of the oviduct which is convoluted and secretes an albuminous coating to ova. This region is highly glandular.

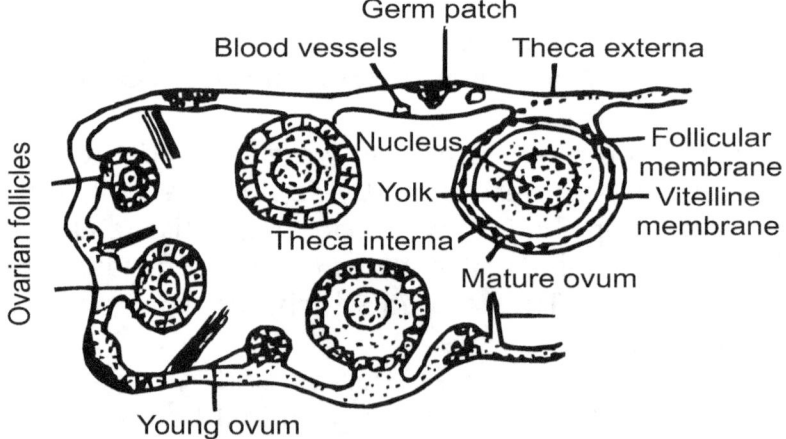

Fig. 4.9: Frog, T.S. of Ovary

(iii) Ovisacs: This is the distal dilated part of the oviducts called ovisac. This part temporarily stores the eggs till they are discharged into the cloaca. The oviducts open dorsally into the cloaca on the raised muscular *genital* papilla situated infront of the opening of ureters.

(3) Cloaca: The cloaca is a median sac or chamber into which ovisacs open. It serves as a common passage for faeces, gametes and urine. It opens out by the *cloacal aperture,* guarded by the cloacal spincter which help in releasing ova only at the time of *aplexus*.

(4) Fat bodies: Towards the anterior end of the ovaries, ribbon or finger like yellow or orange coloured structures called fat bodies are present. Their main function is to provide nourishment to the developing ova during hibernation. The fat bodies also reduce the specific gravity and help to maintain floating in water.

Gametogenesis

Gametes are the sex cells responsible for sexual reproduction. They are formed in the ovary and testes. Gametes are *haploid* and are formed by meiosis or reduction division. The process by which gametes are formed in the gonads is called *gametogensis*. There are two types of gametes, the *male gamete* or *sperm* and the *female gamete* or *ovum*. The process of formation of male gametes or sperms in the *testes* is called *spermatogenesis* and the formation of female gametes or ova in the ovary is called *oogenesis*.

It is a well known fact that as a result of meiotic division of cells, which takes place in germ cells only, the number of chromosomes become half or haploid in the daughter cells. The chromosome number in the parent is *2n* or diploid but due to meiotic division the chromosome number becomes half i.e. haploid or *n*. By the fusion of haploid gametes (ova and sperm) the number of chromosomes in the zygote becomes diploid. In all plant and animal species diploid number of chromosomes is always definite and thus during gametogenesis it becomes half or haploid, otherwise the chromosome number will be further doubled which will give rise to a large number of chromosomes and then there will be no end to it.

Spermatogenesis

The process in which sperms or spermatozoa are produced from primordial germ cells of the testes is called *spermatogenesis*. It starts a little before the breeding period and the entire process takes place in the testes in three phases.

(i) Phase of multiplication, (ii) Phase of growth and (iii) Phase of maturation.

(a) Phase of multiplication: In the testes, the germinal epithelial cells of the seminiferous tubule give rise to primordial or primary germ cells. These cells undergo repeated meiotic divisions producing a large number of diploid (2n) cells called *spermatogonia*. These cells are also called sperm mother cells. They possess diploid or *2n* chromosomes.

(b) Phase of growth: The spermatogonia undergo a slight increase in size, in this phase. These cells accumulate food material in their bodies thus increasing in size. These cells are called *primary spermatocytes*.

(c) Phase of maturation:

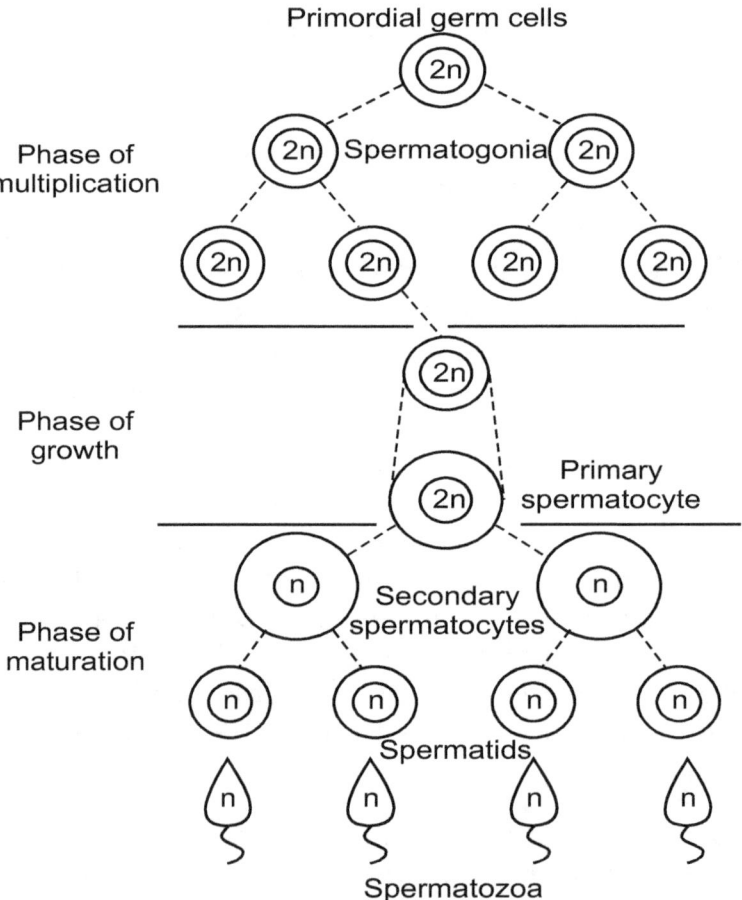

Fig. 4.10: Frog - Spermatogenesis

In this phase, each primary spermatocyte undergoes *meiosis* or *maturation* division. In the phase of maturation, two successive cell divisions take place. The 'first maturation division' is reduction division which results in the formation of two haploid cells called *secondary spermatocytes*. The homologous pair of chromosomes begins to separate and the primary spermatocytes divide into two. After division the homologous chromosomes reach the daughter cells but the chromatids of each chromosome do not separate. Thus, in the first maturation division two secondary spermatocytes are formed. After sometime the secondary spermatocytes divide so that the chromatids also become separate and go to the daughter cells. These daughter cells are called *spermatids* and this division is called 'second maturation division'.

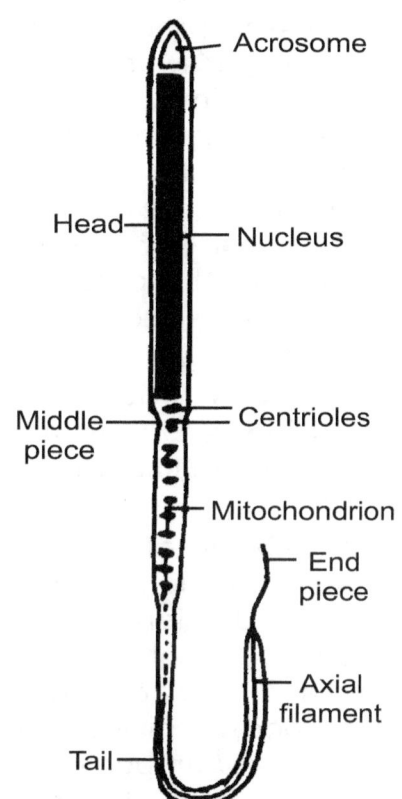

Fig. 4.11: Frog - Spermatozoon

The spermatids are haploid or with 'n' number of chromosomes. In this way one spermatogonium gives rise to four spermatids. The spermatids do not divide further because cell division stops and spermatids undergo metamorphosis. In metamorphosis, the spermatids are transformed into spermatozoa. This process is called *spermatogenesis*. During the process the round spermatid elongates and its posterior end forms a tail or flagellum. This form is called spermatozoon.

Structure of Spermatozoon: The male gamete or sperm is a microscopic initiative and motile structure measuring about 0.03 to 0.04 mm in length. It can be distinguished into three parts:

(i) head,
(ii) middle piece and
(iii) the tail.

The *head* is elongated and contains the nucleus. It forms the anterior part of the sperm. On the head there is a cone like structure called *acrosome*. The acrosome is probably the source of lysin, that helps in the penetration of the sperm into the ovum. The middle piece is the short region and contains proximal and distal centrioles.

The axial filament originates from the distal centrioles and continues into the tail. The middle piece also contains mitochondria which provide energy for movement of the sperm. The tail is the long vibratile part made up of cytoplasmic membrane which contains an axial filament continuous with the distal centriole. The terminal part of the tail without cytoplasmic membrane is called *end piece or flagellum*. The structure of the axial filament is almost the same as that of a cilium or flagellum. It is a hollow tube which possess nine pairs of microfibrils situated equidistantly along its wall. In the centre, there is only one pair of microfibrils.

Oogenesis: The process in which female gamete or ova are formed in the ovaries from the cells of germ patches is called *oogenesis*. This process is partly completed in the ovary, partly in the oviduct and partly after entry of the sperm into the ovum outside the body of the animal.

Like spermatogenesis, in oogenesis also there are three phases: (i) Phase of multiplication, (ii) Phase of growth and (iii) Phase of maturation.

(a) Phase of multiplication: By repeated division in the germinal epithelial cells of the ovary a large number of oogonia cells are formed. These cells are diploid cells.

(b) Phase of growth: From the number of oogonia cell only one cell stops dividing and enters the phase of growth. It gets enlarged in size due to accumulation of yolk. This is called *primary* oocyte. The remaining cells surround the primary oocyte to form an ovarian follicle.

(c) Phase of maturation: The primary oocyte undergoes maturation divisions. There are two maturation divisions. The first maturation division takes place in the oviduct while the second maturation division takes place after the entry of sperm into the ovum. The first maturation division is reduction division in which the primary oocyte divides into two haploid but unequal cells. The chromosome number is haploid i.e. *n*. The larger one is called the secondary oocyte while the smaller one is called the *first polar body*. The second maturation division is equational in which *secondary* oocyte divides unequally to form a large *mature ovum* and a small *second polar body* or second *polocyte*. The first polar body may divide to form two more polar bodies. But they are incapable of reproduction and are thus destroyed. Thus, unlike spermatogenesis a single primary oocyte produces only one functional ovum. The polar bodies eventually disintegrate.

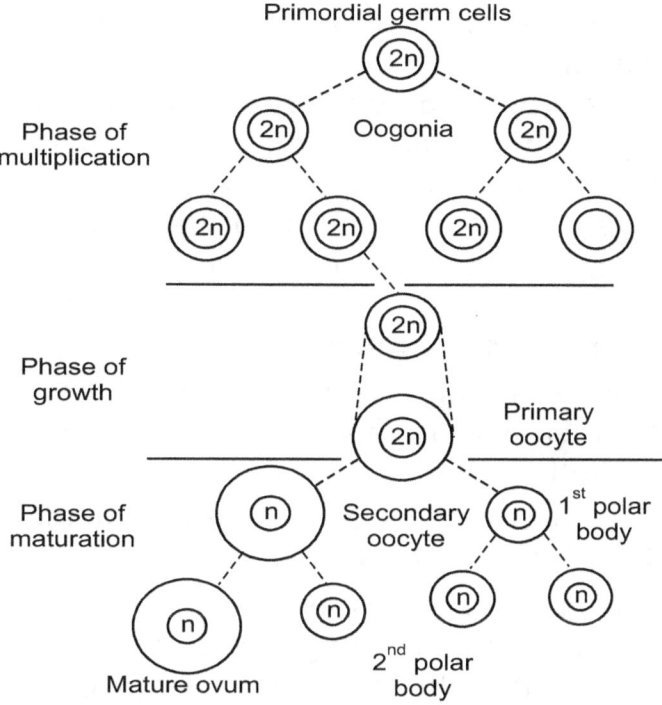

Fig. 4.12: Frog - Oogenesis

Structure of Ovum: The female gamete or egg or ovum is large, non-motile and spherical in shape. Its diameter is about 0.18 to 2 mm. When the egg enters the oviduct it is in a primary oocyte condition. It undergoes division (1st maturation) and divides into large secondary oocyte and first polar body. The polar body is completed only after the sperm enters the eggs. The egg of the frog is *telolecithal* showing an upper *animal pole* in which nucleus cytoplasm, cell organelles and pigment granules are present.

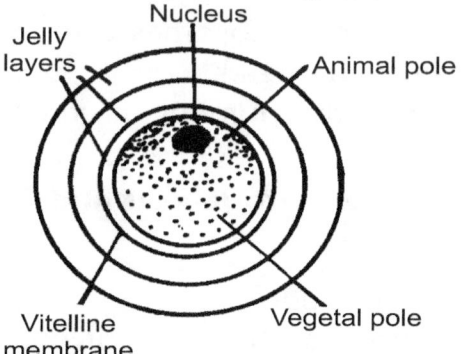

Fig. 4.13: Frog - Egg or Ovum before Fertilization

The lower coloured part is called *vegetal* pole in which a large amount of yolk is present.

The ovum is surrounded by a very thin membrane called *vitelline membrane* or egg membrane. After the entry of sperm it is converted into a *fertilization membrane* which prevents the entry of other sperms. Thin layers of albumin surround the entire ovum. When it is released in water, the albumin layers swell to form jelly or tertiary membranes.

Functions of Tertiary Membranes
1. The jelly or tertiary membranes help the eggs to attach to each other and to aquatic plants so that they are not washed off.
2. The jelly makes eggs distasteful to aquatic animals hence getting protection from enemies.
3. The membranes act as lenses therefore their temperature increases by concentrating the sun's rays on it. This helps in development of the frog in cold weather.
4. Jelly protects eggs from mechanical injuries.
5. The algae adhere to the membrane which carry out photosynthesis and provide oxygen necessary for development.

Significance of Gametogenesis
1. In the process of gametogenesis haploid male and female gametes are produced from testes and ovaries.
2. The gametes are essential for fertilization and production of a new individual.
3. The doubling of chromosomes takes place by the union of male and female gametes.
4. It helps to keep the number of chromosomes constant in that individual.

Comparison between Spermatogenesis and Oogenesis

Spermatogenesis	Oogenesis
1. It is a process of formation of sperms from germ mother cells in testes.	1. It is a process of formation of ova from germ cells in ovaries.

Spermatogenesis	Oogenesis
2. This entire process takes place in testes.	2. It partly takes place in the ovary, partly in oviduct and partly after the entry of the sperm into the ovum.
3. All spermatogonia are active and enter the phase of growth.	3. Only one oogonium from each group undergoes the growth phase.
4. First reduction division is equal. Two equal secondary spermatocytes are formed.	4. First reduction division is unequal, one large secondary oocyte and one small first polar body is formed.
5. Second maturation division (cytoplasmic) is equal and each secondary spermatocyte forms two equal size spermatids.	5. Second maturation division (cytoplasmic) is unequal. A secondary oocyte forms a large ovum and two small polar bodies. First polar body forms two small (equal) polocytes.
6. No polar bodies are formed.	6. Polar bodies are formed.
7. Spermatozoon is formed by metamorphosis of spermatid.	7. There is no metamorphosis in the formation of the mature ovum.
8. The spermatids form small tailed mobile spermatozoa.	8. Ovum is large, without tail and immobile.
9. One spermatogonium forms four spermatozoa.	9. One oogonium forms one ovum only.

Breeding

The success of reproduction depends on special breeding habits in animals. In frogs, the breeding season lasts from June to September. During breeding season both males and females become highly excited. They show peculiar behaviour during this period. The male frogs generally gather in shallow water pond in considerable number and during night time start croaking in chorus.

Due to the presence of vocal sacs the croaking sound is amplified in males. This croaking sound is mainly for recognition of sex but also serves as an invitation or call to female for coming to the breeding ground. This sound attracts females from the surrounding areas of the pond. When they come in the pond, the male selects a gravid female and mounts on her back clasping her firmly behind her forelimbs.

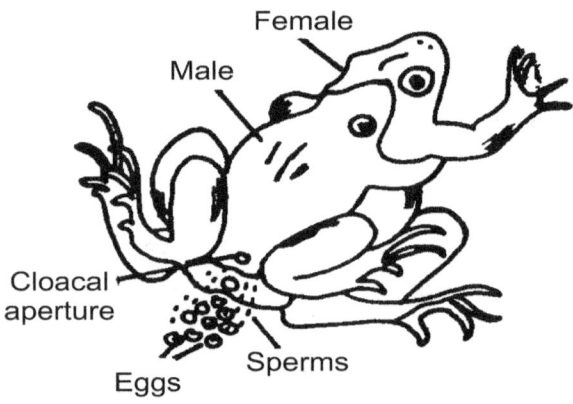

Fig. 4.14: Frog Amplexus

The nuptial pads in males are well developed during the breeding season which help in firmly gripping the female. The mounting of the male on the back of the female is called *amplexus* or *sexual embrace*. There is no true copulation in frog hence it is called *pseudo copulation*. The stimulation for mounting comes from a *hormone* secreted by the *anterior pituitary* lobe.

Amplexus is an instinctive behaviour and a spinal reflex. Sometimes, the clasping instinct of the male frog is so strong that the female is killed by the violent embrace. During amplexus the male is smaller in size than the female hence it remains passive and easily carried by the female. Female frogs remain in the vicinity of the pond water and swim.

The amplexus continues for many days during which the female is coaxed to lay eggs. When eggs are laid by the female in water the male sheds spermatic fluid over them and the mates then separate.

Spawning

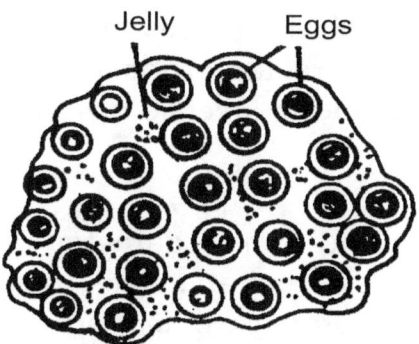

Fig. 4.15: Frog - Spawn

The process of releasing eggs in bunches or groups in the surrounding water is called *spawning* or *oviposition*. This occurs during amplexus. When the eggs are released in water the thin layers of albumin swells-up forming a sticky jelly. This jelly binds the eggs together into one large gelatinous frothy mass called spawn. Thus, in the spawn spermatozoa and eggs are present. The expulsion of eggs by a female may take place in a single act or by repeated expulsions. In spawn the pigmented area of the eggs is always in the upper half while the heavy yolk laden portion lie below. The jelly covering is useful for eggs in many ways.

- The jelly glues the eggs together and protects the eggs from cold, attack of microorganisms and aquatic insects.
- The distasteful jelly makes spawn inedible to fish and birds. The jelly and pigmented part of the egg absorbs solar heat and makes the eggs warmer than the water.
- The spawn is usually laid in heavy aquatic vegetation to which their jelly covering makes them adherent.

Embryology

After fertilization of the egg it undergoes development and forms the organism. Before hatching or birth the early stage of the development of an organism is called *embryo*. *Embryology* is that branch of biology which deals with the development of embryo. Fertilized eggs or the zygote undergoes many events which follow one after another. These events change a simple zygote into a new individual. This tiny structure carries large number of potentialities of producing a complex organism.

The series of events which convert the very small and tiny zygote into an organism are fertilization, cleavage, blastulation, gastrulation, organogeny. Growth and metamorphosis are two post embryonic events through which a young juvenile or larval stage matures into a new adult.

Fertilization

The union of male and female gametes i.e. sperm and ovum is called fertilization. It is external and takes place in the surrounding water after mating or amplexus. During amplexus, female frog deposits eggs in water in bunches called spawn and at the same time the male frog also sheds the spermatic fluid over the spawn. Thus, both the gametes are in close association and hence the sperm enters the egg before the jelly covering coat of egg absorbs the surrounding water and swells. The unfertilized egg dies in a short period but because of fertilization the life of the egg is saved and it undergoes further changes. Thus, fertilization makes the egg immortal.

Fertilization is considered as a two fold process: first *activation* and second *amphimixing* i.e. mixing of hereditary (nuclear and chromosomal) material. The sperm enters the egg usually in the animal pole within 40 degrees. Generally, the sperm penetrates at the spot which is the elevation of the vitelline membrane away from the egg. The acrosome present on the head of the sperm also secretes an enzyme which facilitates penetration of the sperm.

Only the head and the middle piece of the sperm enter, the tail breaking away. Immediately after sperm entry, the vitelline membrane surrounding the egg is converted into the *fertilization membrane*. This is nothing but the activation of the egg. This fertilization membrane prevents the entry of other sperms. Thus, there is no polyspermy or multiple sperm invasion of the egg. This is achieved by negative chemical and/or physical reaction of the egg towards any extra spermatozoa after one of them has made contact with the egg surface.

During fertilization generally only one sperm nucleus normally fuses with the egg nucleus. If any additional sperms are successful in invading, the egg attempts to divide independently of the egg nucleus and then degenerate. Extensive polyspermy which may occur in aged eggs, interferes drastically with the cleavage mechanism and the eggs reach an early cytolysis and death. After the entry of the sperm, the second maturation division is completed. As a result, the ovum and the second polar body are formed.

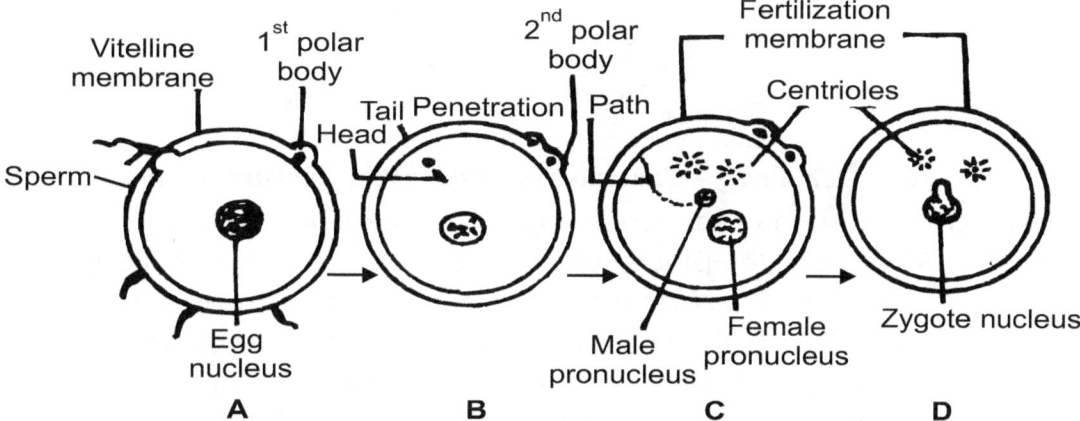

Fig. 4.16: Frog - Process of Fertilization of Egg.
A. Egg and Sperm, B. Entry of Sperm, C. Male and Female Pronucleus
D. Formation of Zygote Nucleus

The sperm contact and penetration of the egg has two immediate effects. The *first* effect is to allow the superficial jelly to swell to its maximum by *imbibition*. Due to the swelling of the jelly the thickness of the three jelly layer is several times the diameter of the egg. The *second* effect is an almost immediate loss of water from one egg so that a space appears between the egg surface and the enveloping vitelline membrane or fertilization membrane. This space is called *perivitelline space,* filled with a fluid, within which the egg is free to rotate.

Penetration path and copulation path: The sperm head generally makes a direct perpendicular contact with the egg cortex through the unswollen jelly and the vitelline membrane. Usually, the entire sperm i.e. head and middle piece enters the egg, but the tail is left behind. As the sperm moves towards the egg nucleus, its path is marked from the surface of the egg. The initial path taken by the sperm is called *penetration path* which is usually along the egg radius. The path taken by the sperm later on to meet the egg nucleus is called *copulation path.* When a sperm enters the egg it takes along with it some of the pigment granules of the surface or cortical layer.

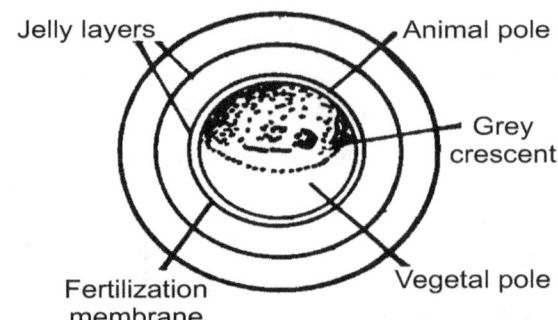

Fig. 4.17: Frog - Structure of Egg after Fertilization

Thus, a cone shaped penetration path can be seen. This path is straight. The middle piece of the sperm containing centrioles separates from the head or male nucleus. The sperm nucleus in the egg is now called male pronucleus and the egg nucleus is called female pronucleus. The male and female pronuclei approach each other and fuse to form a *zygote nucleus* without the nuclear membrane. Then the zygote moves towards the centre and forms the *cleavage path*. After fertilization the zygote nucleus contains diploid (2n) number of chromosomes. In frog *Rana tigrina* the diploid number of chromosomes are 26. If fertilization does not take place within 24 hours, the sperms and ova die.

After an hour of zygote formation in between the animal and vegetal pole, there is loss of pigment from the surface of the egg which is neither black nor white but is grey. This crescentic area of grey colour is called grey crescent which is formed due to migration of pigments. It is formed exactly opposite to the point of entry of the sperm. It establishes the grey crescent plan and it transforms the radial symmetry of the zygote to a bilateral symmetry. The grey crescent is entirely a surface phenomenon and is no way concerned with fusion of nuclei.

It is the response to sperm penetration. The region of the grey crescent will become the posterior side and the opposite i.e. the region of sperm entrance will become the anterior side of the future embryo. The grey crescent also marks the point of formation of *blastopore* which indicates the posterior end of the future embryo. Thus, the grey crescent is significant in the following respects:

(i) It marks the posterior end of the embryo,
(ii) It indicates the plane of first cleavage,

(iii) It converts radial symmetry of the zygote into bilateral symmetry and
(iv) It indicates that the egg is fertilized.

Significance of Fertilization

Fertilization brings about the following changes in the zygote for further development:

1. The activation of the egg takes place by the entry of the sperm.
2. The grey crescent appears opposite the entry of the sperm.
3. The volume of the egg decreases by water loss and perivitelline space is formed; filled with fluid, within which the egg is free to rotate.
4. After entry of the sperm the vitelline membrane is converted into the fertilization membrane which prevents further entry of sperms. Thus, polyspermy is avoided.
5. The centrioles are introduced due to fertilization which are lacking in the mature egg.
6. After the entry of the sperm, the second maturation division is completed in which the mature ovum and second polar body are formed from the secondary oocyte.
7. By the fusion of two haploid gametes diploid condition is restored.
8. Due to fertilization new genetic combination is formed, which is responsible for variations and
9. Fertilization stimulates egg to undergo cleavage.

Structure of a Fertilized egg (Zygote)

The fertilized egg or zygote of the frog *Rana tigrina* is round and its diameter is about 0.18 cm. The zygote is now surrounded by a fertilization membrane and three jelly coats (layers) which are thicker than the diameter of the zygote. The fertilized egg is called telolecithal egg because cytoplasm is at the animal pole and yolk at the vegetal pole. The cytoplasmic pole is pigmented and is called animal pole while the cream coloured yolk laden pole is called vegetal pole.

In between the animal and vegetal pole a crescentic area of grey colour is present called *grey crescent*. This area is formed opposite to the entry of the sperm due to migration of pigment. In the zygote due to immediate loss of water from the egg space appears between the egg surface and the enveloping vitelline membrane now known as the fertilization membrane. This space is known as perivitelline space containing a fluid which facilitates rotation of egg. Polar bodies are present in the perivitelline space.

Development of Frog

The fertilized egg or zygote undergoes development. Development is a complicated process in which gradual and orderly change of zygote into a multicellular organism takes place. In case of frog *Rana tigrina* development takes place in two phases. They are:

1. Embryonic development: In this phase, the zygote undergoes series of stages such as cleavage, blastulation, gastrulation, formation of three germinal layers and organogeny. During this phase the zygote is transformed into the embryo which is ready to hatch.

2. Post-embryonic development: When the embryo escapes by rupturing the fertilization membrane. It is called hatching. The newly hatched young is called larva which is dissimilar to the parents. The changes from larva to the juvenile frog is called post-embryonic development. It includes metamorphosis.

Embryonic Development

Embryonic development includes the following important stages:

1. Cleavage

- The mitotic division of an unicellular zygote or fertilized egg into multicellular embryo takes place by a process called *cleavage* or *segmentation*.
- In frogs, cleavage is *holoblastic* and *unequal*. It is holoblastic because during each division the zygote divides completely from pole to pole, but unequal because the cells formed are unequal in size.
- The cleavage always begins at the animal pole where less amount of yolk is present. The cleavage follows certain laws.
- There are four major cleavage laws, known by the names of those who first emphasized their importance. They are:

1. Pfluger's law: According to this law the spindle elongates in the direction of least resistance.

2. Balfour's law: The rate of cleavage tends to be governed by the inverse ratio of the amount of yolk present in holoblastic cleavage. The yolk tends to impede division of both the nucleus and the cytoplasm.

3. Sach's law: Cells tend to divide into equal parts and each new plane of division tends to bisect the previous plane at right angles.

4. **Hertwig's law:** The nucleus and its spindle are generally found in the centre of active protoplasm and the axis of any division spindle lies in the longest axis of the protoplasmic mass. Divisions tend to cut the protoplasmic masses at right angles to their axes.

The First Cleavage

It is at right angles to the grey crescent and meridonial i.e. the cleavage is vertical but passes through the centre. This divides the zygote into two equal cells called blastomeres. The first cleavage starts after 2.5 hours after fertilization. There appears a very short inverted fold near the centre of the pigmented and slightly depressed animal pole cortex.

This depression is extended in both directions and in the animal pole which is nothing but the first cleavage furrow. In the beginning, furrow is very superficial, it later extends from centre of the animal pole around the zygote towards the vegetal pole. This is the first vertical cleavage.

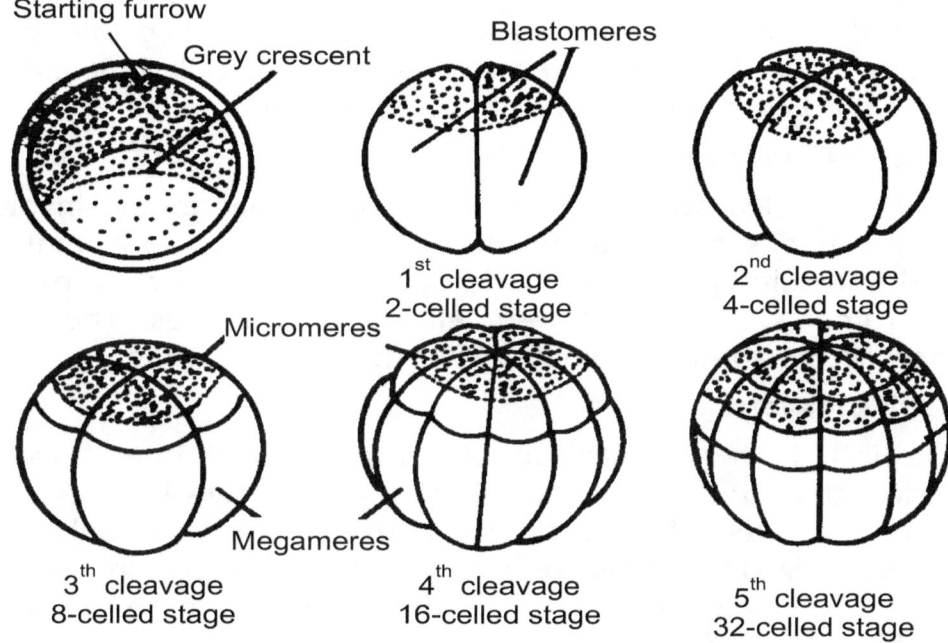

Fig. 4.18: Frog - Cleavage of Egg

The Second Cleavage

Before the first cleavage furrow has completely encircled the zygote a second furrow begins at the centre of the animal pole and at right angles to the first furrow. Thus, second cleavage is also meridonial or vertical but at right angles to the first cleavage plane. It divides the zygote into four blastomers. The second cleavage first begins to appear at about one hour after the completion of the first cleavage. The four blastomeres which are formed after the second cleavage are not qualitatively identical. Because the two blastomeres contain part of the grey crescent while two are without any part of the grey crescent.

The Third Cleavage

The third cleavage begins about 30 minutes after the second is completed. The cleavage rate is accelerated with each division. The third cleavage is *horizontal* but *latitudinal* i.e. a little above the equatorial plane and at right angles to both the first and second cleavages. It is slightly above the level of equator, above 60° to 70° from the centre of the animal pole. This shifting of the cleavage plane towards the animal pole is due to the presence of more cytoplasm and less yolk in this region. Yolk is generally resistant to cleavage. The third cleavage divides the zygote into eight cells of which the four slightly smaller cells at the animal pole are called *micromeres* and four large ones towards the vegetal pole are called *megameres*. Thus, the third cleavage forms eight unequal cells.

The Fourth Cleavage

The fourth cleavage is meridonial but generally double, involving two simultaneous cleavages in meridonial plane at right angles to each other resulting in the formation of 16 cells of which upper cells are micromeres and the lower cell are megameres. The fourth cleavage occurs about 20 minutes after the third cleavage.

The Fifth Cleavage

The fifth cleavage is also double but latitudinal, one above and one below the third division; forming in all 32 - cells in four tiers of eight each. After this, the cleavage becomes irregular. The micromeres divide rapidly due to cytoplasm in them but the megameres divide slowly due to the presence of a large quantity of inert yolk.

2. Blastulation

As a result of cleavage a single walled hollow ball of cells is formed. Internally, at the 8-celled stage a small cavity is formed at the animal pole called *segmentation cavity* or *blastocoel* and the embryo is called *blastula*. This process is called blastulation. Blastulation starts at the 8-celled stage. As the cells go on dividing their number increases and the segmentation or blastocoel cavity inside also increases. The cavity is filled with an albuminous fluid arising from the surrounding cells. The blastula is called *coeloblastula* as the blastocoel is relatively large. The blastocoel is eccentric as it is more towards the animal pole.

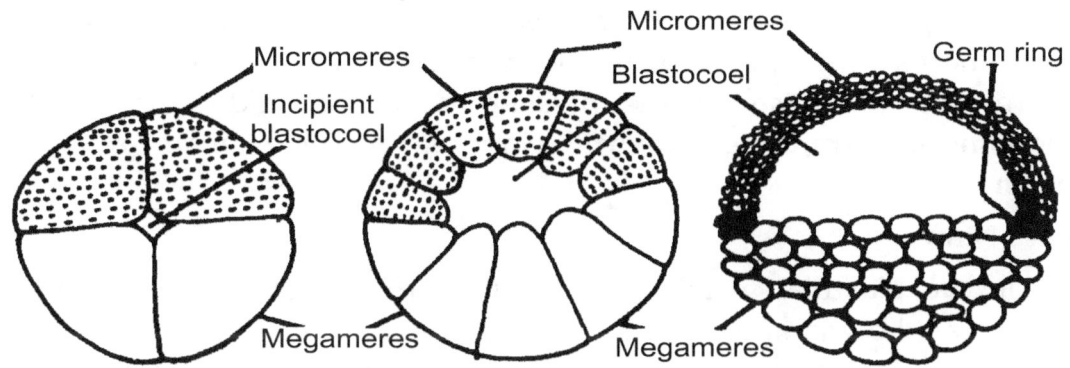

Fig. 4.19: V.S. of 8-celled Stage, V.S. of Early Blastula, V.S. of Late Blastula

The blastula is distinguished into early blastula and the late blastula.

Early blastula

The early blastula consists of a single layer of cells. The cells are 32 in number at this stage. The pigmented micromeres are present towards the animal pole and yolky megameres are seen below, towards the vegetal pole. The macro and megameres enclose the small blastocoel in between them.

The late blastula

The repeated cleavages result into the formation of a large number of cells. The blastocoel inside the blastula also increases. The blastocoel has an arched roof and flat floor and is located in the anterior half of the blastula or in the animal pole. The arched roof of the blastula is made up of 2 to 3 layers of pigmented micromeres. The floor of the blastocoel is formed by few layers of large yolky cells or megameres. Between the micromeres and the megameres and along the equator of the blastula, the cells are of intermediate size. These cells form the *marginal belt* or marginal zone or *germ ring*.

It is believed that here the yolk is actively transformed into cytoplasm and the cells divide more rapidly than the other cells. This germ ring is also concerned with the formation of the lips of the future blastopore. The marginal zone or germ ring is formed in the region of grey crescent. Opposite to this grey crescent region the wall of the blastula appears to contain relatively more layers of cells and is therefore somewhat thicker. These changes are essential for the next process in embryonic development called *gastrulation*. The micromeres form the *ectoderm* or the outer layer. The cells of the germ ring give rise to the *mesoderm* or the middle layer. The megameres form the *endoderm* or inner layer. These layers are called germ layers.

Fate Maps

In the blastula, certain areas called presumptive organ forming areas can be marked out. These areas are so called because it is presumed that they give rise to particular organs or tissues of the adult frog. The arrangement of the presumptive organ forming areas in the blastula has been mapped out. Such maps are called *fate maps* since they indicate the fate of the presumptive areas.

Fate maps are prepared at the blastula stage by removing certain groups of cells or by injecting certain areas of the blastula with vital dyes like Nile blue sulphate, Janus green and Neutral red and then following the movement of the coloured cells during development. In the blastula, the anterior half of the blastula consists of pigmented *ectoderm* cells, the posterior half of yolky *endoderm* cells with a ring of *mesoderm* in between. The ectoderm is divided into two regions, the *presumptive epidermis* and the *presumptive neural plate region*. The presumptive epidermis is present on the anterior, ventral and lateral parts of the anterior or animal pole.

The presumptive neural plate occupies the dorsal and lateral part of the animal pole. The head develops from the anterior parts of the neural plate and epidermal regions. In the epidermal region of the head are formed paired presumptive areas of *suckers*, *lenses* and *ears*. The presumptive *eye* region occupies the mid dorsal part of the neural plate region of the head.

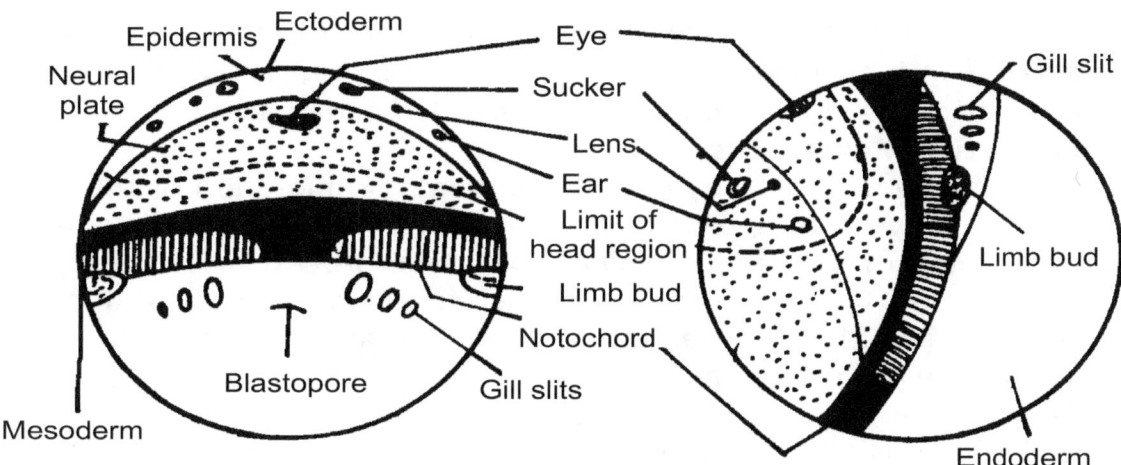

Fig. 4.20: Fate Maps

The mesoderm forms a ring between the ectoderm and the endoderm. It is divided into *presumptive notochordal* and somites region. The presumptive notochord occupies the dorsal part of the ring, with a pair of arms extending laterally. The somites form a band encircling almost the entire ring except for the dorsal part occupied by the presumptive notochord. The endoderm (yolky cells) occupies the posterior half or vegetal pole of the blastula with three pairs of visceral pouches.

3. Gastrulation

Gastrulation is a process of rearrangement and reorganisation of the cells of blastula in which the three germ layers are formed. Thus, gastrulation is a conversion of the single walled blastula into the double walled stage called *gastrula*. The presumptive organ forming areas get rearranged and reorganised to take their respective position. Once gastrula is formed, the cells of the three germ layers i.e. ectoderm, endoderm and mesoderm are no more in the presumptive stage. The fate of these cells becomes definite. Another feature of gastrulation is the formation of the *archenteron* or gut cavity. The commencement of gastrulation is marked by a small depression.

This is the beginning of *archenteron formation* and the opening of the archenteron is called dorsal lip of *blastopore*. At this stage, blastocoel is well developed. It is roofed dorsally by the *neural plate*. Behind the neural plate is the *notochordal plate*. The *epidermis* lies on the anterior, lateral and ventral side. The *mesoderm* is present on the equator in the form of a dorsally incomplete ring. The posterior half consists of the yolky *endoderm*. This is called early gastrula.

Formative Movements

Gastrula is formed by mass movements or migration of cells of a determinative nature, called *formative movements*. These movements are mainly of two types 'epiboly' or over growth and emboly or invagination. Both processes take place simultaneously. In addition to this closure of blastopore, rotation and elongation are the processes which take place simultaneously.

Epiboly

Epiboly is the overgrowth of cells. This takes place because the micromeres contain more cytoplasm than megameres, and divide rapidly. It involves overgrowth of ectoderm forming cells over and around the endoderm forming region. In other words, it is the encroachment of micromeres over megameres. In the beginning, the ectodermal cells move towards the grey crescent and then the movement continues laterally and ventrally from all sides. Finally, because of the encroachment of the ectodermal cell the entire embryo is covered by pigmented micromeres except for a small area of megameres called yolk plug.

In the region of the *yolk plug* the micromeres instead of growing forward turn inwards forming dorsal, lateral and ventral lips which join to form a circular groove called *blastopore* around the yolk plug described in emboly. Thus, epiboly results in the formation of a complete outer layer of micromeres called *ectoderm* and also marks the future end of the embryo (blastopore).

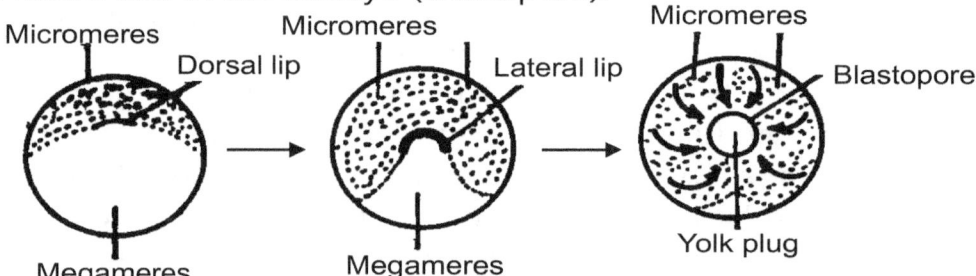

Fig. 4.21: Epiboly

Emboly

This is another type of formative movement which includes two processes, namely, invagination and involution. Both the processes occur simultaneously.

1. Invagination: The insinking of the cells in the region of grey crescent is called invagination. First, a small depression or crescentic groove forms a cavity called archenteron in the area of the grey crescent. The archenteron is also called gastrocoel or secondary body cavity which is nothing but the beginning of future gut. The external opening of the archenteron is called the blastopore. During invagination, the archenteron increases the size and the blastocoel is reduced to a small slit like cavity.

2. Involution: The inturning and inspreading of invaginated cells from the margin of the blastopore through archenteron is called *involution*. The in-rolling of the cells start above the archenteron forming a double walled fold called dorsal lip. As more and more cells turn inwards, the dorsal lip extends downwards forming lateral lips resulting in a horse shoe shaped groove which meet ventrally to form the *ventral lip*. Thus, a circular groove called *blastopore* is formed through which endodermal cells are seen as the yolk plug.

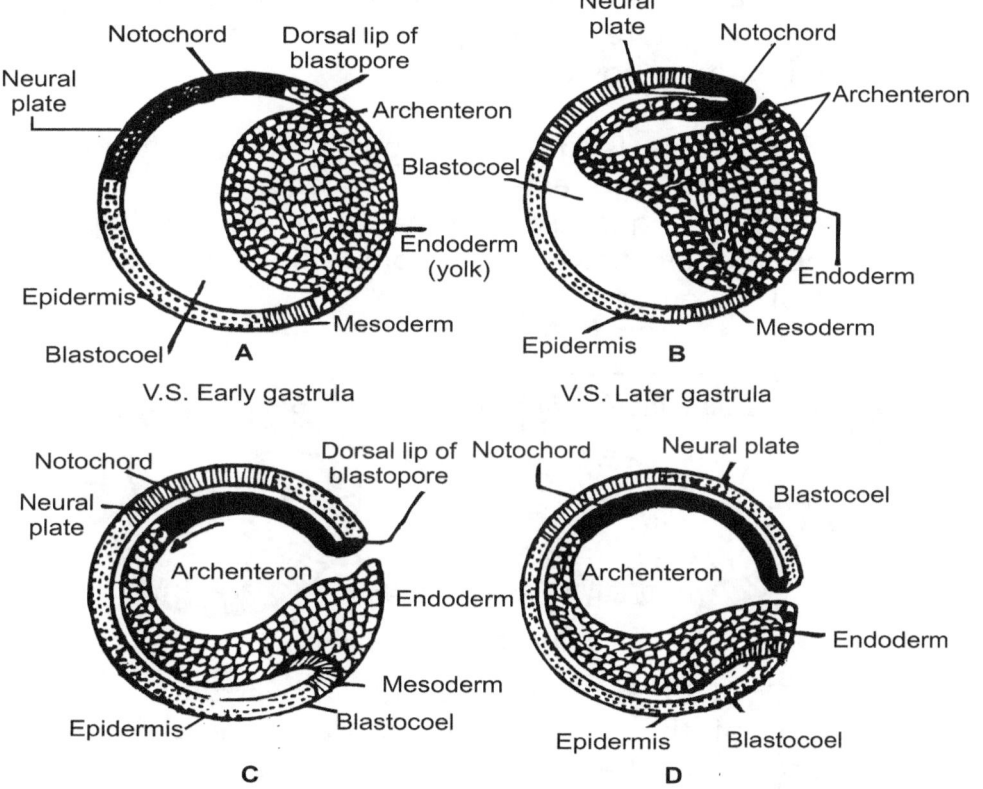

Fig. 4.22: V.S. through Various Stages of Gastrula

At first the endoderm cells are invaginated, i.e. endodermis material turn inwards. The cells of the notochord and mesoderm which were external, now turn inwards from the margin of blastopore and become internal. As the epiboly advances, the emboly also advances simultaneously involving more and more cells inside. As a result, the archenteron or gastrocoel goes on decreasing till its existence is lost and reduced to a slit like cavity. The involuted cells form a distinct second layer called *chorda mesentoderm* on the roof of the archenteron differentiated into middle notochordal and lateral mesodermal sheets, the cells of which were formerly external and on one side endodermal cells form the anterior and ventral wall of the archenteron.

Rotation

During gastrulation, the archenteron increases in size and simultaneously the blastocoel decreases in size. The yolk cells are heavy due to the presence of yolk in them. These heavy yolk cells become rearranged. They show displacement on one side. This results in a gradual change in the centre of gravity of the gastrula. The embryo now rotates through more than 90° taking the blastopore to the future posterior end.

Elongation

The embryo shows lengthwise growth. The notochordal and mesodermal cells undergo extending movements. As a result of extension, the spherical gastrula becomes elongated in shape. At this stage the embryo gets flattened on one side marking the future dorsal surface of the embryo.

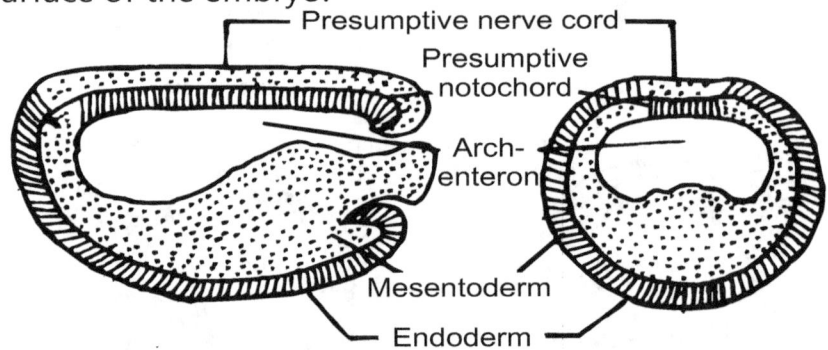

Fig. 4.23: Frog - L.S. and T.S. of gastrula

The margins of the lips of the blastopore now contract. The blastopore becomes oval and gradually disappears. Thus, at the end of gastrulation, the embryo is converted into a double walled stage gastrula showing outer ectoderm with a middorsal neural plate and inner chorda mesentoderm with middorsal notochordal cells and enclosing a new cavity called archenteron.

Late Gastrula or Three Germinal Layers Stage

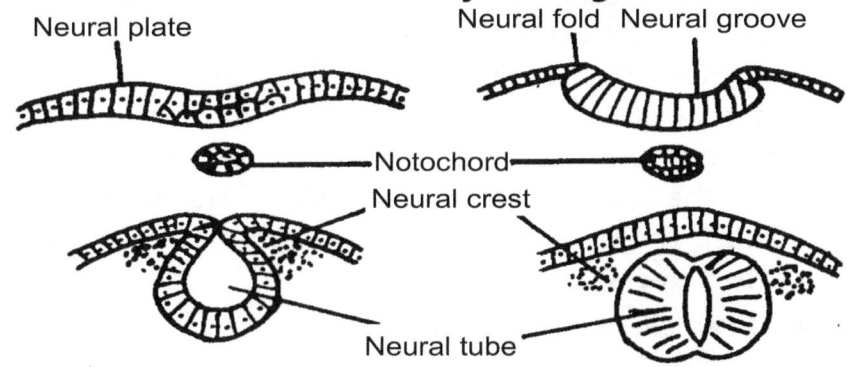

Fig. 4.24: Frog - Formation of Neural Tube

The elongated gastrula becomes flat on the middorsal side to form the *neural plate*. It is continuous on all sides with the epidermis. The notochord lies below the neural plate. The neural plate sinks downwards and undergoes folding. These are called neural folds. The neural folds enclose a neural groove. Later on the neural folds converge dorsally to form a *neural tube*. The cells of the chorda-mesentoderm in mid dorsal line soon get detached and by proliferation give rise to a solid cylindrical rod called *notochord*. Simultaneously, the mesoderm grows downwards and meets in the midventral line. A split begins to appear in the dorsal mesoderm, which then extends ventrally.

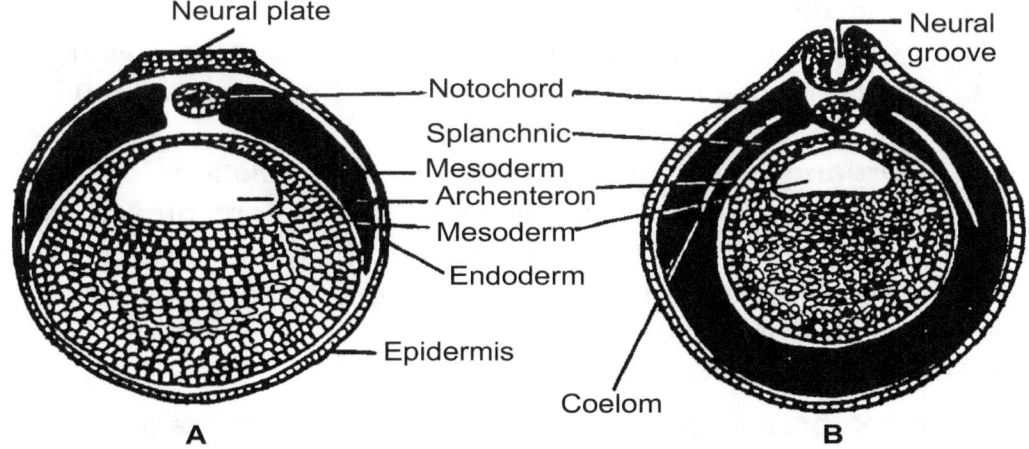

Fig. 4.25: A. Neural Plate Stage. B. Neural Groove Stage

This separates the outer *somatic mesoderm* from an inner *splanchnic mesoderm*. The space between the two form the coelom. The lateral mesoderm cells extend downwards and meet midventrally to form complete mesoderm layer. The endodermal cells placed ventrally and laterally further divide, grow upwards along the sides, converge and meet middorsally below the notochord to form the complete inner layer of endoderm enclosing a cavity now called *enteron*. The embryo now at the end of gastrulation show three distinct layers, the outer ectoderm, middle mesoderm and inner endoderm. These three layers are called germinal layers because all the cells of these layers are capable of division.

Fate of the Three Germinal Layers

The ectoderm, endoderm and mesoderm are the three germinal layers which give rise to definite tissues and organs in a frog. Each germinal layer gives rise to organs as stated below:

1. Ectoderm: The ectoderm consists of the neural plate and the epidermis region. The epidermis forms the outer layer of the skin, lining of the stomodaeum and proctodaeum, cornea, lens and retina of the eye. The neural plate gives rise to the brain, spinal cord i.e. nervous system.

2. Mesoderm: It gives rise to the dermis of the skin, the muscular, skeletal system, circulatory system, excretory system, connective tissues, peritoneum, urinogenital systems including organs like kidneys, gonads and heart.

3. Endoderm: The endoderm forms the lining of the alimentary canal, digestive glands like liver and pancreas with their ducts, endocrine glands and the lining of the lungs and urinary bladder.

4. Organogeny: At the end of gastrulation ectoderm, endoderm and mesoderm and give rise to different organs called organogeny. Thus, the embryo before hatching develops muscles, alimentary canal, liver, tympanic cavities, eustachian tubes, tail, gills, suckers, eye, mucous gland etc.

Post Embryonic Development

In the embryonic period, the embryo remains in the fertilization membrane. After completion of embryonic development the embryo ruptures the fertilization membrane and this process is called hatching. After hatching the young one, which is quite different from its parents, is called *larva*. The larva of the frog is called 'tadpole larva'. The larva is aquatic. Post embryonic development leads to the formation of the juvenile frog from the larva.

Metamorphosis

Metamorphosis is the process in which the larva undergoes series of external and internal changes to attain the juvenile frog stage. These modifications or changes are termed as metamorphic changes. There are many larval forms which are transitional stages in the life history of the frog. These are stages in adaptation to changes in habitat and the type of food available. Following are the types of important stages:

1. Newly hatched tadpole: The hatching of the tadpole takes place about 14 days after fertilization. The newly hatched larva has a fish like appearance. The tadpole is about 5 to 7 mm in length. It shows a large head, fusiform body, short stumy tail and two pairs of rudimentary gills on the lateral sides behind the head. The larva neither has a mouth for feeding nor tail for swimming.

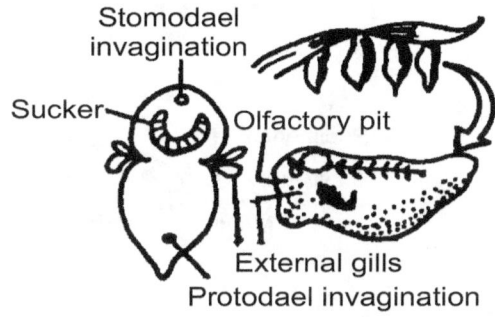

Fig. 4.26: Newly Hatched Tadpole (ventral view)

Hence, it remains attached to aquatic weeds by an horse shoe-shaped *sucker* or cement gland situated on the ventral side of the head. During this period the yolk is utilised as food material and the skin and two pairs of gills assist for respiration.

The stomodaeum and proctodaeum are also seen as depressions ventrally at the anterior and posterior ends.

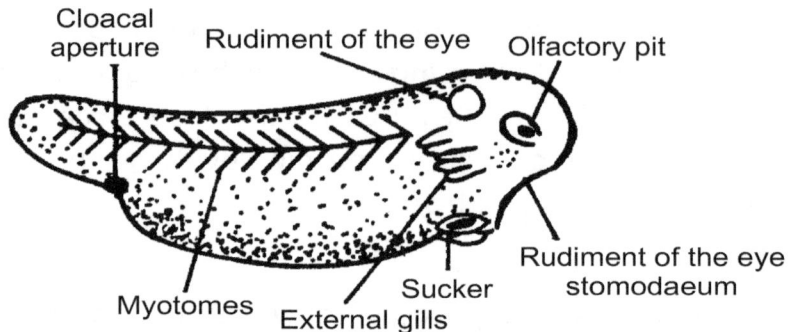

Fig. 4.27: Frog - Tadpole on Hatching

2. Tadpole with three pairs of external gills: As the tadpole larva grows, a third pair of external gills appear. These gills become branched getting a rich vascular supply. The larval body is divided into the trunk and tail region. The tail is elongated and shows myotomes or muscle segments and develops dorsal and ventral fin folds. Thus, the tail is used for locomotion. The stomodaeum opens infront by a mouth provided with a pair of horny jaws and posteriorly proctodaeum opens by an anal aperture. The mouth is used for feeding and the tail for swimming; thus a tadpole larva leads a free swimming life. It also shows rudimentary eyes and nasal pits on the head. It feeds on aquatic vegetable matter. The intestine gets elongated and at the same time the suckers go on diminishing and is ultimately lost.

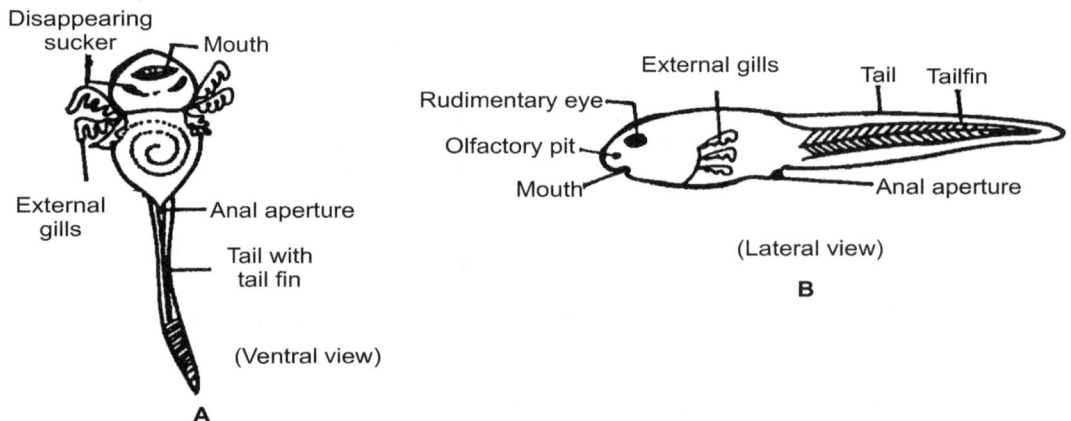

Fig. 4.28: A Tadpole with Three Pairs of External Gills

3. Tadpole with internal gills: At this stage the external gills begin to disappear and in place of these gill slits or branchial clefts are formed. Internal gills are formed within the gill slits. The length of the tadpole is about 11 mm. A fold of skin appears called *operculum* which covers the internal gills. It encloses a cavity called *opercular cavity*. This cavity opens only on the left side by a single aperture called spiracle. The tadpole now breathes like a fish. Water is drawn into the pharynx through the mouth and pumped out over the internal gills. A constant current of water is maintained by the lowering and raising of the floor of the pharynx coupled with the opening and closing of the mouth. Like a fish it also develops a two chambered heart and lateral line sense organs. They also get elongated with increased number of myotomes. At this stage the tadpole also shows limb buds. Hindlimb buds are clearly visible but forelimb buds are hidden in the opercular chamber. The tadpole feeds on vegetable matter, the intestine elongates further and is seen as a double spiral through the semi-transparent skin of the ventral side.

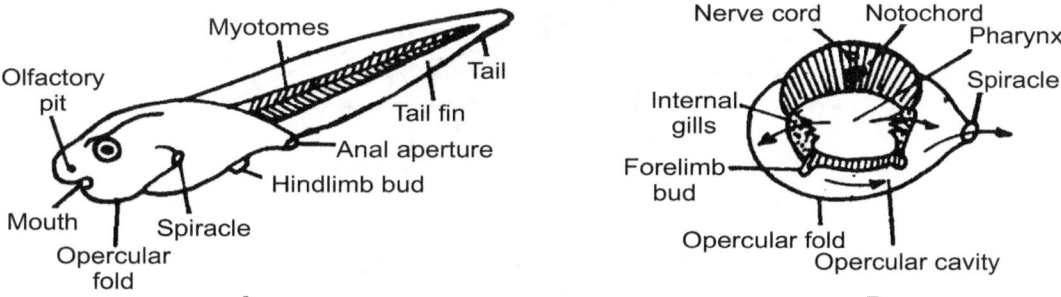

**Fig. 4.29: A. Fish-like Tadpole, Internal Gill Stage
B. T.S. through Opercular Fold**

4. **Tadpole with hind limbs:** As development proceeds the hindlimb buds gradually develop into hindlimbs and as seen first. The forelimb buds also grow but remain hidden beneath the operculum. The internal gills begin to degenerate and eyes start bulging out.

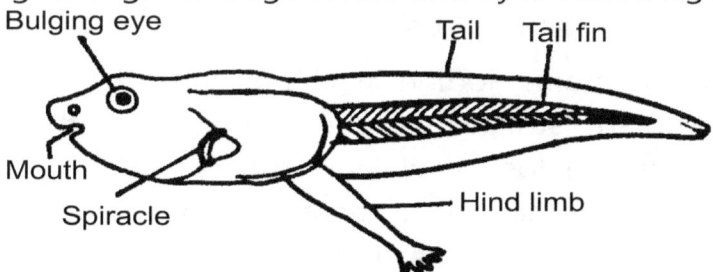

Fig. 4.30: Hindlimb Stage

5. Tadpole with forelimbs: It is also called climatic metamorphosis which prepares the tadpole for semi-aquatic or amphibious life. At this stage the forelimb buds develop into forelimbs. The left forelimb comes out through the spiracle while the right forelimb comes out by rupturing the opercular fold. The internal gills degenerate completely, gill slits close down and the opercular fold fuses with the skin of the head. The lungs appear as a pair of out growths from the gut. The nasal pits break through as *internal nares* into the mouth cavity. At this stage the tadpole often comes to the surface of water to engulf air. The mouth begins to become wider and the tadpole turns carnivorous to increase protein intake.

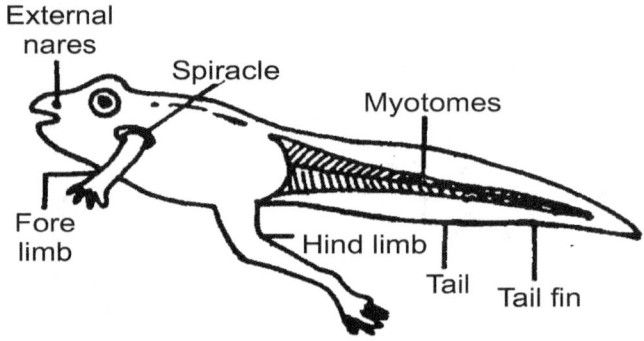

Fig. 4.31: Forelimb Stage

6. Juvenile frog: The actual metamorphosis is transformation of the last larval stage into a juvenile frog. The final changes in metamorphosis take place rapidly. The first sign of metamorphosis is when the tadpole stops feeding. Its food requirement is fulfilled by the tissue of the tail. Thus, the tail goes on reducing by autolysis. Thyroxine hormone secreted by the thyroid gland also plays an important role in metamorphosis.

Thyroxine contains iodine which accelerates metamorphosis. These changes are striking as some organs of the tadpole are modified, others are lost, while still others which are formed are totally new. The external and internal changes which take place in metamorphosis are described as follows.

Fig. 4.32: Juvenile Frog

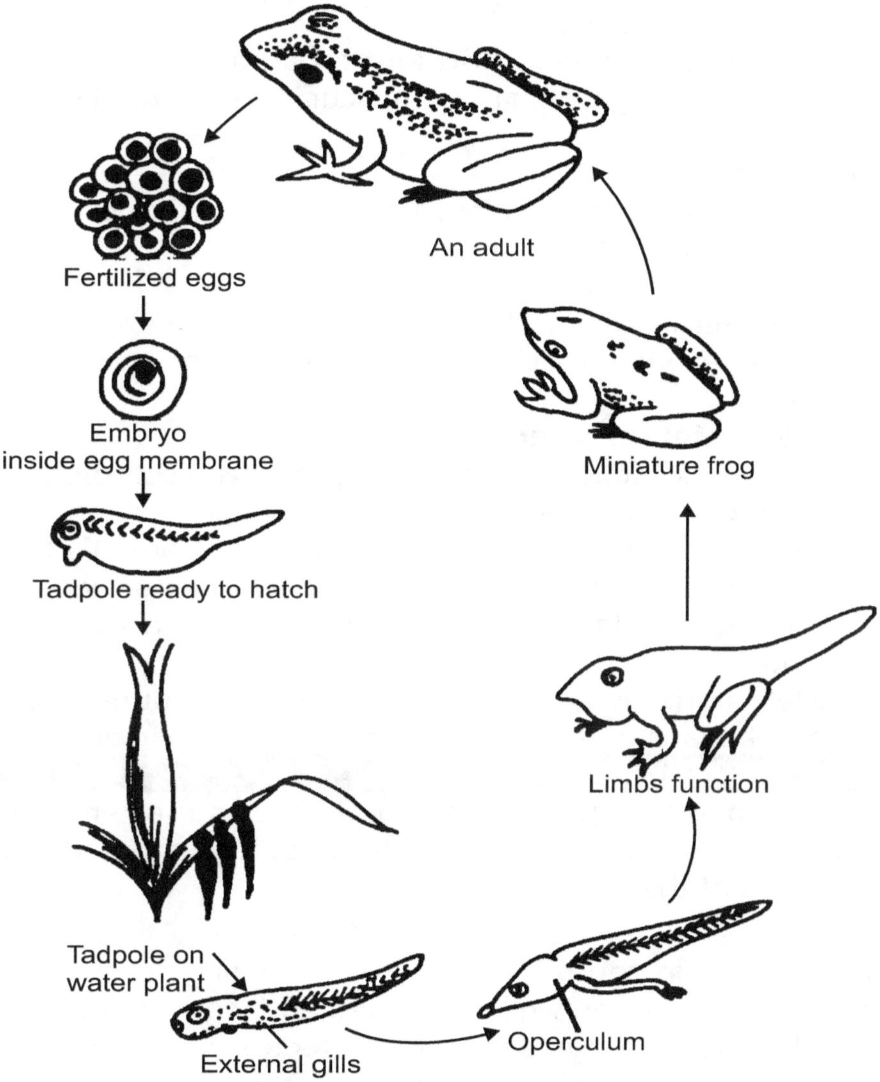

Fig. 4.33: Frog - Life Cycle

External Changes
1. The tail begins to disappear as it is reabsorbed into the body by autolysis.
2. The ciliated larval skin is lost, characteristic mottled skin is formed.
3. The mouth becomes wide, horny jaws and lips are replaced by true jaws.
4. The tongue becomes elongated and functional for catching prey.
5. The eyes become prominent, bulge out and tympanum becomes distinct.
6. The body becomes short and broad and the limbs develop further. They become muscular and hindlimbs show webbed toes.

Internal Changes
1. The cartilagenous skeleton is replaced by bones.
2. The heart becomes three chambered.
3. The liver, stomach and lungs develop.
4. The internal gills and gill slits totally degenerate.
5. The intestine gets shortened in adaptation to a carnivorous diet.

Significance of Metamorphosis
1. The larval stages exhibit adaptations according to their habitat and food available.
2. Due to metamorphosis an aquatic, tailed, aquatic breathing, herbivorous tadpole is gradually transformed into an amphibious, tailless, air-breathing and carnivorous juvenile frog.
3. Metamorphosis clearly indicates that during evolution amphibians must have evolved from fish-like ancestors.

4.4 Central Nervous System

The brain and the spinal cord together form the central nervous system. This system is a hollow tubular structure situated along the mid-dorsal axis of the animal.

(A) Brain

Brain is the main controlling and co-ordinating centre of all body activities. It is the anterior, well developed and well differentiated part of the central nervous system. It is protected in a hard bony box called *cranium*. Inside the cranium brain is further enclosed by three membranes called *meninges*. The outer brown fibrous tough and protective membrane which lines the cranium is called *dura matter*.

The innermost membrane closely applied to the brain is a thin, delicate and pigmented membrane called *pia matter*. The narrow space between the membranes and the inner cavities of the brain are filled with a clear, watery cerebro-spinal fluid. The meninges protect the brain from mechanical shocks and injuries. The cerebro spinal fluid works as a lubricant and shock absorber.

This cerebro spinal fluid supplies oxygen and is also nutritive in function. It prevents desiccation of brain and also helps the feebly rigid brain to withstand stress. The nervous tissue of the brain is differentiated into inner grey matter which is surrounded by white matter.

The brain of the frog is differentiated into three main parts, namely:
1. Fore brain or prosencephalon,
2. Midbrain or mesencephalon and
3. Hindbrain or rhombencephalon.

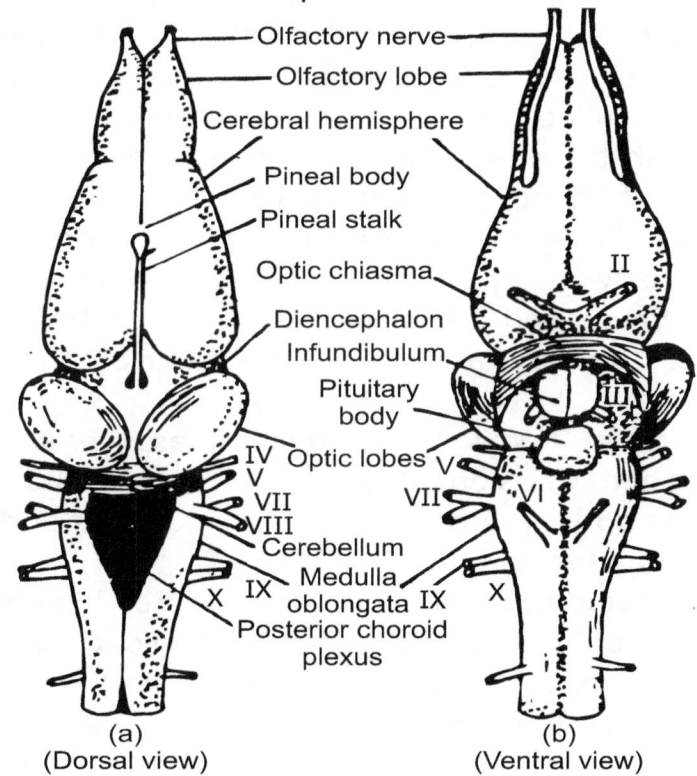

(a) (Dorsal view) (b) (Ventral view)

Fig. 4.34: Brain

1. The Fore Brain or Prosencephalon

It is the anterior part of the brain and consists of *olfactory* lobes, *cerebral hemispheres* and diencephalon or thalamencephalon.

(a) Olfactory Lobes: These are a pair of small lobes projecting anteriorly from the cerebral hemispheres. Dorsally they are completely fused with each other but differentiated by longitudinal and transverse grooves. Each olfactory lobe sends an olfactory nerve to the nasal chamber of its side. They are with sensory nerves. Internally each lobe contains a small cavity, the *olfactory ventricle or rhinocoel.*

Olfactory lobes are concerned with the sense of smell.

(b) The Cerebral Hemispheres: The cerebral hemispheres or cerebrum lie behind the olfactory lobes. They are seperated by a shallow transverse groove. They form the major parts of the brain. These are long, oval and smooth structures, narrow in front but broad behind and separated from one another by a deep mid-longitudinal groove or fissure. Each hemisphere encloses a cavity called the *lateral ventricle.* (or the left first and the right second ventricle). They are also called *paracoels* and are continuous anteriorly with olfactory ventricles. Posteriorly they unite with each other and with the diocoel of diencephalon by a common passage, the *foramen of Monro.* The floor of ventrolateral walls of the lateral ventricles are thickened to form the *corpora striata (*singular corpus striatum). The two corpora striata are interconnected by a tract of transverse fibres called the *anterior commissure.* The roof and dorso-lateral walls of the lateral ventricles are relatively thin and known as *pallium.*

The cerebral hemispheres function as the seat of memory, intelligence and decision. It also controls voluntary actions (will power) of the body. The corpus striatum regulates body temperature in cold blood animals.

(c) Diencephalon: Behind the cerebral hemispheres lies an unpaired diencephalon. It is a short, rhomboid, depressed region on the dorsal surface of the brain. The dorsal and ventral walls of the diencephalon are thin, but the lateral walls are thick and bulging called *optic thalami* (singular thalamus). On the roof of the diencephalon lies anterior *choroid plexus.* It is a non-nervous and highly vascular structure. From the posterodorsal side of the diencephalon arises a hollow stalk known as the *pineal stalk*. It bears at its free end a knob like structure called *pineal body*. It is considered to be a vestigeal third eye.

On the ventral side of the diencephalon is a median bilobed projection called *infundibulum*. Attached to the ventral surface of the infundibulum is a small rounded structure called *hypophysis* or *Rathke's pouch*. The infundibulum and hypophysis collectively form the pituitary body. Anterior to the pituitary body optic nerves cross each other forming a X-shaped structure called the *optic chiasma*. Diencephalon encloses the *third ventricle* or *diocoel*. The floor of the third ventricle is called the *hypothalamus*.

The function of diencephalon is to control spontaneous (involuntary) movements of the body. It also regulates body temperature, reproductive activities and sleep. The pituitary gland is the most important endocrine gland controlling all other endocrine glands. It secretes a number of hormones. The secretion of the pituitary body, control the general growth of the body as well as pigmentation of the skin. Diencephalon also works as a relay centre for conducting impulses to cerebral hemispheres. The pineal body is the functionless vestigeal third eye. The optic thalami of the diencephalon act as association centres for the sense of sight.

2. Midbrain or Mesencephalon

It forms the middle part of the brain and consists of *optic lobes* and *crura cerebri*.

(a) Optic lobes: Optic lobes are also known as corpora bigemina (singular - corpus bigeminum). They are a pair of prominent oval and hollow bodies diverging anteriorly and converging posteriorly, situated on the dorsal side of the brain. They, however, project on the sides so that they are partly visible from the ventral side also. Each optic lobe contains a cavity called the *optocoel*. Both the optocoels are connected with each other and also to the third ventricle in front and the fourth ventricle behind by a narrow space called *iter* or aqueduct of *Sylvius*. From the ventral side of each optic lobe arises the *optic nerve*. The optic nerves of either side cross each other in front of infundibulum to form the *optic chiasma*.

The optic lobes are concerned with the sense of sight, co-ordination of movements and checking of spinal reflexes. Because of crossing of optic nerves, each optic lobe controls the opposite side of the body.

(b) Crura cerebri: These are pair of thick longitudinal bands of nervous tissue situated ventrally on the floor of the iter. Structurally and functionally they connect forebrain to the hindbrain transmitting impulses to and fro.

3. Hindbrain or Rhombencephalon

It consists of *cerebellum* and *medulla oblongata*.

(a) Cerebellum: The cerebellum is a poorly developed narrow transverse solid ridge or band, placed dorsally just behind the optic lobes.

The function of cerebellum is to maintain equilibrium of the body and along with cerebrum it controls and co-ordinates muscular movements of the body.

(b) The medulla oblongata: It is the posterior most part of the brain. It is slightly broad at the anterior end and narrow posteriorly where it continues into the spinal cord without any line of demarcation. On the dorsal side it shows a highly vascular patch of piamatter called *posterior choroid plexus*. It nourishes the posterior part of the brain. The medulla oblongata encloses the fourth ventricle or metacoel which is continued behind in the spinal cord as the cerebrospinal canal. The floor of the fourth ventricle is very thick.

As regards the functions, the medulla oblongata controls most of the important involuntary vital functions of the body such as heart beats, peristalsis, blood pressure, respiratory movements etc. It is also concerned with catching and swallowing of prey, croaking, digestive reflexes like secretion of gastric and pancreatic juices.

The posterior choroid plexus secretes cerebro spinal fluid and provides nourishment as well as oxygen to the internal parts of the hind brain by giving offshoots. The medulla oblongata forms a bridge connecting the spinal cord to the brain. The removal of medulla oblongata or damage to it soon results in death.

Ventricles of Brain

The brain is hollow, its cavity being enlarged or reduced at places to form ventricles. They are filled with cerebrospinal fluid.

Frog brain shows the following ventricles.

1. **Rhinocoels or olfactory ventricles:** These are pair of cavities in the olfactory lobes.
2. **Paracoels or lateral ventricle:** These are pair of narrow ventricles present in the cerebral hemispheres. They open into the third ventricle behind through a common aperture called *foramen of Monro*.
3. **Dioecoel or third ventricle:** It is a narrow median ventricle present in diencephalon.
4. **Optocoels or optic ventricles:** These are present in the optic lobes. They are connected to the third ventricle in front and to the fourth ventricle behind through a narrow space called 'Iter' or 'Aqueduct of Sylvius'.
5. **Iter or Aqueduct of Sylvius:** It is a narrow space connecting the optocoels as well as the third ventricle in front and the fourth ventricle behind.
6. **Metacoel or fourth ventricle:** It is the spacious cavity present in the medulla oblongata. It posteriorly continues into the spinal cord as the cerebrospinal or central canal.

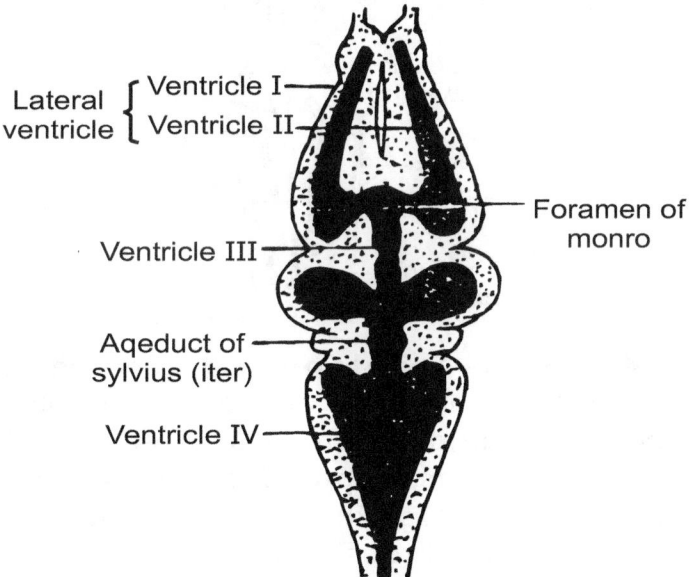

Fig. 4.35: H.L.S. Showing Ventricles

Spinal Cord

The spinal cord is a part of the central nervous system and extends from the medulla of the brain mid-dorsally through the neural canal of the vertebral column. It is protected within the vertebral column and covered by two meninges, the outer dura matter and inner pia matter enclosing cerebro spinal fluid in between.

In frog, the spinal cord is short because of the absence of a tail. It is short, thick, cylindrical, somewhat flattened and white in colour. Posteriorly, it terminates into a fine, non-nervous filament, the *filum terminale*. The spinal cord is slightly thicker in the region of the fore and hind limbs. The thickened part of the spinal cord of the forelimb is called *brachial plexus* while in the region of hindlimbs the swelling or thickened part is called *sciatic plexus*. These swellings have more nerve bodies than elsewhere.

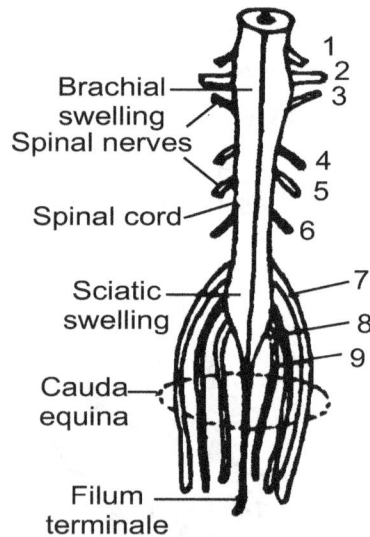

Fig. 4.36: Frog – Spinal Cord and spinal nerves

The spinal cord is cylindrical and dorsoventrally flattened. It shows two median longitudinal grooves called dorsal and ventral fissures running all along its length. The ventral fissure is a deep longitudinal groove whereas the dorsal fissure is a shallow longitudinal groove. A thin fibrous partition the *dorsal septum,* lies in the thickness of the cord beneath the dorsal fissure. The dorsal septum and the ventral fissure, incompletely divide the spinal cord into symmetrical right and left halves. The spinal cord encloses a very narrow cavity known as the *central canal*. The central canal is lined with a single layered columnar epithelium called *ependyma*. It opens into the *fourth ventricle* or *metacoel* of the brain in front but is closed posteriorly. It is filled with cerebrospinal fluid.

Histology: Like the brain, the spinal cord is also formed of grey matter and white matter. The grey matter surrounds the central canal and outer to white matter is grey matter. In the transverse section of the spinal cord the outermost membranous covering is called *dura matter* and the inner covering is called *piamatter*. Between the two membranes is a fluid called *cerebro-spinal fluid* which protects the spinal cord from external shocks.

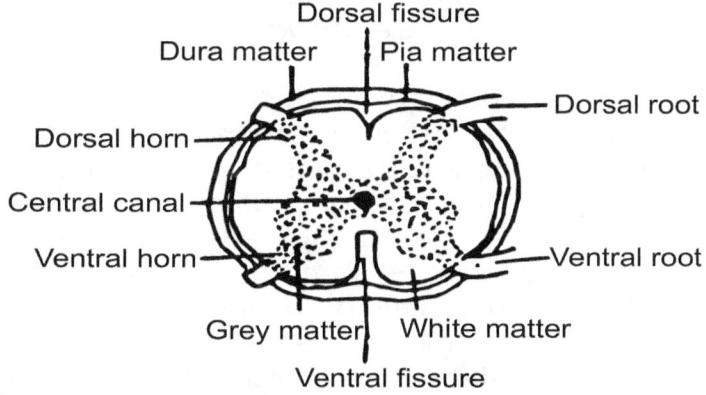

Fig. 4.37: Frog - T. S. Spinal Cord

The grey matter which surrounds the central canal contains *cytons* or cell bodies of neurons, whereas the white matter contains *axons* or nerve fibres. The myelin sheaths of the glistening white in colour, are responsible for its white appearance. Extending from the central mass of grey matter are four *horns* or *cornua* two dorsally (the *dorsal horns*) and two ventrally, (the *ventral horns*). Thus, the grey matter appears H-shaped. From these horns, the dorsal and ventral roots of the spinal nerves take their origin. The dorsal root is made of sensory fibres and ventral root of motor fibres. The dorsal root carries a ganglion called *dorsal root* ganglion. The spinal cord gives rise to 10 pairs of spinal nerves.

Functions of Spinal Cord
1. The spinal cord serves as a pathway for the conduction of impulses to and fro between the brain and different parts of the body.
2. The spinal cord is a chief motor effector.
3. It also serves as a centre for many reflex actions.

Peripheral Nervous System

The peripheral nervous system consists of nerves arising from the brain and spinal cord. The nerves arising from the brain are called *cranial nerves* and those taking their origin from the spinal cord are known as *spinal nerves*. These nerves are white thread like structures acting as the lines of communication between the different organs in the body and the central nervous system. There are three types of nerves:

1. **Sensory or afferent nerves:** The nerves which carry impulses from the sense organs to the central nervous system are called *sensory nerves* or *afferent nerves*.
2. **Motor or efferent nerves:** The nerves which carry impulses from the central nervous system to the effector organ, such as muscles or glands are known as *motor nerves* or *efferent nerves*.
3. **Mixed nerves:** The nerves which include both sensory and motor fibres are called *mixed nerves*.

Cranial Nerves: There are 10 pairs of cerebral nerves which arise from the brain. Since, they emerge out through the openings or foramina in the cranium, they are called cranial nerves. Of these nerves some are purely sensory, some are purely motor and rest of the nerves are of mixed type i.e. containing both sensory and motor nerve fibres. The nerves which have their origin from the ventral roots are purely motor, while those which have their origin from the dorsal roots are sensory. The mixed nerves are dorsal roots but have ganglia and hence they are mixed nerves. The cranial nerves are numbered I to X as well as names are assigned to them. The number, name, origin, nature and distribution of the cranial nerves is given below in tabular form.

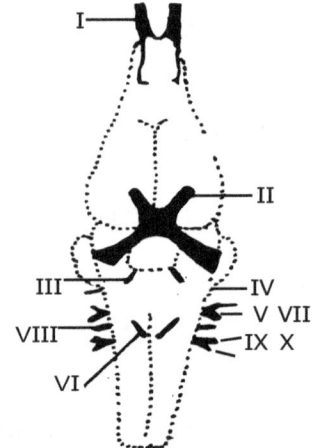

Fig. 4.38: Cranial Nerves

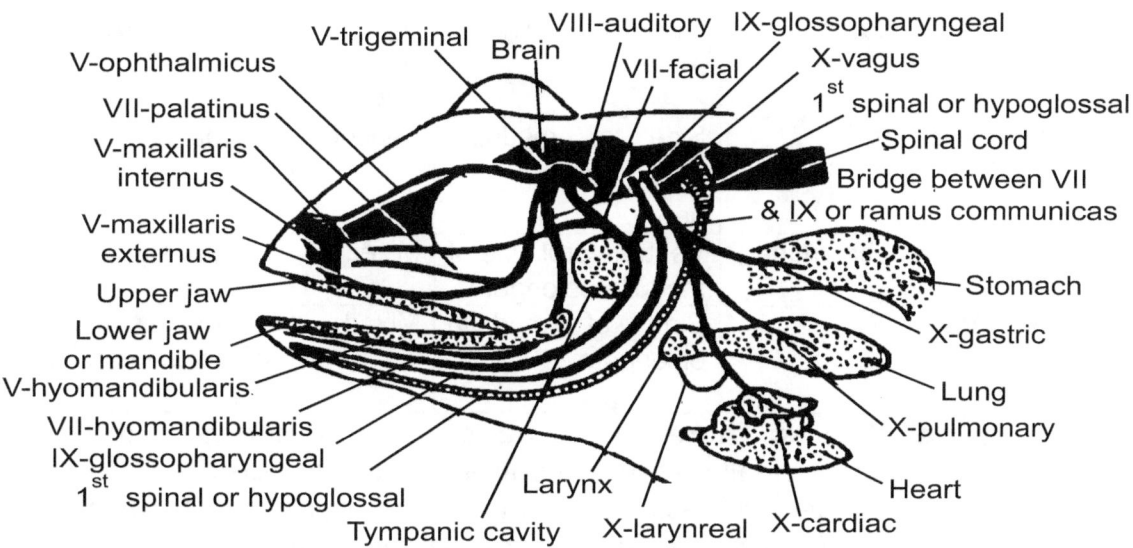

Fig. 4.39: Frog - dissection of cranial nerves in left view

Sr. No.	Name	Centre of origin	Nature of nerve fibres	Distribution
I	Olfactory	Olfactory lobes	Sensory	Olfactory epithelium of nasal chamber
II	Optic	Optic lobes	Sensory	Retina of eyes
III	Oculomotor	Floor of midbrain	Motor	Four muscles of eye ball
IV	Trochlear of pathetic	From dorsal surface between optic lobes and cerebellum	Motor	One eye muscle
V	Trigeminal (i) Ophthalmic (ii) Maxillary (iii) Mandibular	Medulla oblongata	Mixed	Skin of snout, orbit. Upper jaw, lips, lower eye lid. Skin of lower jaw, tongue muscle, muscles of lower jaw.
VI	Abducens	Midventral surface of medulla oblongata	Motor	Eye muscle and nictitating membrane.
VII	Facial divided into (i) Palatinus (ii) Hyomandibular	Sides of medulla oblongata	Mixed Mixed	Roof of buccal cavity. Skin of lower jaw and tongue.

Sr. No.	Name	Centre of origin	Nature of nerve fibres	Distribution
VIII	Auditory	Side of medulla, behind 7th cranial nerve.	Sensory	Internal ear
IX	Glossopharyngeal	Ventrolateral side of medulla oblongata	Mixed	Tongue and pharynx
X	Vagus	Side of medulla oblongata	Mixed	Larynx, oesophagus, stomach, heart lungs etc.

Spinal Nerves: There are 10 pairs of spinal nerves in the frog. They arise symmetrically from the spinal cord between the successive vertebrae. The nerves pass out from the neural canal through the *internal vertebral foramina.* Each of the spinal nerves is a mixed nerve as it is formed by joining of the dorsal root which is sensory and the ventral root which is motor. The dorsal and the ventral roots unite with each other before coming out of the inter vertebral foramen. At the exit of the spinal nerves there are calcarious white patches called *Glands of Swammerdam* or *Periganglionic glands.* The dorsal root has a ganglion containing sensory neurons, thus its fibres are only of a sensory type. They carry impulses from the receptor (sense organs) to the cells of the central nervous system. The ventral root has only motor fibres whose cell bodies are situated in the spinal cord. They carry impulses from the central nervous system to the effector organs such as muscles or glands.

Each spinal nerve, soon after its formation, divides into three branches, namely.

(i) The short dorsal branch or *ramus dorsalis* going to the skin and muscles of the back.

(ii) The prominent ventral branch or *ramus Ventralis* supplying the skin and the muscles of ventral and lateral parts of the body.

(iii) The short *ramus communicans* which joins the spinal nerve with the corresponding sympathetic ganglion. The posterior spinal nerves 6th, 7th, 8th, 9th and 10th come out of intervertebral foramina and run parallel to the filum terminal. These nerves show brush like appearance resembling a horse's tail. Therefore, it is called *cauda equina.*

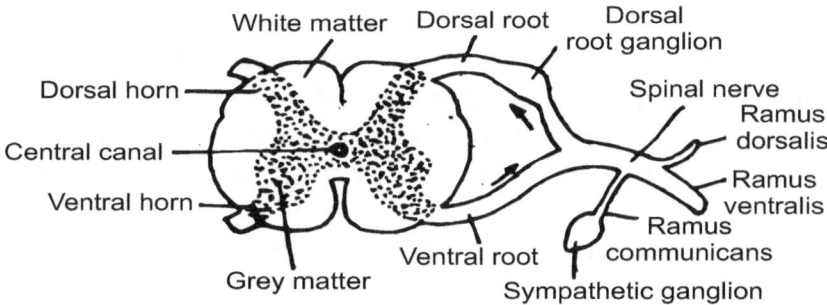

Fig. 4.40: Origin and branches of spinal nerve

The nature of the spinal nerve is mixed because each of the three branches receives fibres from both the dorsal and ventral roots. The course of the dorsal branches and the rami communicans (pleural of ramus communican) is similar in all the spinal nerves. The ventral branches, however, differ in their course in different spinal nerves. Their distribution is described as below.

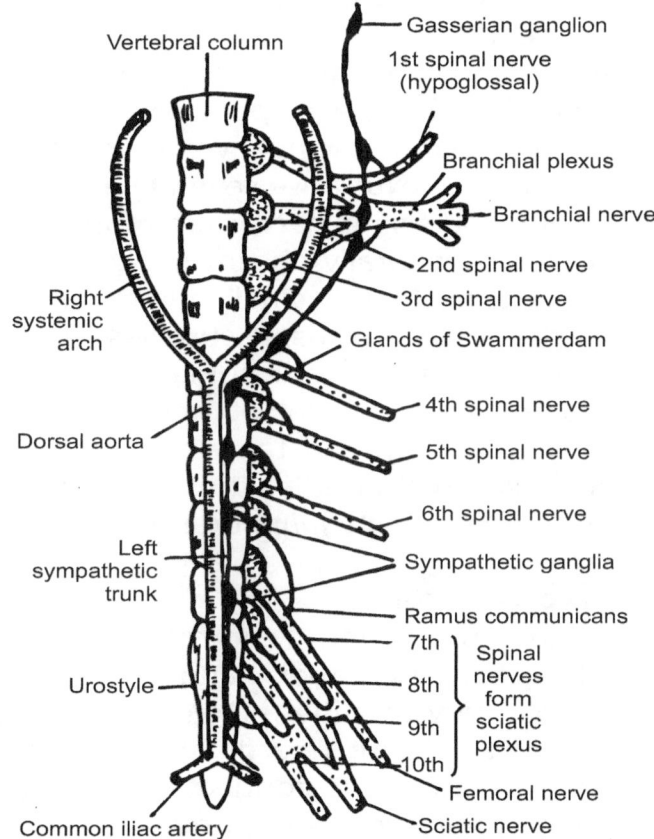

Fig. 4.41: Frog. Dissection showing spinal nerves 1-10 and sympathetic trunk on the left side only

The *first spinal nerve* called *hypoglossal* comes out of the neural canal between the first and second vertebrae. It is a thin nerve. It shows only ventral root, because the dorsal root disappears during metamorphosis. The nerve turns anteriorly to supply muscles of the tongue. It is motor in nature. The *second spinal nerve* comes out between the second and the third vertebrae. It is a large and stout nerve which runs straight outwards. It is soon joined by the third spinal nerve and a small branches from the hypoglossal nerve. Thus, it forms a network or a junction called the *cervico-brachial plexus* and then forms the *brachial nerve* which supplies arms innervates the skin and muscles. The *third spinal nerve* emerges between the third and the fourth vertebrae. It is a small nerve. Beyond the brachial plexus it resembles the next three nerves. The *fourth, fifth, and sixth* nerves escape between the fourth and fifth, the fifth and sixth and the sixth and seventh vertebrae respectively. All of them are slender nerves and innervate the skin and muscles of the belly. The *seventh, eighth* and *ninth* nerves are large nerves, which come out between the seventh and eighth vertebrae, the eighth and ninth vertebrae and ninth vertebrae and the urostyle respectively. All these nerves run backward and unite by oblique connectives to form the *lumbo sacral* or *sciatic plexus*. From this plexus arise several nerves, which enter the hind limb. The femoral and sciatic nerves are more prominent nerves. The *tenth spinal nerve* is generally absent in *Rana tigrina* or may be present only on one side. It is a small nerve called the *coccygeal nerve*. It also joins the sciatic plexus. It supplies the urinary bladder, cloaca and other parts. The last four spinal nerves (7th, 8th, 9th and 10th) do not leave the neural canal at once. They run backwards within the neural canal for some distance from their origin to reach the points of their exit. The bundle, thus formed by them in the neural canal, is called the *cauda equina* due to its resemblance with a horse's tail.

Autonomous Nervous System

The central nervous system controls almost all voluntary activities of the frog. On the other hand the autonomic nervous system controls involuntary activities; such as heart beat, breathing, peristalsis etc. Thus, this system is partly independent of the central nervous system even though it is connected to it. It deals with the internal environment of the body. Autonomous system is divided into two parts: (A) Sympathetic Nervous System and (B) Parasympathetic Nervous System.

Sympathetic Nervous System

The sympathetic nervous system consists of sympathetic cords, sympathetic ganglia, rami communicans and plexuses. The sympathetic nervous system includes a pair of long, delicate thread like cords called *sympathetic cords* running beneath the vertebral column, one on the either side of the dorsal aorta. They are continued forward along the outer sides of the systemic arches. Both the cords enter the cranium and join the *vagus ganglia* of X nerve and then forward again where they join the *Gasserian ganglia* of V or trigeminal nerve where they finally end there. Each sympathetic cord contains 10 sympathetic ganglia which are pigmented. The ganglia are connected with adjacent spinal nerves by small nerves called *rami communicans*.

The ganglia are connected with the brain and the spinal cord on the one hand and the organs supplied with nerves on the other hand. The nerve fibres which connect central nervous system to the autonomic ganglia are called *preganglionic fibres* and they are short and of a medullated nature. The fibres which connect the visceral organ and the ganglia are called *post ganglionic* fibres and these are long and of non-medullated nature.

A large network of nerve fibres is given out from sympathetic nerves arising from the sympathetic ganglia called *plexus*. The nerve fibres of the 3rd to 6th pair of ganglia form networks called *solar plexus*. This plexus is present on the side of the coeliaco-mesenteric artery. The solar plexus innervates the alimentary canal and associated glands. *Iliac plexus* arising from the nerves given out from the 9th and 10th ganglia supplies nerves to kidney, testes or ovaries and oviducts. The *cardiac plexus* is formed by the nerves coming from the 1st ganglia. It supplies nerves to the heart and the bases of nearby blood vessels. The preganglionic fibres are *cholinergic* i.e. they release acetylcholine. The post-ganglionic fibres are *adrenergic* i.e. they release epinephrine (adrenaline).

This chemical is also called sympathin, which generally stimulates these organs, e.g. increase of heart beats, decrease of secretion of saliva etc.

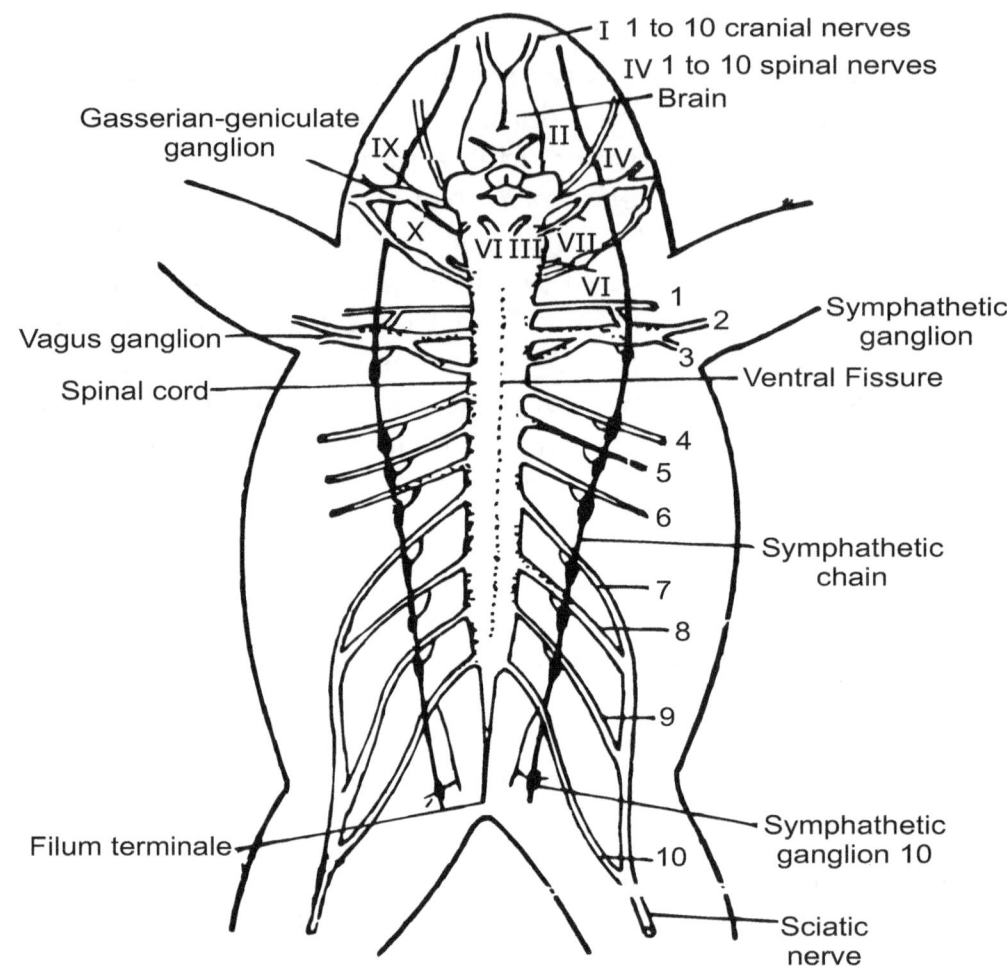

Fig. 4.42: The Central and Peripheral Nervous System of the Frog (Ventral View)

Parasympathetic Nervous System

This system is formed by the parasympathetic ganglia and parasympathetic nerve fibres. The parasympathetic ganglia are situated close to or in the organ. They give out preganglionic fibres which are very long and post-ganglionic fibres which are short. These fibres innervate the same organs which are innervated by the sympathetic fibres. The parasympathetic nerve fibres are *cholinergic* i.e. they release *acetylcholine*.

This system consists of *cranial and sacral* out flow of parasympathetic nerve fibres. The cranial outflow is connected to the medulla oblongata and innervates the organs such as larynx, lungs, heart and digestive organs. The sacral outflow is connected to the posterior part of the spinal cord and supplies nerves to the large intestine, kidneys and urinary bladder.

Working of the Autonomous Nervous System

All the visceral organs in the body are innervated by two sets of nerves of both the sympathetic and parasympathetic nerves. The parasympathetic fibres secrete *acetylcholine*. It has an inhibitory effect on organs which is antagonistic to that of the sympathetic nerves. The sympathetic nerves secrete adrenaline and have excitatory effect. If sympathetic fibres accelerate any activity, the parasympathetic fibres would inhibit the same. For example, if sympathetic stimulus accelerates heart beat, the parasympathetic stimulus inhibits or slows down heart beats.

Parasympathetic stimulus brings about the dilation of blood vessels, whereas sympathetic stimulus brings about the constriction of blood vessels. Thus, they bring about balanced functioning of all visceral organs.

Mechanism of Nervous Action

The function of the nervous system is done through three types of neurons, (i) the *sensory neuron* which conducts impulses towards the central nervous system, (ii) the *adjustor neuron* which hands over the impulse to the proper neuron and (iii) the *motor neuron* which conducts the impulse away to the effector organ. The stimulus enters the neuron through the dendronic end. It is then converted into an impulse which leaves through its axonic end. The neurons are interconnected in such a way that axon of one is always in contact with endron of other.

The place where the axon and dendrite branches meet connecting one neuron with another is called *synapse*. The terminal swollen parts of the axon is called the synaptic knob. Between the knob and membrane of the dendrite a little space is present called *synaptic cleft*. In the knob a chemical substance *acetylcholine* is present which is called *neurochemical transmitter*.

Whenever a nerve impulse is to arise this chemical is released in the synaptic cleft. Accumulation of acetylcholine in the synaptic cleft is responsible for generating nerve impulse. It also receives the enzyme *cholinesterase* which prevents lingering and intermixing of impulses. The synapse serves as a switchboard receiving many impulses and transmitting them to proper motor neurons.

Reflex Action

A reflex is an inborn, quick and automatic response to a particular stimulus. The term *reflex action* is defined as a quick, automatic and involuntary response of the central nervous system to a stimulus received from the receptors. It is so called because the action is so quick as if the stimulus is reflected back in the form of a response. All nervous activities performed by the central nervous system are reflex actions in which stimuli reaching the central nervous system are reflected back in the form of responses.

Knee jerk as a result of a sharp tap below the knee cap, closing of eye lids on the approach of an object, withdrawal of the hand when burned or pricked are examples of reflex actions. The physiological definition of a reflex action is, an action brought about by *efferent* or *motor neuron* due to the stimulation of an *afferent* or *sensory* neuron. The path followed by an impulse during a reflex action is called the *reflex arc*. It is the structural and physiological unit of the nervous system and the simple reflex arc contains atleast three neurons, i.e. sensory neuron, adjustor or connector neuron and motor neuron communicated through synaptic connections.

The components of a reflex action are as follows.
1. **Receptor organ:** It is the point of stimulus or the sense organ which receives the stimulus and converts it into an impulse e.g. skin, tongue, eye etc.
2. **Sensory or afferent neuron:** It is situated in the dorsal root ganglion. It carries an impulse from the receptor organ to the central nervous system.
3. **Adjustor or connector neuron:** It is the intermediate neuron situated in the grey matter of the spinal cord. It receives the impulse, analyses it and generates an appropriate impulse which is transmitted to the proper motor neuron.
4. **Motor or efferent neuron:** It is the neuron which carries impulses from the adjustor neuron to the effector organ.
5. **Effector organ:** It is the organ which ultimately receives the impulse and gets excited and shows response to the stimulus e.g. glands or muscles.

In frog, most actions are reflex actions. For example, shooting of tongue at the sight of a flying insect, hopping on land at the sight of danger and withdrawal of the leg when pricked. In pricking the skin (receptor organ) receives the stimulus and converts it into an impulse. The impulse is carried through the sensory neuron to the spinal cord.

In a reflex action quick action is required without consulting the brain, the spinal cord gives order through the motor neuron to the muscles of the legs which is immediately withdrawn. This reflex action takes place even if the brain is cut off.

Advantages of Reflex Action:
1. It is executed without loss of time, thus helps the animal to adapt itself to the changing environment.
2. It is very important from the point of view of safety and survival of the animal.
3. A reflex action gives relief to the brain to some extent as most of the reflex actions are spinal reflexes. Thus, it is a short-cut without consulting the brain.

Types of Reflex Actions:
Reflex actions are of two types, namely -
(i) Unconditional or simple reflex action and
(ii) Conditional reflex action.

(i) Unconditional reflex action: Unconditional reflexes are inborn or inherited responses to stimulus from the environment. Closing of eyelids on the approach of an object, withdrawal of hand when pricked or burned are the unconditional reflexes. An animal is not conscious or aware of these reflexes. These reflexes control the secretions of the glands, breathing, heart rate and so on.

(ii) Conditional reflex action: These reflexes are not inborn. These are acquired and depend on past experience and training. This is called 'learning'. Cycling, swimming are examples of conditional reflexes. These help the animal to adapt to varying and changing environmental conditions.

4.5 Sense Organs

There are number of specialised sensitive structures in the body of the animal which receive the stimuli. They are called *receptors* or sense organs. Receptors are responsible for making the frog aware of its environment. They are the cells or organs specialised to take the impressions of a stimulus and transmit the impressions to the brain for interpretation. This is called *sensation*. The nature of the stimulus is interpreted by the centre in the brain and not by the receptor. Thus, they are not responsible for sensations.

For example, the sweet taste of sugar, it is the taste centre present in the brain and not the tongue that is responsible. The receptors or sensory organs are composed of a particular type of cells forming organs which receive only a particular stimulus. This is Muller's law. According to this law, taste buds are capable of perceiving the taste, the photoreceptors perceive light and both of these cannot perceive sound. The ear or auditory organ is responsible for perception of sound and they can not perceive light and taste. Thus, each receptor is adapted for a specific type of stimulus. In lower animals the receptors are scattered while in higher animals they are grouped together with some other tissues to form *sense organs*.

There are five sense organs in the frog, they are for touch, smell, taste, sight and hearing which are stimulated by the environment. These sense organs are called *external receptors* or *exteroceptors*.

There are also other sense organs found in the body which detect temperature, pain, hunger, thirst, fatigue etc. called internal receptors or *enteroceptors*. Receptors can be classifed with the type of stimulation and location.

Sr. No.	Type of receptor	Type of stimulation	Location
1.	Mechanoreceptors or Tangoreceptors	Mechanical (Touch, pressure and tension)	Skin
2.	Chemoreceptors	Chemical (Taste, smell)	Tongue, Nose
3.	Photoreceptors	Light (sight)	Retina of eye
4.	Phonoreceptors	Sound (hearing)	Internal ear
5.	Thermoreceptors	Thermal (heat or cold)	Skin
6.	Proprioreceptors	Fatigue, muscle tones, Visceral pain.	Muscles joints and visceral organs
7.	Enteroreceptors	Hunger, thirst	Alimentary canal
8.	Statoreceptors	Change in body equilibrium	Internal ear

In case of the frog, *Rana tigrina* skin, nasal chambers, tongue, eyes and ears are the most important sense organs.

1. Tangoreceptors: Tangoreceptor organs are the organs of touch. The frog has numerous microscopic cutaneous sense organs or tangoreceptors present under epidermis of the skin. They are either in the form of simple networks of *nerve endings* scattered among cells or as compact groups of cells forming *tactile patches*. In higher animals, tactile patches are specialised differently for cold, hot, pressure, pain etc. Nerve endings lie a few cells below the surface thus any stimulus has to pass through the outer cells before they reach the nerve endings. They are sensitive to various types of stimuli such as touch, chemicals, temperature, humidity, light, pain etc. The tadpole has a lateral line system which is absent in the adult frog.

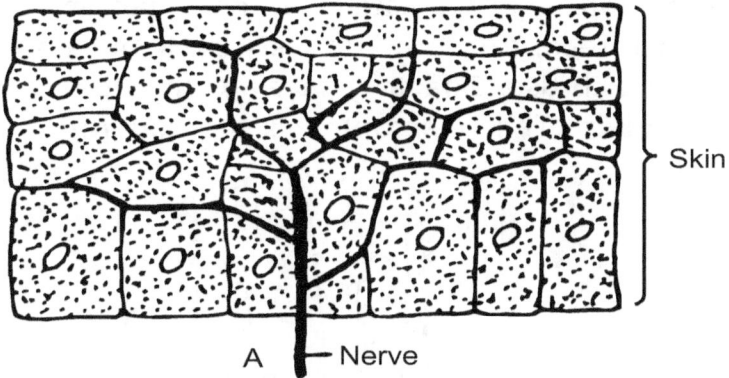

Fig. 4.43: Frog - Free nerve ending in the skin

2. Gustatoreceptors: Gustatoreceptors or taste buds are organs of taste. They are in the form of taste buds present in small papillae on the tongue and floor and roof of the buccal cavity. They are lined with a mucous membrane and the taste buds are present in mucous membrane. Each taste bud is almost club-shaped structure consisting of two types of cells. The elongated spindle like receptor cells or sensory cells end in fine hair like processes for sampling food which is taken into mouth. Receptor cells are innervated by fibres of the VII and IX cranial nerves. The other type of cells are called supporting cells. Taste buds are stimulated only by liquid food. A substance in the liquid form touches the sensory hairs from where the stimulus goes to the brain through the nerves. There are four fundamental sensations of taste, sweet, salty, bitter and sour.

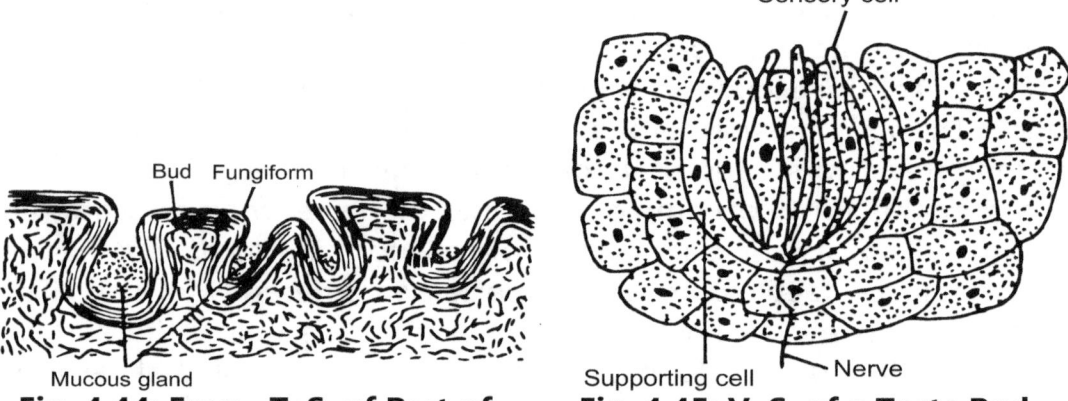

Fig. 4.44: Frog - T. S. of Part of Tongue

Fig. 4.45: V. S. of a Taste Bud

3. **Olfactoreceptor:** Olfacto-receptors are the organs of *smell*. These olfactoreceptors are located in the olfactory sac. In *Rana tigrina* the olfactoreceptors are not very well developed, because they are not of much use. Olfactory sacs are situated in the olfactory lobes inside cranium. The olfactory sacs are separated by an inter-nasal septum.

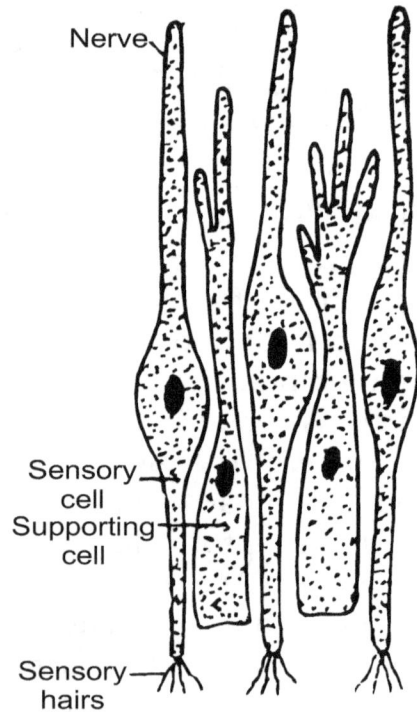

Fig. 4.46: Frog - Olfactory Epithelial Cells

Each sac is perforated by two apertures - an *internal nare* which communicates with the buccal cavity and *external nare* which communicates with the exterior. The nasal sac is lined with mucous epithelium. The cells of the epithelium are columnar. In between these cell *neurosensory cells* are present and each cell is like a *bipolar neuron*. The proximal end of the cell is broad and terminates into sensory hairs. Nerve fibres are attached to their inner ends. Nerve fibres unite to form the olfactory nerve which carries the sensations of odours to the brain.

In between the sensory cells lie supporting cells. These cells are without sensory hairs but may possess nerve fibres. There are also mucous secreting cells in the olfactory epithelium which secrete mucous and thus keep the sensory hairs epithelium moist. Sensory cells are affected by the odour of odoriferous substances and from here through the olfactory nerve the sense of smell is carried to the brain.

4. Photoreceptors: Eyes are photoreceptor organs which are sensitive to light. Eyes of the frog are large and rounded structures situated in the skull in deep depressions called *orbits*. In frogs, the orbits are present on the lateral sides of the skull. Therefore, each eye covers a different visual field. This is called *monocular vision*. In monocular vision a greater visual field is covered which is of advantage when escaping from the enemy. When eyes are situated in front of the cranium, vision is called *binocular vision* e.g. man. Each eye is made up of a spherical *eye ball* protected in the bony socket of the cranium called orbit and guarded in front by a pair of *eyelids* and a transparent *nictitating membrane*. The upper eyelid is thick and slightly movable while the lower eyelid is thin and movable while the lower eyelid is thin and immovable. The eyelids are nothing but simple folds of integument. The third eyelid or nictitating membrane is attached to the lower eyelid and covers the eye and protects it when the frog is burrowing or is under water. It can be drawn over the eye or withdrawn and can remain folded under the lower eyelid.

Eye Muscles

The eye ball is held in the orbit and is moved with the help of six external (extrinsic) muscles. The *retractor* and *levator bulbi* push the eye ball out of the orbit and pull it in the orbit. The names of the muscles, origin and insertion are given in the following table.

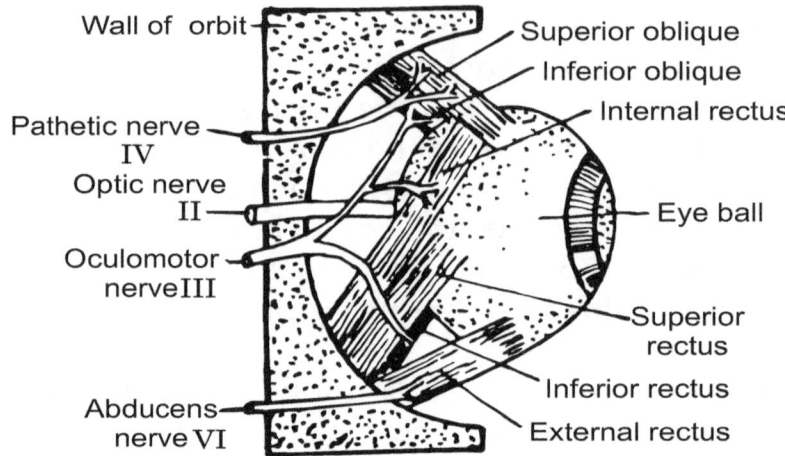

Fig. 4.47: Frog - Dissection of Right Eye ball in Dorsal view showing Eye Muscles and their Nerve Supply

Sr. No.	Name of the muscle	Origin	Insertion	Innervation
1.	Anterior rectus	Anterio-dorsal part of the orbit	Lateral wall of the eye ball	3rd cranial nerve (oculomotor)
2.	Posterior rectus	Posterior part of the orbit	Posterior wall of the eye ball	6th cranial nerve (Abducens)
3.	Superior rectus	Mid-dorsal part of the orbit	Posterior wall of the eye ball	3rd cranial nerve
4.	Inferior rectus	Basal part of the orbit	Basal part of the eye ball	
5.	Superior oblique	Dorsal surface of the orbit	Anterior wall of the eye ball	4th cranial nerve (Trochlear)
6.	Inferior oblique	Ventral part of the orbit	Anterior wall of the eye ball	3rd cranial nerve

The rectus muscles move the eyeball upward, downward, forward and backward. The oblique muscles rotate the eyeball along its axis.

Structure of Eye

Each eye ball is made up of three concentric layers or coats - (1) the sclerotic (2) the choroid and (3) the retina.

1. Sclerotic: It is the outermost layer made up of dense fibrous connective tissue and hyaline cartilage forming a kind of protective capsule for the inner delicate structures. Most of its portion is opaque; except the anterior part which slightly, bulge out of orbit. This transparent part is called *cornea*. The cornea is covered by a transparent membrane called *conjunctiva*; which is kept moist by the secretion of *Harderian glands* situated below the lower eyelid. The gland also lubricates the nictitating membrane. The eye muscles are attached to this layer.

This coat performs the following functions:
  (i) to protect the inner delicate layers.
  (ii) to provide attachment to the eye muscles.
  (iii) to admit light into the eye ball through the cornea.

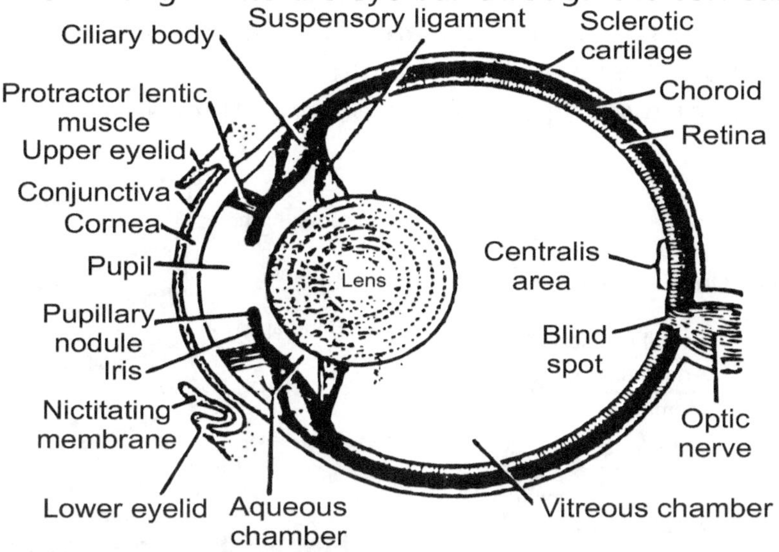

Fig. 4.48: Frog - Diagrammatic V. S. of Eye ball

2. Choroid: This is the middle layer of the eye ball present below the sclerotic coat. It is pigmented externally and vascular internally. This is an incomplete layer on the anterior side. Behind the cornea it is deflected into form a circular diaphragm called *iris*; leaving an oval aperture called *pupil* in the centre. In frog, the iris has a golden yellow colour and is provided with circular and radial muscles for controlling the diameter of the pupil. Just behind the iris, is a thickened edge of the choroid called *ciliary* body or *suspensory ligament*. It contains muscle fibres which run parallel to the edges of the lens.

This layer performs different functions which are:
(i) to provide nourishment to the cells of the eye ball.
(ii) to provide attachment to the lens and that of the iris to control the diameter of the pupil controlling the amount of light entering the eye.

3. Retina: It is the innermost, incomplete and modified layer of the eyeball. The retina is the only layer which is sensitive to light forming the visual part of the eye. The retina is made up of two layers; an outer thin pigmented layer and inner thick sensory layer. The pigmented layer is made up of a single layer of thin flattened and pigmented cells. However, the sensory layer is made up of *rods and cones* sensitive to light and colour, the *bipolar nerve* cells. The axonic fibres of these ganglionic nerve cells join to form the optic nerve. The rods and cones are elongated photoreceptor cells arranged below the layer of pigment cells of the retina. Each rod and cone consists of two segments, the outer and inner.

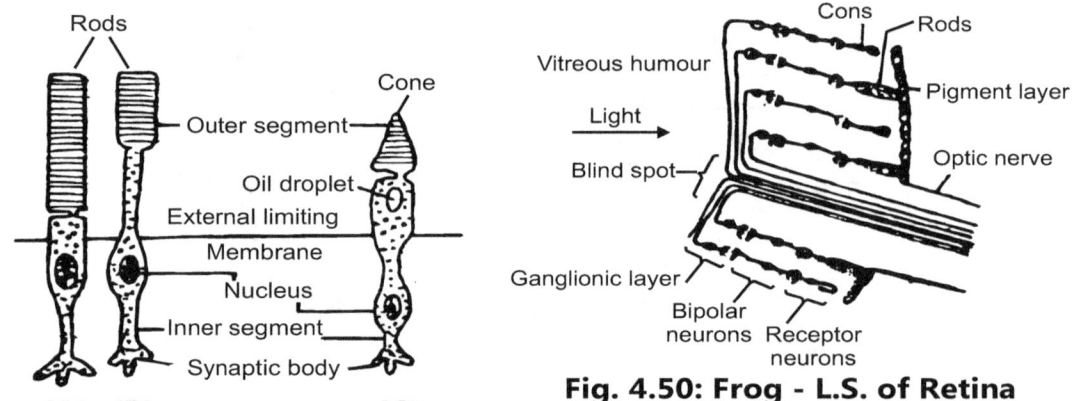

Fig. 4.49: Frog - Rod and Cones
A. B. Rods, C. Cones

Fig. 4.50: Frog - L.S. of Retina showing arrangement of Cellular Layers

The outer segment of rods and cones contains pigments while the inner segment contains nucleus and synaptic connections. In case of rods the outer segment is broad and cylindrical and contains the pigment *rhodopsin* while that of a cone cell is short and conical and contains the pigment *iodopsin* and oil droplet. There are two types of rods found in frogs, namely, *red rods* with a long outer segment containing the pigment *visual purple* or *rhodopsin* and *green rods* with a short outer segment containing the pigment *visual green*.

Rhodopsin consists of a protein *opsin* and *retinene*, an aldehyde of vitamin A. In cones the visual pigment is called *opsin*. The rods are sensitive to dim light, give blurred images and are responsible for black and white vision.

The cones are sensitive to bright light, give sharp images and are concerned with distinguishing colours. In frog, rods are numerous compared to cones. The posterior part of the retina from where the fibres of the optic nerve emerges out is called *blind spot*. The blind spot does not contain any rods or cones. Just below the layer of rods and cones is a layer of *bipolar neurons*. The bipolar neurons with their dendrites form the synapses with rods and cones. Their axons form synapses with the cells of the ganglionic layer. In the layers of *ganglionic cells* the dendrites form the synapses with the axons of bipolar neurons. The axons of the ganglionic cells form fibres of the optic nerve.

At the exit of the optic nerve there are no rods and cones, hence this area is called blind spot, as no image is perceived in this region. Just above the blind spot there is a thickened area called *area centralis* corresponding to the yellow spot in mammals. This is the area of acute vision due to concentration of cones. Just behind the iris, is a spherical, transparent crystalline *lens* which is slightly flattened in front. It is protected by a thin membrane of connective tissue called *lens capsule*.

The *lens* is held in position by suspensory ligaments attached to the ciliary body projecting from the choroid coat. The lens divides the cavity of the eye ball into the anterior space, *aqueous chamber* filled with the watery, *aqueous humour* and posterior, *space vitreous* chamber filled with viscous fluid called *vitreous humour*. The latter helps to maintain the globular shape of the eye ball and keep the retina well flattened. In frog, since the lens is more rigid and incapable of changing its focal length, slight accommodation is attained by moving the lens forward and backward by a pair of *protractor lentis muscles* and the *retractor lentis muscles*.

The contraction of protractor move the lens closer to the cornea, while that of the retractor moves the lens away from the cornea. The ability to focus the objects of different distances is called accommodation. It is usually done by changing the shape of the lens (focal length). However, in frogs, shape of the lens cannot be changed.

Working of Eye

The structure of the eye is similar to that of a camera and thus its working is also the same. In the eye, the light rays travel through the cornea and aqueous chamber, the lens and vitreous humour transfer them to the retina. The aperture of iris and distance of lens from cornea could be adjusted with the help of protractor and retractor lentis muscles respectively. The image which is formed on the retina is inverted.

As a result, the rods and cones are stimulated and the impulse is carried through the optic nerve to the visual centre in the brain which interprets the correct image of the object. Frogs can see the object which is at a particular distance only, hence, frogs depends much on the side and the movement of the object to detect the prey or enemy.

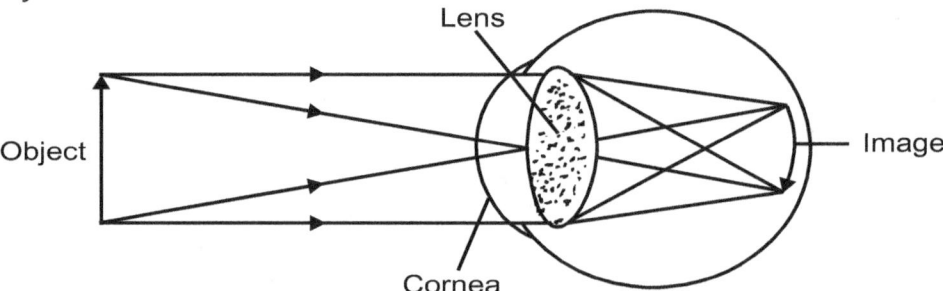

Fig. 4.51: Frog - Image Formation

Statoacoustic Organs or Ear

The statoacoustic organs are organs of hearing as well as of *balancing* or *equilibrium*. The ear of frog is divided into two parts: (i) The middle ear and (ii) the internal ear. The frog has no *external ear* or *pinna* which is found in mammals.

1. Middle Ear

It encloses a tubular space and is also called tympanic cavity, which is closed externally by a thin tympanic membrane. Externally, it appears more or less a circular patch on the side of the head, just behind the eye. Attached to the inner surface of the tympanic membrane is a slender rod like structure called *columella*. The inner end of the columella fits into a small apertue called *fenestra ovalis*. This part of the columella which fits into fenestra ovalis is called *stapes* or *stapedial plate*.

From the lower end of the tympanic cavity arises the *Eustachian tube*. It runs downwards and opens into the pharynx. The Eustachian tube helps to keep equal pressure in the middle ear cavity with that of outside.

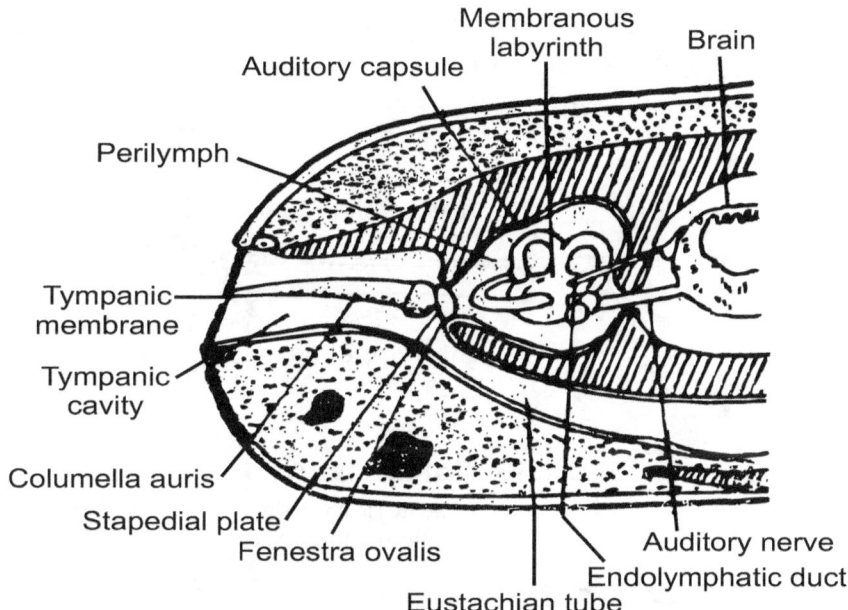

Fig. 4.52: Frog - Section of Head passing through Ear

2. Internal ear

The internal ear is enclosed in the auditory capsule. It is also called *membranous labyrinth* and is supposed to be the sensory part of the ear. It is lodged in the bony auditory capsule surrounded by a watery fluid called *perilymph*. The membranous labyrinth is externally differentiated into two parts, the dorsal *utriculus* and the ventral *sacculus*.

The utriculus bears three *semicircular canals* arranged in three planes at right angles to each other, each showing a swelling called *ampulla* at one end. Of these, the anterior and posterior canals are vertically placed and at right angles to each other, while the third is placed horizontally. One end of each semi-circular canal is dilated into a small rounded swollen structure called *ampulla*. The adjacent ends of the two vertical canals are united before opening into the *utriculus*. The sacculus of frogs is peculiar. It gives rise to two small bulgings called *lagena* and *pars basilaris*. These bulgings have sensory cells which are sensitive to sound vibrations.

From the sacculus arises a narrow duct, *the ductus endolymphaticus*. It pierces the auditory capsule, enters the cranial cavity and expands to form an *endolymphatic sac* on the hind brain. The auditory capsule contains a fluid called *perilymph* in which floats the membranous labyrinth. The fluid inside the membranous labyrinth is called *endolymph*. The endolymph contains many calcarious particles, called *otoliths*.

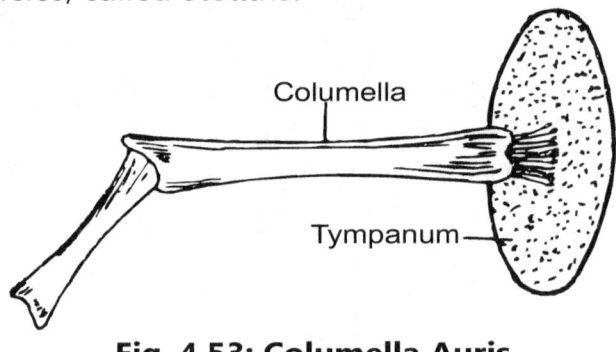

Fig. 4.53: Columella Auris

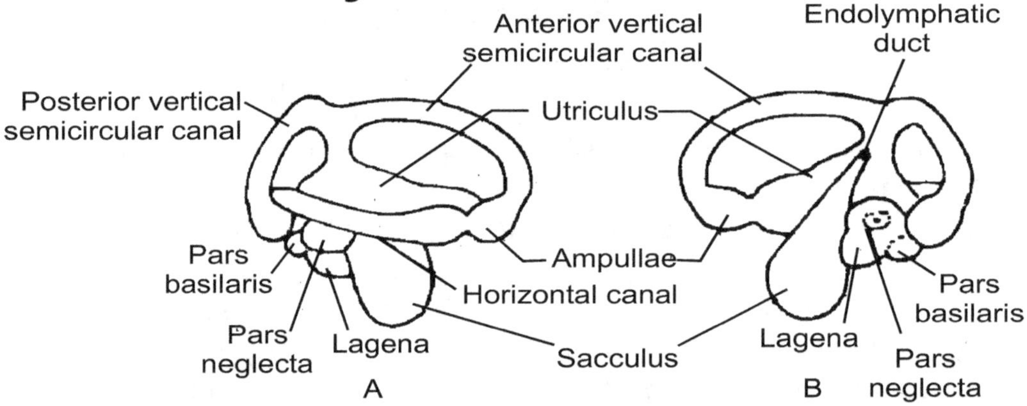

Fig. 4.54: Frog. Membranous labyrinth. (a) Outer view, (b) Inner view

The membranous labyrinth for most of the part is lined with cubical cells, but at certain places the cells are elongated. The elongated cells possess at their free ends long, stiff, hair-like processes. The places where the groups of these sensory cells are present is known as *acoustic spots*. Each ampulla has an acoustic spot, while the utriculus and the sacculus contains number of acoustic spots. These sensory spots are innervated by the fibres of *auditory nerve*.

Histology of Membranous Labyrinth

The wall of the membranous labyrinth is formed of (i) outer layer of *connective tissue* and (ii) inner layer of *cubical epithelium*. The wall of the ampullae is slightly pushed inwards, within the vestibule forming the *acoustic ridge*. The sensory cells with long sensory hair are present in the region of the acoustic ridge. The group of cells in the ampullae are called *cristae*, and those found in the utriculus and sacculus are known as *maculae*.

The macula of the utriculus is known as *pars neglecta* and that of lagena (sacculus) is known as *basilar papilla* or *macula lagena*. The endolymph contains a large number of calcium carbonate and protein particles called *otolith* or *otoconia*. The sensory hair of cristae and maculae also lie in the endolymph.

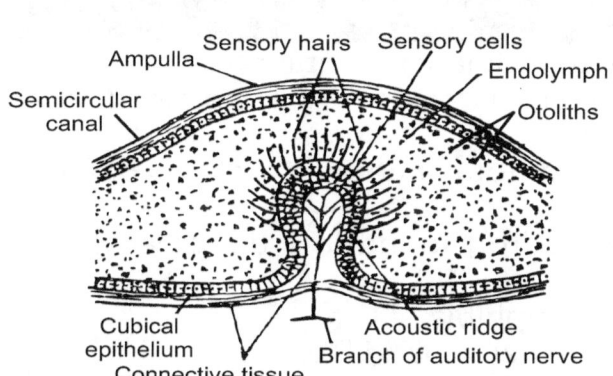

Fig. 4.55: Frog - V. S. of ampulla through an acoustic ridge or crista

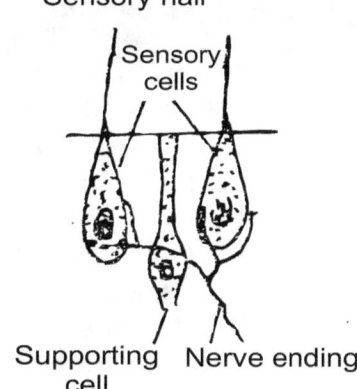

Fig. 4.56: Frog - Sensory epithelial cells or acoustic spot

Working of Ear

Ears perform two important functions, (i) Hearing and (ii) Equilibrium or balancing.

1. Hearing

Hearing is mainly due to sacculus. Sound waves from the surrounding atmosphere strike against the tympanic membrane which starts vibrating. These vibrations are conducted through the columella and stapedial plate to the perilymph of the internal ear. From the latter the vibrations are further received by the endolymph. Here the sensory cells of acoustic spots set impulses which are passed on to the auditory nerve. The nerve further conducts the impulses to the auditory centre of the brain where they are perceived as sound.

2. Equilibrium

The equilibrium or balancing is maintained by the semi-circular canals, utriculus which are arranged in three different planes at right angles to each other. Thus, the change of movement in any direction is recorded. Any change in the position of the body disturbs the suspended otoliths which stimulate the sensory hair cells of utriculus and its three canals.

Impulses are carried by auditory nerves to the brain. The brain immediately sends the necessary message to the muscles. Various muscles act in co-ordination to bring a frog back to its normal position. The semicircular canals are also concerned with the velocity of movements and the sense of direction.

Summary

- Amphibian also show extraordinary parental care.
- When embryonic or larval characters are maintained in an adult body called neoteny.
- Partially, intermediate and total neoteny are the different types of neoteny.
- *Rana tigrina* is the largest frog found in India called Indian bull frog.
- It is the member of class Amphibia.
- It is adapted for aquatic as well as land life.
- Frog feed on living prey with its sticky tongue.
- In hot summer it undergoes summer sleep called aestivation and in severe cold undergoers winter sleep.
- Sexual dimorphism is prominent.
- It exhibits cutaneous and pulmonary respiration.
- Digestive system consists of alimentary canal and associated glands.
- Circulatory system consists of venous system and arterial system.
- Heart is three chambered.
- Hepatic portal and renal portal systems are present.
- The central nervous system is well developed and it includes brain and spinal cord.
- Well developed sense organs are present.
- Male reproductive system consists of testes, vasa efferentia, urinogenital ducts, cloaca.
- Female reproductive system consists of pair of ovaries, pair of oviducts and cloaca.
- Fertilization is external and show embryonic and post embryonic development.

- In embryonic development it includes cleavage, blastula, gastrula, epiboly, emboly, rotation stages.
- In post embryonic development tadpole, tadpole with external gills, tadpole with internal gills, tadpole with hindlimbs and forelimbs and juvenile frog.

Review Questions

1. Describe the digestive system of frog and add a note on food and feeding habits and physiology of digestion.
3. Describe the structure and working of the heart of frog.
4. Describe the arterial system of the frog.
5. Give an account of venous system of the frog.
6. What is portal system? Give an account of hepatic or renal portal system in the frog.
7. Give an account of lymphatic system in the frog.
8. Describe the male reproductive system of frog and add a note on the structure of a sperm.
9. Give an account of the female reproductive system and add a note on the structure of the ovum.
10. Give the functions of blood in frog.
11. Describe the reproductive organs of male and female frog.
12. Describe the histological structure of ovary and testis of the frog.
13. What is gametogenesis? Give an account of the process of spermatogenesis or oogenesis. Tabulate the similarities and differences in the process of spermatogenesis and oogenesis.
14. What is fertilization? Give an account of fertilization in frog. Add a note on the significance of fertilization.
15. Write short notes on:
    (1) Clotting of blood
    (2) Truncus arteriosus
    (3) Spermatogenesis
    (4) Oogenesis
    (5) Copulation
    (6) Frog spawn
    (7) Penetration, copulation and cleavage path
    (8) Structure of sperm and ovum
    (9) Amplexus
    (10) Hibernation
    (11) Aestivation

(12) Lungs of frog
(13) Brain of frog
(14) Cutanous respiration
(15) Pulmonary respiration
(16) Buccopharyngeal respiration
(17) Sound producing organs
(18) Spinal cord
(19) Tongue
(20) Ear of frog
(21) Sexual dimorphism in frog
(22) Buccal cavity of frog
(23) Functions of skin of frog
(24) Dorsal and ventral view of heart of frog
16. Draw well labelled diagrams only:
(1) Dorsal and ventral view of heart
(2) Internal structure of the heart
(3) Arterial system
(4) Venous system
(5) Male reproductive organs of the frog
(6) Female reproductive organs of frog.
(7) T.S. of ovary
(8) T.S. of liver
(9) T.S. of the stomach
(10) T.S. of intestine
(11) V.S. of skin
(12) Brain of frog
(13) Ventricles of brain
17. Explain:
(a) Brow spot
(b) Vocal sacs
(c) Cloaca
(d) Oesophagus
18. Describe the respiratory system and add the mechanism of respiratory in frog.
19. Give an account of Central Nervous System.
20. Give an account of sense organs of frog.
21. Describe the mechanism of pulmonary respiration in frog.
22. Give an account of peripheral nervous system of frog.
23. Give an account of autonomous nervous system.
24. Describe the structure of eye and add note on working of eye.
25. Describe the structure and function of ear.

Chapter 5...

Neoteny in Amphibia

5.1 Neoteny in Amphibia
5.2 Parental Care in Amphibia
✍ Summary
✍ Review Questions

5.1 Neoteny in Amphibia

Neoteny and paedogenesis are two different evolutionary developmental processes. But many times these two terms are often considered as synonyms, which is not correct. There is clear distinction between these two terms.

1. Neoteny: When larval or embryonic characters are maintained in an adult body, this is called neoteny. For example, urodel amphibian *Salamander* show larval gill in adults. Another example is retention of embryonic cartilaginous skeleton in adult Chondrichytes.

2. Paedogenesis or Paedomorphosis: It refers to the development of gonads and production of young ones by the larval or premature animal. There are several examples of paedogenesis found in different groups of animals. For example, gall fly and salamanders. Thus, in case of neoteny embryonic or larval features, the characters are retained in the body of adult individual, whereas paedogenesis stresses precocious development of gonads in larval body.

Amphibia and Neoteny

Some urodel amphibians show this remarkable phenomenon of neoteny. *Amblystoma* is the very well studied classical example of neoteny. Some aquatic larval urodels delay or fail to metamorphose but still become sexually mature. They mate and produce fertile eggs.

The adults and larval urodels are very much similar because the adults have retained many larval characters. Here question arises, do these urodel amphibians represent neoteny paedomorphosis? In case of the amphibians, the distinction between these two processes shows overlapping. It becomes difficult to distinguish these processes.

If the individuals of these amphibians are considered as adults which retain certain larval characteristics but are not metamorphosed then the process is called neoteny or if they may be considered as larvae in which reproductive organs develop precociously, then the process is called paedogenesis or paedomorphosis.

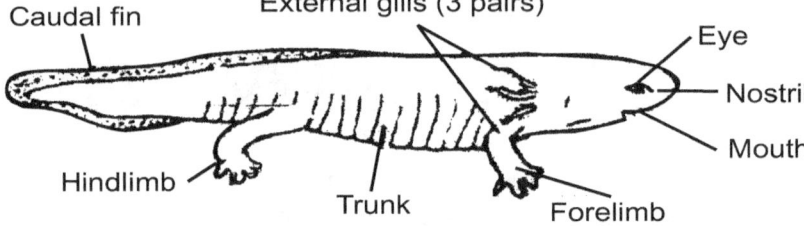

Fig. 5.1: Axolotl larva of Tiger Salamander, *Amblystoma tigrinum*

Axolotl larva of tiger salamander *Amblystoma* is the classical and best studied example of neoteny and paedogenesis among Amphibia. *Amblystoma maxicanum* is found in the mountain lakes of Mexico and Central America. Another closely related species *A. tigrinum* called Tiger Salamander found in high altitudes of Colorado of North America is a black salamander with yellow spots. The adult has no external gills or tail fin. Generally, they go through typical, external gilled larval stages then to metamorphosis, to transform into adult air breathing form. In 1865 some axolotl larvae were brought to Paris, their gills were discarded and they underwent metamorphosis to become adult terrestrial salamander. Axolotls are used as important laboratory experimental animals.

Thus, the ability of larva to reproduce is called neoteny. In *Amblystoma* both the adult and the larva can reproduce but metamorphosis can be induced in the axolotl by injecting thyroid extract.

Environmental Factors and Neoteny

Neoteny is a remarkable process found in Amphibians, however, its significance and causes are not properly understood. The environmental factors affect metamorphosis in several ways. The scarcity of food, cold temperature, insufficient iodine (component of thyroxine hormone which induces amphibian metamorphosis) are the factors responsible for failure of axolotl larva which has three pairs of external gills and a caudal fin. In the normal course axolotl larva undergoes metamorphosis, loses its external gills and caudal fin, lungs become functional and it changes into a terrestrial adult. If the food is scarce, water drying up and a lack of iodine in the water, then the axolotl larva leaves water for land and becomes an adult without metamorphosis.

If however, food and water are abundant with iodine compounds, the axolotl larva does not change into an adult but remains in the larval form and becomes sexually mature to start reproducing. This sexually mature but morphologically immature larval stage with external gills is called an axolotl larva. This name was given by natives of Mexico who captured them for food. It is called Aztec axolotl means servant of water. The larva when first discovered was called separate genus Siredom axolotl (Wagler 1830) metamorphosis and larval characters are retained. This is indicated by the fact that drying up of swamps, lack of food and rise in temperature in surrounding water induce axolotls to metamorphose.

This is experimentally proved that the axolotls breed in Mexico and Southern Parts of U.S.A. when transferred to the eastern states or injected with thyroxine or TSH, these axolotls lose their external gills, assume lungs and become adult airbreathing native tiger salamanders. As the temperature of surrounding water drops, the response of the larval tissue to thyroid hormone also diminishes and there is no response entirely below 5°C. The genetic basis for metamorphosis seems to be multifactorial, variable and subject to selective pressures.

Genes for transformation have become suppressed in neotenic populations but not entirely absent for there is occasional appearance of metamorphosed individuals.

Types of Neoteny: There are three types of neoteny found in amphibians:

(i) **Partial Neoteny:** When metamorphosis is delayed due to temporary ecological or physiological changes in environment it is shown by tadpoles and larvae tiding over winter.

(ii) Intermediate Neoteny: It is found in axolotls which also reproduce sexually but undergo metamorphosis in suitable conditions. Under experimental conditions in laboratories it is possible to produce either axolotls or transformed individuals.

(iii) Total Neoteny: In this condition the individuals remain forever in larval stage. Though thyroxine treatment is given to their larvae they fail to induce metamorphose. This is because there is no response to larval tissue to the hormone.

Significance of Neoteny: According to **Weismann** (1875), neoteny is considered as a case of retarded evolution or atavism i.e. reversion to ancestral condition. But now this is regarded as a secondary specialisation, a physiological adaptation of advantage. This is also proved by the great heterogeneity of all neotenous perennibranchiate forms.

5.2 Parental Care in Amphibia

Amphibians show extraordinary parental care to save as many as possible. The frogs and toads lay large number of eggs. In some cases about 10,000 eggs are laid per year just to save at least a few hundreds of them. Frog eggs are relished by fish, turtle and even other frog. The lucky ones which survive and turn into tadpoles are not so lucky either, for the tadpoles are constantly preyed upon by fish turtles, birds, otters and snakes. It is really hard for an egg to transform into an adult frog after overcoming all these hurdles. Hence, parents try to protect their eggs from enemies. All the groups of amphibians show instances of parental care.

Urodeles: These are the tailed amphibians. *Amphiuma*, *Salamanders* exhibit parental care. In *Amphiuma* the congo eel, the mother carefully guards the eggs by coiling her body around them.

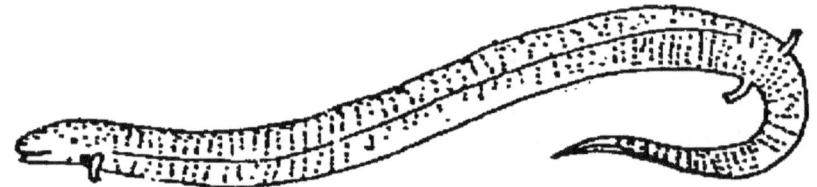

Fig. 5.2: *Amphiuma*

In *Desmognathus fuscus*, the dusky salamander, the female carries the eggs attached round her neck. The female of *Salamandra, Salamandra* of the European 'frog', retains her few eggs within her body for 10-12 months and gives birth to the larvae. These larvae complete their development in water. In the European alpine salamander *Salamandra atra,* the mother retains her one or two eggs that develop fully before birth.

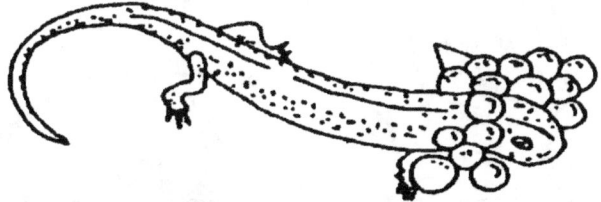

Fig. 5.3: Dusky salamander with eggs

Anurans: Frogs and toads show the highest degree of parental care. Most of the frogs step into water for laying eggs, some have abandoned ponds altogether for this purpose. They deposit their eggs on plants overhanging ponds and in moist places near ponds.

Fig. 5.4: A - *Hyla*, B - *Rhacophorus*

A South African tree frog *Phyllomedusa* glues its eggs to the leaves hanging over a pond and on hatching, the tadpoles roll down straight into the water below where they undergo further development. The another tree frogs lay their eggs high upon the trees. During rainy seasons, the leaves hold water and these frogs lay their eggs in 'leaf - ponds'. Although the eggs are then relatively safe from predators, they are often destroyed by winds and heavy rains. Many frogs and toads build nests in which the eggs are laid and the young ones are developed.

A Brazilian tree frog *Hyla fabre* lays eggs in mud craters called the nurseries which the male builds in shallow water by moving in a ring and pushing up mud. A nursery is about 30 cm. in diameter and its rim is a little higher than the level of water.

(a) Nurseries of *Hyla fabre*   (b) Nest of *Rhacophorus sehelegeli*
Fig. 5.5

The eggs and the larvae that emerge from them remain safe in the nurseries from the predatory fishes and insects. Spawning is so timed that in a few days rain water submerges the nurseries and the larvae spreads in the pond. Another tree frog *Hyla restinfictrix* lines a cavity in a tree trunk with beeswax brought from the combs of stingless bees and lays eggs in this cavity. When full of rain water, the tadpoles can develop here without any fear of enemies.

Some tropical frogs have another interesting strategy to protect their eggs. The male, while sheding his semen over the eggs, kicks his hind legs vigorously to produce a frothy mixture of air, water, semen and eggs. The outer layer of this froth soon hardens ensuring protection to the eggs till they hatch.

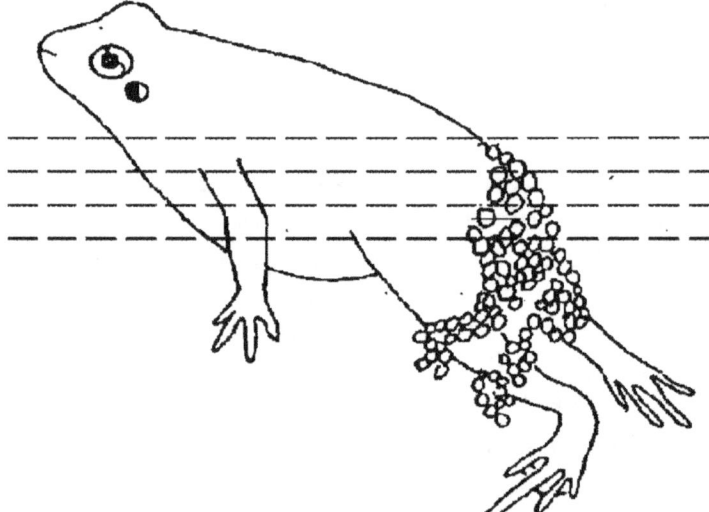

Fig. 5.6: The mid wife toad *Alytes obstetricians*

In *Rhacophorus schelegeli* of Japan, pairing male and female frogs burrow deep on the bank of a pond. Eggs are laid in a froth. The parent then retire through a tunnel dug sloping straight down into the pond water. By the time the tadpoles hatch, the froth changes into fluid that flows with the larvae down into the pond water. Thus, tadpoles reach the appropriate environment. *Hyla nebulosa* has left water altogether. It lays eggs in a nest made by dry leaves and tiny adults emerge from eggs, there being no larval stage.

Male of the European midwife toad *Alytes obstericians* takes the eggs along with it to protect them. The male of this toad winds the string of eggs around his hind feet and burrows into moist soil. It periodically comes out to feed and moisten the eggs. When the larvae are ready to hatch, it shifts to a nearby pond to release the larvae.

The *Pipa* species have a more interesting way of protecting their eggs. Female *Pipa dorsigera* undergoes certain changes during the breeding season. The egg carrying tube, oviduct, elongates and protrudes out to reach the skin on its back.

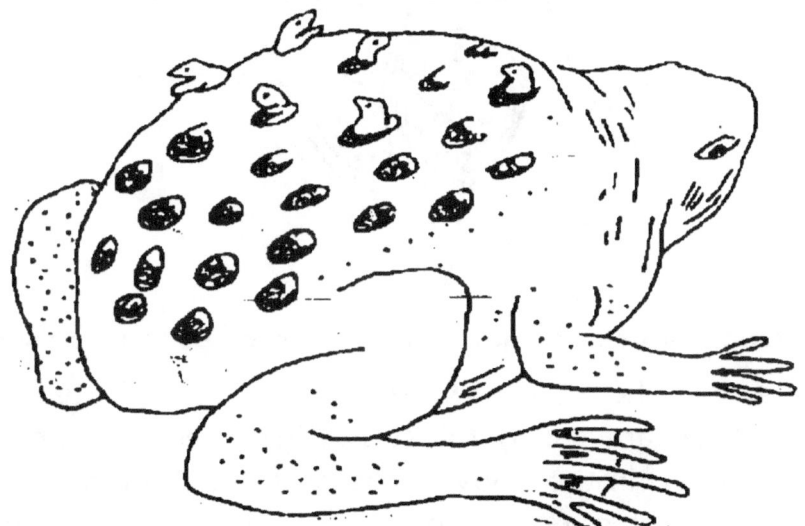

Fig. 5.7: Suriman toad *Pipa dorsigera*

After laying eggs on its own back the female allows the male to fertilize and spread the eggs evenly on its back. The dorsal skin then develops many pouches to enclose the eggs. For about ten weeks the female carries the embryos on her back. After the tadpoles emerges breaking open the pouches, her skin returns to its normal state.

Some frogs protect their eggs and tadpole as well. *Rhinoderma darwini*, a South American frog, is one such and is called the mouth breeding frog. It is also called as Darwin's frog because Charles Darwin discovered it during his voyage on the Beagle. In most of the male frogs, the vocal sacs blow up like balloons to act as resonating chambers during croacting. But in mouth-breeding frogs, the elongated vocal sacs are used for an altogether different purpose, to breed the tadpoles. The eggs are guarded by several males till they are about to hatch. At that time each male carefully takes them into his mouth and slips them into vocal sacs. The eggs hatch into tadpoles and remain in the vocal sacs till they metamorphose into tiny froglets. Then the male 'coughs' them out from his mouth.

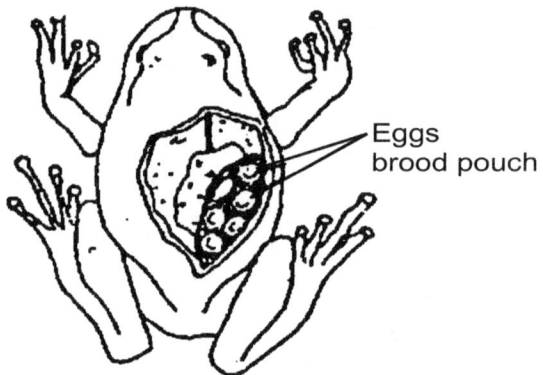

Fig. 5.8: Brood pouch of female *Gastrotheca* cut open to show eggs

Female of the *Gastrotheca* shows complicated breeding technique. These are called marsupial frog because the eggs and larvae are retained in the body of the mother. The female has in her back skin a special pouch or brood pouch with a slit opening. It opens a little in front of the cloacal aperture. Fertilized eggs are transferred into this pouch where further development occurs. About 200 tadpoles are born at a time. Another marsupial frog *Gastrotheca ovifera* lays only about 20 eggs which develop into young frogs.

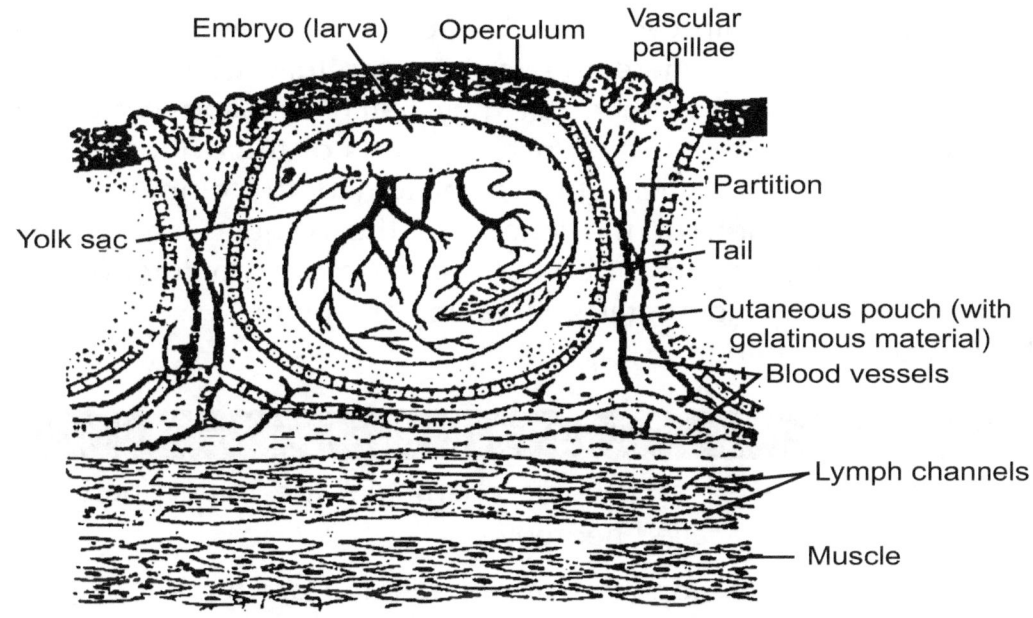

Fig. 5.9: Developing larva of *Pipa*

A more striking mode of a protection is seen in the Suriman toad, *Pipa americana*. In breeding season female skin becomes soft and spongy. During amplexus, oviduct protrudes out and passes under male's belly. Eggs are forced out of the oviduct one by one with the strokes of the male. Each egg sinks into a small pocket that gets covered by an operculum formed from a remant of egg coat, reinforced by skin secretions. Thus the young develop safely in the moist maternal tissue. Richly vascular papillae develop between the pockets. The embryo developes a yolk sac and a broad vascular tail, but no gills. The tail perhaps acts as a placenta for metabolic exchanges between maternal and embryonic tissues. Tiny toads emerge from the pockets after about 80 days.

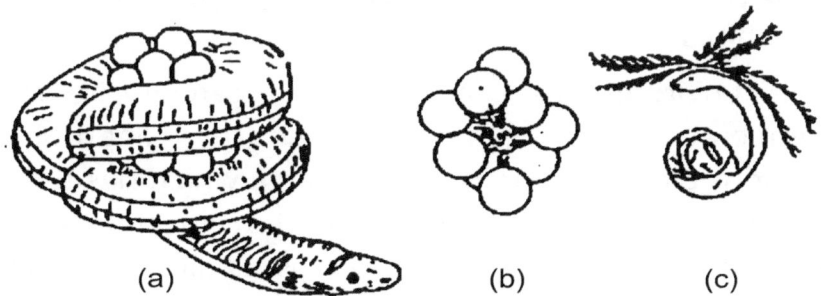

Fig. 5.10: (a) *Ichthyophis glutinosa* (b) Bunch of eggs (c) Almost ripe embryo

Caecilians: Certain caecilians, like *Ichthyophis* and *Hypogeophis*, lay eggs in burrows, where the mother carefully guards them by coiling her body around them till they hatch. In *Geotrypetes,* large yolky eggs are retained in the posterior parts of the oviducts, where development occurs. When yolk is consumed the embryos hatch. These spread throughout the length of the oviducts and develop further, deriving nourishment by the oral absorption of 'uterine milk'. The oviducal wall and foetal epithelium are highly vascular, which allow gaseous exchange.

Summary

- When larval or embryonic characters are maintained in an adult body, is called neoteny.

- When the development of gonads and production of young ones by the larval or premature animal is called as paedogenesis.

- Urodel amphibian *Amblystoma* shows remarkable phenomenon of neoteny.

- Some aquatic larval urodels delay or fail to metamorphose but still become sexually mature. They mate and produce fertile eggs.

- The adults and larval urodels are very much similar because the adults have retained many larval characters. *Axolotl* larva of tiger Salamander *Amblystoma* is the classical and best studied example of neoteny and paedogenesis among Amphibia.

- The environmental factors like scarcity of food, cold temperature and insufficient iodine (thyroxine hormone) are responsible for failure of axolotl larva which has three pairs of external gills and a caudal fin; but in normal course of metamorphosis the axolotl larva losses gills and caudal fin.

- Three types of neoteny found in amphibians namely, partial neoteny, intermediate neoteny and total neoteny.

- According to **Weismann** (1875), neoteny is considered as a case of retarted evolution or atavism i.e. reversion to ancestral condition significantly.
- Amphibians show extraordinary parental care to save as many as possible.
- Urodel *Amphiuma* salamanders mother carefully guards the egg by coiling her body around them. And the dusky Salamander, *Desmognathus fuscus* female carries the eggs attached round her neck.
- Anurans (frogs and toads) shows degree of parental care. Most of frogs laying their eggs in water or on plants overhanging ponds. The tree frogs lay their eggs high upon the trees because during rainy seasons, the leaves hold water.
- *Rhacophorus* of Japan pairing of male and female frogs burrow deep on the bank of pond then eggs are laid in a froth.
- *Gastrotheca* female shows complicated breeding technique. These are called marsupial frog because the eggs and larvae are retained in the body of mother.
- The caecilians, like *Ichthyophis* and *Hypogeophis* lay eggs in burrows, where the mother carefully guards them by coiling her body around them till they hatch.

Review Questions

1. Explain phenomenon of neoteny in Amphibians with suitable examples.
2. What is neoteny? Explain the types of neoteny in amphibains.
3. Write short notes on:
   (a) Neoteny
   (b) Paedogenesis

(c) Environmental factors affecting neoteny
(d) Types of neoteny
(e) Parental care in urodels
(f) Parental care in anurans
(g) Parental care in caecilians

www.ingramcontent.com/pod-product-compliance
Lightning Source LLC
Chambersburg PA
CBHW080428230426
43662CB00015B/2214